首斬り朝

SAMURAI 首斬り朝
EXECUTIONER

Punished is not the man himself,
but the evil that resides in him.

story
KAZUO KOIKE

art
GOSEKI KOJIMA

DARK HORSE MANGA™

translation
DANA LEWIS

lettering & retouch
SNO CONE STUDIOS

publisher
MIKE RICHARDSON

editor
TIM ERVIN

book design
DARIN FABRICK

art director
LIA RIBACCHI

Published by Dark Horse Manga, a division of Dark Horse Comics, Inc.
in association with Soeisha Inc.

Dark Horse Comics, Inc.
10956 SE Main Street, Milwaukie, OR 97222
www.darkhorse.com

First edition: January 2005
ISBN: 1-59307-209-0

1 3 5 7 9 10 8 6 4 2

Printed in Canada

To find a comics shop in your area, call the
Comic Shop Locator Service toll-free at 1-888-266-4226.

首斬り朝

THE HELL STICK

By **KAZUO KOIKE**
& GOSEKI KOJIMA

諸行無常
是生滅法
生滅滅已
寂滅為楽

VOLUME

3

A NOTE TO READERS

Samurai Executioner is a carefully researched re-creation of Edo-Period Japan. To preserve the flavor of the work, we have chosen to retain many Edo-Period terms that have no direct equivalents in English. Japanese is written in a mix of Chinese ideograms and a syllabic writing system, resulting in numerous synonyms. In the glossary, you may encounter words with multiple meanings. These are words written with Chinese ideograms that are pronounced the same but carry different meanings. A Japanese reader seeing the different ideograms would know instantly which meaning it is, but these synonyms can cause confusion when Japanese is spelled out in our alphabet. *O-yurushi o* (please forgive us)!

SAMURAI 首斬り朝 EXECUTIONER

TABLE OF CONTENTS

the ninth

Hellstick

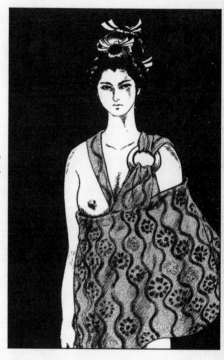

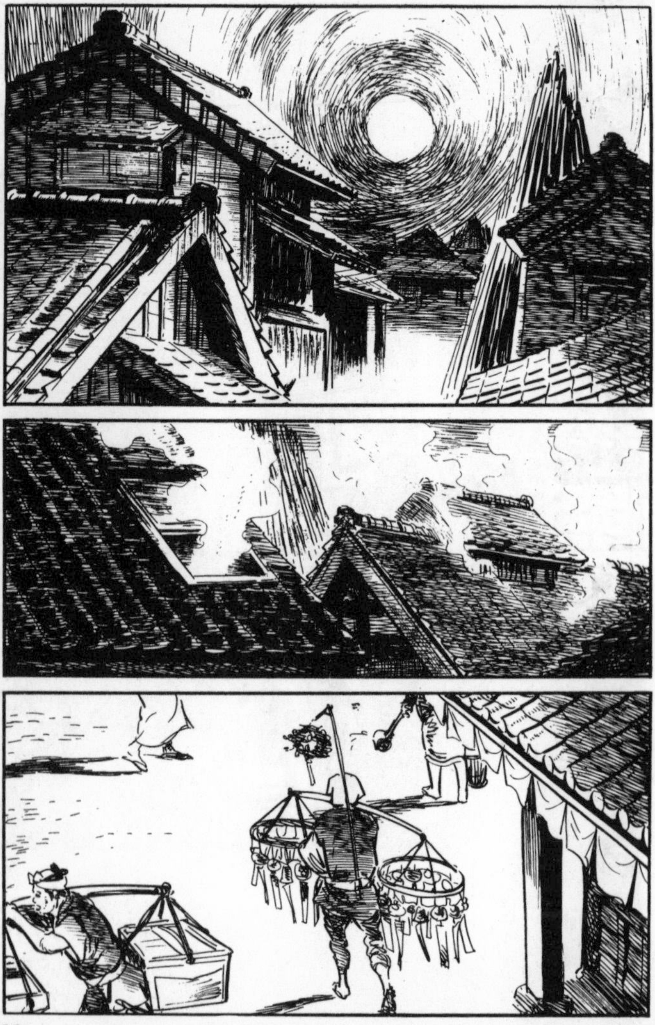

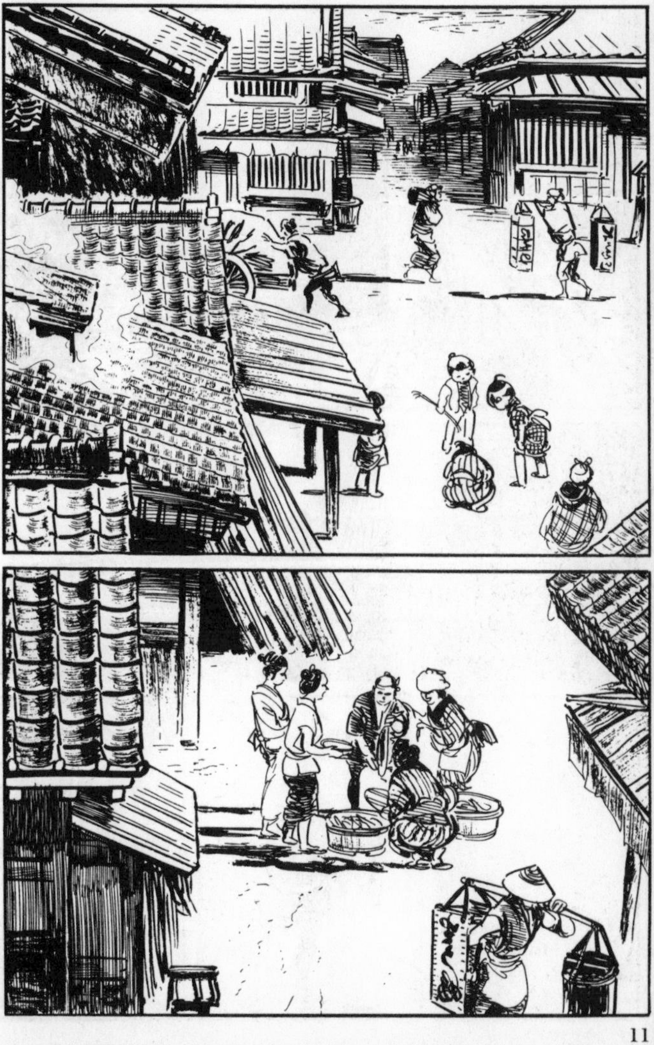

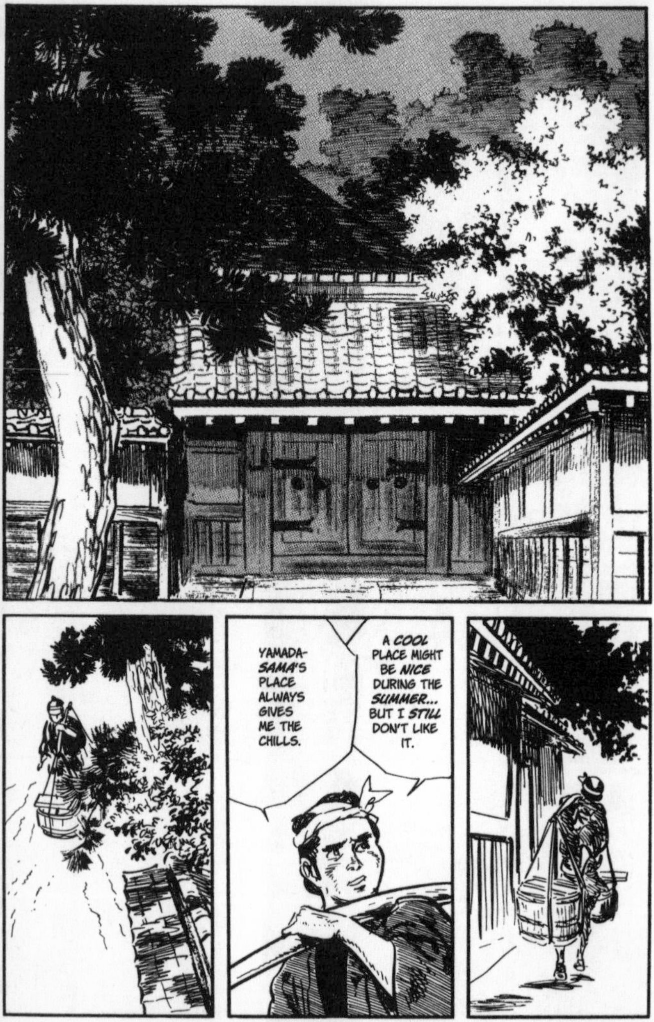
YAMADA-SAMA'S PLACE ALWAYS GIVES ME THE CHILLS.
A COOL PLACE MIGHT BE NICE DURING THE SUMMER... BUT I STILL DON'T LIKE IT.

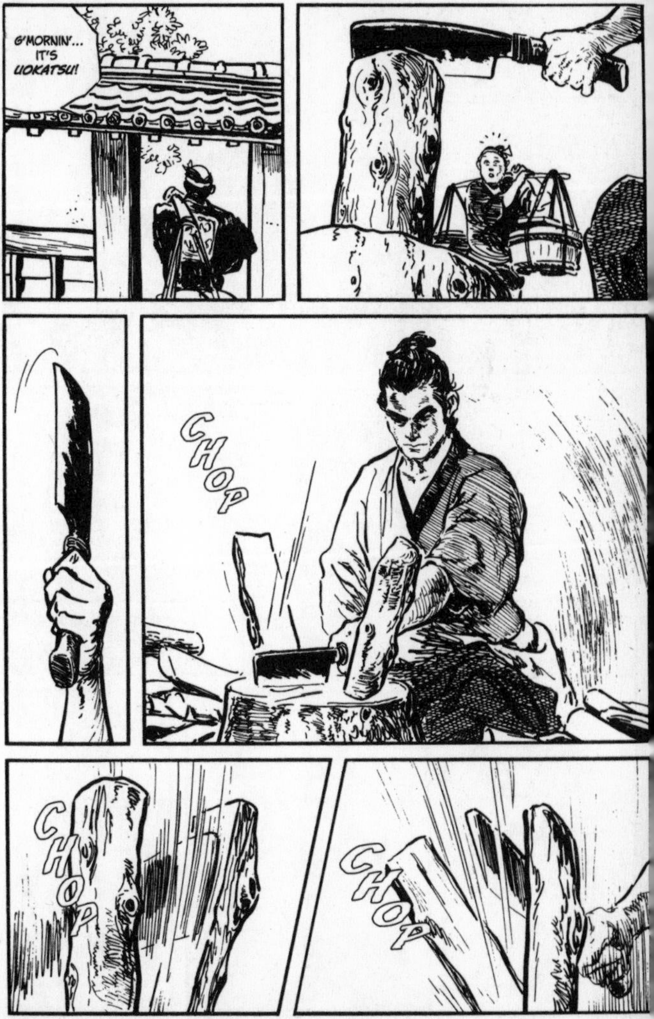
G'MORNIN'... IT'S UOKATSU!
CHOP
CHOP
CHOP

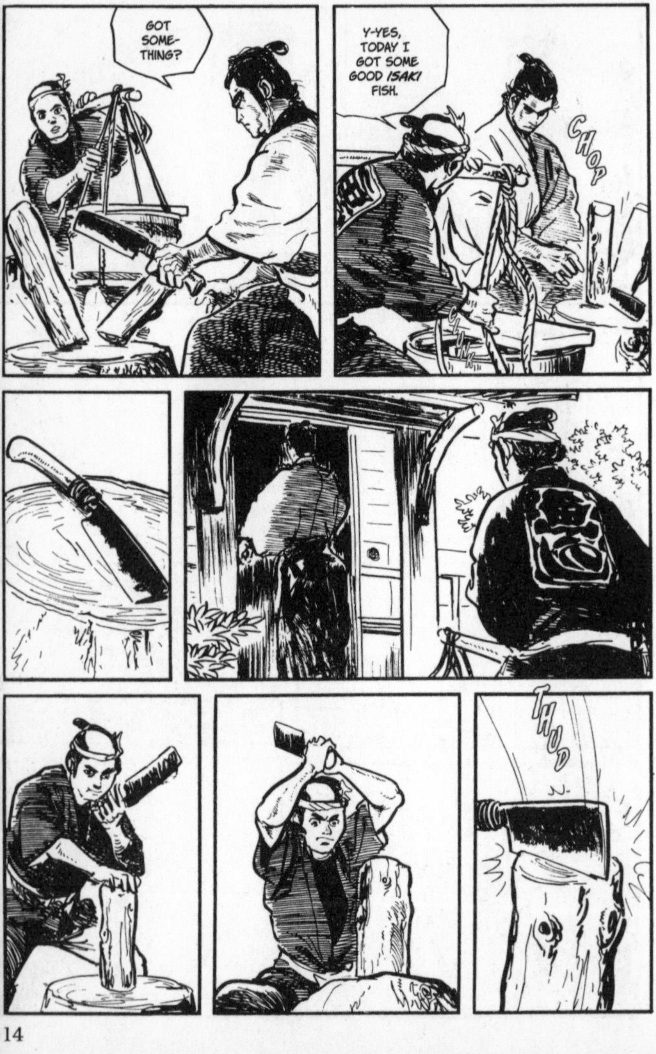
GOT SOME-THING?
Y-YES, TODAY I GOT SOME GOOD *ISAKI* FISH.
CHOP
CHUNK
THUD

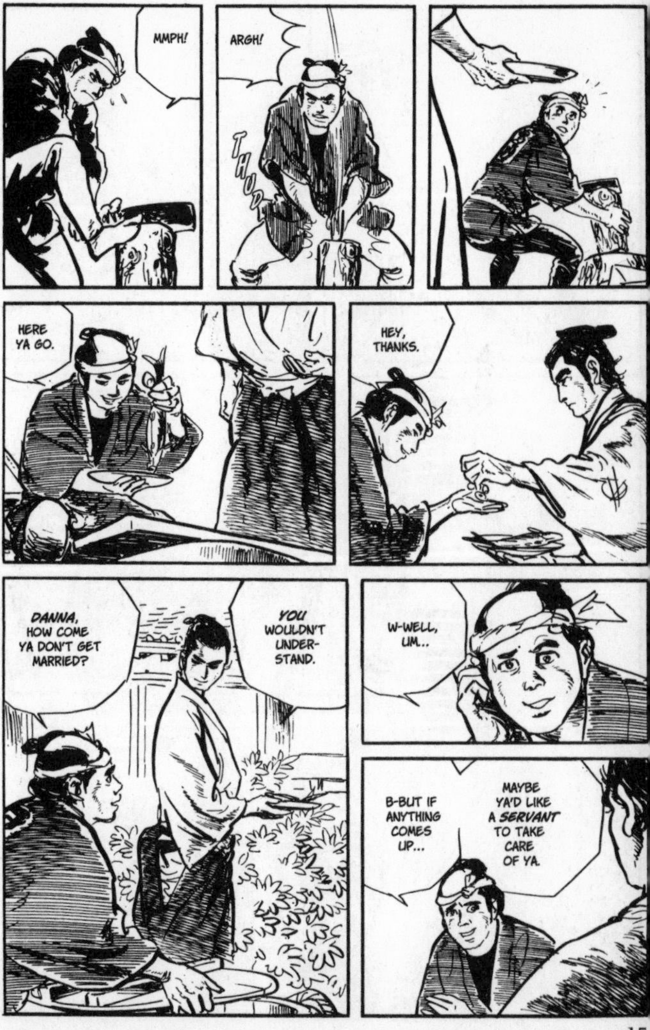

MMPH!
ARGH!
THUD
HERE YA GO.
HEY, THANKS.
DANNA, HOW COME YA DON'T GET MARRIED?
YOU WOULDN'T UNDER-STAND.
W-WELL, UM...
B-BUT IF ANYTHING COMES UP...
MAYBE YA'D LIKE A *SERVANT* TO TAKE CARE OF YA.

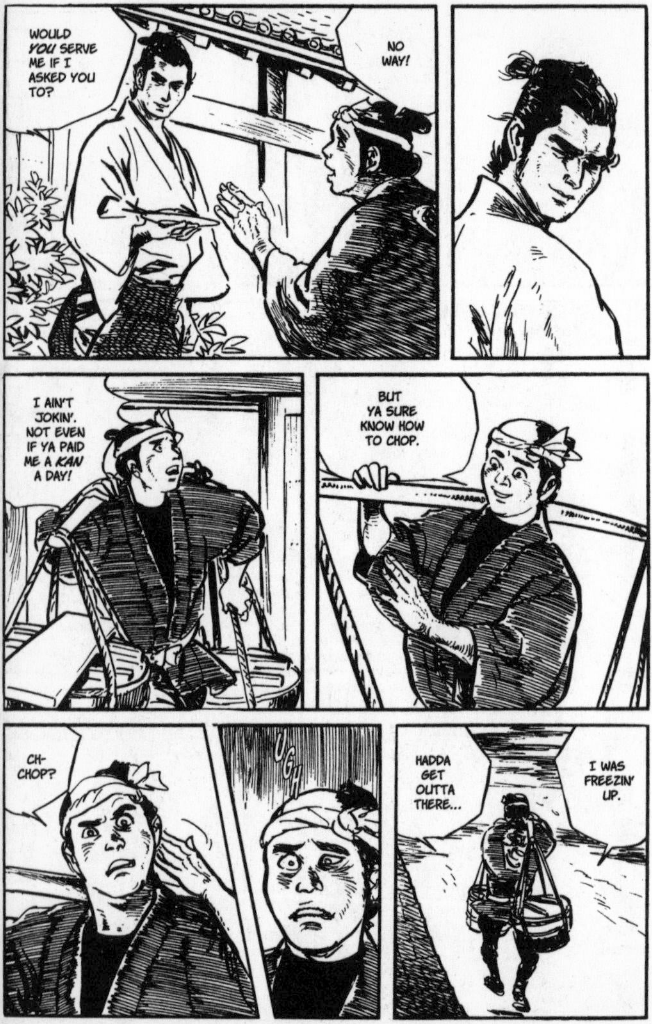
WOULD *YOU* SERVE ME IF I ASKED YOU TO?
NO WAY!
I AIN'T JOKIN'. NOT EVEN IF YA PAID ME A *KAN* A DAY!
BUT YA SURE KNOW HOW TO CHOP.
CH-CHOP?
UGH
HADDA GET OUTTA THERE...
I WAS FREEZIN' UP.

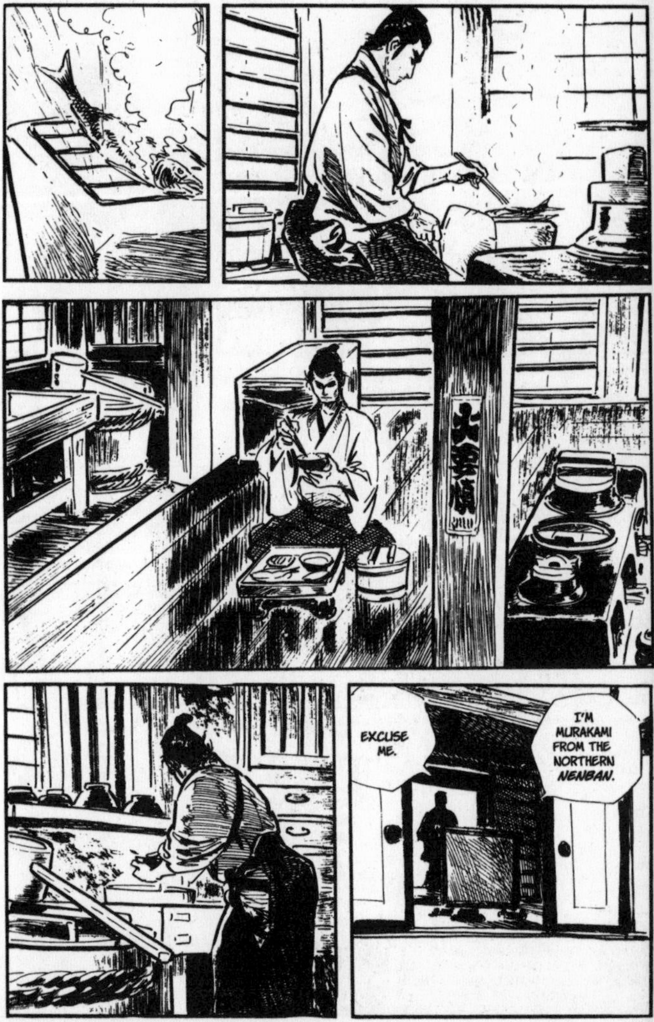
EXCUSE ME.
I'M MURAKAMI FROM THE NORTHERN *NENBAN*.

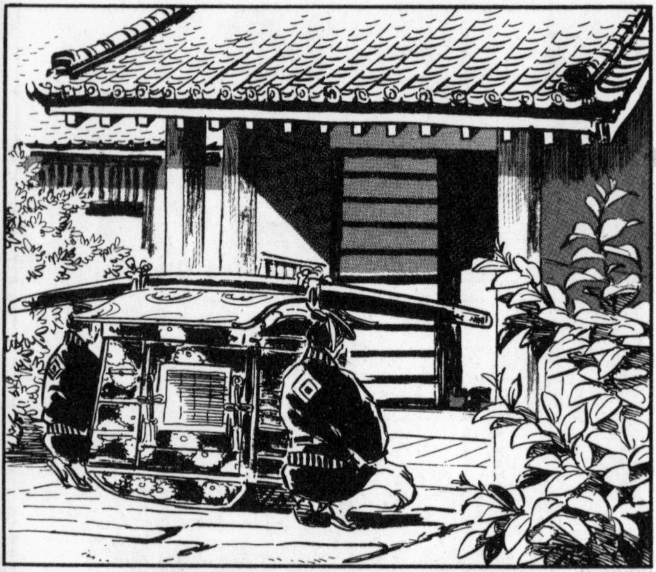

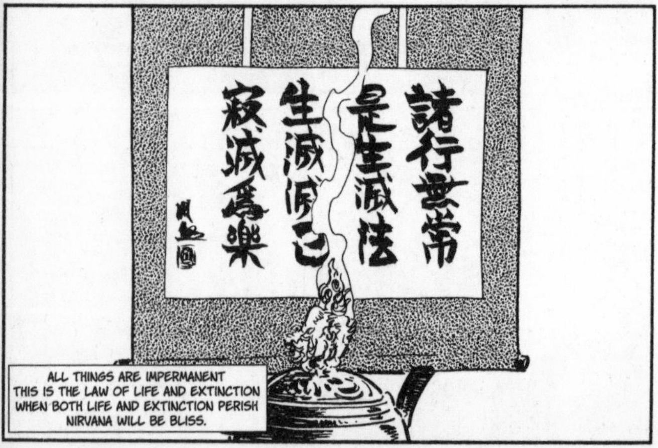
諸行無常
是生滅法
生滅滅已
寂滅爲樂
ALL THINGS ARE IMPERMANENT
THIS IS THE LAW OF LIFE AND EXTINCTION
WHEN BOTH LIFE AND EXTINCTION PERISH
NIRVANA WILL BE BLISS.

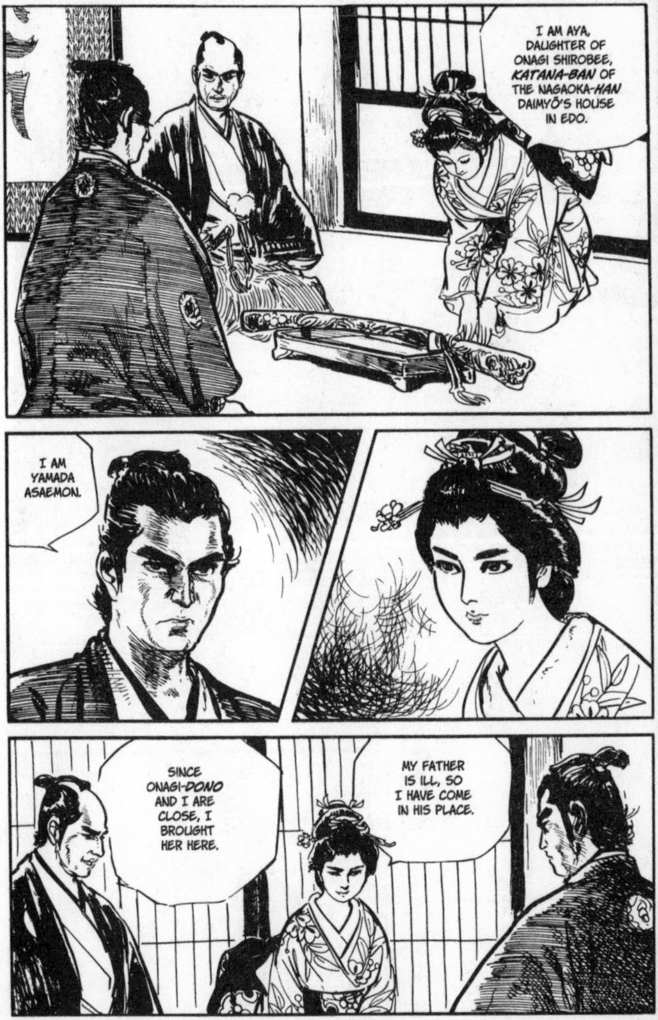

I AM AYA, DAUGHTER OF ONAGI SHIROBEE, *KATANA-BAN* OF THE NAGAOKA-*HAN* DAIMYŌ'S HOUSE IN EDO.
I AM YAMADA ASAEMON.
SINCE ONAGI-*DONO* AND I ARE CLOSE, I BROUGHT HER HERE.
MY FATHER IS ILL, SO I HAVE COME IN HIS PLACE.

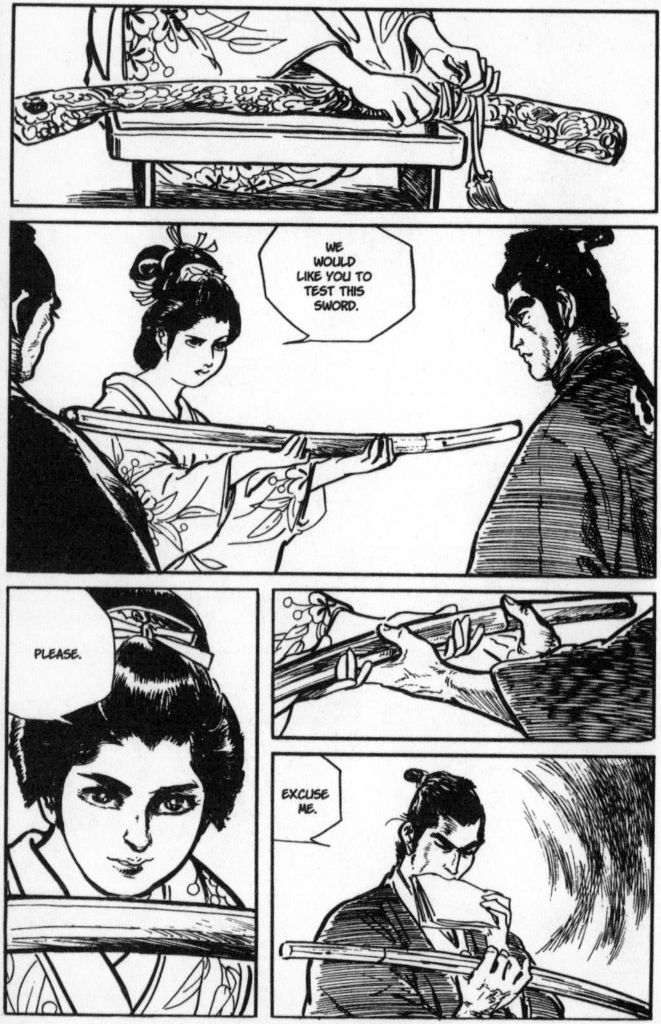
WE WOULD LIKE YOU TO TEST THIS SWORD.
PLEASE.
EXCUSE ME.

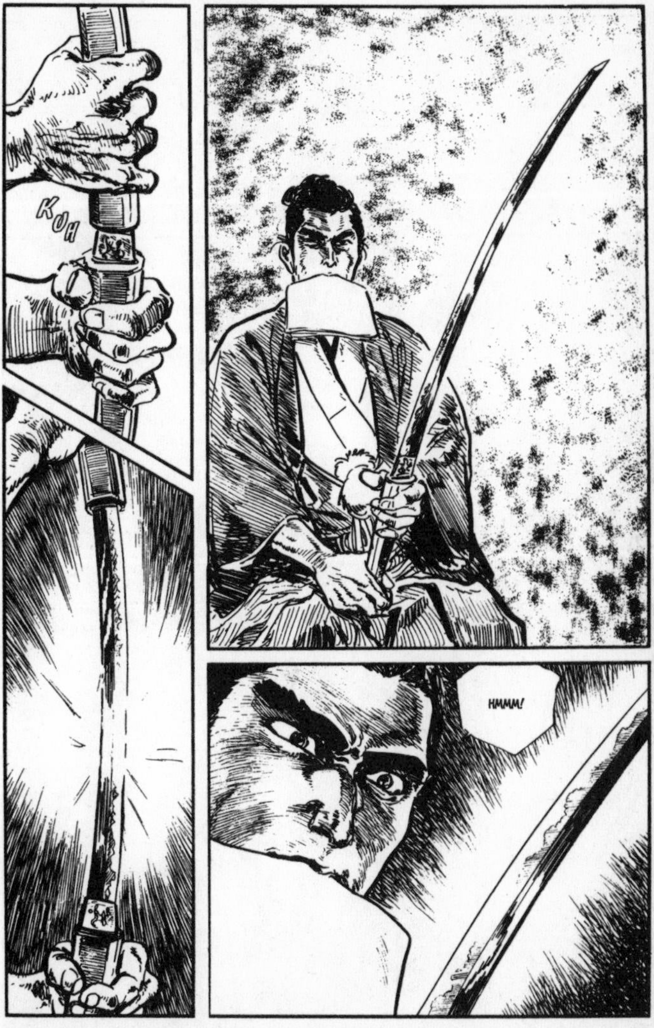
KUH
HMMM!

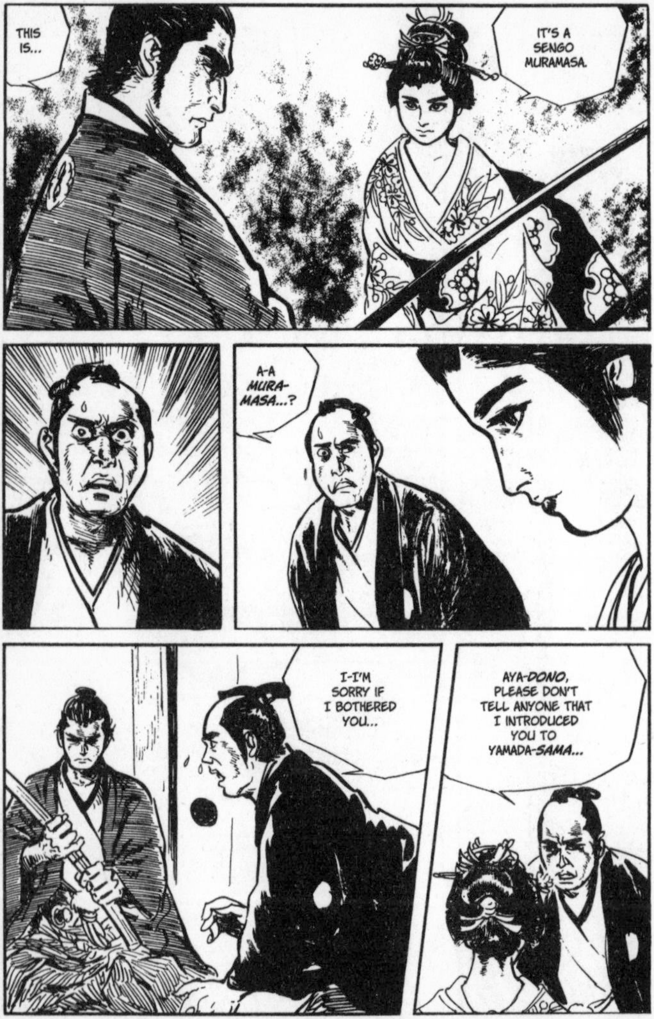
THIS IS...
IT'S A SENGO MURAMASA.
A-A *MURA-MASA*...?
I-I'M SORRY IF I BOTHERED YOU...
AYA-*DONO*, PLEASE DON'T TELL ANYONE THAT I INTRODUCED YOU TO YAMADA-*SAMA*...

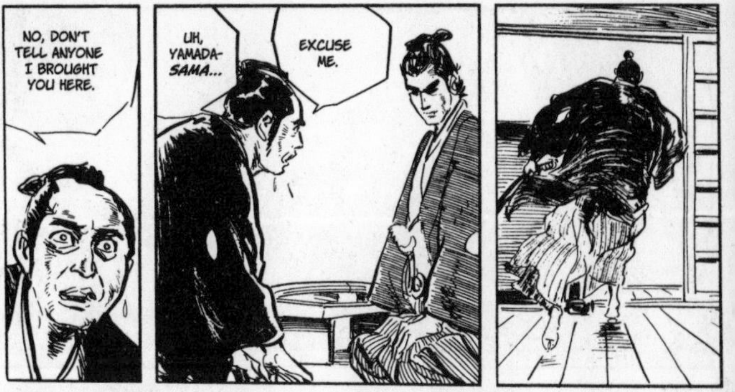
NO, DON'T TELL ANYONE I BROUGHT YOU HERE.
UH, YAMADA-*SAMA*...
EXCUSE ME.

YORIKI MURAKAMI OF THE *NENBAN* OF THE NORTH *MACHI-BUGYŌSHO* HAS EVERY REASON TO BE PANIC-STRICKEN.

THE INFAMOUS SWORDS OF SENGO MURAMASA WERE SAID TO BE CURSED. THEY WERE SHUNNED AND DETESTED BECAUSE THEY INVITED DISASTER TO THE TOKUGAWA FAMILY. THE *DAIMYO* AND *HATAMOTO* WERE HESITANT TO EVEN UTTER THEIR NAME, MUCH LESS POSSESS THEM.

IN THE THIRD MONTH OF THE FOURTEENTH YEAR OF TENMON, TOKUGAWA IEYASU'S FATHER HIROTADA WAS STABBED IN THE CROTCH BY HIS HEREDITARY VASSAL IWAMATSU HACHIYA.

IN THE THIRD YEAR OF TENSŌ, IEYASU'S ELDEST SON NOBUYASU COMMITTED *SEPPUKU*. HIS *KAISHAKUNIN* TENPO YAMASHIRO NO KAMI'S *WAKIZASHI* WAS A MURAMASA.

MOREOVER, IN THE SEVENTH MONTH OF THE FIFTH YEAR OF KEICHŌ, KAGAI HIDEMOCHI, A VASSAL OF ISHIDA MITSUNARI, ATTEMPTED TO ASSASSINATE IEYASU BUT FAILED, KILLING IEYASU'S STAND-IN MIZUNO TADASHIGE INSTEAD--USING A MURAMASA.

IN THE NINTH YEAR OF KAN'EI, IEYASU'S GRANDSON SURUGA *DAINAGON* TADANAGA COMMITTED SUICIDE IN JŌSHŪ TAKASAKI CASTLE--USING A MURAMASA *TANTŌ*.

THE DISASTERS THAT MURAMASA SWORDS HAVE BROUGHT UPON THE TOKUGAWA FAMILY ARE TOO NUMEROUS TO LIST.

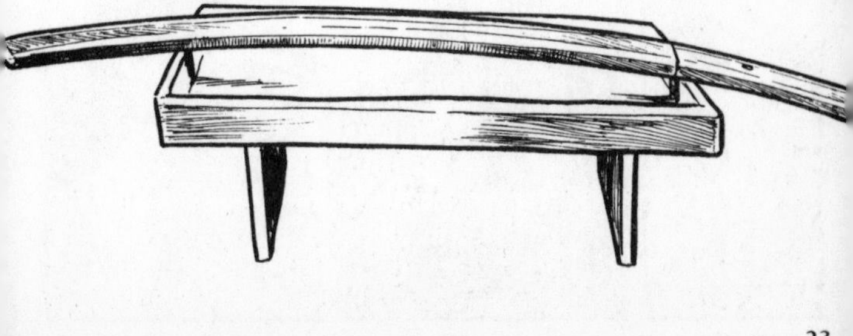

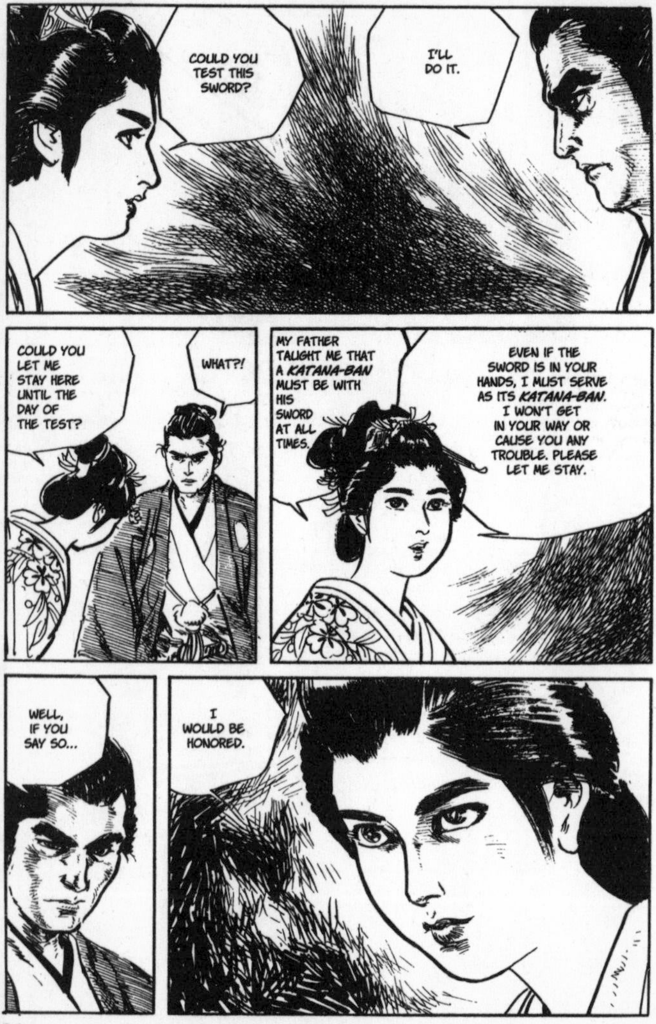
COULD YOU TEST THIS SWORD?
I'LL DO IT.
COULD YOU LET ME STAY HERE UNTIL THE DAY OF THE TEST?
WHAT?!
MY FATHER TAUGHT ME THAT A *KATANA-BAN* MUST BE WITH HIS SWORD AT ALL TIMES.
EVEN IF THE SWORD IS IN YOUR HANDS, I MUST SERVE AS ITS *KATANA-BAN*. I WON'T GET IN YOUR WAY OR CAUSE YOU ANY TROUBLE. PLEASE LET ME STAY.
WELL, IF YOU SAY SO...
I WOULD BE HONORED.

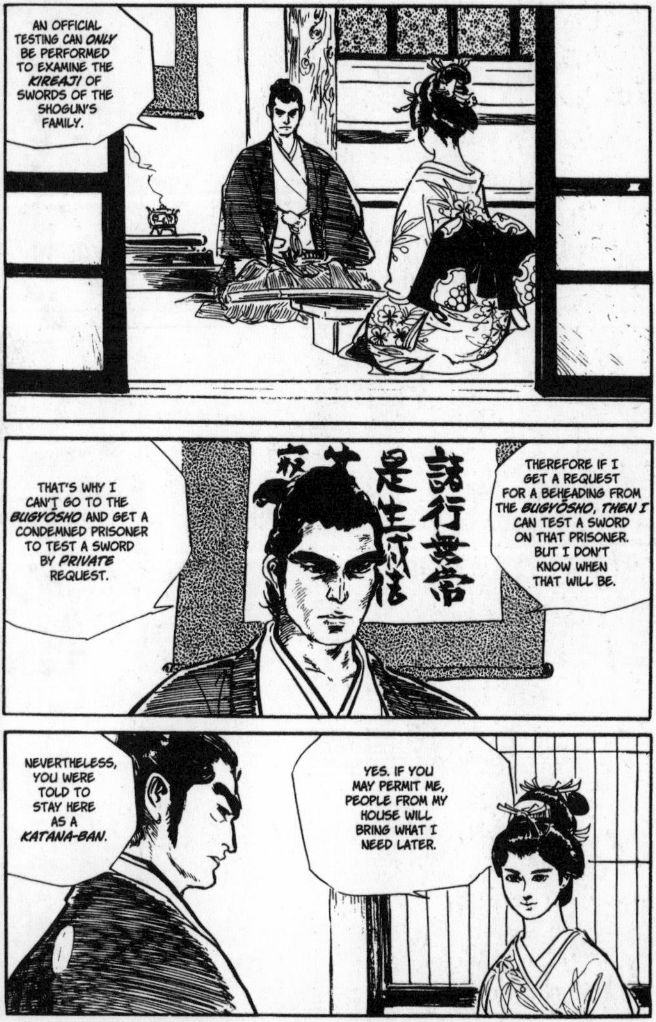
AN OFFICIAL TESTING CAN *ONLY* BE PERFORMED TO EXAMINE THE *KIREAJI* OF SWORDS OF THE SHOGUN'S FAMILY.
THAT'S WHY I CAN'T GO TO THE *BUGYŌSHO* AND GET A CONDEMNED PRISONER TO TEST A SWORD BY *PRIVATE* REQUEST.
諸行無常
是生滅法
THEREFORE IF I GET A REQUEST FOR A BEHEADING FROM THE *BUGYŌSHO, THEN I* CAN TEST A SWORD ON THAT PRISONER. BUT I DON'T KNOW WHEN THAT WILL BE.
NEVERTHELESS, YOU WERE TOLD TO STAY HERE AS A *KATANA-BAN*.
YES. IF YOU MAY PERMIT ME, PEOPLE FROM MY HOUSE WILL BRING WHAT I NEED LATER.

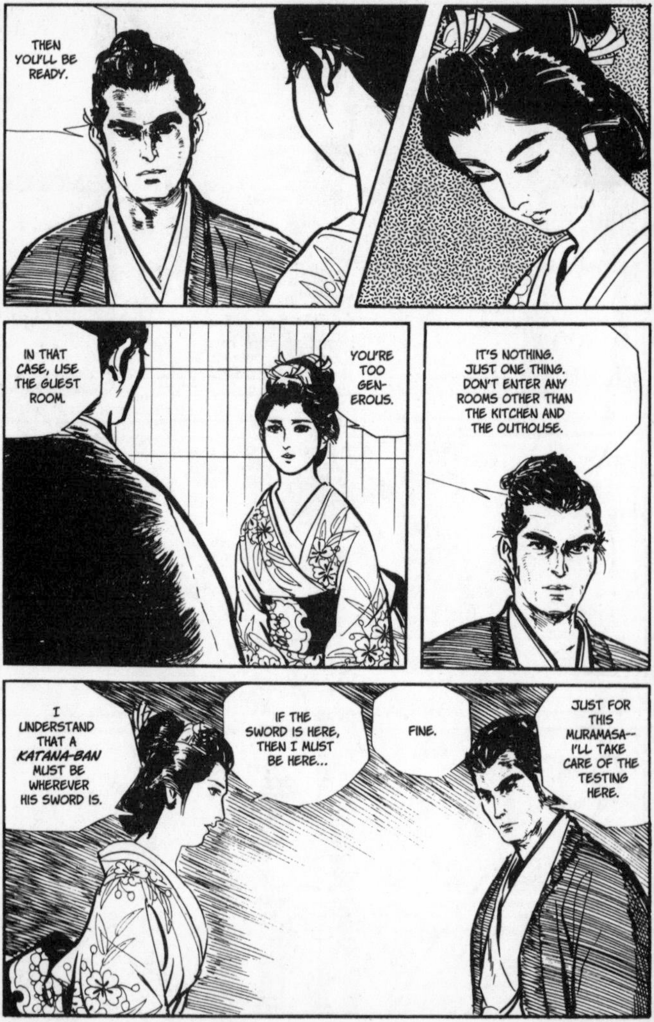
THEN YOU'LL BE READY.
IN THAT CASE, USE THE GUEST ROOM.
YOU'RE TOO GEN-EROUS.
IT'S NOTHING. JUST ONE THING. DON'T ENTER ANY ROOMS OTHER THAN THE KITCHEN AND THE OUTHOUSE.
I UNDERSTAND THAT A *KATANA-BAN* MUST BE WHEREVER HIS SWORD IS.
IF THE SWORD IS HERE, THEN I MUST BE HERE...
FINE.
JUST FOR THIS MURAMASA-- I'LL TAKE CARE OF THE TESTING HERE.

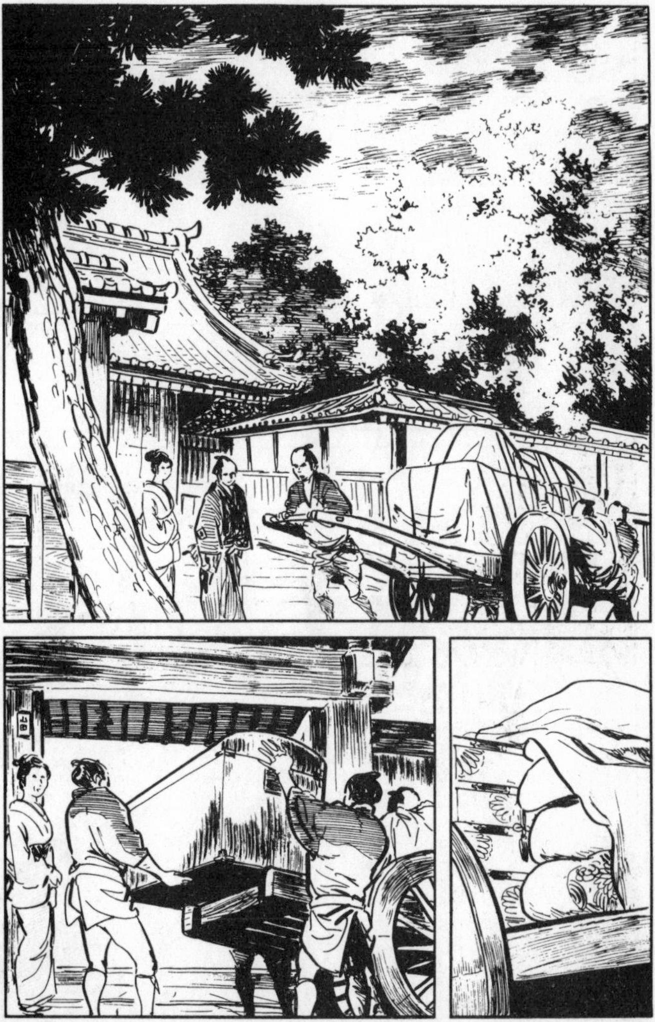

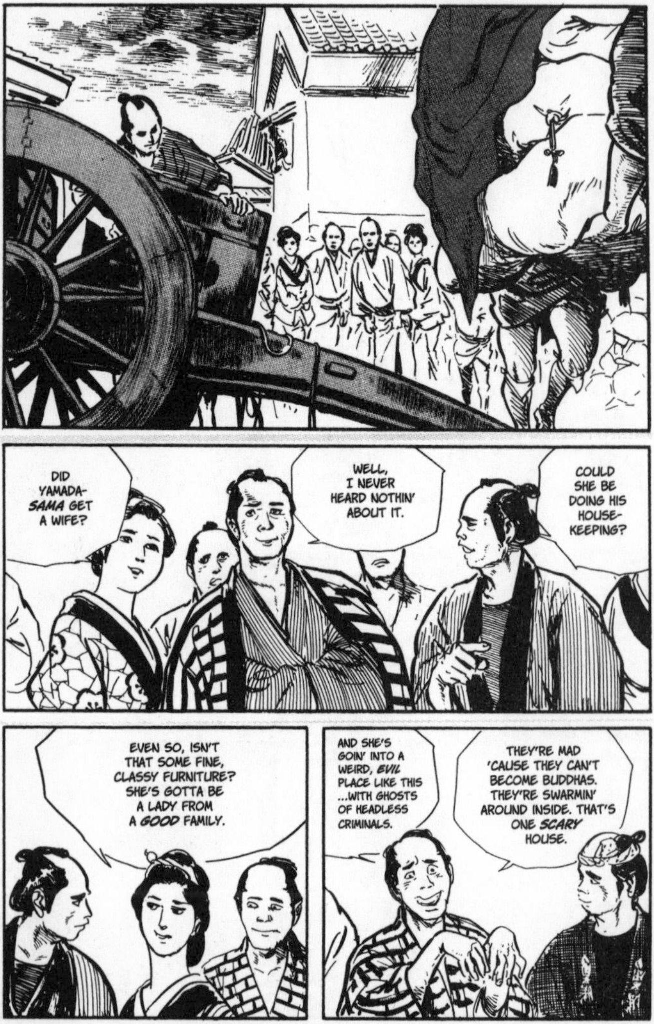
DID YAMADA-SAMA GET A WIFE?
WELL, I NEVER HEARD NOTHIN' ABOUT IT.
COULD SHE BE DOING HIS HOUSE-KEEPING?
EVEN SO, ISN'T THAT SOME FINE, CLASSY FURNITURE? SHE'S GOTTA BE A LADY FROM A GOOD FAMILY.
AND SHE'S GOIN' INTO A WEIRD, EVIL PLACE LIKE THIS ...WITH GHOSTS OF HEADLESS CRIMINALS.
THEY'RE MAD 'CAUSE THEY CAN'T BECOME BUDDHAS. THEY'RE SWARMIN' AROUND INSIDE. THAT'S ONE SCARY HOUSE.

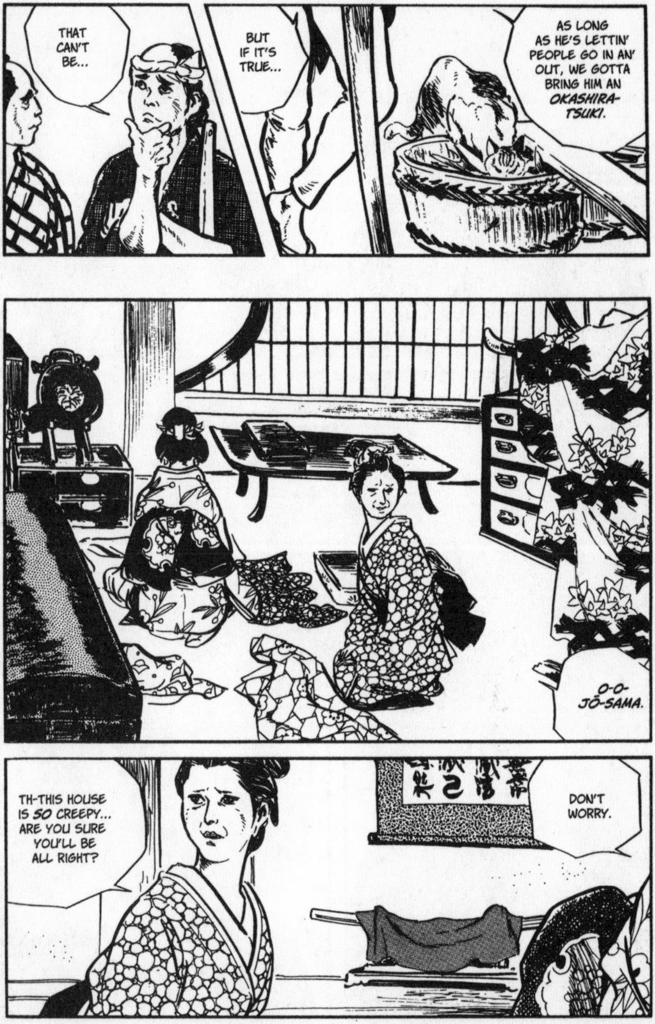
THAT CAN'T BE...
BUT IF IT'S TRUE...
AS LONG AS HE'S LETTIN' PEOPLE GO IN AN' OUT, WE GOTTA BRING HIM AN *OKASHIRA-TSUKI*.
O-O-JŌ-SAMA.
TH-THIS HOUSE IS *SO* CREEPY... ARE YOU SURE YOU'LL BE ALL RIGHT?
DON'T WORRY.

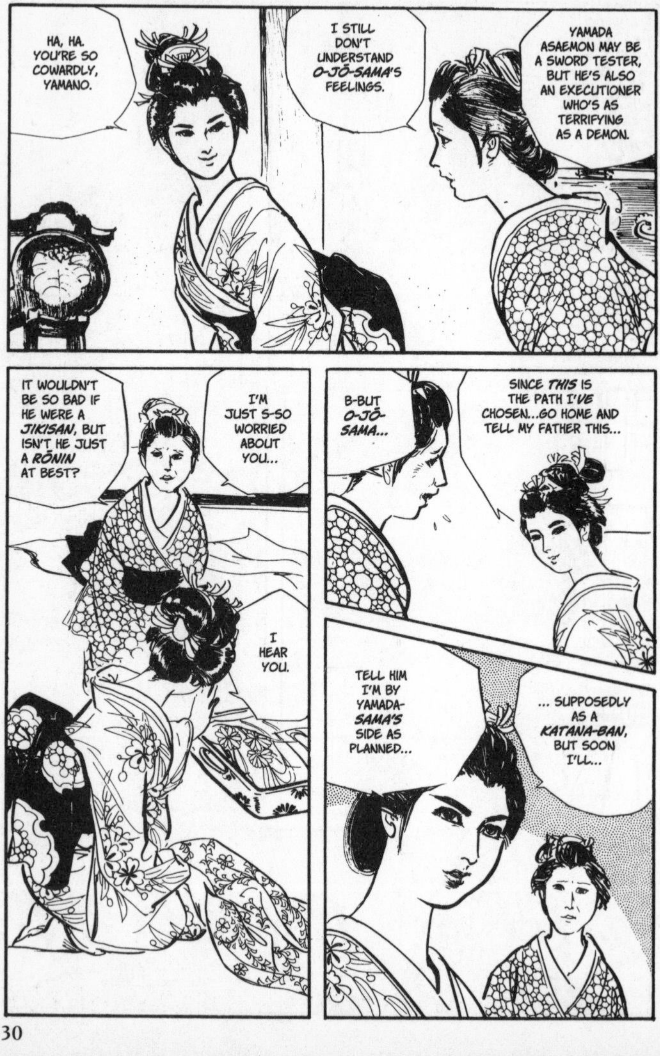
HA, HA. YOU'RE SO COWARDLY, YAMANO.
I STILL DON'T UNDERSTAND *O-JŌ-SAMA*'S FEELINGS.
YAMADA ASAEMON MAY BE A SWORD TESTER, BUT HE'S ALSO AN EXECUTIONER WHO'S AS TERRIFYING AS A DEMON.
IT WOULDN'T BE SO BAD IF HE WERE A *JIKISAN*, BUT ISN'T HE JUST A *RŌNIN* AT BEST?
I'M JUST S-SO WORRIED ABOUT YOU...
I HEAR YOU.
B-BUT *O-JŌ-SAMA*...
SINCE *THIS* IS THE PATH *I'VE* CHOSEN...GO HOME AND TELL MY FATHER THIS...
TELL HIM I'M BY YAMADA-*SAMA'S* SIDE AS PLANNED...
... SUPPOSEDLY AS A *KATANA-BAN*, BUT SOON I'LL...

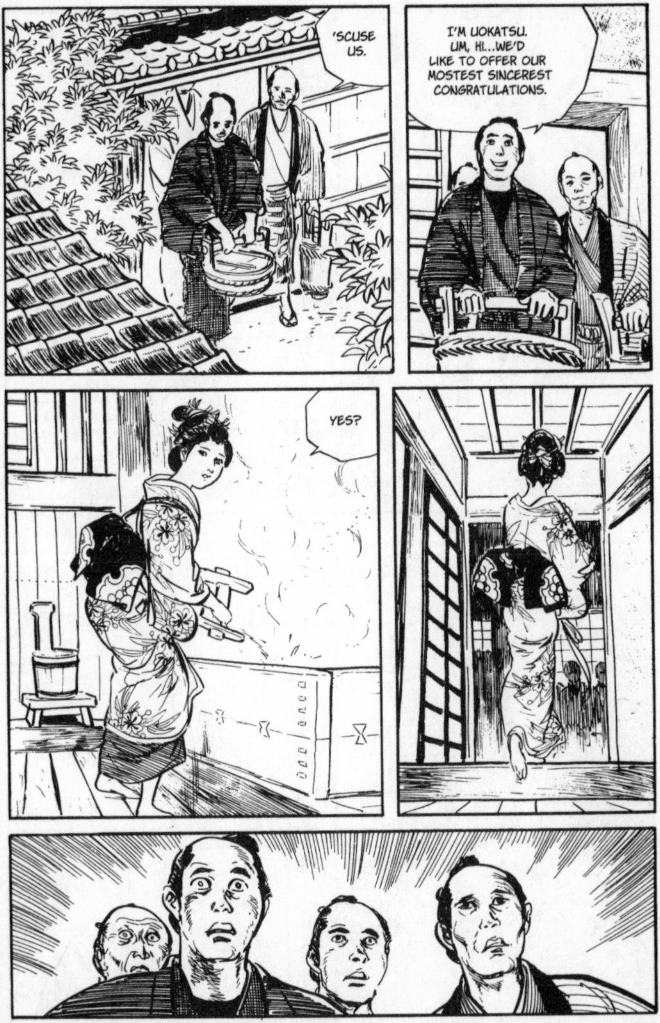
'SCUSE US.
I'M UOKATSU. UM, HI...WE'D LIKE TO OFFER OUR MOSTEST SINCEREST CONGRATULATIONS.
YES?

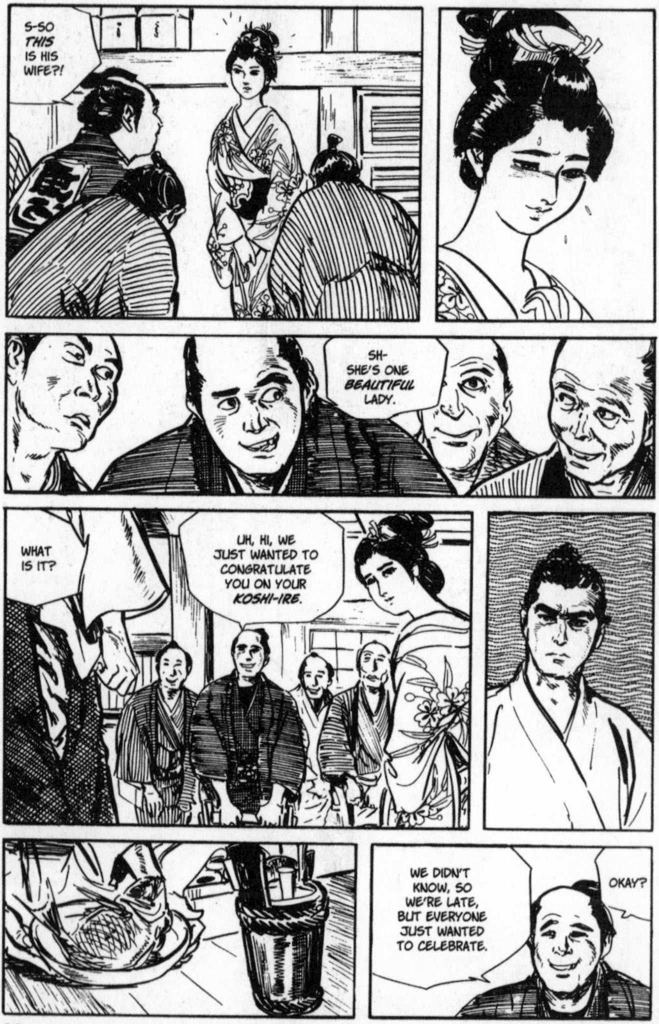
S-SO *THIS* IS HIS WIFE?!
SH- SHE'S ONE *BEAUTIFUL* LADY.
WHAT IS IT?
UH, HI, WE JUST WANTED TO CONGRATULATE YOU ON YOUR *KOSHI-IRE*.
WE DIDN'T KNOW, SO WE'RE LATE, BUT EVERYONE JUST WANTED TO CELEBRATE.
OKAY?

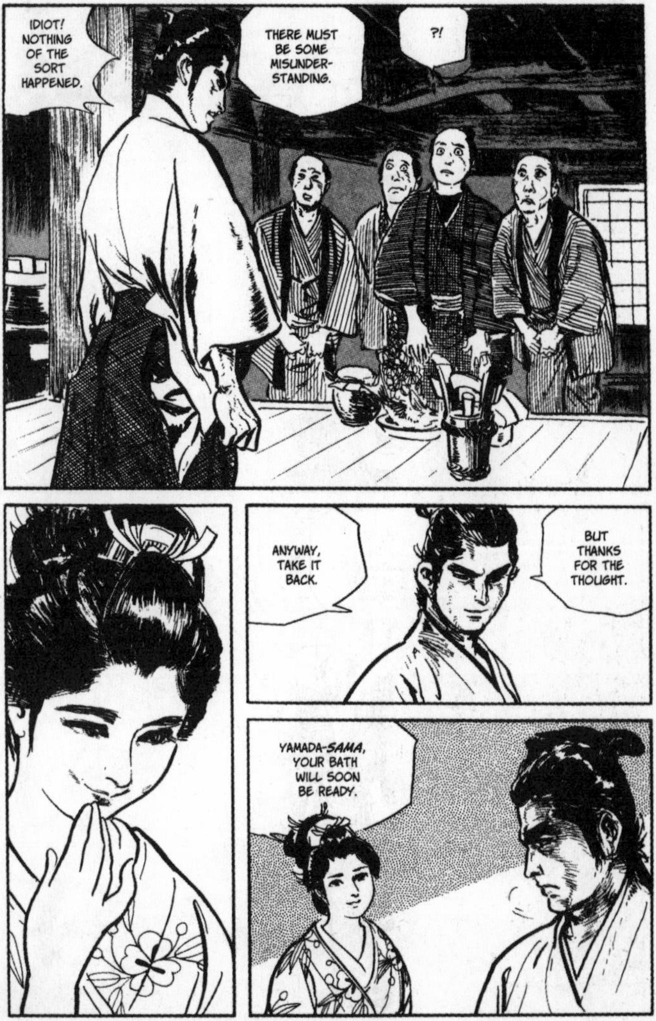

IDIOT! NOTHING OF THE SORT HAPPENED.
THERE MUST BE SOME MISUNDER-STANDING.
?!
ANYWAY, TAKE IT BACK.
BUT THANKS FOR THE THOUGHT.
YAMADA-*SAMA*, YOUR BATH WILL SOON BE READY.

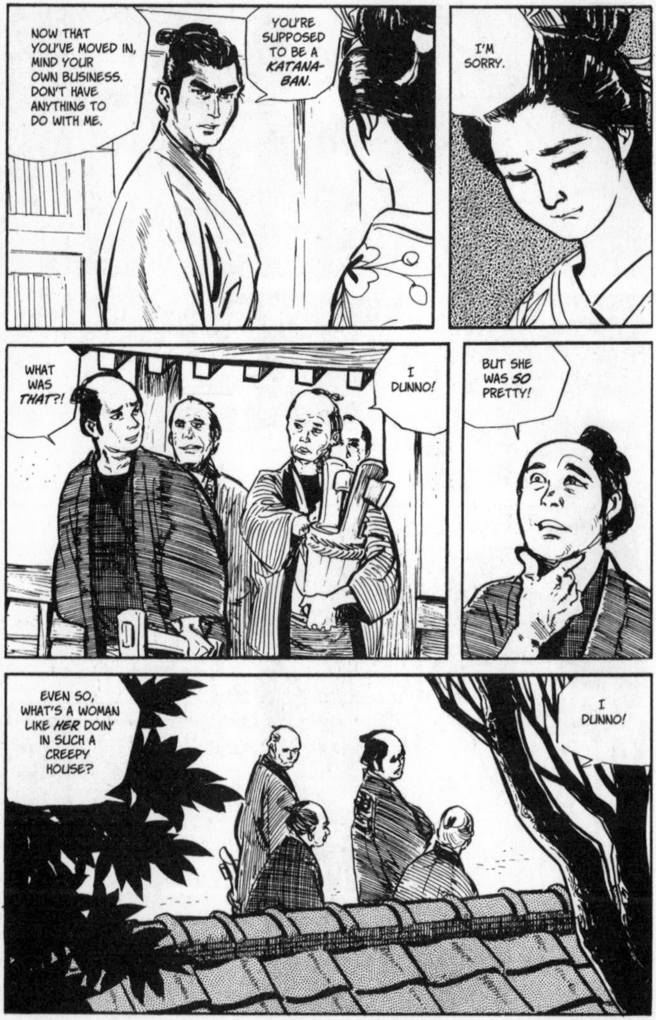
NOW THAT YOU'VE MOVED IN, MIND YOUR OWN BUSINESS. DON'T HAVE ANYTHING TO DO WITH ME.
YOU'RE SUPPOSED TO BE A *KATANA-BAN.*
I'M SORRY.
WHAT WAS *THAT?!*
I DUNNO!
BUT SHE WAS *SO* PRETTY!
EVEN SO, WHAT'S A WOMAN LIKE *HER* DOIN' IN SUCH A CREEPY HOUSE?
I DUNNO!

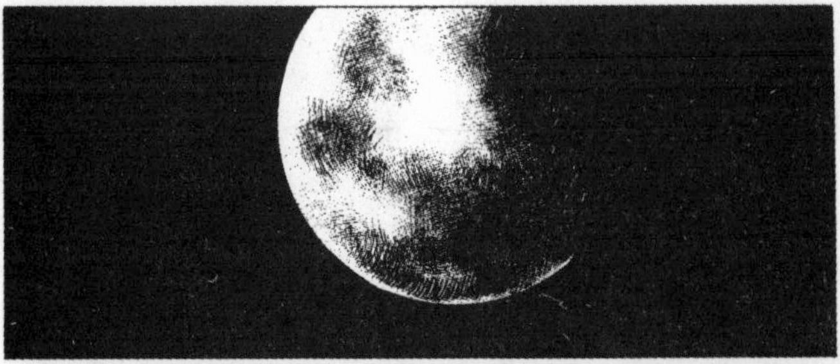
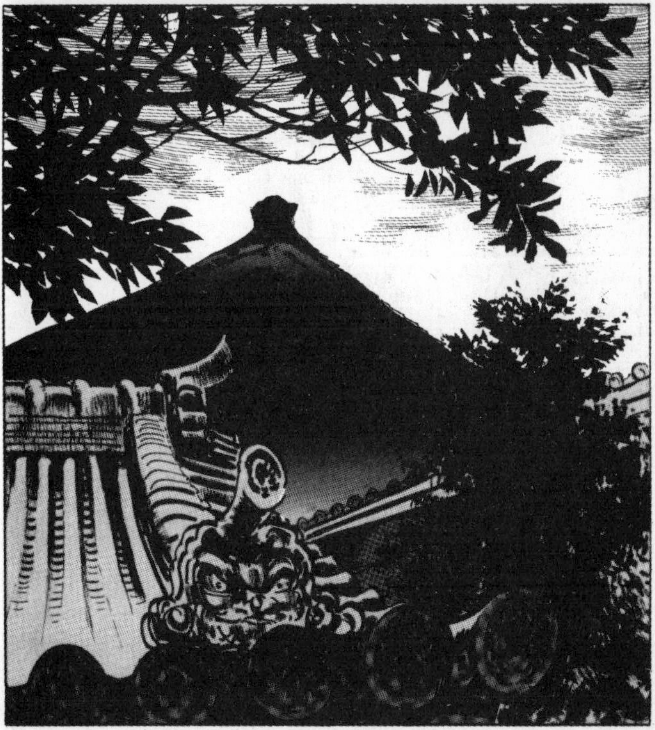

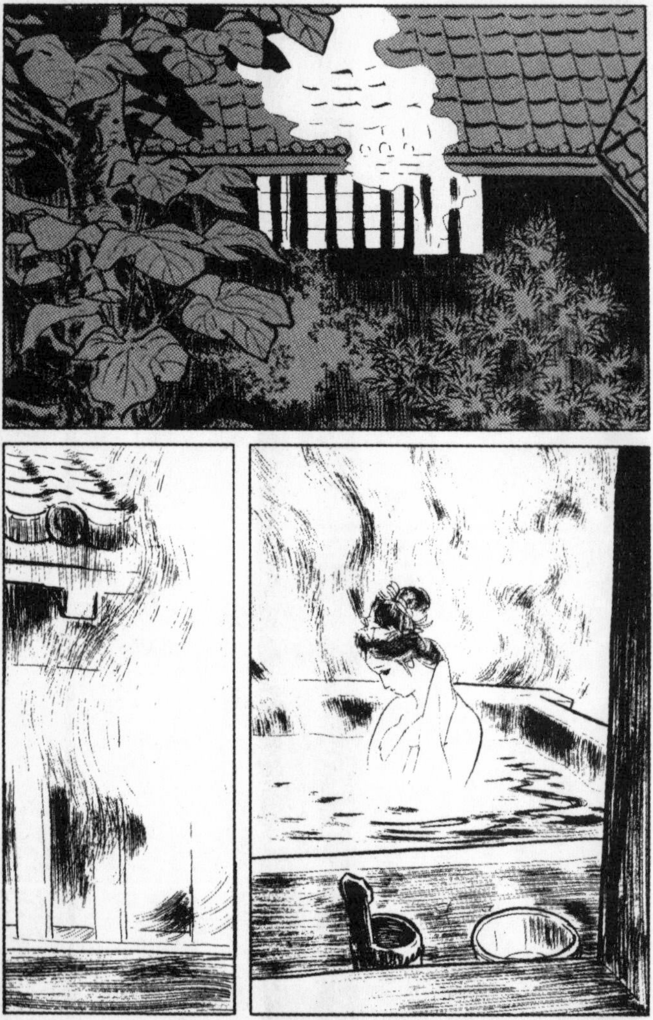

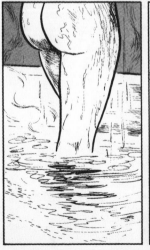

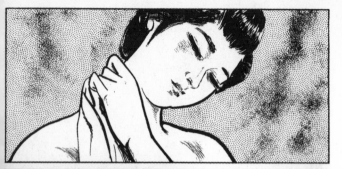

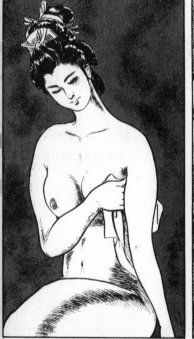

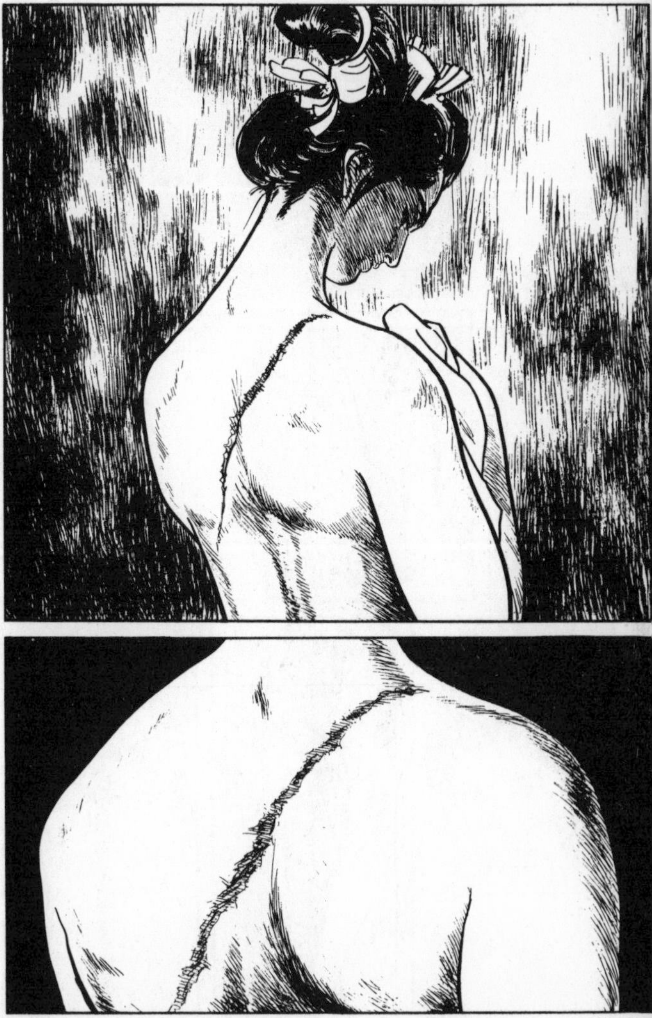

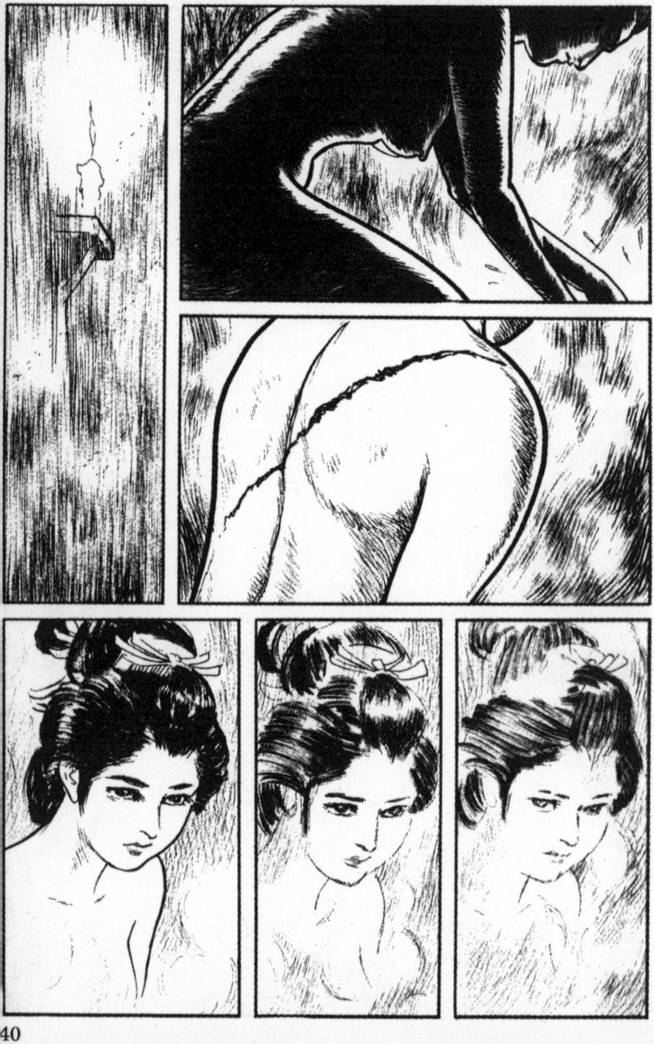

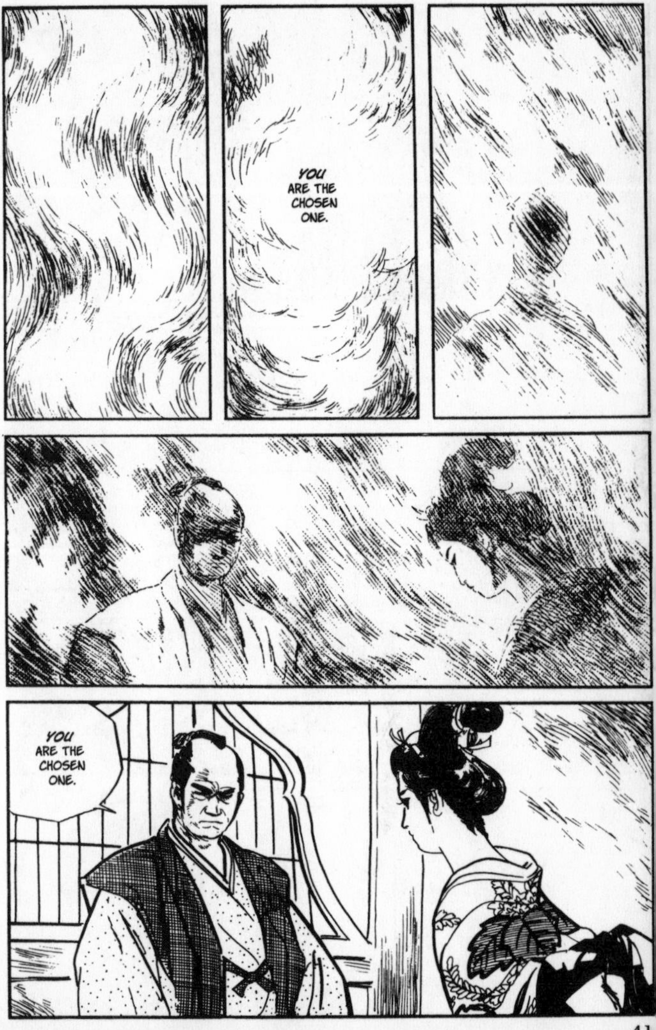
YOU ARE THE CHOSEN ONE.
YOU ARE THE CHOSEN ONE.

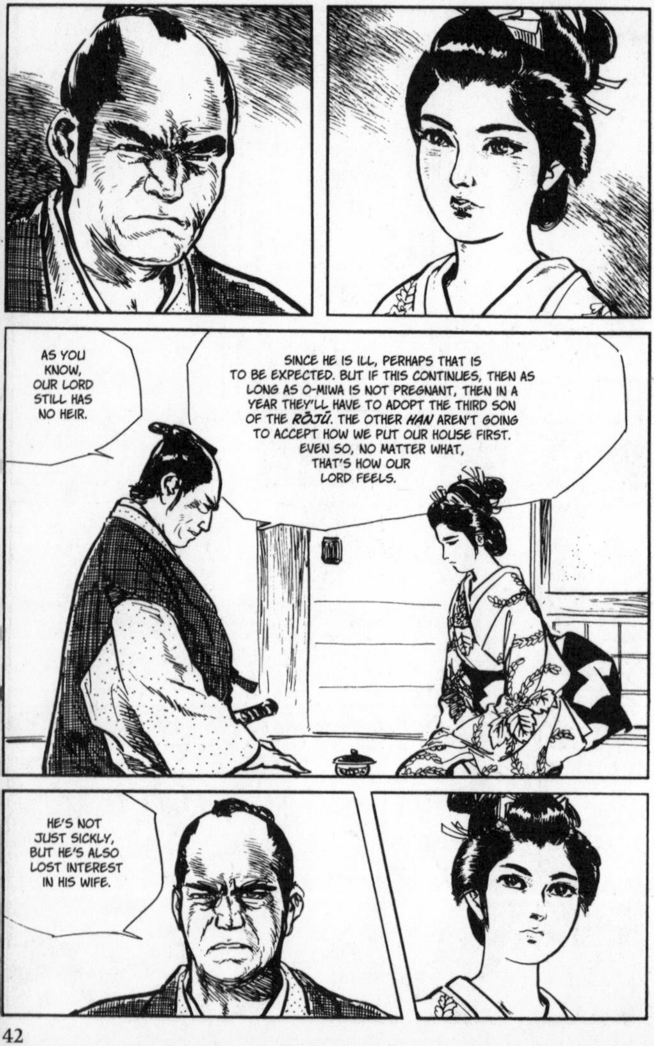
AS YOU KNOW, OUR LORD STILL HAS NO HEIR.
SINCE HE IS ILL, PERHAPS THAT IS TO BE EXPECTED. BUT IF THIS CONTINUES, THEN AS LONG AS O-MIWA IS NOT PREGNANT, THEN IN A YEAR THEY'LL HAVE TO ADOPT THE THIRD SON OF THE *RŌJŪ*. THE OTHER *HAN* AREN'T GOING TO ACCEPT HOW WE PUT OUR HOUSE FIRST. EVEN SO, NO MATTER WHAT, THAT'S HOW OUR LORD FEELS.
HE'S NOT JUST SICKLY, BUT HE'S ALSO LOST INTEREST IN HIS WIFE.

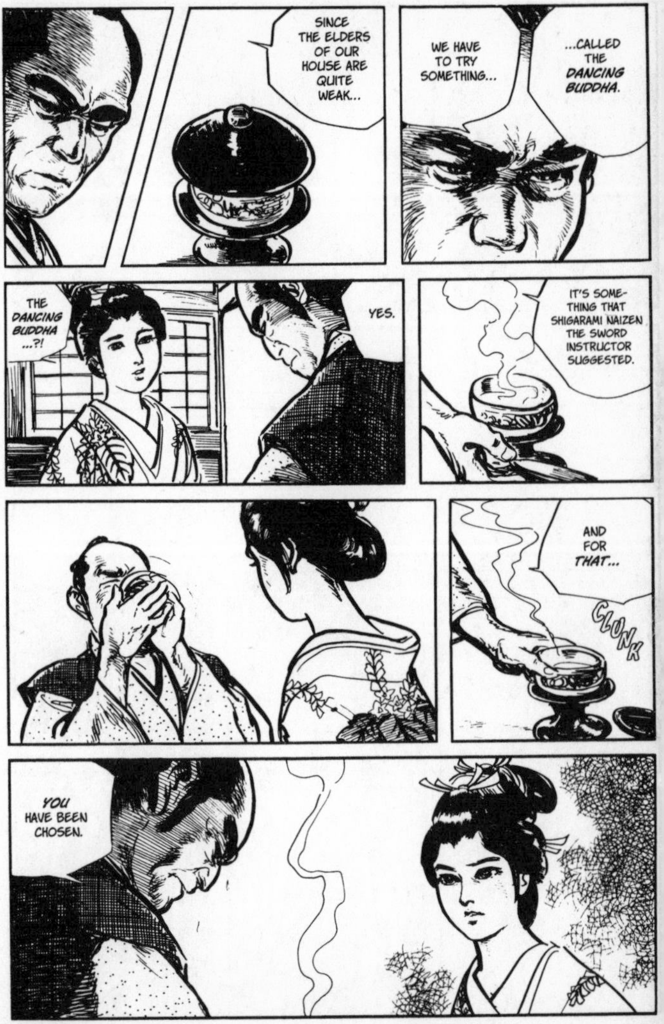
SINCE THE ELDERS OF OUR HOUSE ARE QUITE WEAK...
WE HAVE TO TRY SOMETHING...
...CALLED THE *DANCING BUDDHA*.
THE *DANCING BUDDHA* ...?!
YES.
IT'S SOMETHING THAT SHIGARAMI NAIZEN THE SWORD INSTRUCTOR SUGGESTED.
AND FOR *THAT*...
CLUNK
YOU HAVE BEEN CHOSEN.

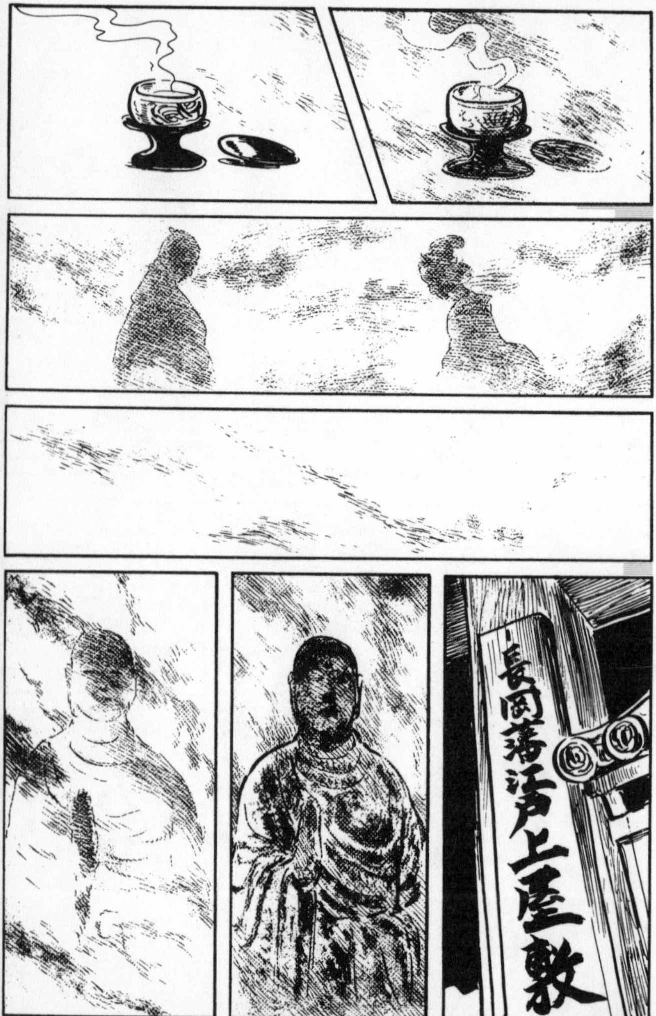
長岡藩江戸上屋敷

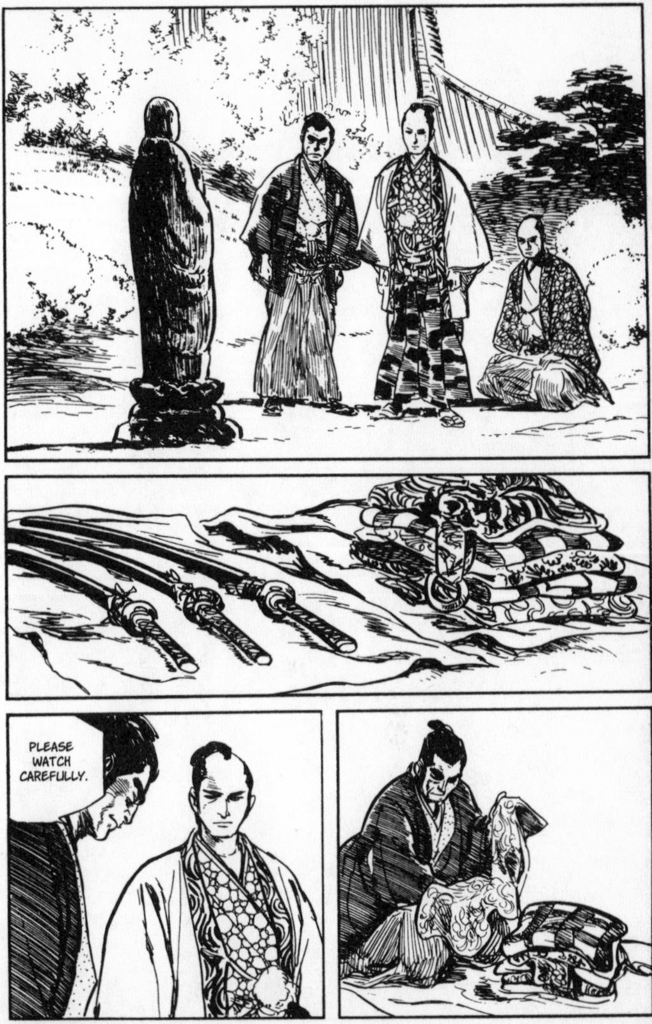
PLEASE WATCH CAREFULLY.

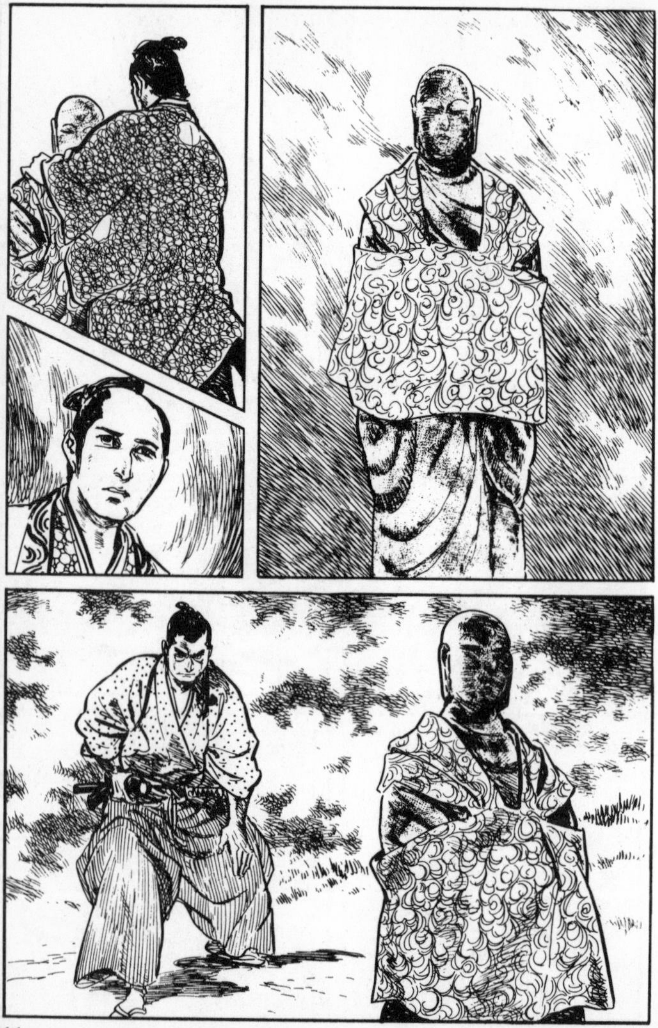

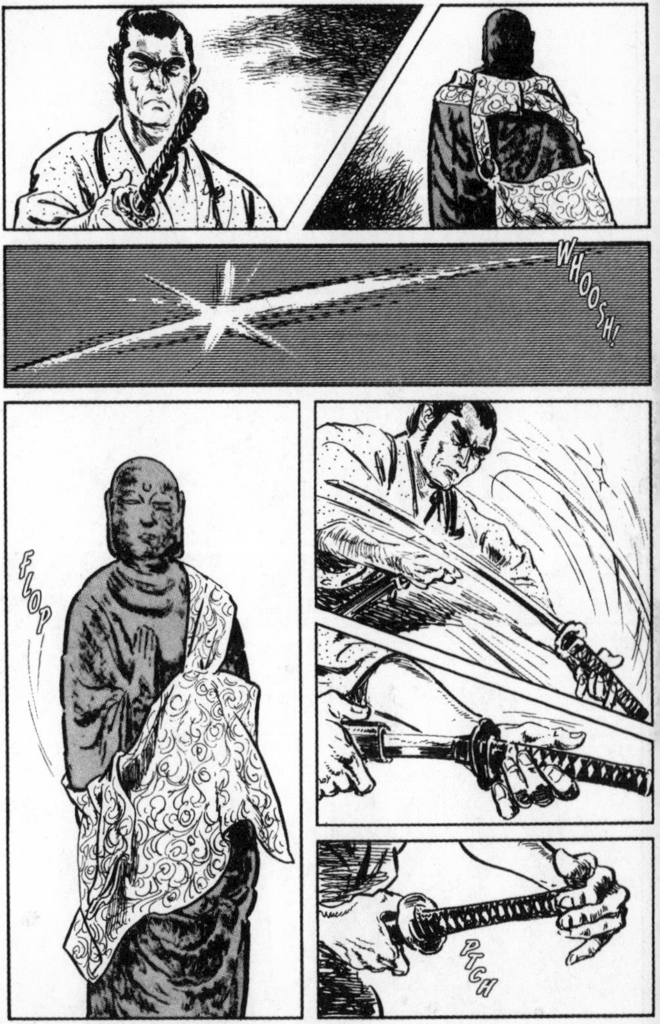
WHOOSH!
FLOP
PTCH

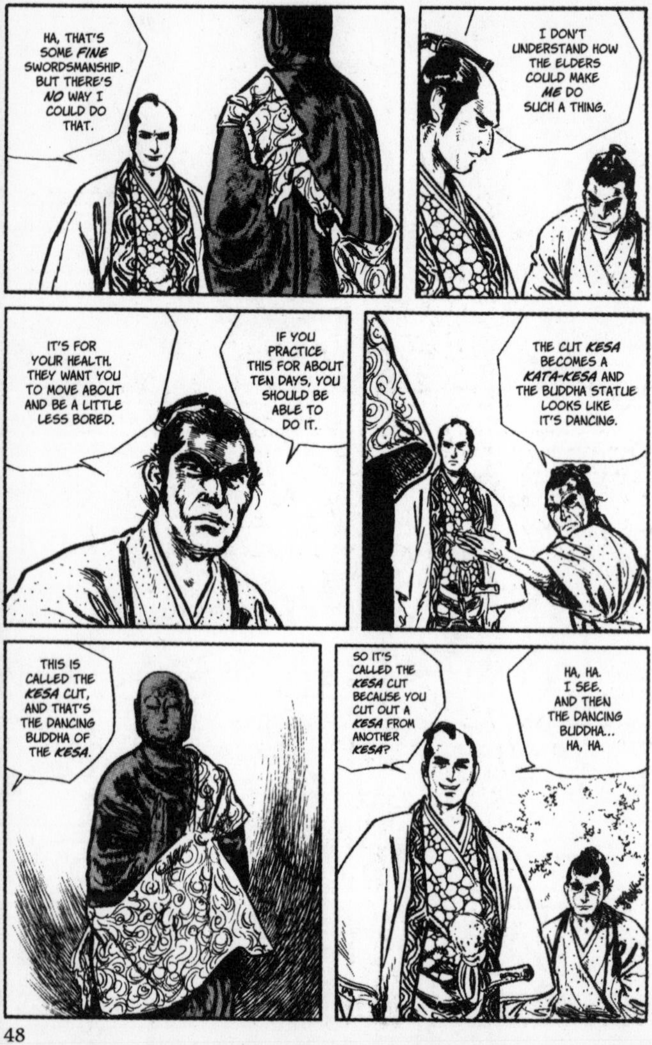
HA, THAT'S SOME *FINE* SWORDSMANSHIP. BUT THERE'S *NO* WAY I COULD DO THAT.
I DON'T UNDERSTAND HOW THE ELDERS COULD MAKE *ME* DO SUCH A THING.
IT'S FOR YOUR HEALTH. THEY WANT YOU TO MOVE ABOUT AND BE A LITTLE LESS BORED.
IF YOU PRACTICE THIS FOR ABOUT TEN DAYS, YOU SHOULD BE ABLE TO DO IT.
THE CUT *KESA* BECOMES A *KATA-KESA* AND THE BUDDHA STATUE LOOKS LIKE IT'S DANCING.
THIS IS CALLED THE *KESA* CUT, AND THAT'S THE DANCING BUDDHA OF THE *KESA*.
SO IT'S CALLED THE *KESA* CUT BECAUSE YOU CUT OUT A *KESA* FROM ANOTHER *KESA*?
HA, HA. I SEE. AND THEN THE DANCING BUDDHA... HA, HA.

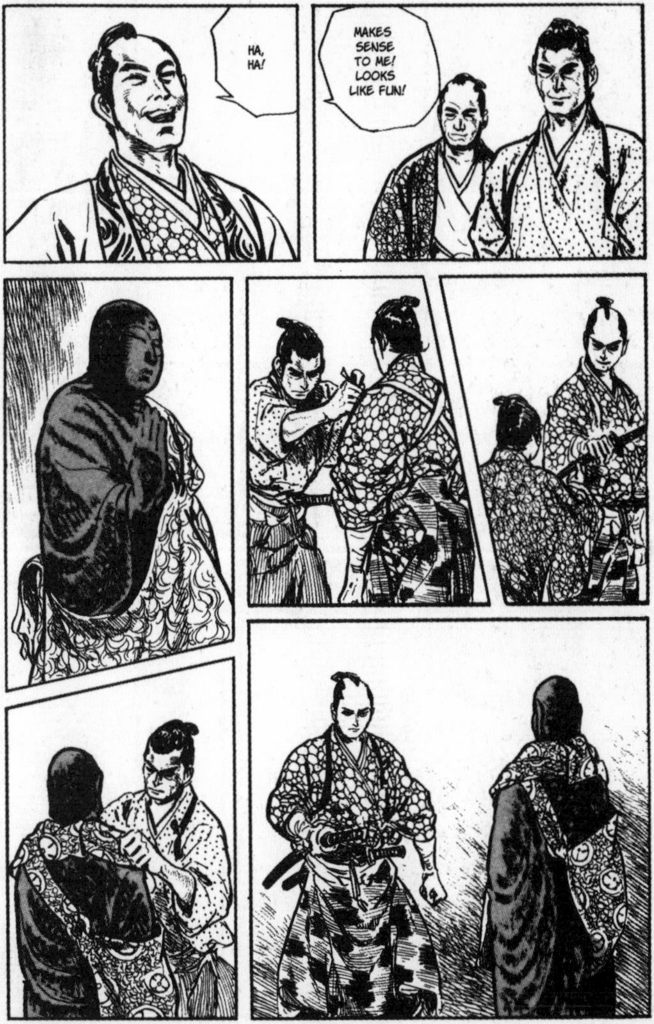
HA, HA!
MAKES SENSE TO ME! LOOKS LIKE FUN!

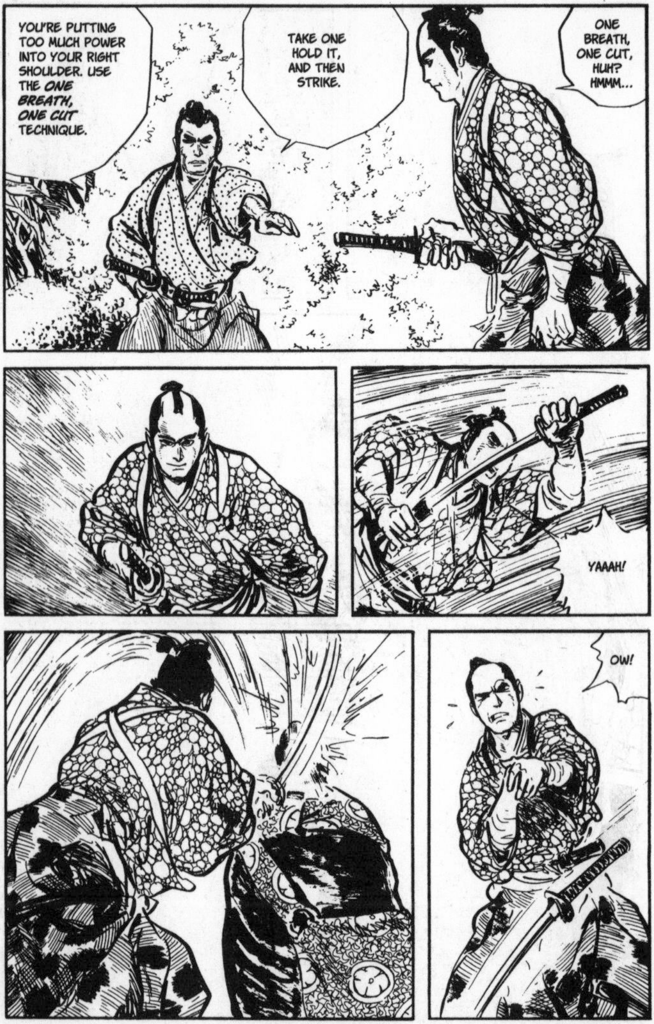
YOU'RE PUTTING TOO MUCH POWER INTO YOUR RIGHT SHOULDER. USE THE *ONE BREATH, ONE CUT* TECHNIQUE.
TAKE ONE HOLD IT, AND THEN STRIKE.
ONE BREATH, ONE CUT, HUH? HMMM...
YAAAH!
OW!

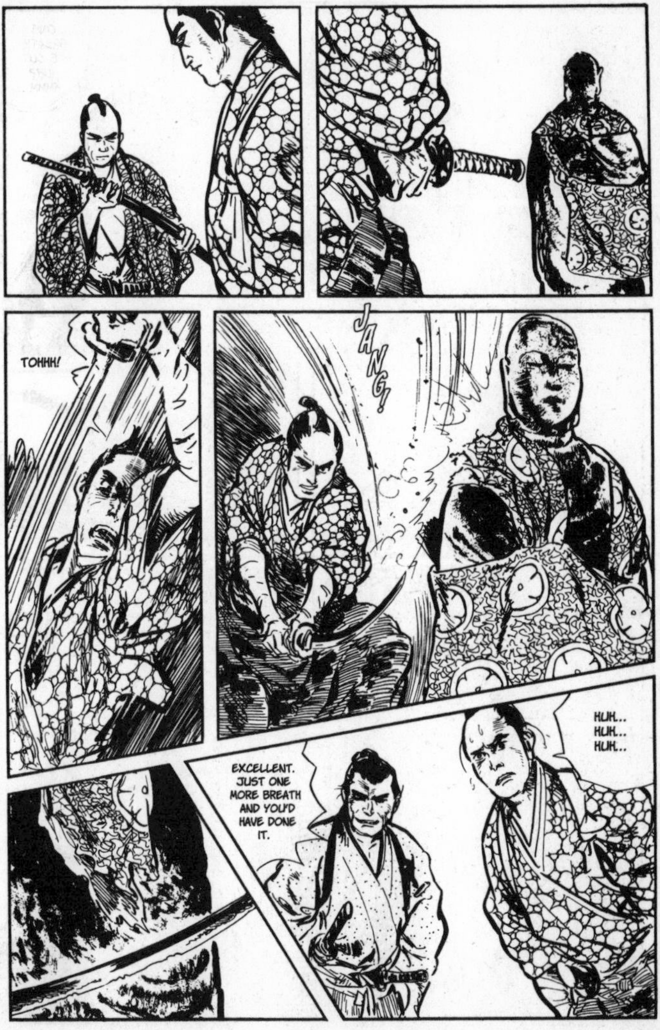
TOHHH!
JANG!
EXCELLENT. JUST ONE MORE BREATH AND YOU'D HAVE DONE IT.
HUH... HUH... HUH...

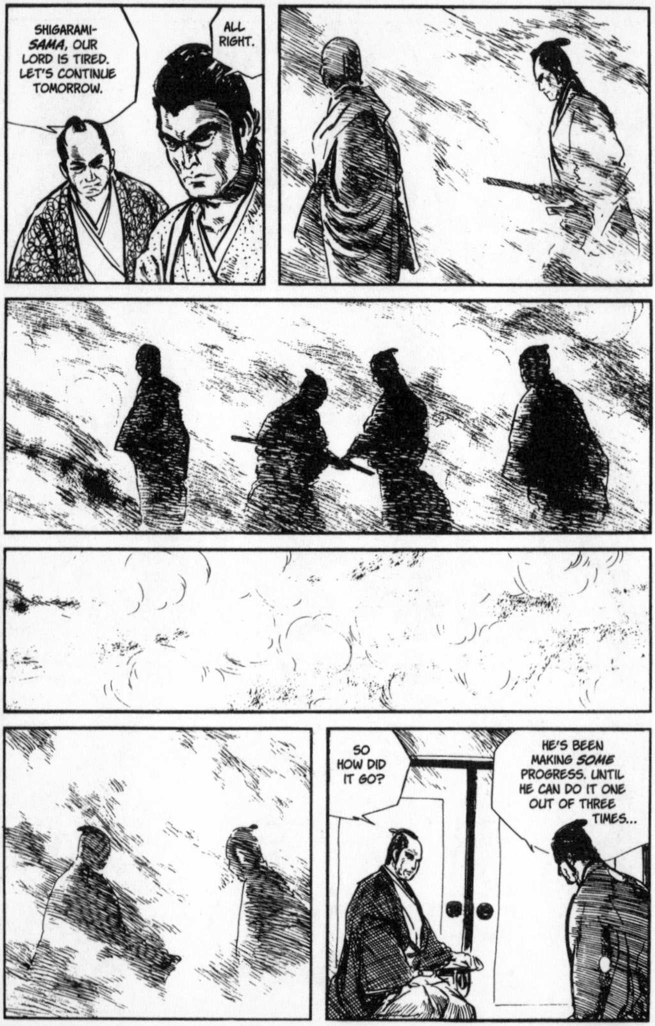
SHIGARAMI-*SAMA*, OUR LORD IS TIRED. LET'S CONTINUE TOMORROW.
ALL RIGHT.
SO HOW DID IT GO?
HE'S BEEN MAKING *SOME* PROGRESS. UNTIL HE CAN DO IT ONE OUT OF THREE TIMES...

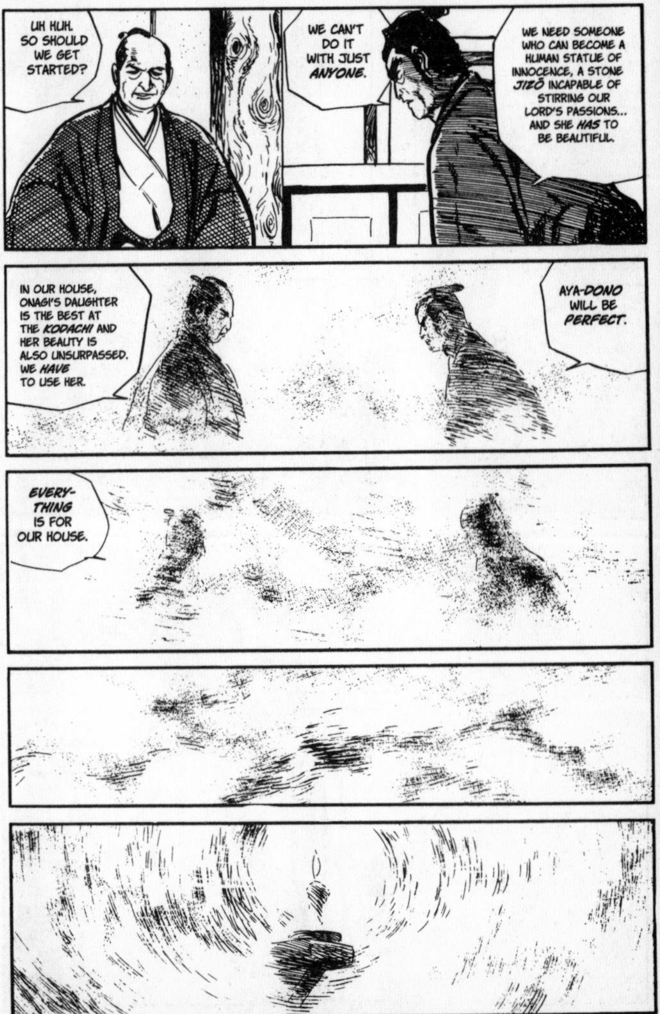
UH HUH. SO SHOULD WE GET STARTED?
WE CAN'T DO IT WITH JUST *ANYONE*.
WE NEED SOMEONE WHO CAN BECOME A HUMAN STATUE OF INNOCENCE, A STONE *JIZŌ* INCAPABLE OF STIRRING OUR LORD'S PASSIONS... AND SHE *HAS* TO BE BEAUTIFUL.
IN OUR HOUSE, ONAGI'S DAUGHTER IS THE BEST AT THE *KODACHI* AND HER BEAUTY IS ALSO UNSURPASSED. WE *HAVE* TO USE HER.
AYA-*DONO* WILL BE *PERFECT*.
EVERY-THING IS FOR OUR HOUSE.

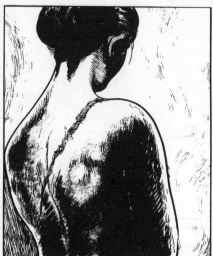

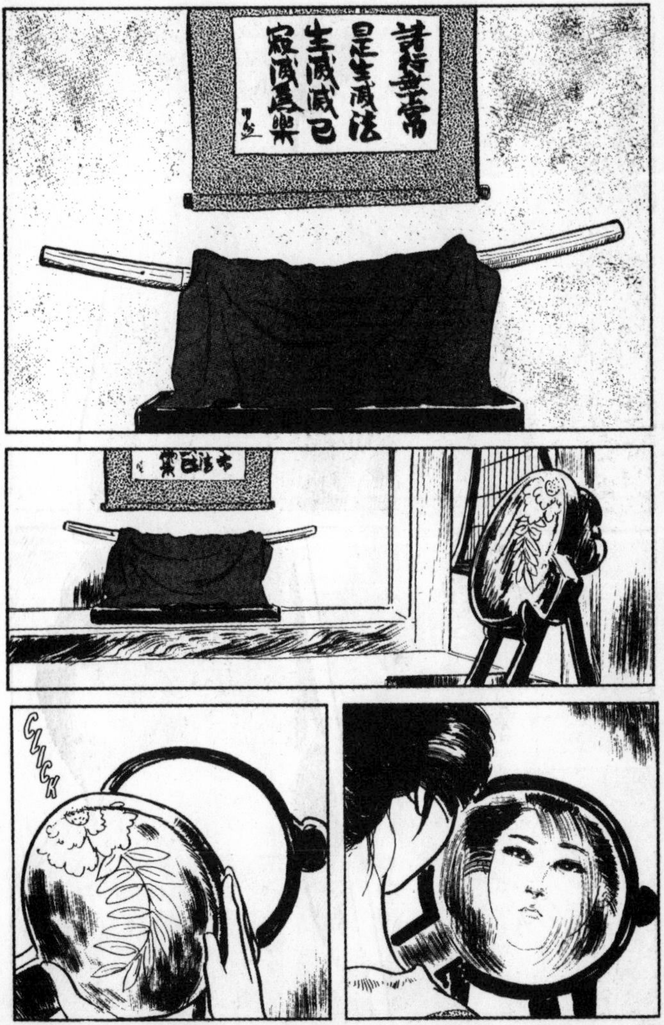
諸行無常
是生滅法
生滅滅已
寂滅為楽
CLICK

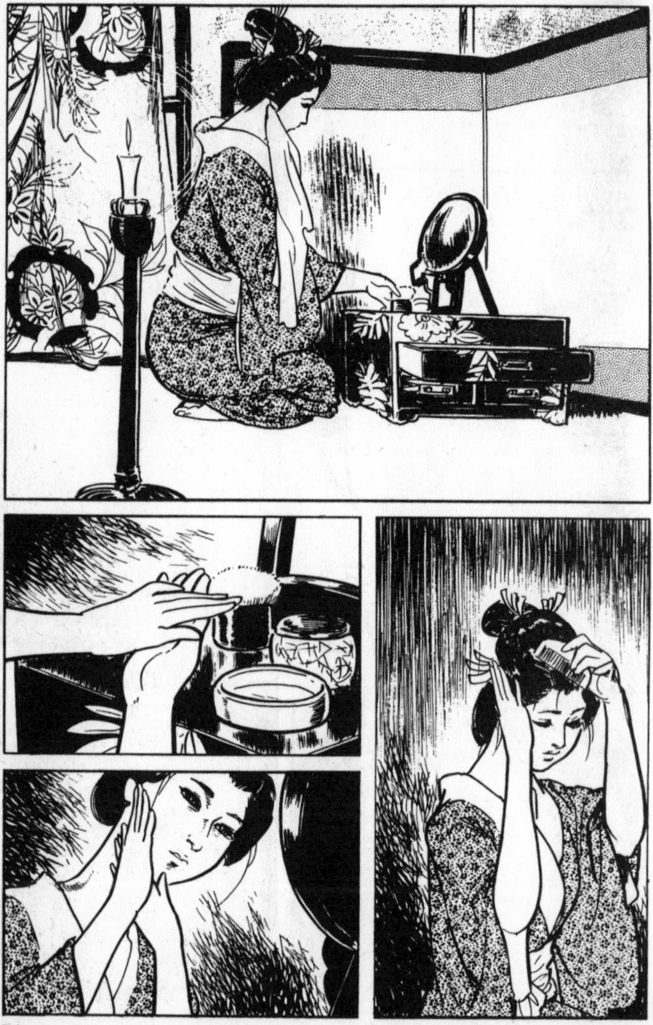

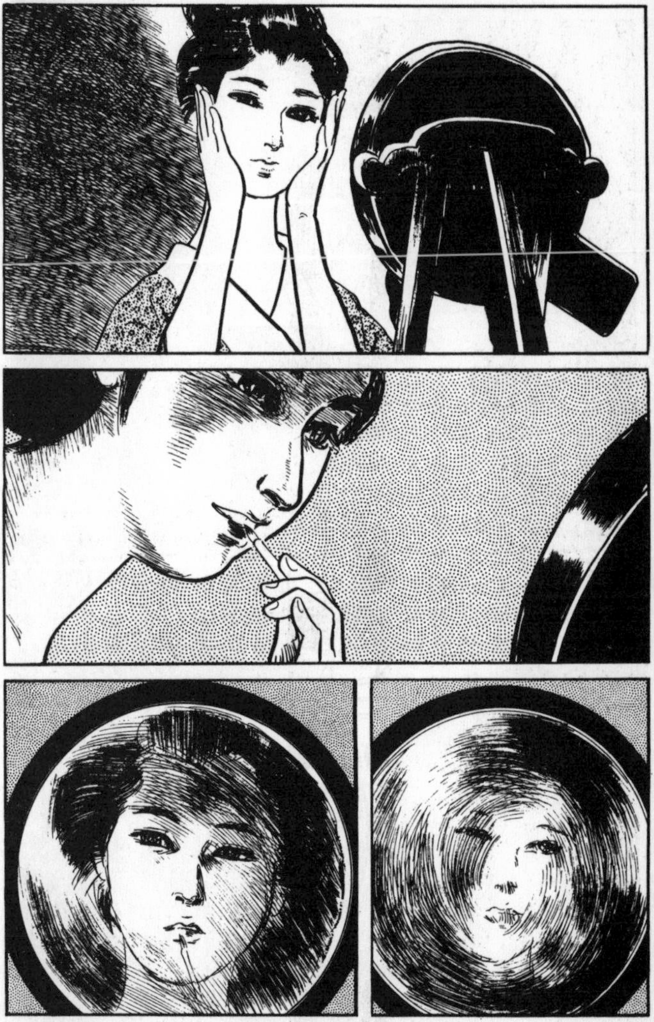

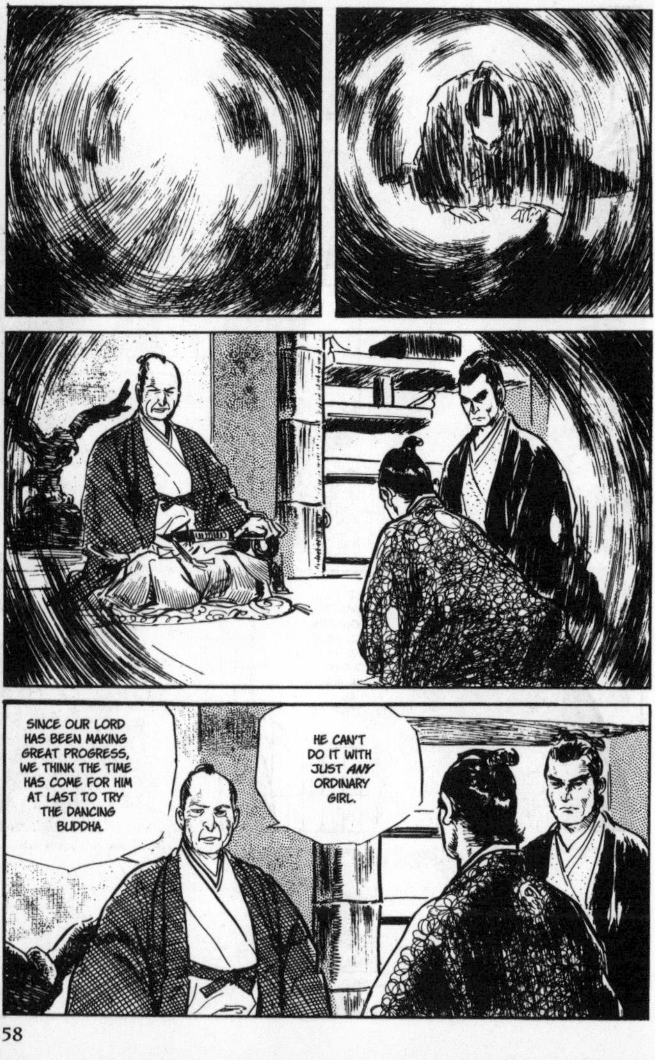
SINCE OUR LORD HAS BEEN MAKING GREAT PROGRESS, WE THINK THE TIME HAS COME FOR HIM AT LAST TO TRY THE DANCING BUDDHA.
HE CAN'T DO IT WITH JUST *ANY* ORDINARY GIRL.

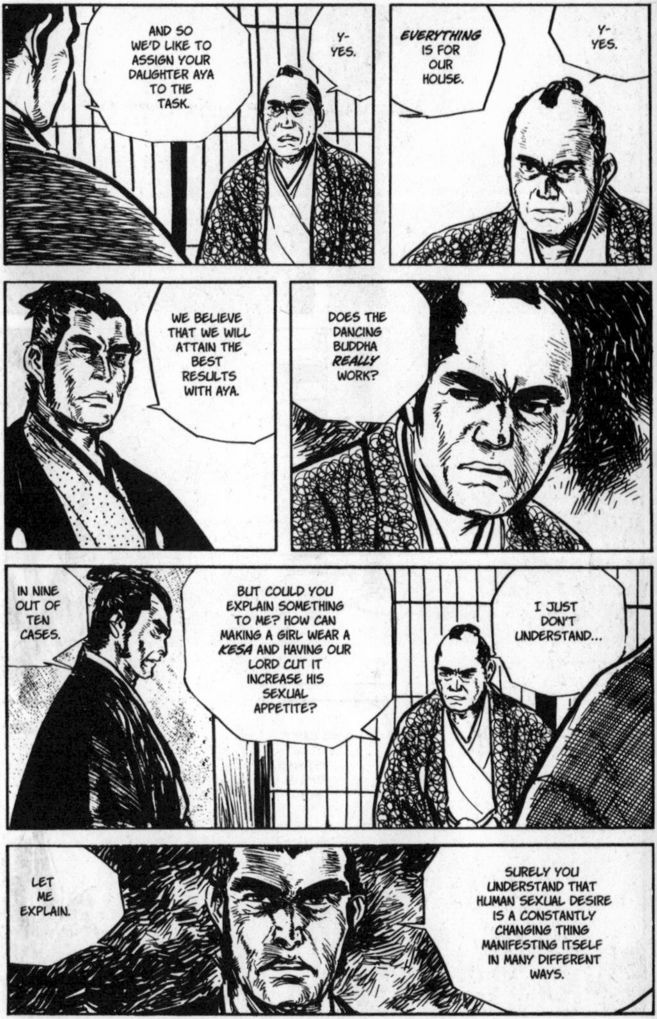
AND SO WE'D LIKE TO ASSIGN YOUR DAUGHTER AYA TO THE TASK.
Y-YES.
EVERYTHING IS FOR OUR HOUSE.
Y-YES.
WE BELIEVE THAT WE WILL ATTAIN THE BEST RESULTS WITH AYA.
DOES THE DANCING BUDDHA *REALLY* WORK?
IN NINE OUT OF TEN CASES.
BUT COULD YOU EXPLAIN SOMETHING TO ME? HOW CAN MAKING A GIRL WEAR A *KESA* AND HAVING OUR LORD CUT IT INCREASE HIS SEXUAL APPETITE?
I JUST DON'T UNDERSTAND...
LET ME EXPLAIN.
SURELY YOU UNDERSTAND THAT HUMAN SEXUAL DESIRE IS A CONSTANTLY CHANGING THING MANIFESTING ITSELF IN MANY DIFFERENT WAYS.

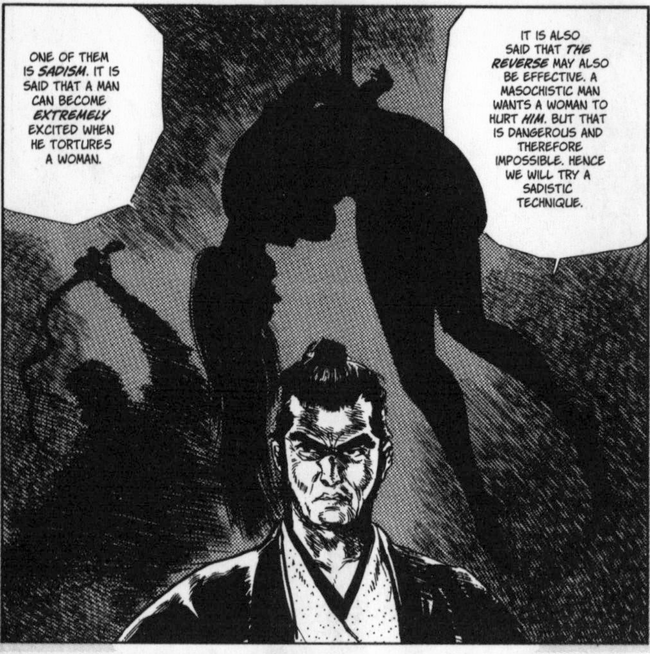
ONE OF THEM IS *SADISM*. IT IS SAID THAT A MAN CAN BECOME *EXTREMELY* EXCITED WHEN HE TORTURES A WOMAN.
IT IS ALSO SAID THAT *THE REVERSE* MAY ALSO BE EFFECTIVE. A MASOCHISTIC MAN WANTS A WOMAN TO HURT *HIM*. BUT THAT IS DANGEROUS AND THEREFORE IMPOSSIBLE. HENCE WE WILL TRY A SADISTIC TECHNIQUE.

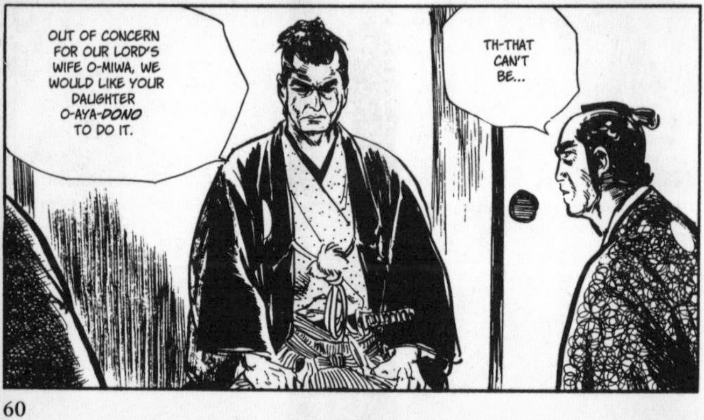
OUT OF CONCERN FOR OUR LORD'S WIFE O-MIWA, WE WOULD LIKE YOUR DAUGHTER O-AYA-*DONO* TO DO IT.
TH-THAT CAN'T BE...

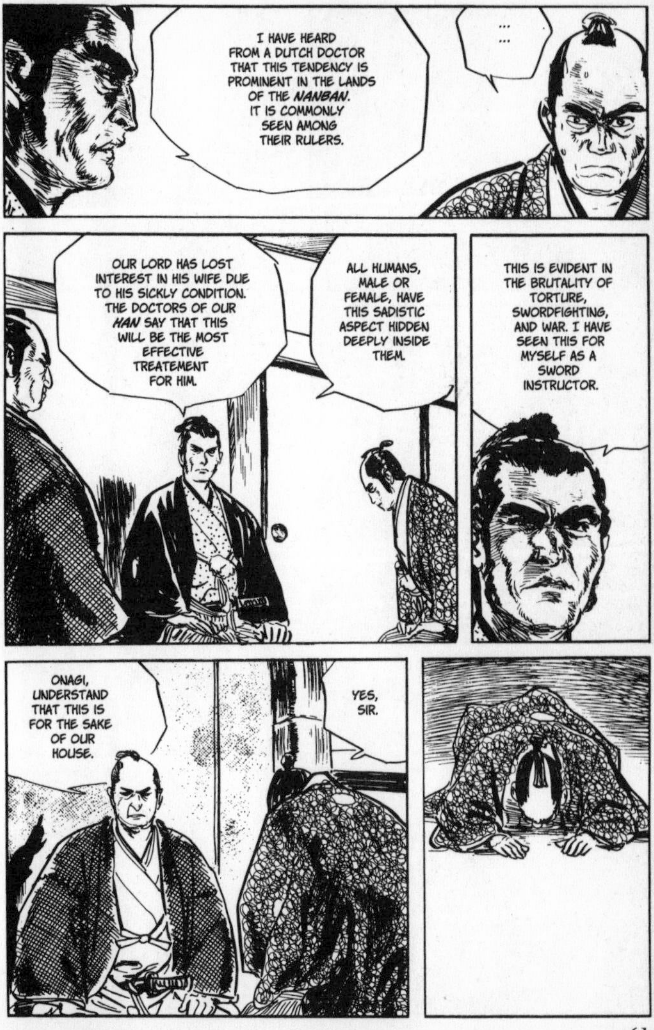

I HAVE HEARD FROM A DUTCH DOCTOR THAT THIS TENDENCY IS PROMINENT IN THE LANDS OF THE *NANBAN*. IT IS COMMONLY SEEN AMONG THEIR RULERS.
...
...
OUR LORD HAS LOST INTEREST IN HIS WIFE DUE TO HIS SICKLY CONDITION. THE DOCTORS OF OUR *HAN* SAY THAT THIS WILL BE THE MOST EFFECTIVE TREATEMENT FOR HIM.
ALL HUMANS, MALE OR FEMALE, HAVE THIS SADISTIC ASPECT HIDDEN DEEPLY INSIDE THEM.
THIS IS EVIDENT IN THE BRUTALITY OF TORTURE, SWORDFIGHTING, AND WAR. I HAVE SEEN THIS FOR MYSELF AS A SWORD INSTRUCTOR.
ONAGI, UNDERSTAND THAT THIS IS FOR THE SAKE OF OUR HOUSE.
YES, SIR.

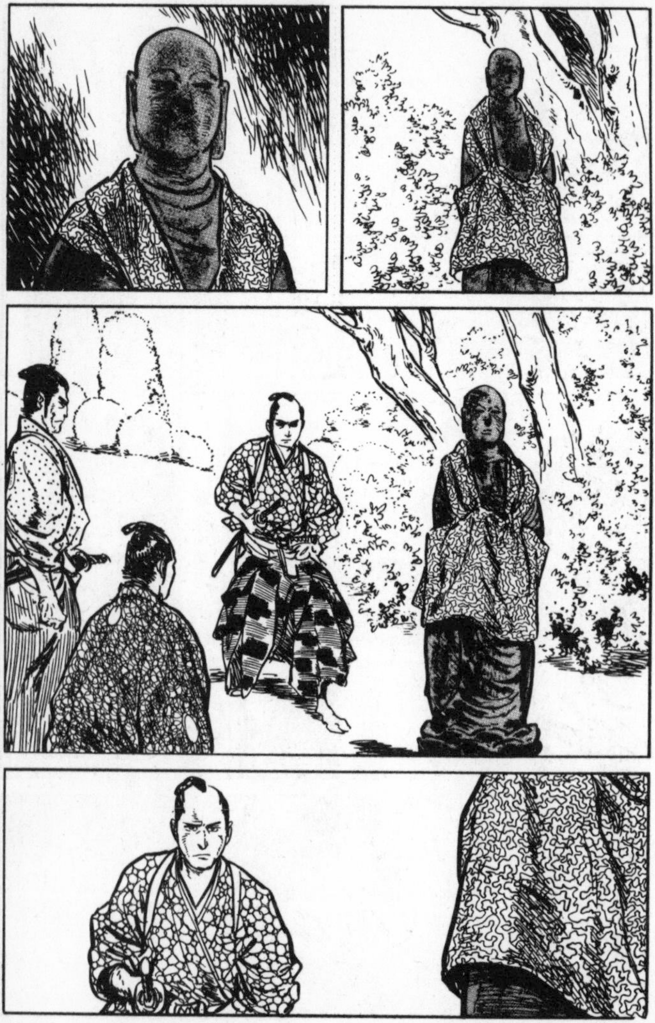

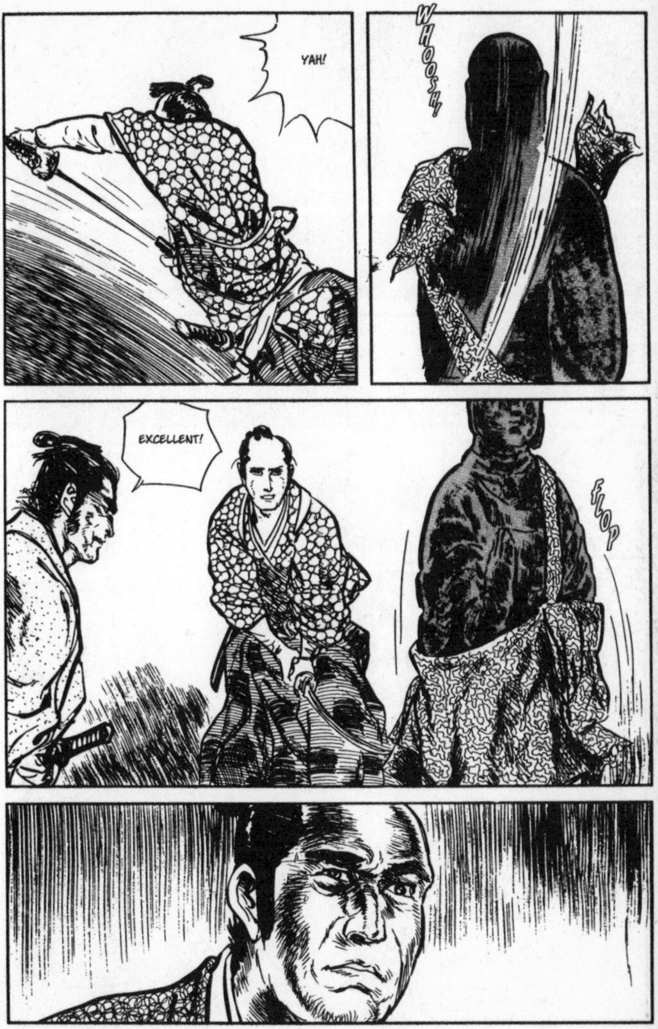
YAH!
WHOOSH!
EXCELLENT!
FLOP

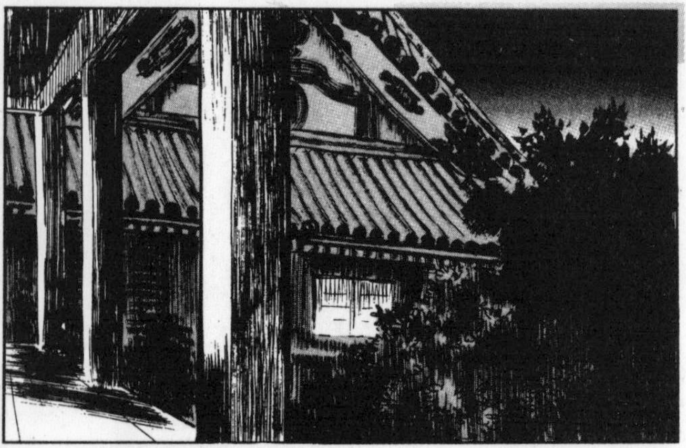

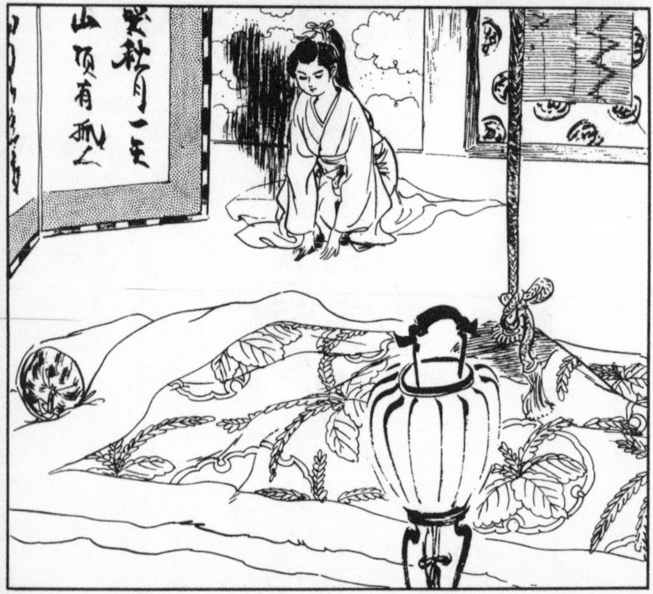
秋月一天
山顶有孤人

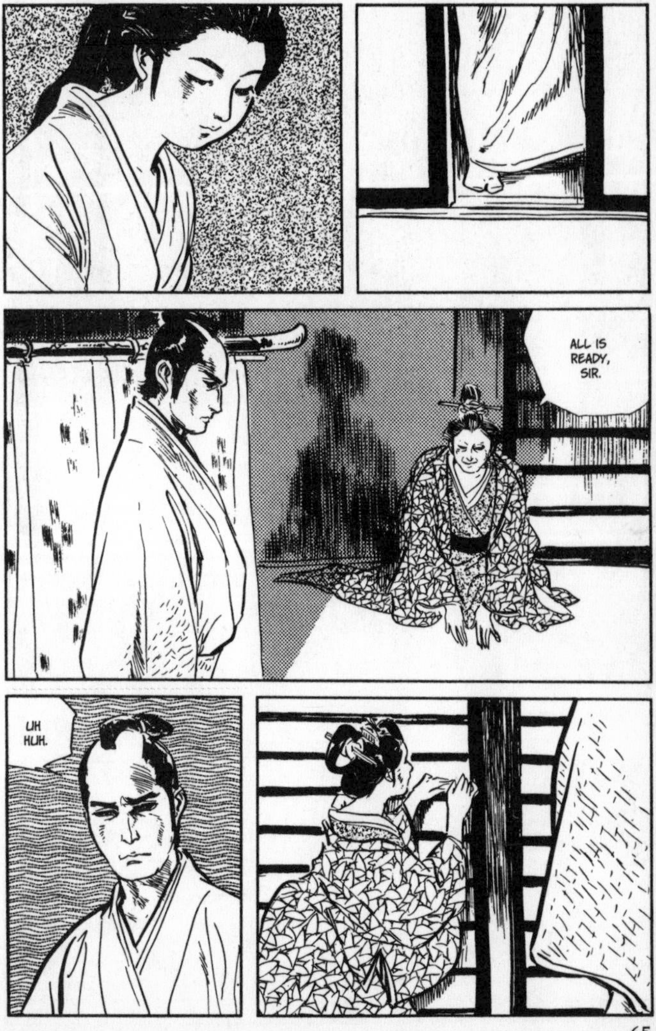
ALL IS READY, SIR.
UH HUH.

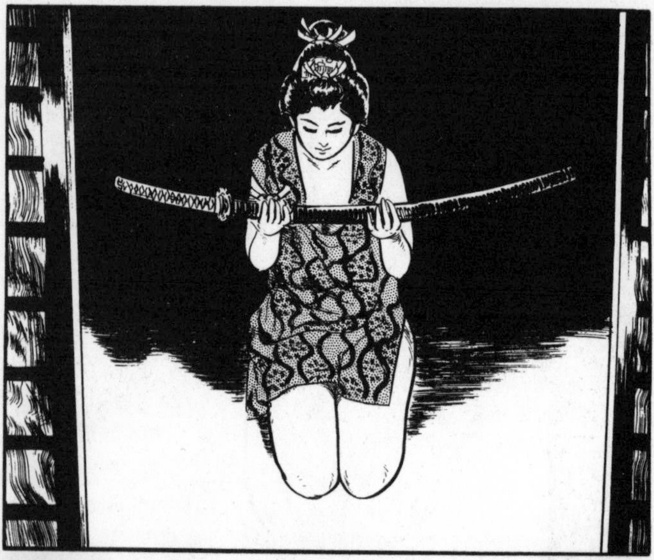
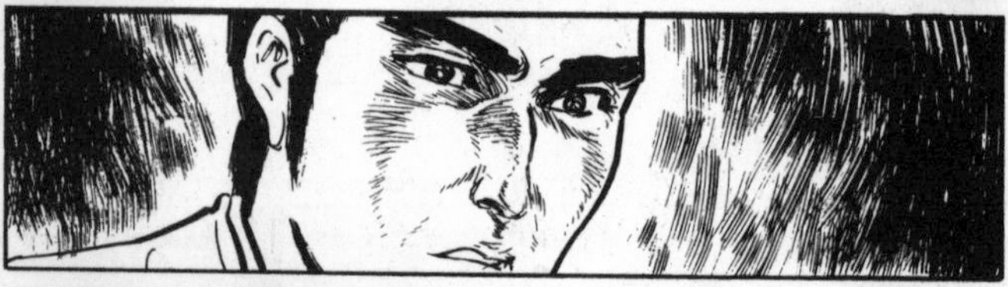
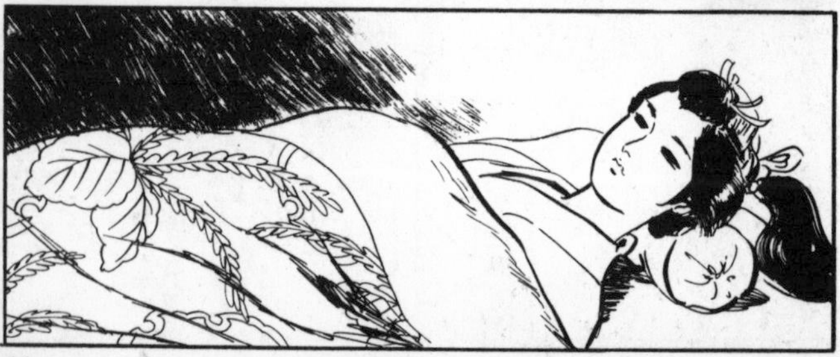

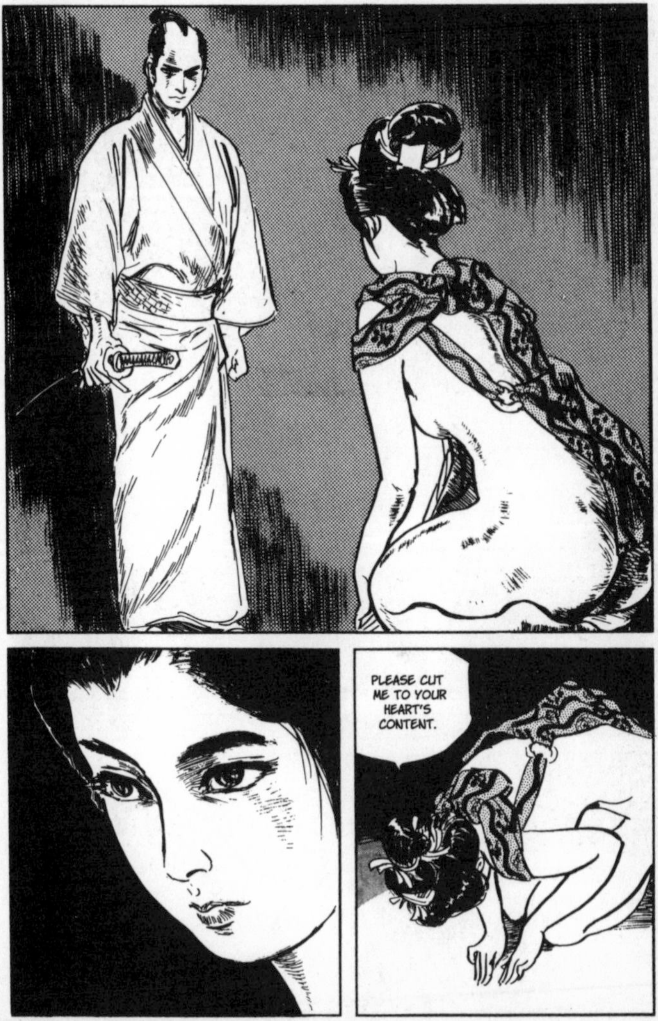
PLEASE CUT ME TO YOUR HEART'S CONTENT.

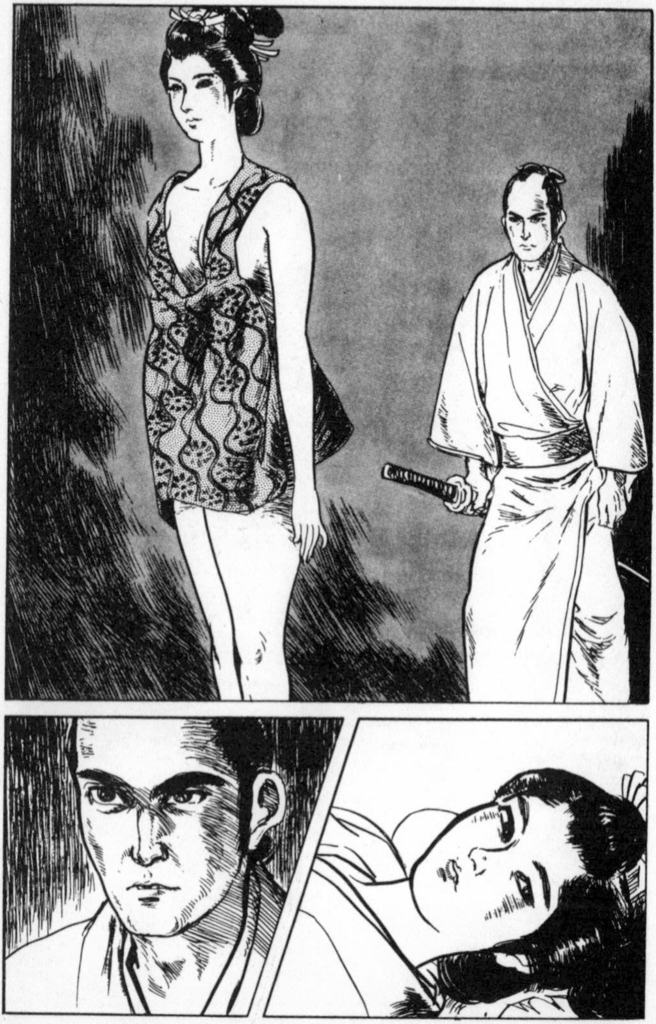

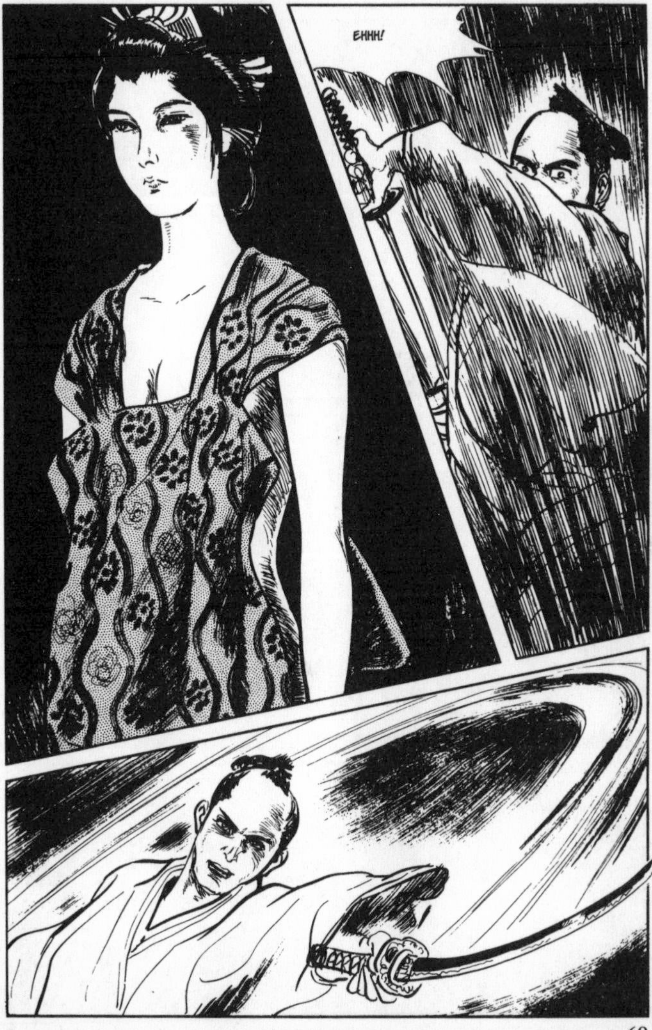
EHHH!

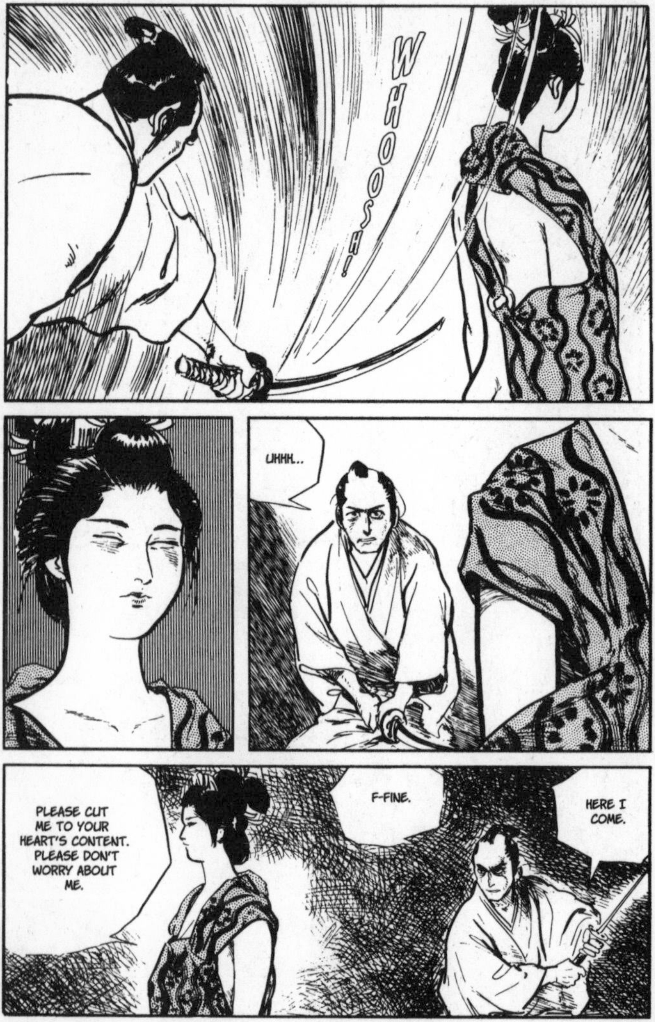
WHOOOSH!
UHHH...
PLEASE CUT ME TO YOUR HEART'S CONTENT. PLEASE DON'T WORRY ABOUT ME.
F-FINE.
HERE I COME.

ALL RIGHT, I'M GONNA DO IT FOR REAL THIS TIME.

YES.

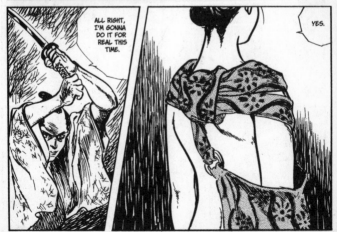

71

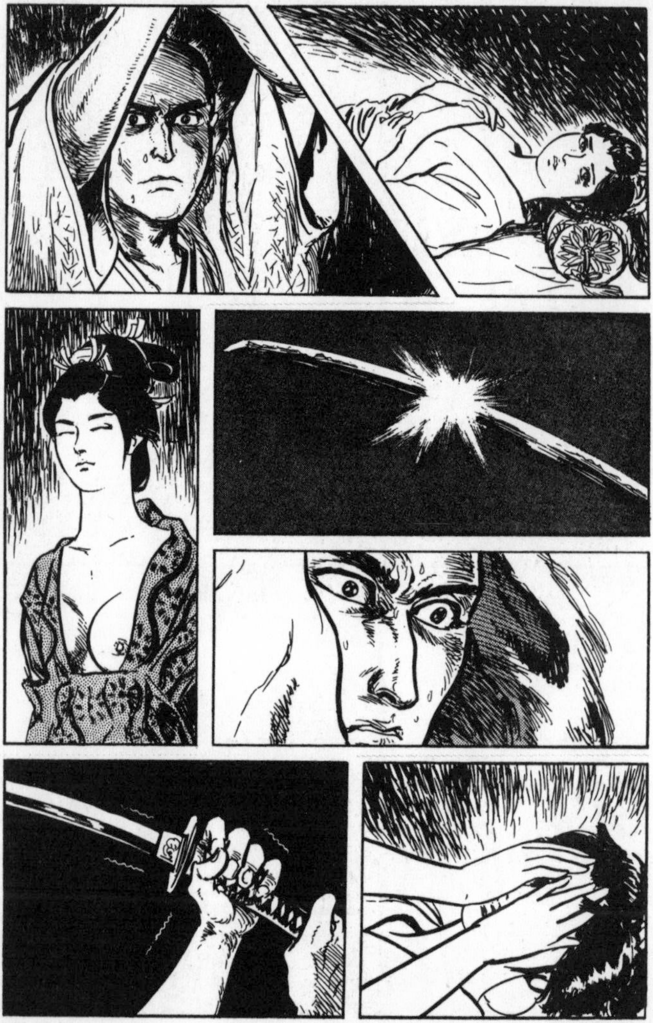

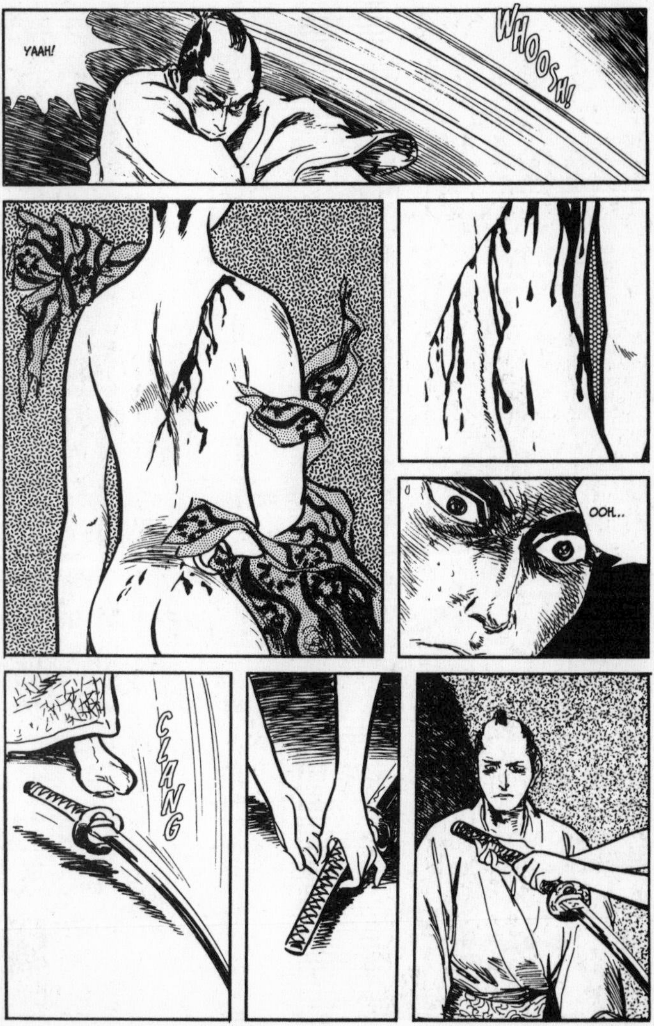
YAAH!
WHOOSH!
OOH...
CLANG

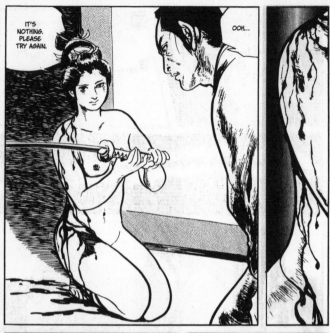

IT'S NOTHING. PLEASE TRY AGAIN.

OOH...

74

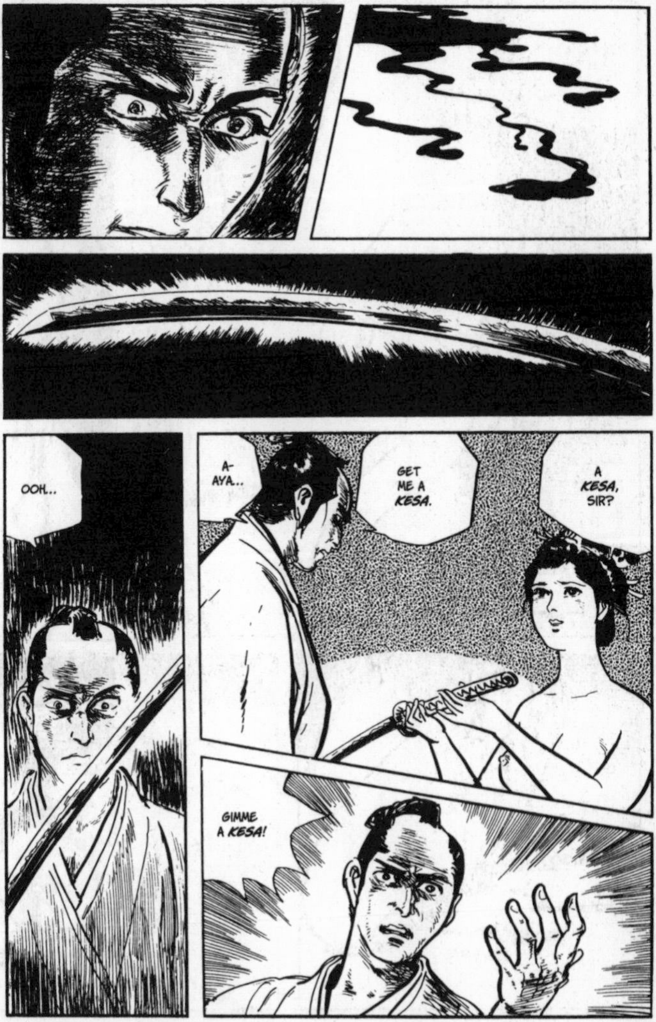
OOH...
A-
AYA...
GET ME A *KESA.*
A *KESA,* SIR?
GIMME A *KESA!*

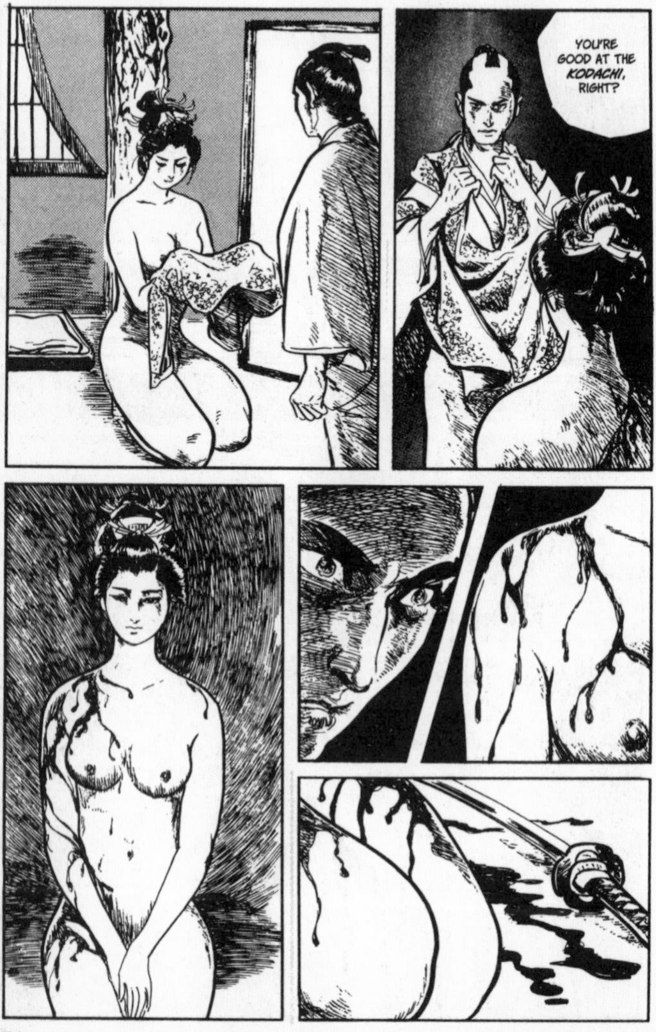
YOU'RE GOOD AT THE *KODACHI*, RIGHT?

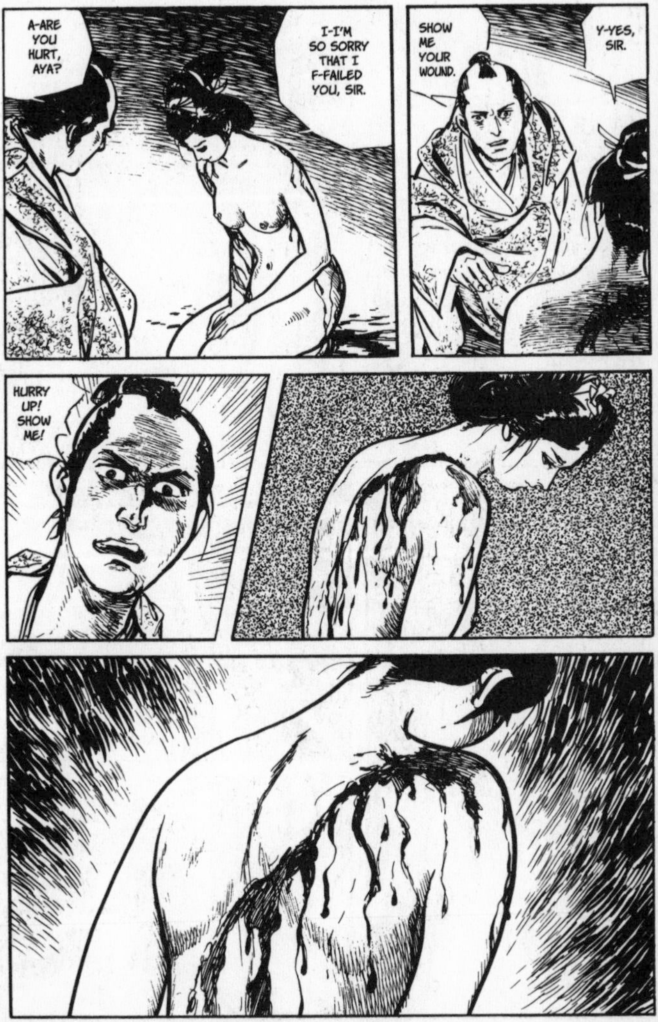
A-ARE YOU HURT, AYA?
I-I'M SO SORRY THAT I F-FAILED YOU, SIR.
SHOW ME YOUR WOUND.
Y-YES, SIR.
HURRY UP! SHOW ME!

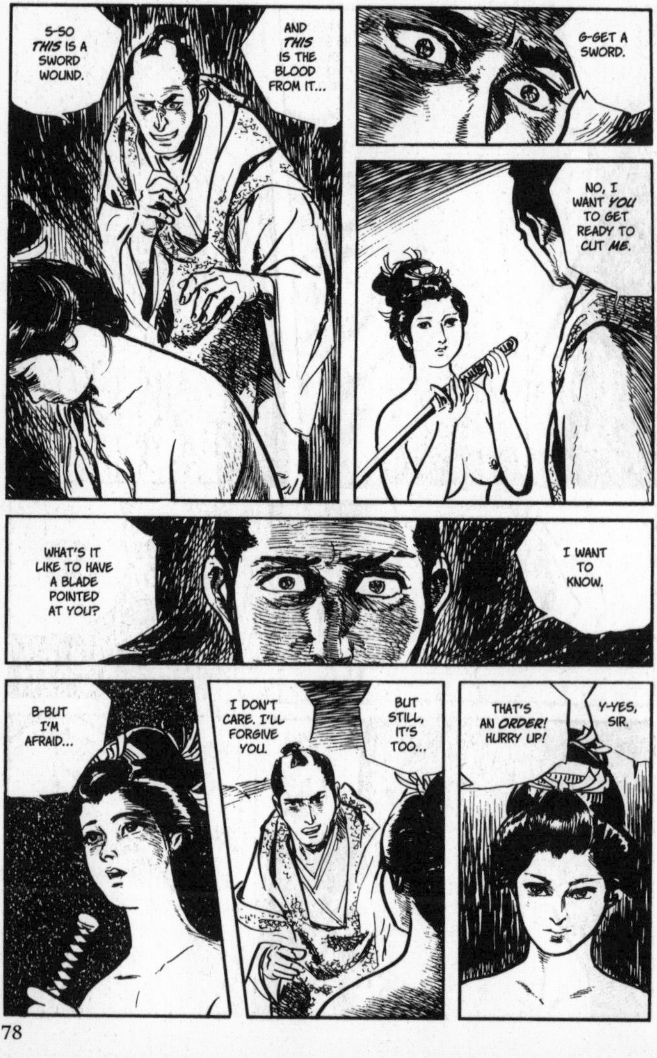
S-SO *THIS* IS A SWORD WOUND.
AND *THIS* IS THE BLOOD FROM IT...
G-GET A SWORD.
NO, I WANT *YOU* TO GET READY TO CUT *ME*.
WHAT'S IT LIKE TO HAVE A BLADE POINTED AT YOU?
I WANT TO KNOW.
B-BUT I'M AFRAID...
I DON'T CARE. I'LL FORGIVE YOU.
BUT STILL, IT'S TOO...
THAT'S AN *ORDER*! HURRY UP!
Y-YES, SIR.

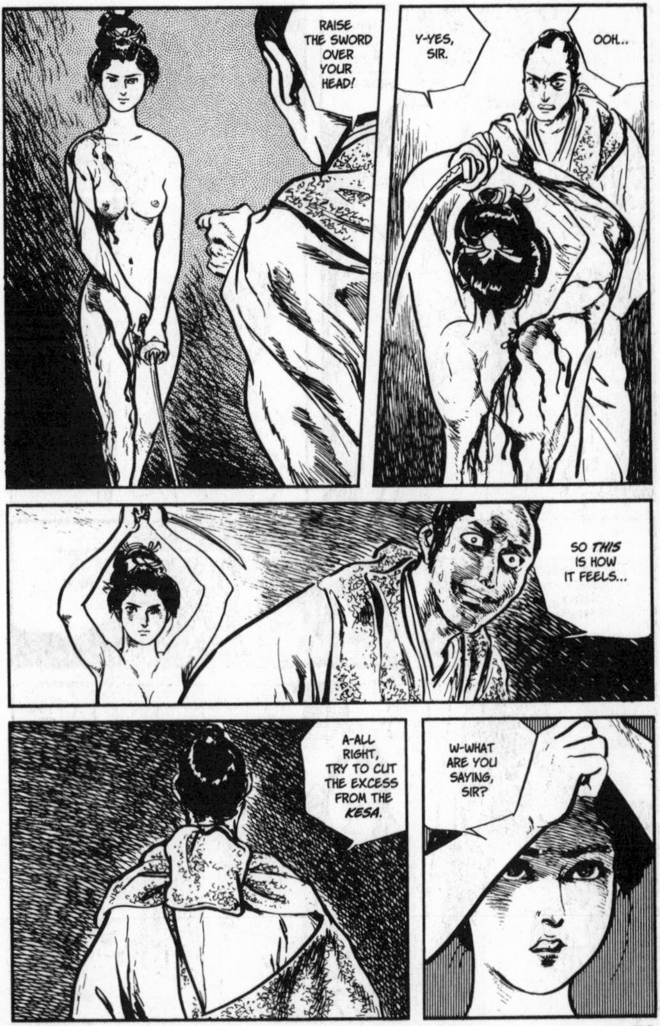

RAISE THE SWORD OVER YOUR HEAD!
Y-YES, SIR.
OOH...
SO *THIS* IS HOW IT FEELS...
A-ALL RIGHT, TRY TO CUT THE EXCESS FROM THE *KESA*.
W-WHAT ARE YOU SAYING, SIR?

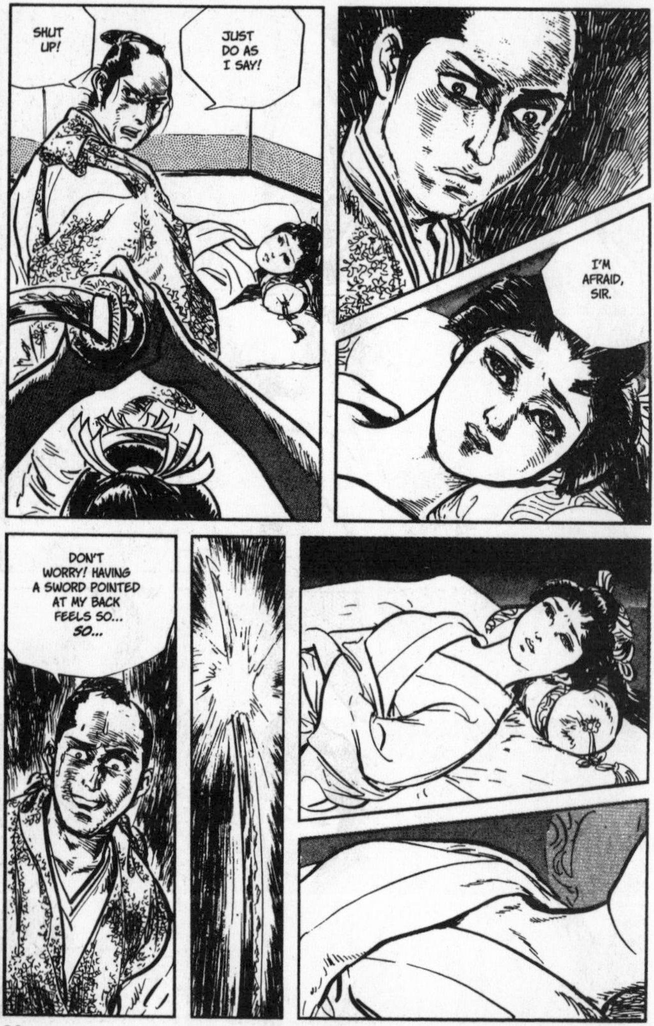
SHUT UP!
JUST DO AS I SAY!
I'M AFRAID, SIR.
DON'T WORRY! HAVING A SWORD POINTED AT MY BACK FEELS SO... SO...

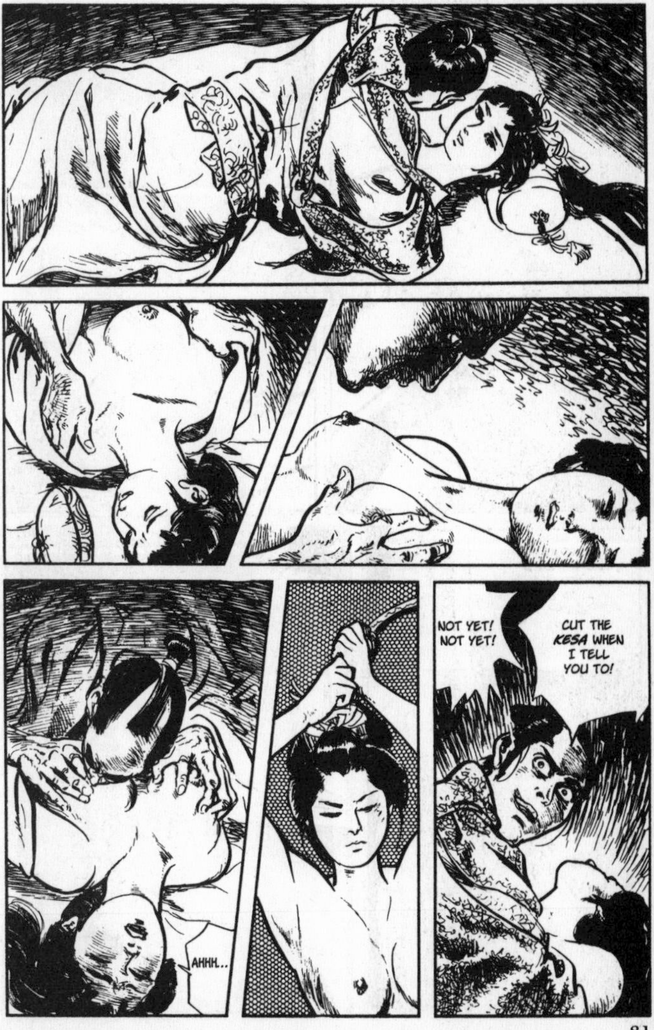
AHHH...
NOT YET! NOT YET!
CUT THE *KESA* WHEN I TELL YOU TO!

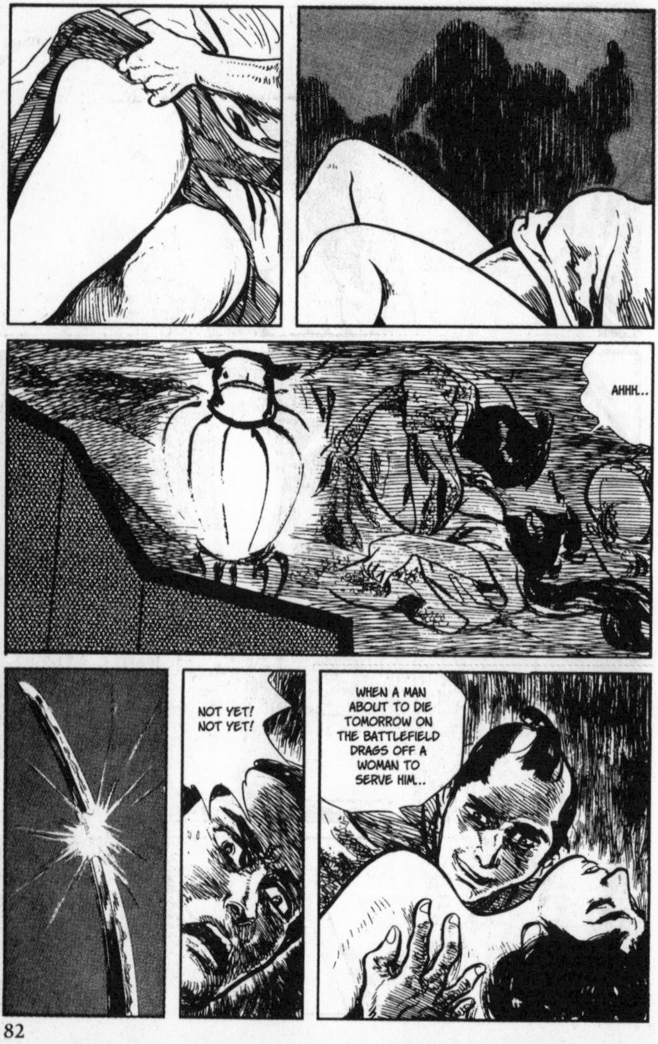
AHHH...
NOT YET!
NOT YET!
WHEN A MAN ABOUT TO DIE TOMORROW ON THE BATTLEFIELD DRAGS OFF A WOMAN TO SERVE HIM...

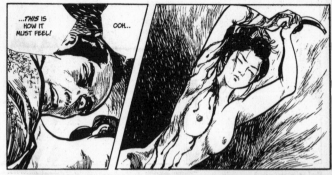

...*THIS* IS HOW IT MUST FEEL!

OOH...

AHHH!

C-CUT THE K-KESA...

83

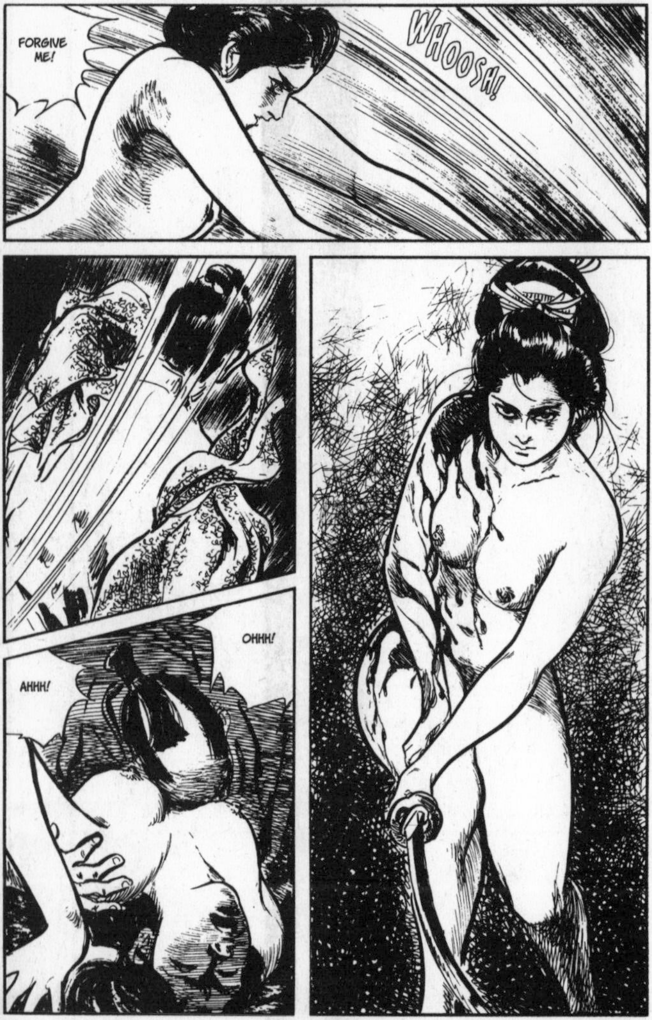
FORGIVE ME!
WHOOSH!
OHHH!
AHHH!

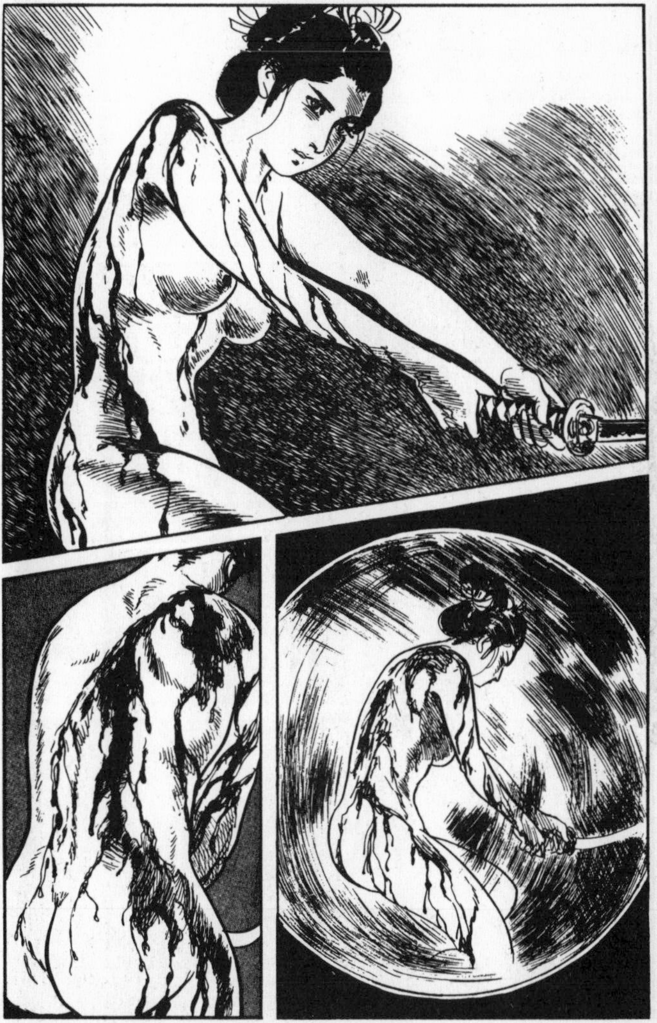

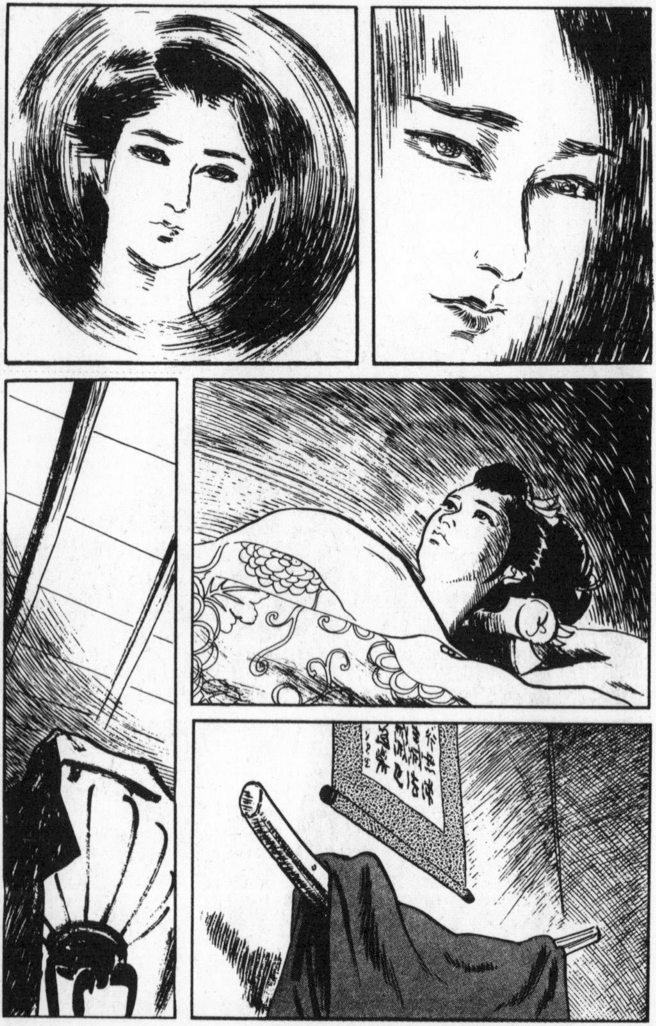

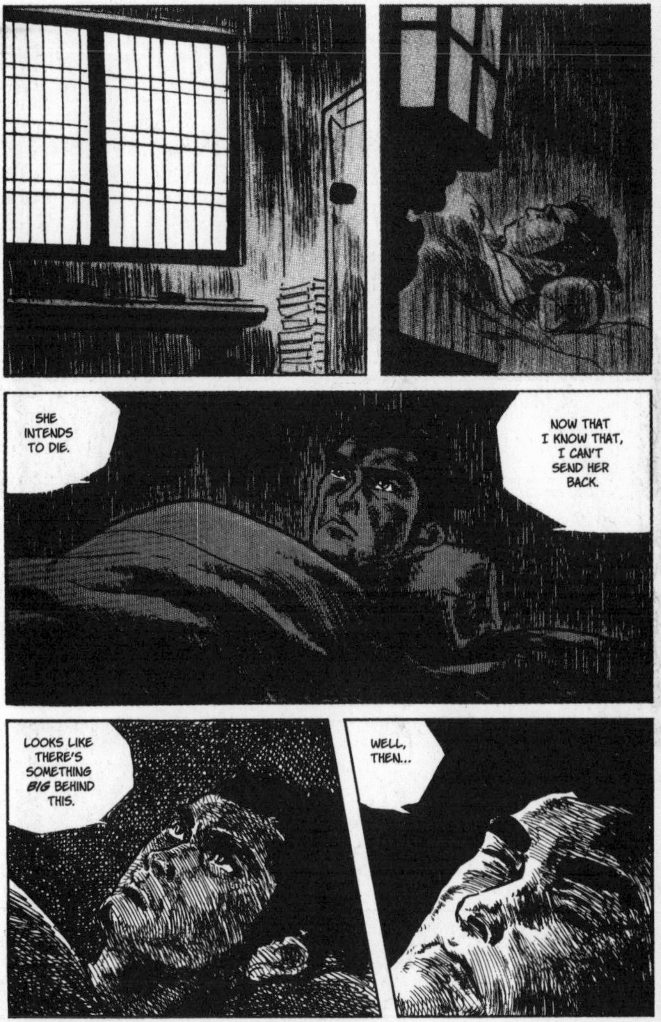
SHE INTENDS TO DIE.
NOW THAT I KNOW THAT, I CAN'T SEND HER BACK.
LOOKS LIKE THERE'S SOMETHING *BIG* BEHIND THIS.
WELL, THEN...

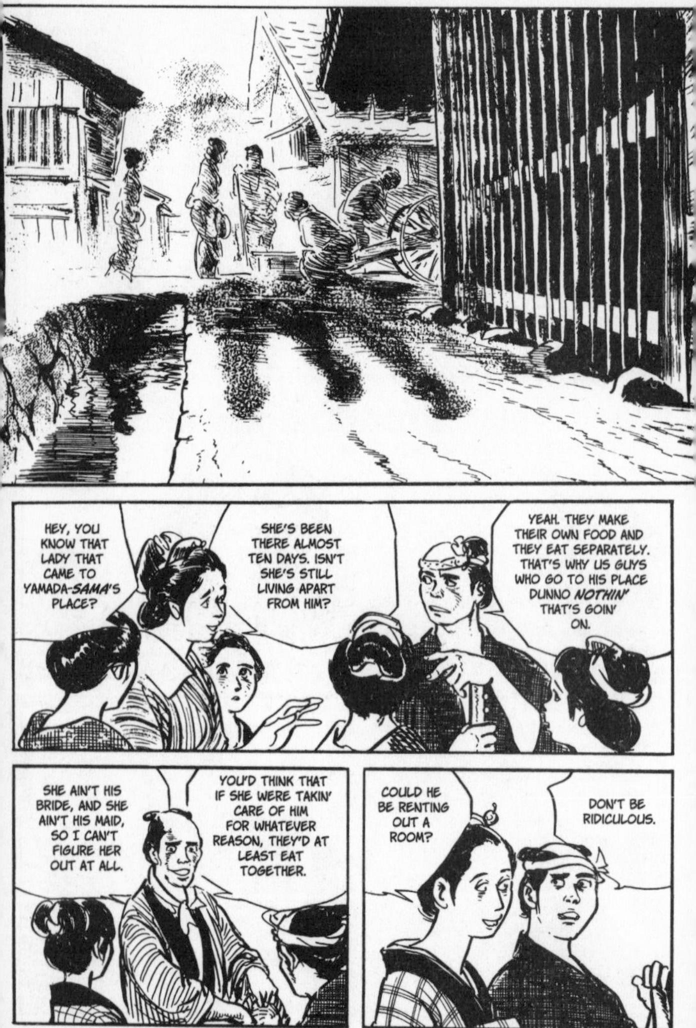
HEY, YOU KNOW THAT LADY THAT CAME TO YAMADA-*SAMA*'S PLACE?
SHE'S BEEN THERE ALMOST TEN DAYS. ISN'T SHE'S STILL LIVING APART FROM HIM?
YEAH. THEY MAKE THEIR OWN FOOD AND THEY EAT SEPARATELY. THAT'S WHY US GUYS WHO GO TO HIS PLACE DUNNO *NOTHIN'* THAT'S GOIN' ON.
SHE AIN'T HIS BRIDE, AND SHE AIN'T HIS MAID, SO I CAN'T FIGURE HER OUT AT ALL.
YOU'D THINK THAT IF SHE WERE TAKIN' CARE OF HIM FOR WHATEVER REASON, THEY'D AT LEAST EAT TOGETHER.
COULD HE BE RENTING OUT A ROOM?
DON'T BE RIDICULOUS.

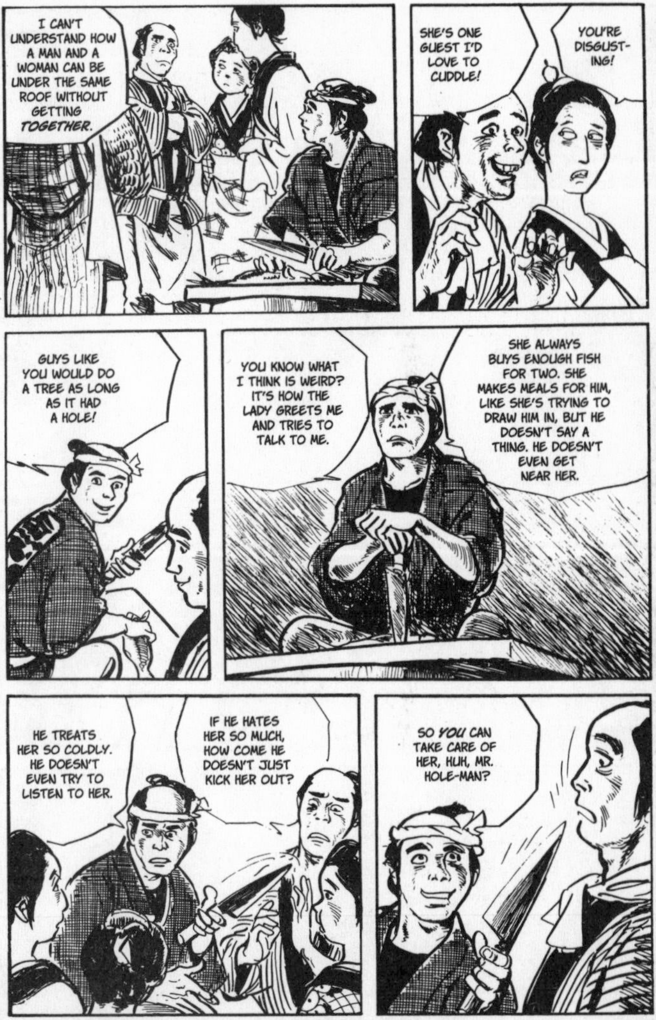
I CAN'T UNDERSTAND HOW A MAN AND A WOMAN CAN BE UNDER THE SAME ROOF WITHOUT GETTING *TOGETHER*.
SHE'S ONE GUEST I'D LOVE TO CUDDLE!
YOU'RE DISGUST-ING!
GUYS LIKE YOU WOULD DO A TREE AS LONG AS IT HAD A HOLE!
YOU KNOW WHAT I THINK IS WEIRD? IT'S HOW THE LADY GREETS ME AND TRIES TO TALK TO ME.
SHE ALWAYS BUYS ENOUGH FISH FOR TWO. SHE MAKES MEALS FOR HIM, LIKE SHE'S TRYING TO DRAW HIM IN, BUT HE DOESN'T SAY A THING. HE DOESN'T EVEN GET NEAR HER.
HE TREATS HER SO COLDLY. HE DOESN'T EVEN TRY TO LISTEN TO HER.
IF HE HATES HER SO MUCH, HOW COME HE DOESN'T JUST KICK HER OUT?
SO *YOU* CAN TAKE CARE OF HER, HUH, MR. HOLE-MAN?

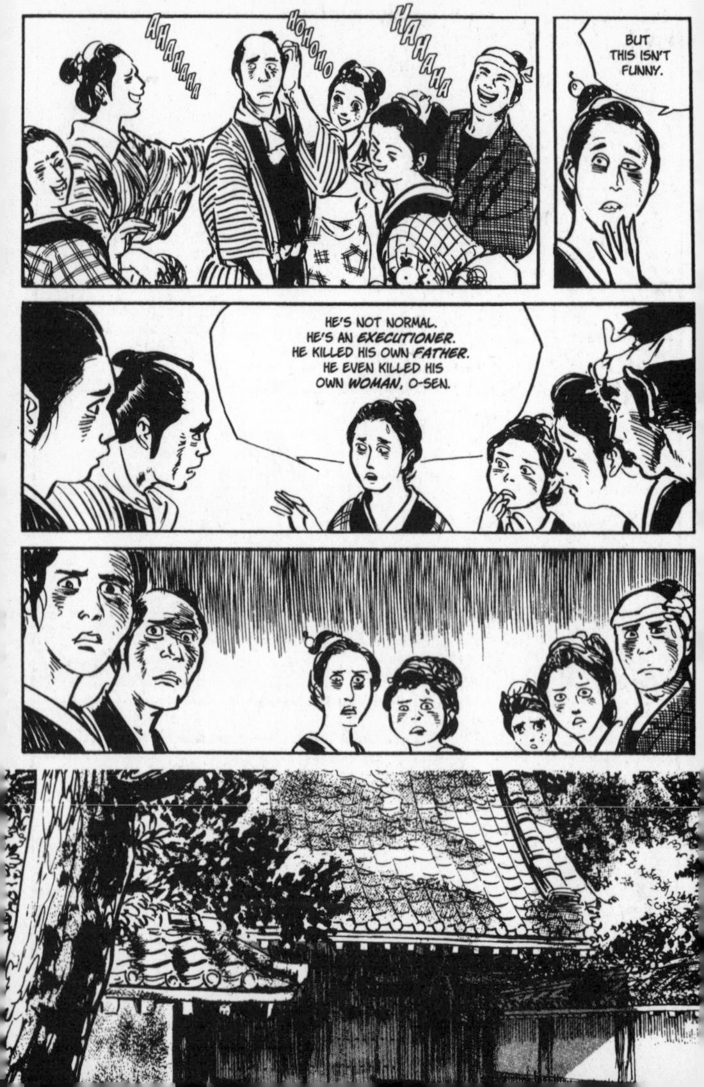
AHAHAHAHA
HOHOHOHO
HAHAHAHA
BUT THIS ISN'T FUNNY.
HE'S NOT NORMAL. HE'S AN *EXECUTIONER*. HE KILLED HIS OWN *FATHER*. HE EVEN KILLED HIS OWN *WOMAN*, O-SEN.

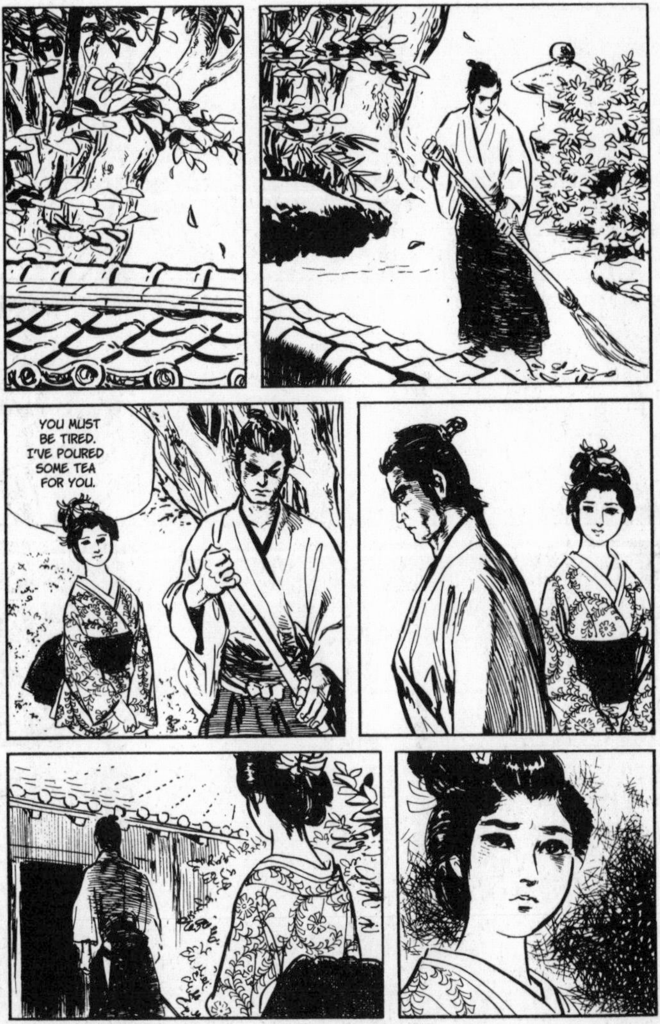
YOU MUST BE TIRED. I'VE POURED SOME TEA FOR YOU.

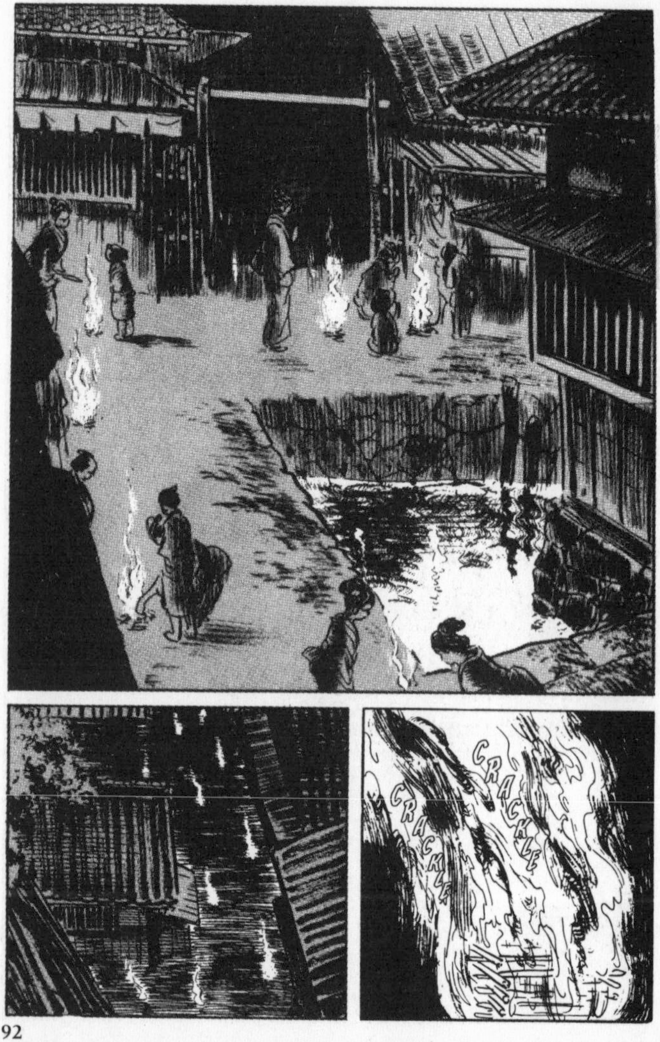
CRACKLE
CRACKLE

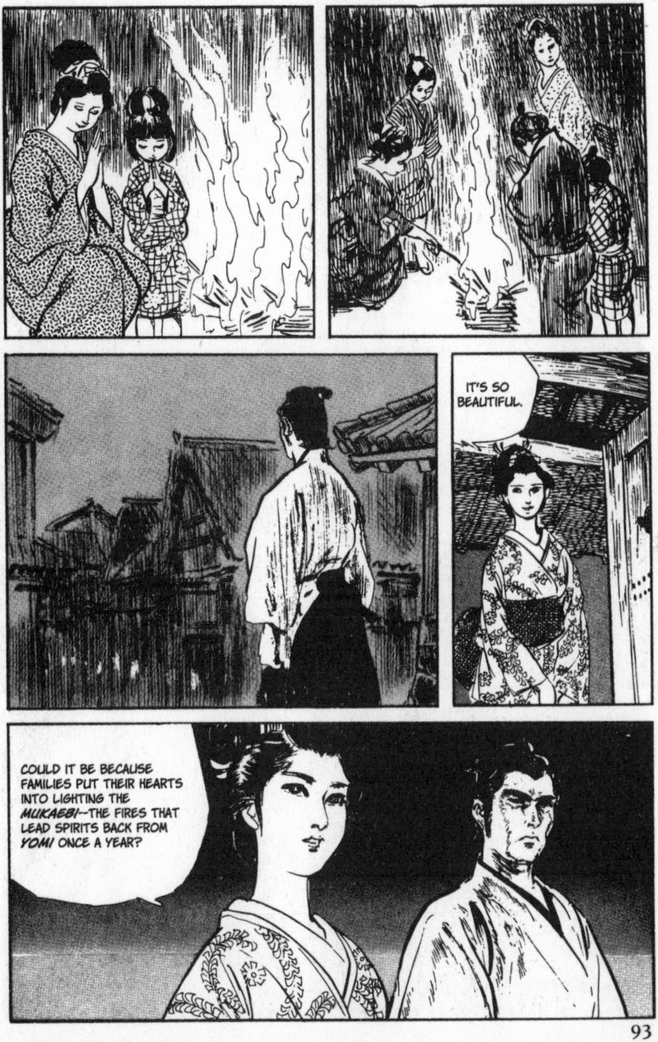
IT'S SO BEAUTIFUL.
COULD IT BE BECAUSE FAMILIES PUT THEIR HEARTS INTO LIGHTING THE *MUKAEBI*--THE FIRES THAT LEAD SPIRITS BACK FROM *YOMI* ONCE A YEAR?

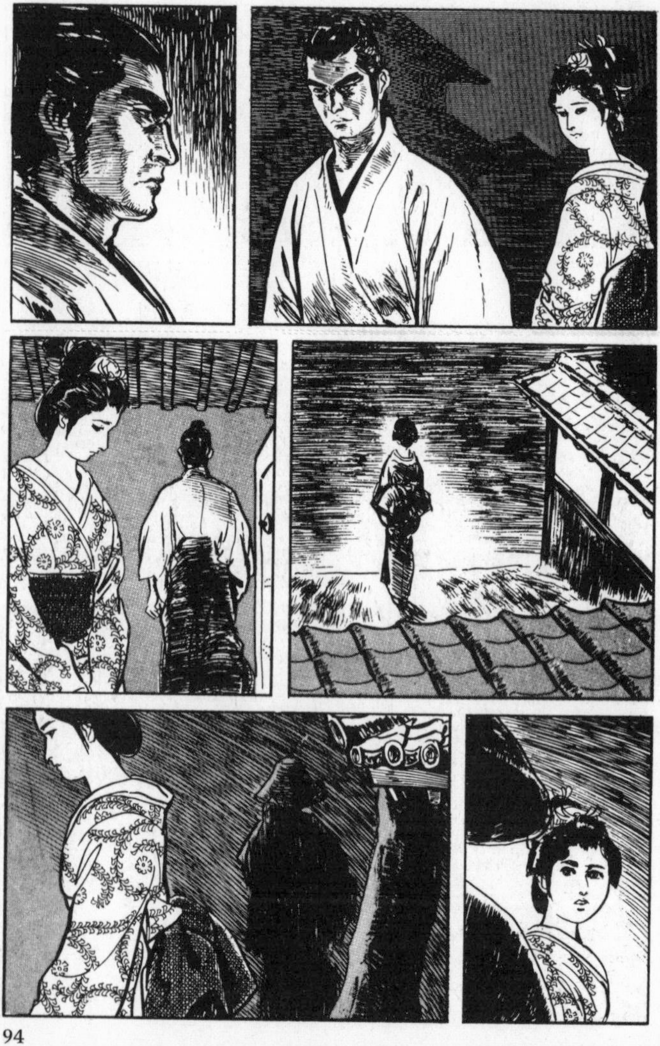

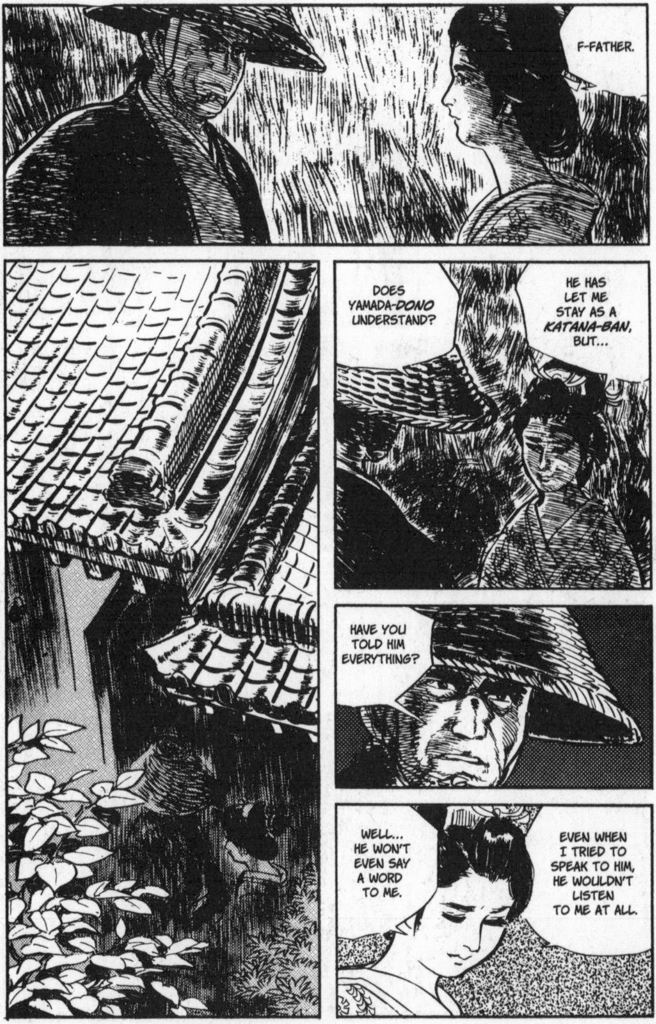
F-FATHER.
DOES YAMADA-*DONO* UNDERSTAND?
HE HAS LET ME STAY AS A *KATANA-BAN*, BUT...
HAVE YOU TOLD HIM EVERYTHING?
WELL... HE WON'T EVEN SAY A WORD TO ME.
EVEN WHEN I TRIED TO SPEAK TO HIM, HE WOULDN'T LISTEN TO ME AT ALL.

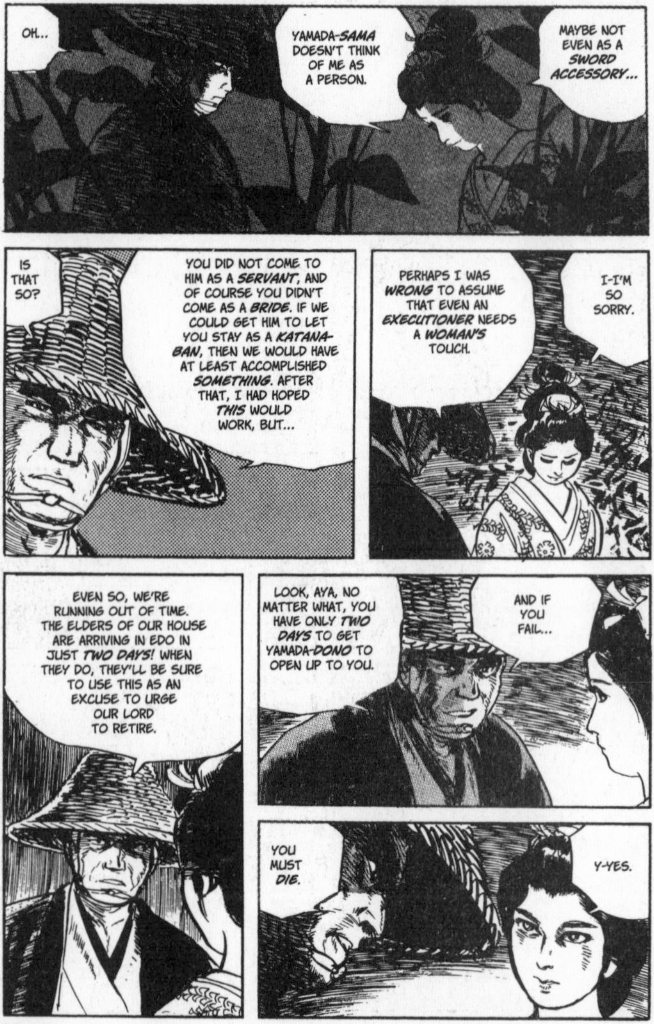
OH...
YAMADA-*SAMA* DOESN'T THINK OF ME AS A PERSON.
MAYBE NOT EVEN AS A *SWORD ACCESSORY*...
IS THAT SO?
YOU DID NOT COME TO HIM AS A *SERVANT*, AND OF COURSE YOU DIDN'T COME AS A *BRIDE*. IF WE COULD GET HIM TO LET YOU STAY AS A *KATANA-BAN*, THEN WE WOULD HAVE AT LEAST ACCOMPLISHED *SOMETHING*. AFTER THAT, I HAD HOPED *THIS* WOULD WORK, BUT...
PERHAPS I WAS *WRONG* TO ASSUME THAT EVEN AN *EXECUTIONER* NEEDS A *WOMAN'S* TOUCH.
I-I'M SO SORRY.
EVEN SO, WE'RE RUNNING OUT OF TIME. THE ELDERS OF OUR HOUSE ARE ARRIVING IN EDO IN JUST *TWO DAYS!* WHEN THEY DO, THEY'LL BE SURE TO USE THIS AS AN EXCUSE TO URGE OUR LORD TO RETIRE.
LOOK, AYA, NO MATTER WHAT, YOU HAVE ONLY *TWO DAYS* TO GET YAMADA-*DONO* TO OPEN UP TO YOU.
AND IF YOU FAIL...
YOU MUST *DIE*.
Y-YES.

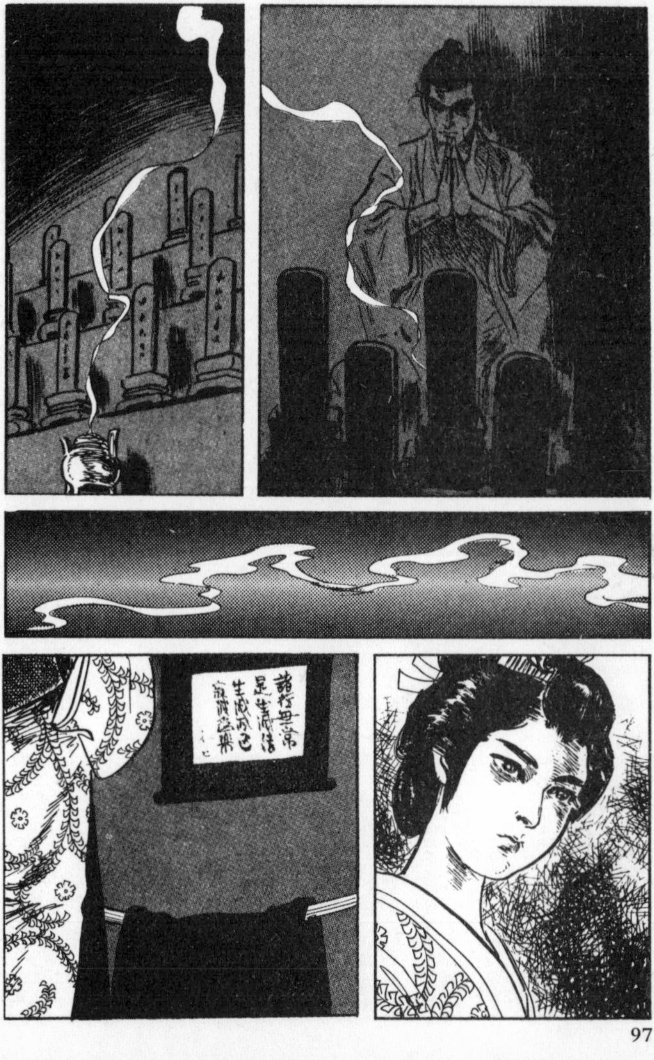
諸行無常
是生滅法
生滅滅已
寂滅為楽

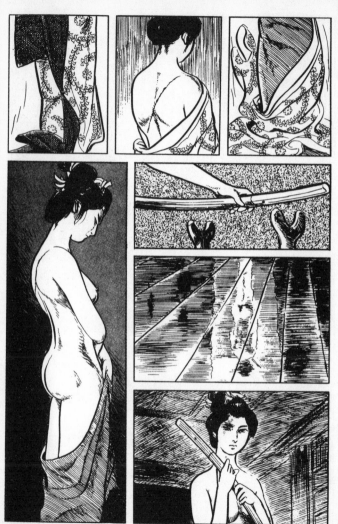

98

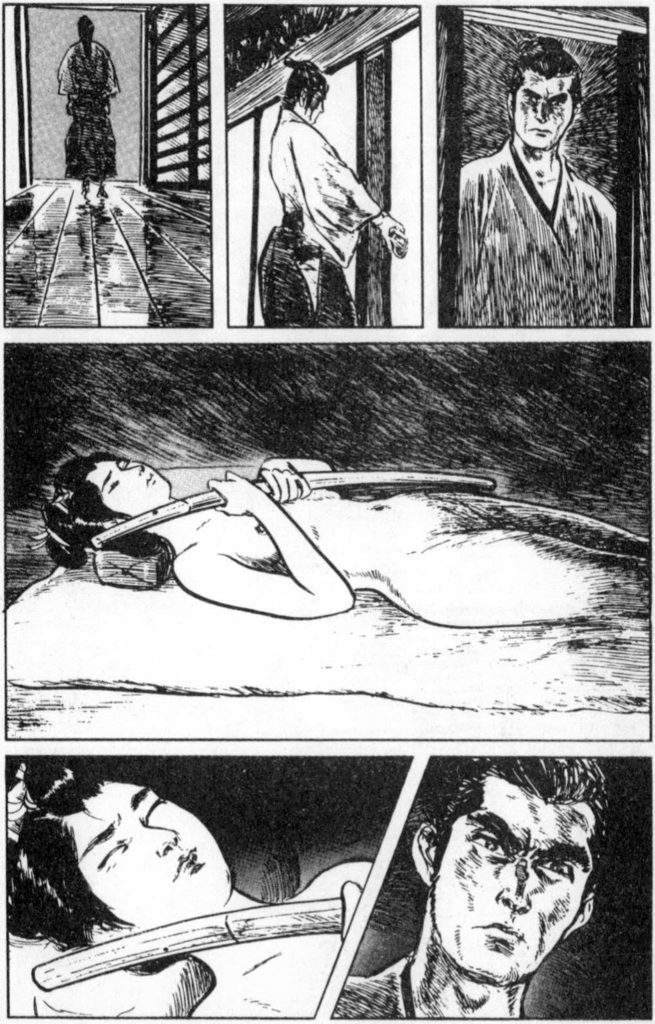

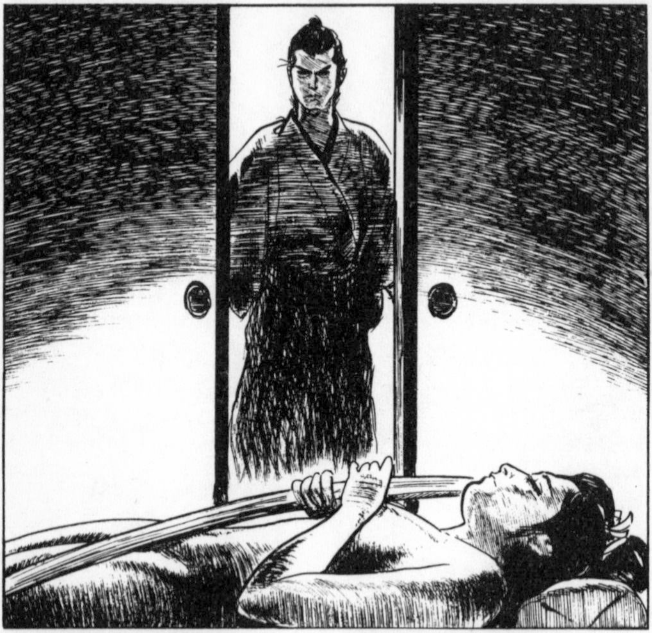
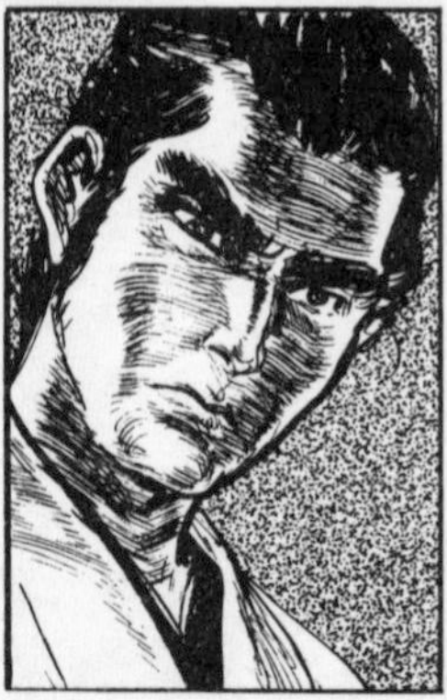
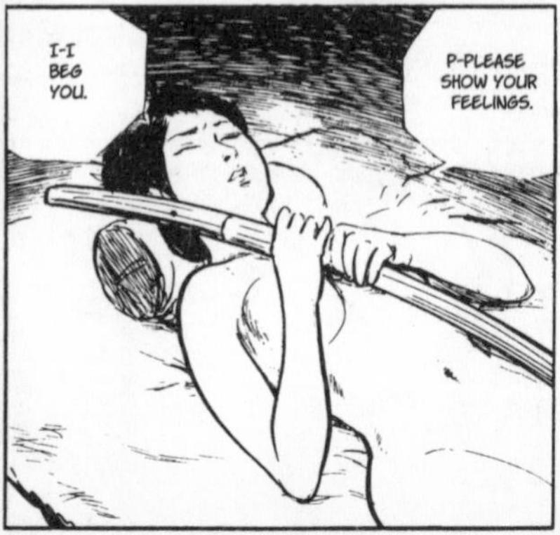
I-I BEG YOU.
P-PLEASE SHOW YOUR FEELINGS.

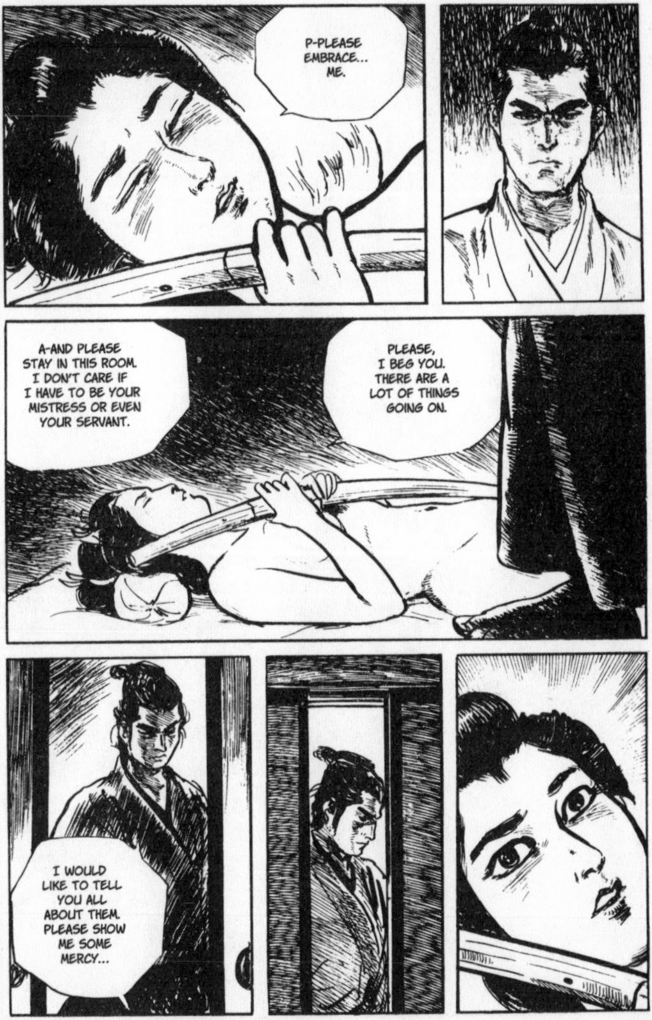
P-PLEASE EMBRACE... ME.
A-AND PLEASE STAY IN THIS ROOM. I DON'T CARE IF I HAVE TO BE YOUR MISTRESS OR EVEN YOUR SERVANT.
PLEASE, I BEG YOU. THERE ARE A LOT OF THINGS GOING ON.
I WOULD LIKE TO TELL YOU ALL ABOUT THEM. PLEASE SHOW ME SOME MERCY...

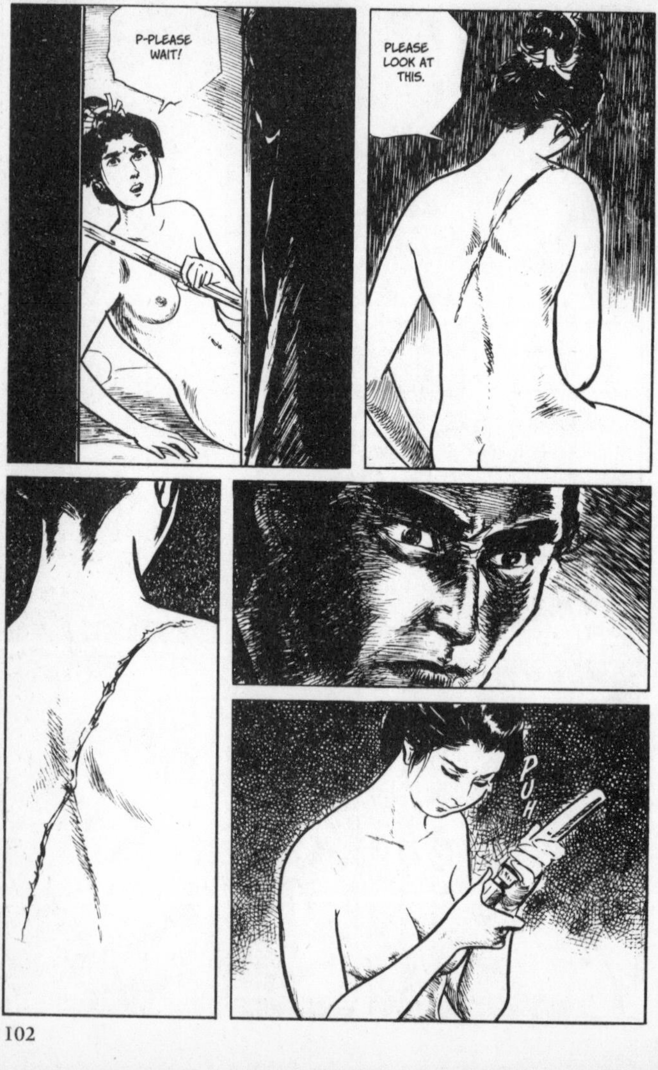
P-PLEASE WAIT!
PLEASE LOOK AT THIS.
PUH

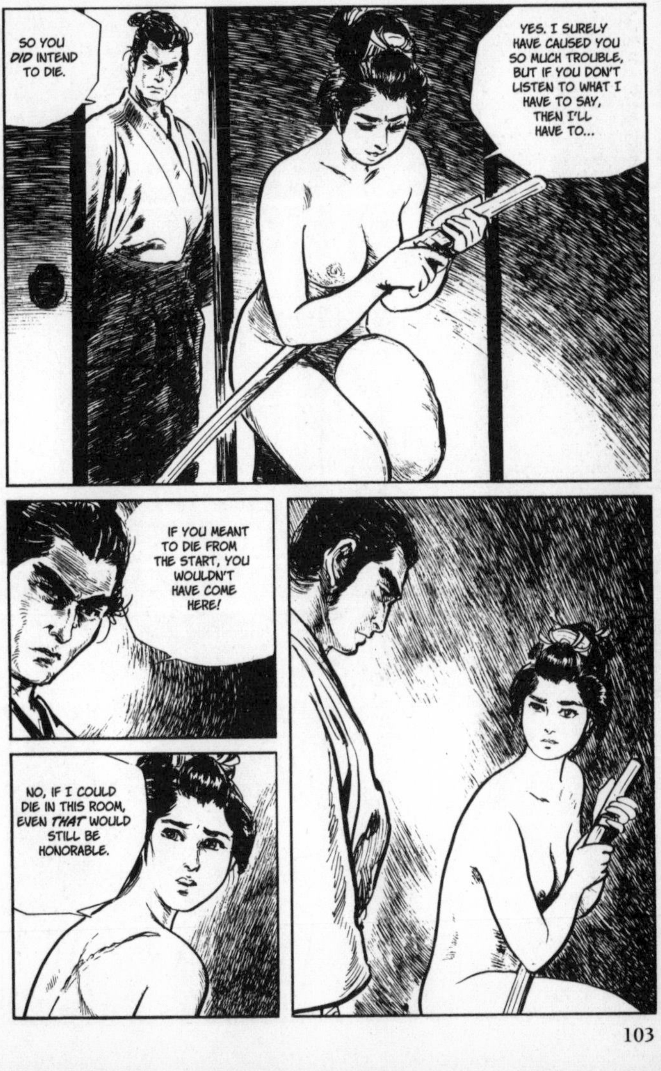
SO YOU *DID* INTEND TO DIE.
YES. I SURELY HAVE CAUSED YOU SO MUCH TROUBLE, BUT IF YOU DON'T LISTEN TO WHAT I HAVE TO SAY, THEN I'LL HAVE TO...
IF YOU MEANT TO DIE FROM THE START, YOU WOULDN'T HAVE COME HERE!
NO, IF I COULD DIE IN THIS ROOM, EVEN *THAT* WOULD STILL BE HONORABLE.

PUT YOUR CLOTHES ON.

Y-YES.

PTCH

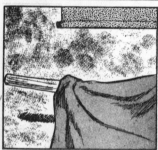

TELL ME WHAT HAPPENED.

TH-THANK YOU.

104

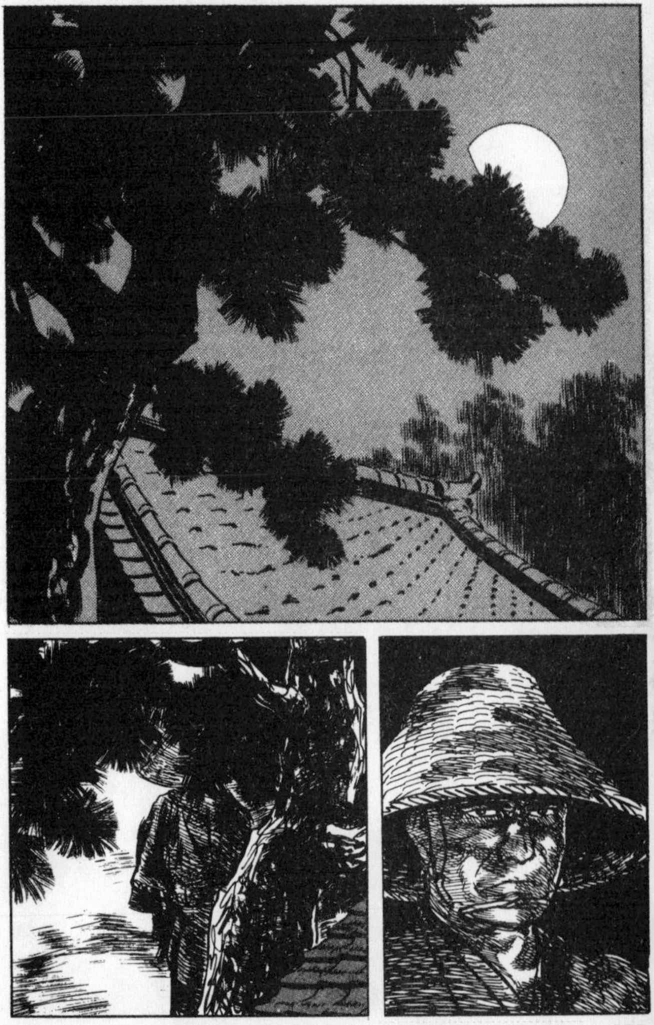

THE DANCING BUDDHA REVITALIZATION TECHNIQUE IS A TOTAL *FRAUD*. IT'S A PLOT BY OUR ELDER RETAINER IWABUCHI SADO BACK HOME AND SAGARAMI NAIZEN TO ADOPT THE SON OF A *RŌJŪ* AND RULE OUR *HAN* THROUGH HIM.

THEY USED OUR LORD'S POOR HEALTH AND LACK OF AN HEIR AS AN EXCUSE TO TEMPT SAKANE-*SAMA*, OUR EDO *KARŌ*.

THEY EVEN DRAGGED MY FATHER INTO THEIR SCHEME SO THAT THEY COULD PIN EVERYTHING ON HIM.

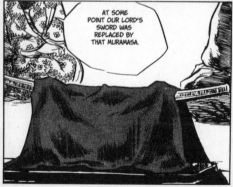

AT SOME POINT OUR LORD'S SWORD WAS REPLACED BY THAT MURAMASA.

AND I...

106

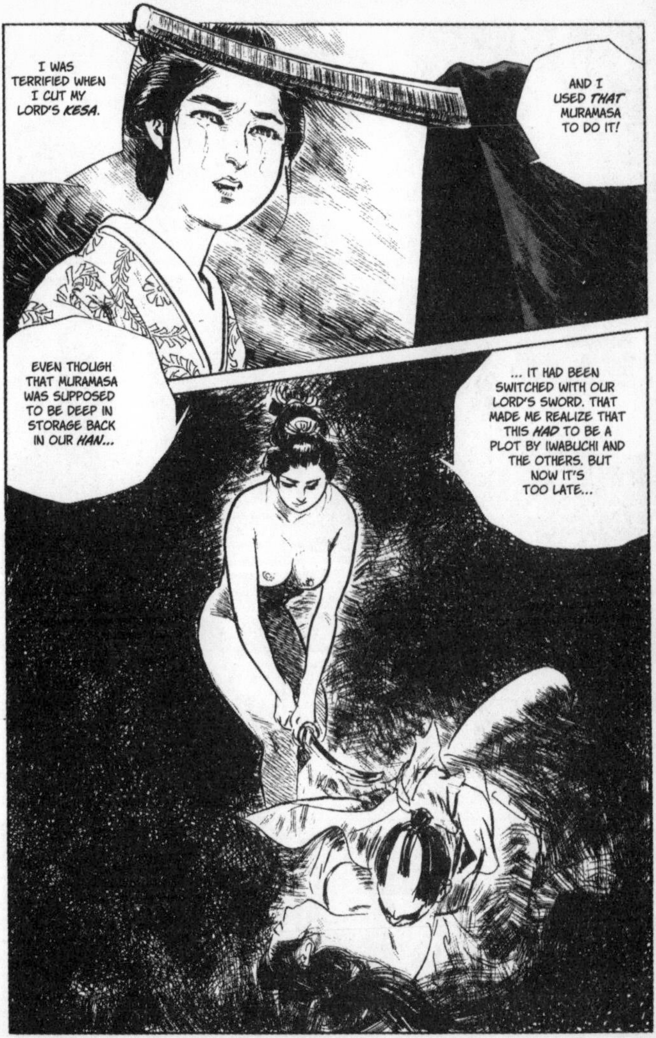
I WAS TERRIFIED WHEN I CUT MY LORD'S *KESA*.
AND I USED *THAT* MURAMASA TO DO IT!
EVEN THOUGH THAT MURAMASA WAS SUPPOSED TO BE DEEP IN STORAGE BACK IN OUR *HAN*...
... IT HAD BEEN SWITCHED WITH OUR LORD'S SWORD. THAT MADE ME REALIZE THAT THIS *HAD* TO BE A PLOT BY IWABUCHI AND THE OTHERS. BUT NOW IT'S TOO LATE...

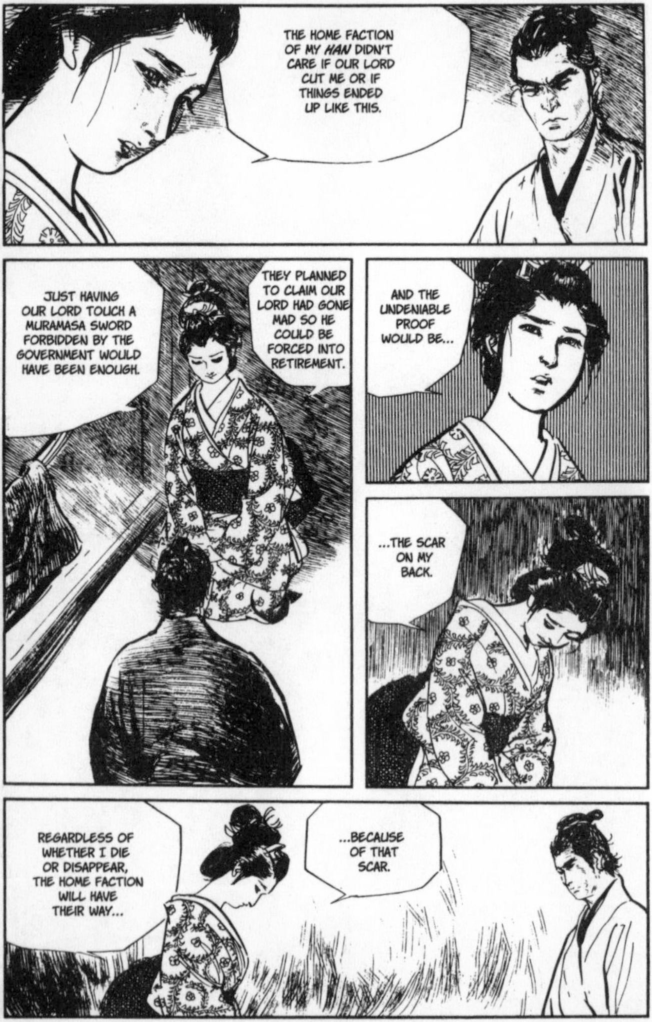
THE HOME FACTION OF MY HAN DIDN'T CARE IF OUR LORD CUT ME OR IF THINGS ENDED UP LIKE THIS.
JUST HAVING OUR LORD TOUCH A MURAMASA SWORD FORBIDDEN BY THE GOVERNMENT WOULD HAVE BEEN ENOUGH.
THEY PLANNED TO CLAIM OUR LORD HAD GONE MAD SO HE COULD BE FORCED INTO RETIREMENT.
AND THE UNDENIABLE PROOF WOULD BE...
...THE SCAR ON MY BACK.
REGARDLESS OF WHETHER I DIE OR DISAPPEAR, THE HOME FACTION WILL HAVE THEIR WAY...
...BECAUSE OF THAT SCAR.

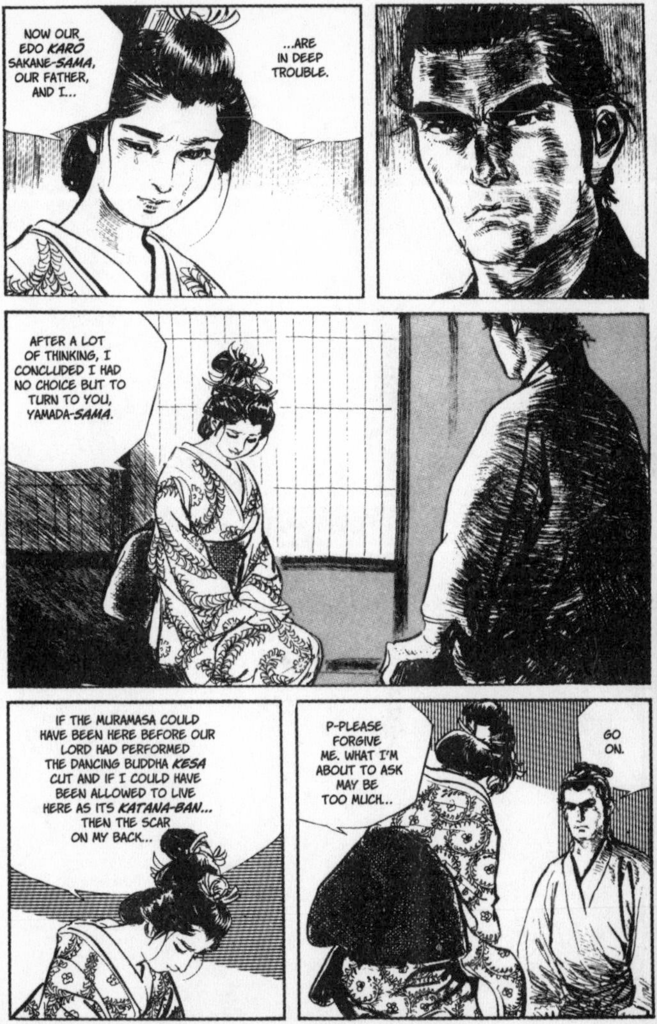
NOW OUR EDO *KARO* SAKANE-*SAMA*, OUR FATHER, AND I...
...ARE IN DEEP TROUBLE.
AFTER A LOT OF THINKING, I CONCLUDED I HAD NO CHOICE BUT TO TURN TO YOU, YAMADA-*SAMA*.
IF THE MURAMASA COULD HAVE BEEN HERE BEFORE OUR LORD HAD PERFORMED THE DANCING BUDDHA *KESA* CUT AND IF I COULD HAVE BEEN ALLOWED TO LIVE HERE AS ITS *KATANA-BAN*... THEN THE SCAR ON MY BACK...
P-PLEASE FORGIVE ME. WHAT I'M ABOUT TO ASK MAY BE TOO MUCH...
GO ON.

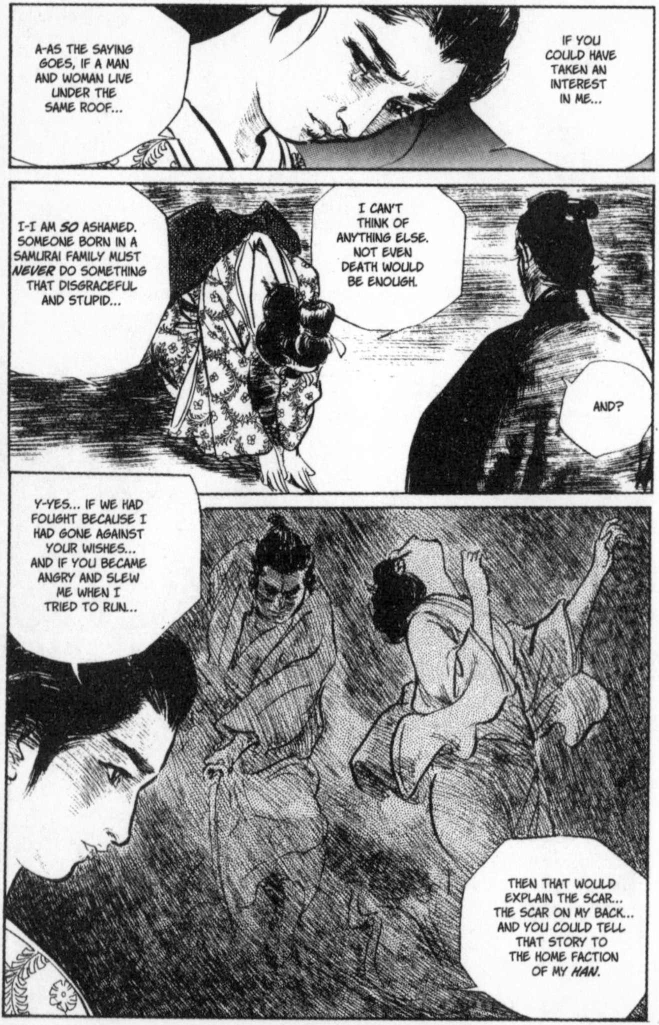
A-AS THE SAYING GOES, IF A MAN AND WOMAN LIVE UNDER THE SAME ROOF...
IF YOU COULD HAVE TAKEN AN INTEREST IN ME...
I-I AM *SO* ASHAMED. SOMEONE BORN IN A SAMURAI FAMILY MUST *NEVER* DO SOMETHING THAT DISGRACEFUL AND STUPID...
I CAN'T THINK OF ANYTHING ELSE. NOT EVEN DEATH WOULD BE ENOUGH.
AND?
Y-YES... IF WE HAD FOUGHT BECAUSE I HAD GONE AGAINST YOUR WISHES... AND IF YOU BECAME ANGRY AND SLEW ME WHEN I TRIED TO RUN...
THEN THAT WOULD EXPLAIN THE SCAR... THE SCAR ON MY BACK... AND YOU COULD TELL THAT STORY TO THE HOME FACTION OF MY *HAN*.

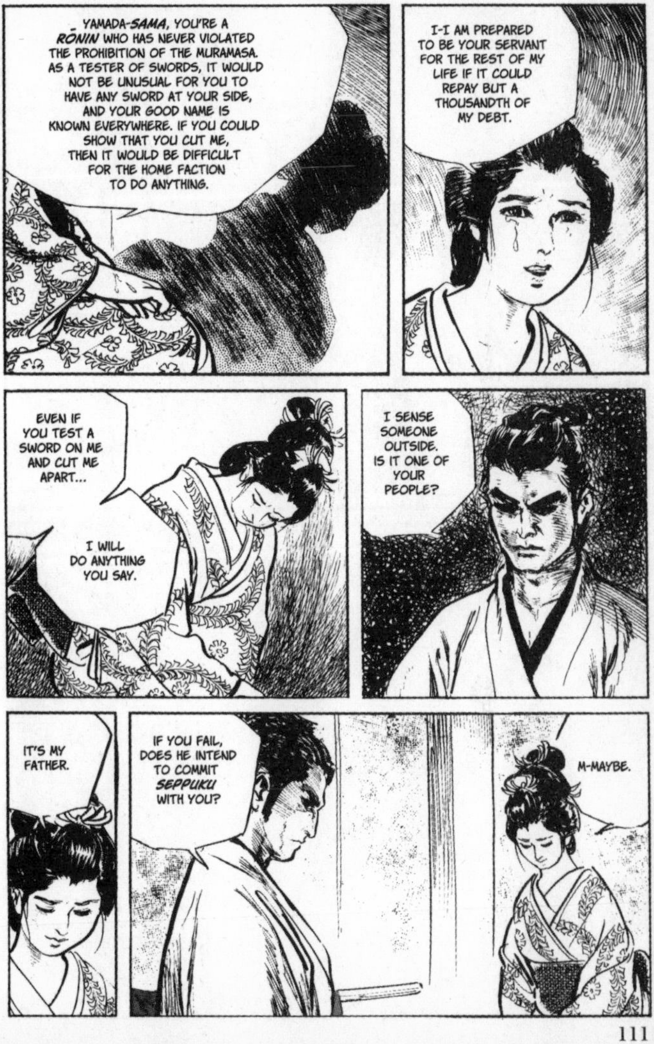
YAMADA-*SAMA*, YOU'RE A *RŌNIN* WHO HAS NEVER VIOLATED THE PROHIBITION OF THE MURAMASA. AS A TESTER OF SWORDS, IT WOULD NOT BE UNUSUAL FOR YOU TO HAVE ANY SWORD AT YOUR SIDE, AND YOUR GOOD NAME IS KNOWN EVERYWHERE. IF YOU COULD SHOW THAT YOU CUT ME, THEN IT WOULD BE DIFFICULT FOR THE HOME FACTION TO DO ANYTHING.
I-I AM PREPARED TO BE YOUR SERVANT FOR THE REST OF MY LIFE IF IT COULD REPAY BUT A THOUSANDTH OF MY DEBT.
EVEN IF YOU TEST A SWORD ON ME AND CUT ME APART...
I WILL DO ANYTHING YOU SAY.
I SENSE SOMEONE OUTSIDE. IS IT ONE OF YOUR PEOPLE?
IT'S MY FATHER.
IF YOU FAIL, DOES HE INTEND TO COMMIT *SEPPUKU* WITH YOU?
M-MAYBE.

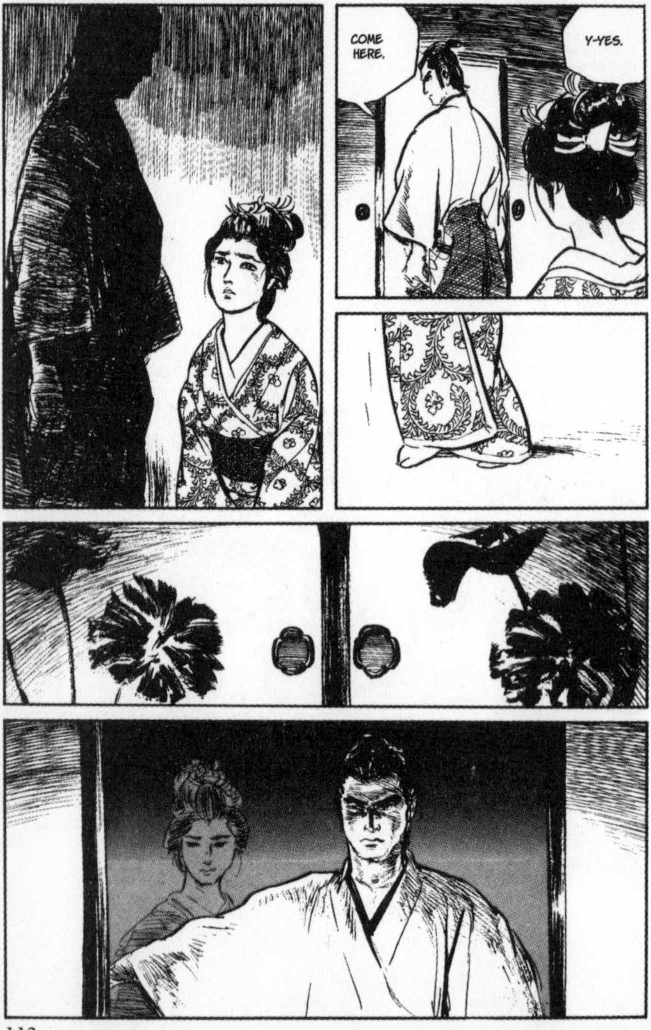
COME HERE.
Y-YES.

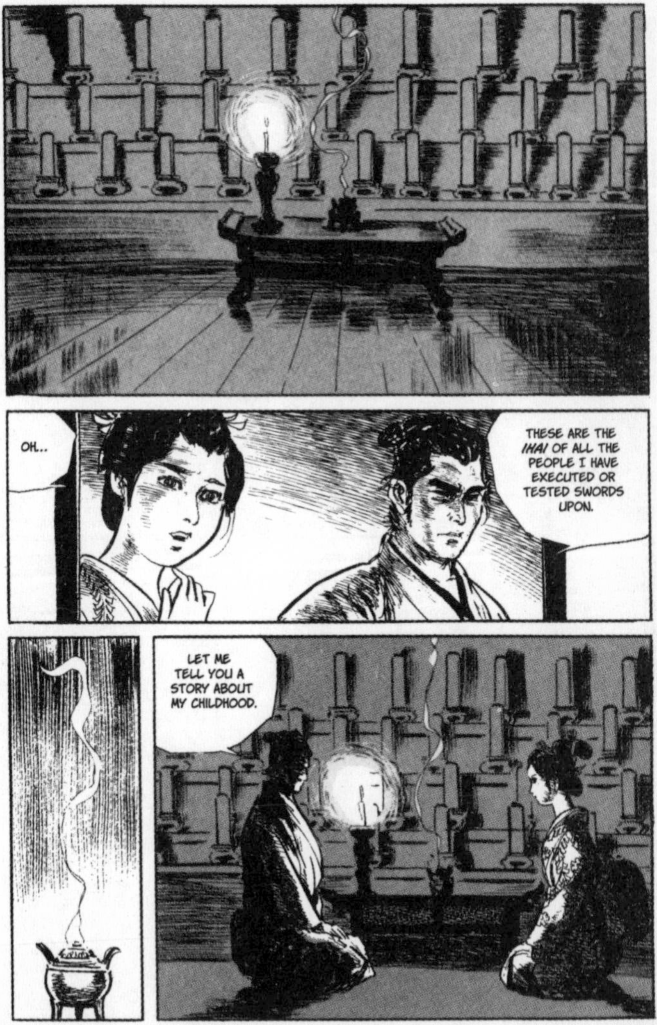

OH...
THESE ARE THE IHAI OF ALL THE PEOPLE I HAVE EXECUTED OR TESTED SWORDS UPON.
LET ME TELL YOU A STORY ABOUT MY CHILDHOOD.

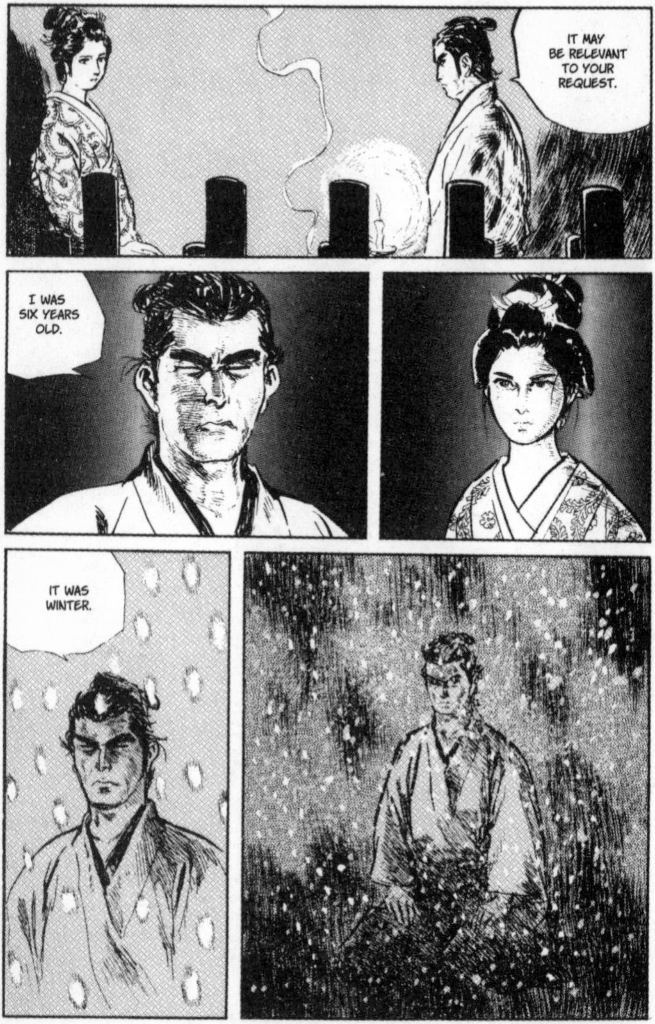
IT MAY BE RELEVANT TO YOUR REQUEST.
I WAS SIX YEARS OLD.
IT WAS WINTER.

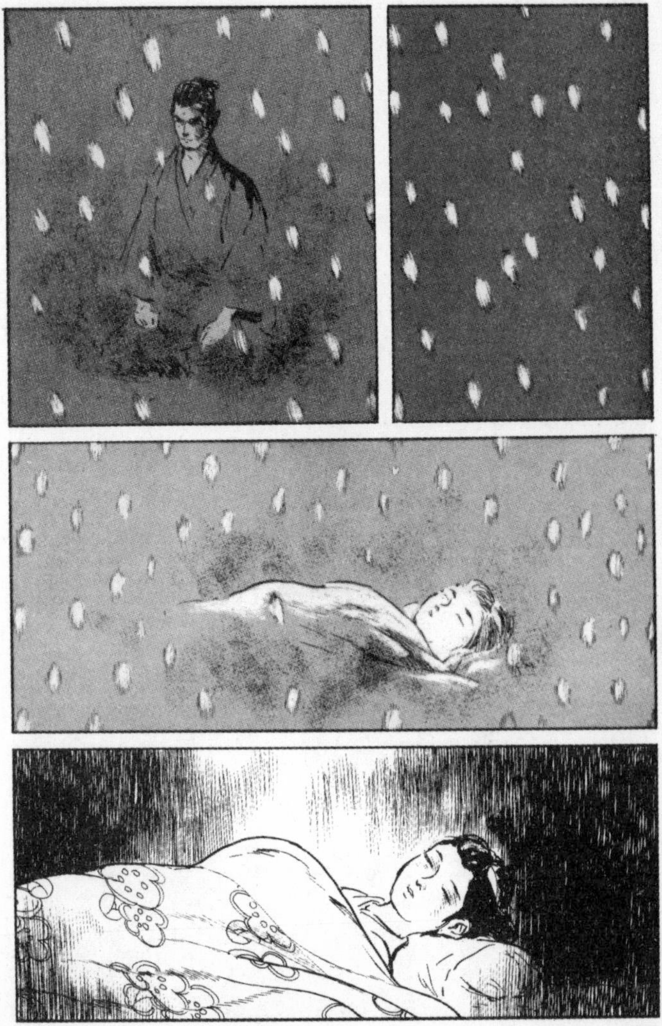

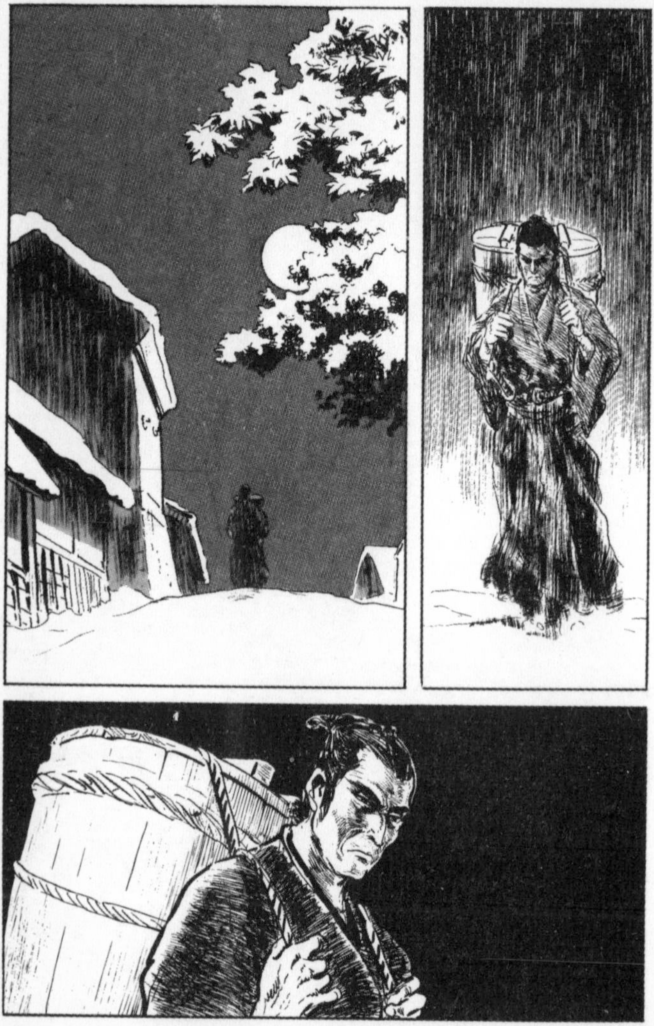

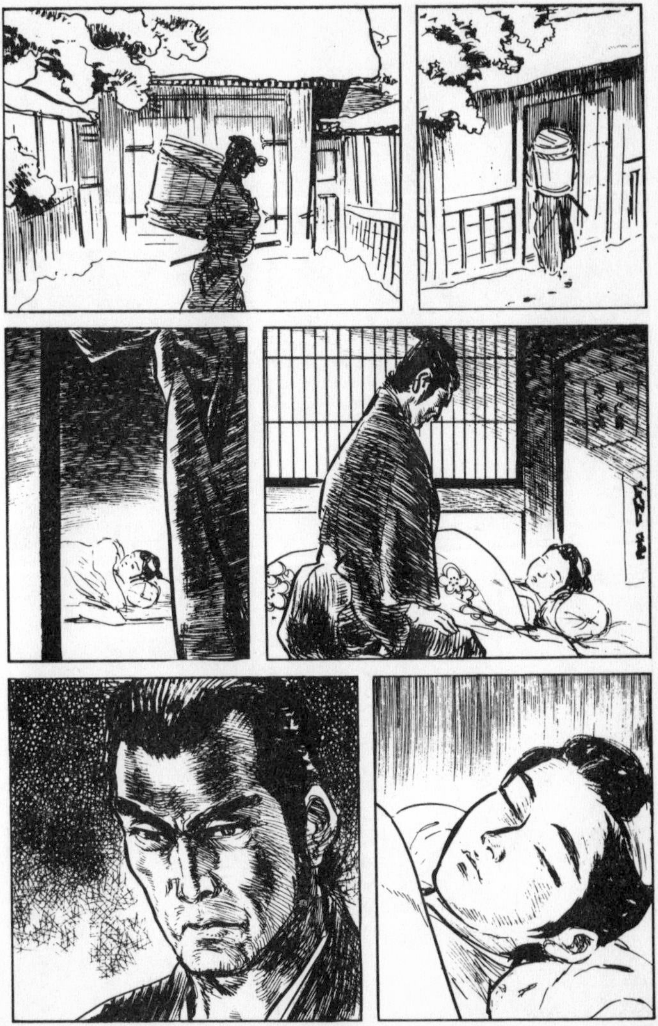

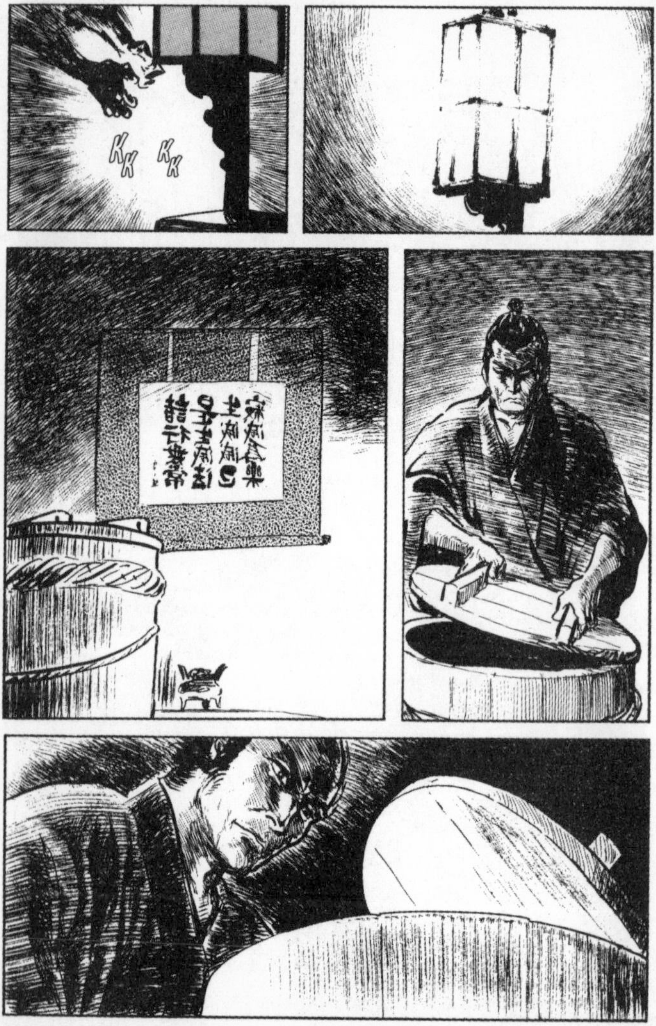
KK
KK

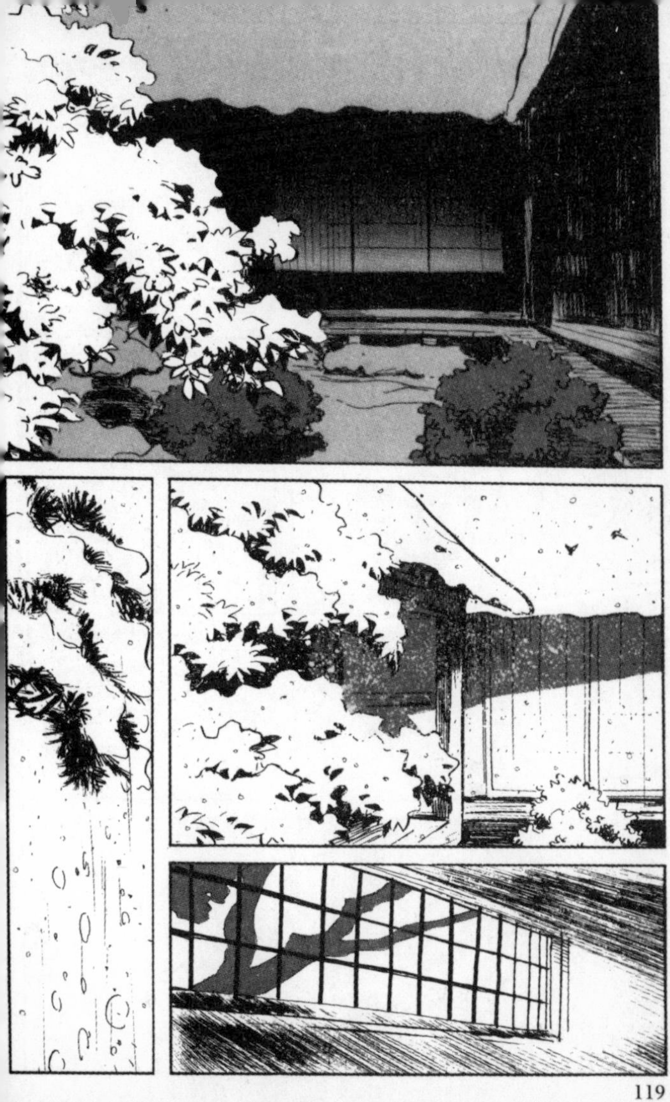

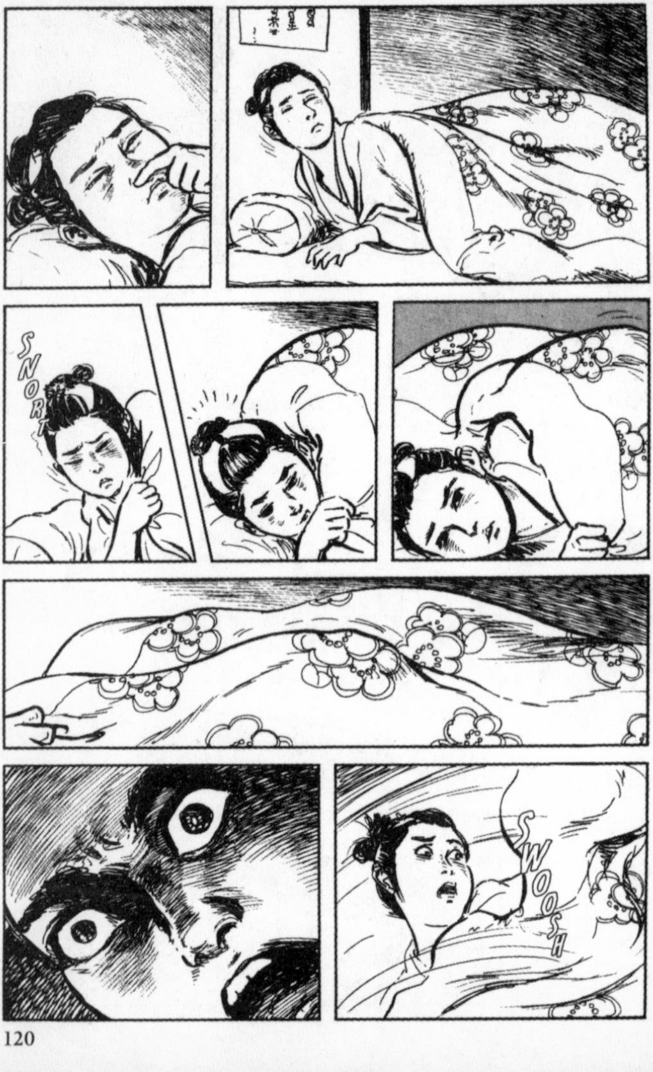
SNORT
SWOOSH

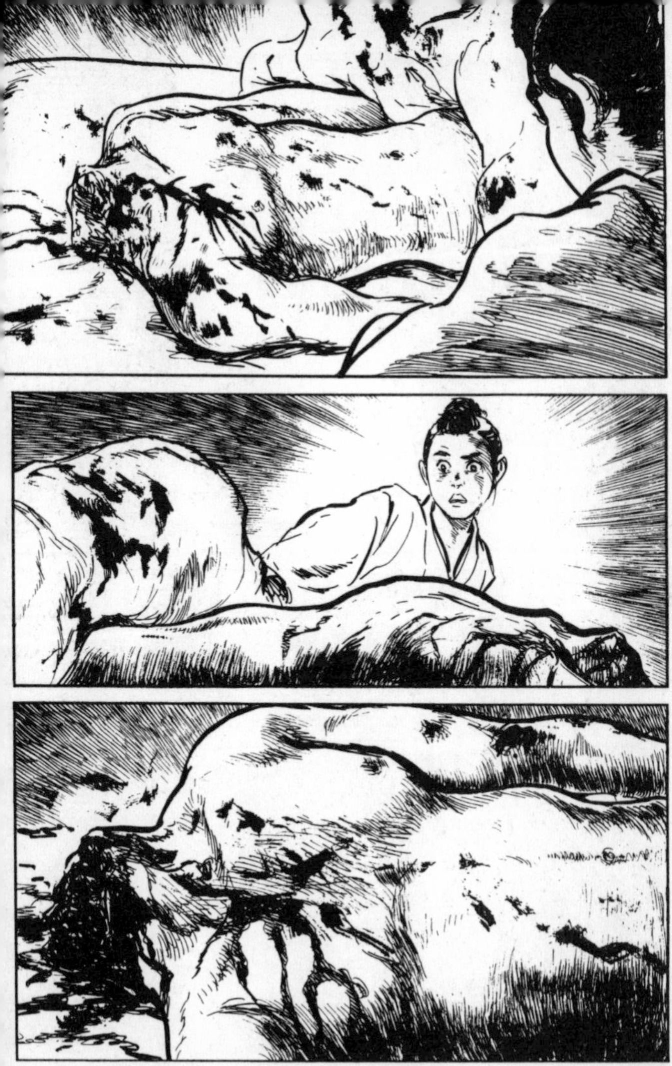

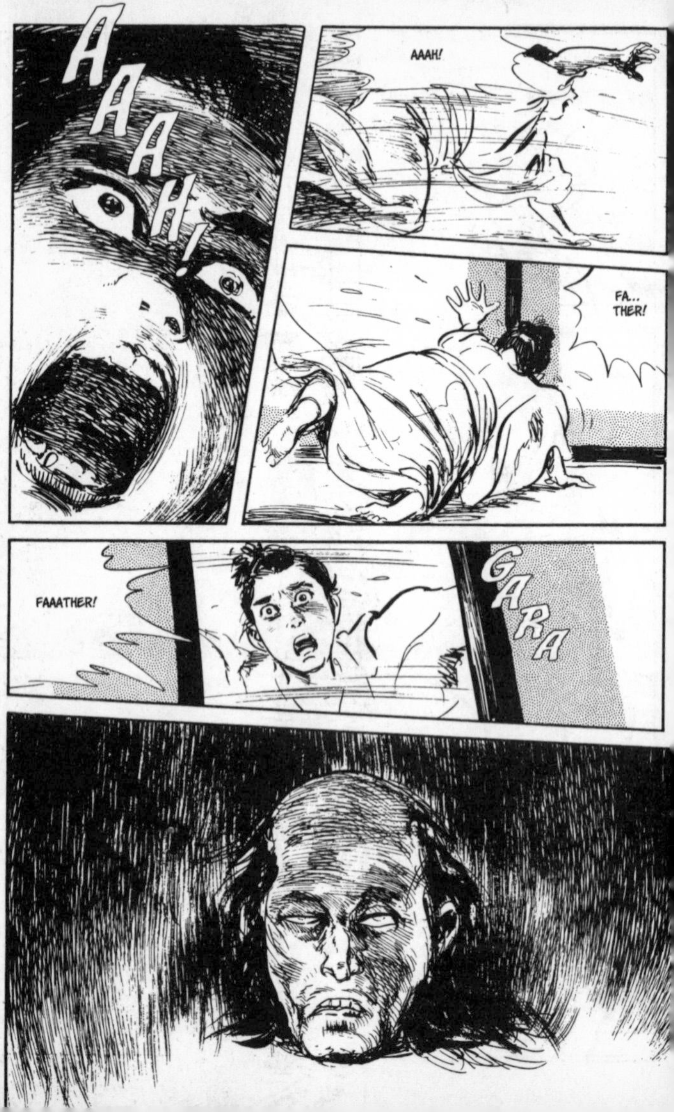
AAAAH!
AAAH!
FA... THER!
FAAATHER!
GARA

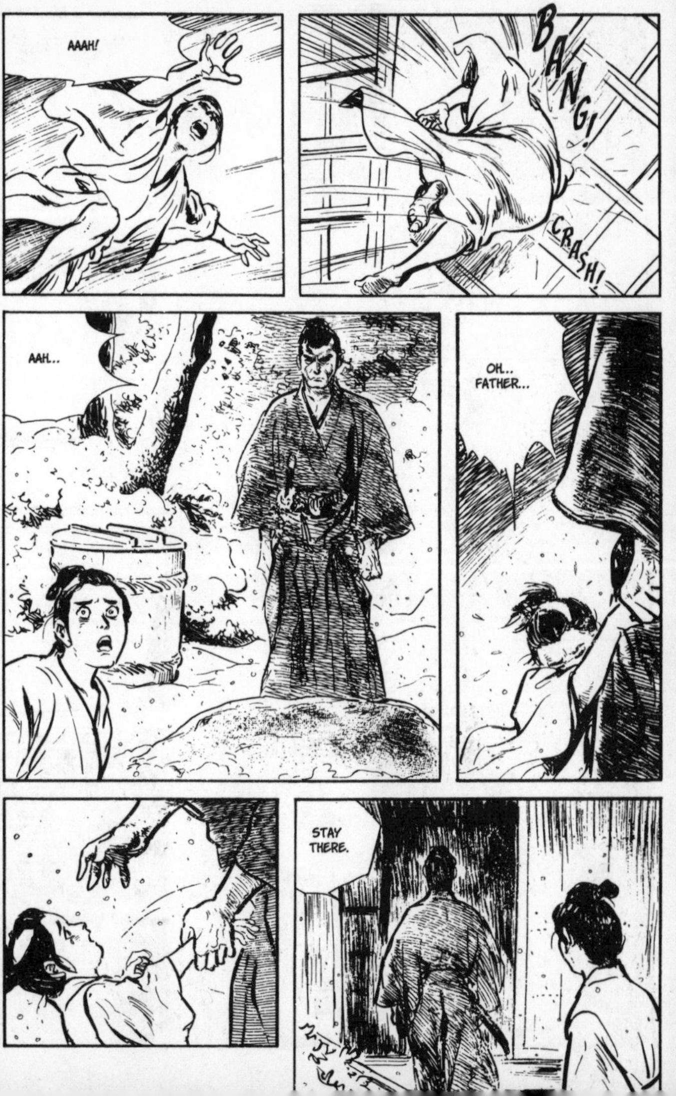
AAAH!
BANG!
CRASH!
AAH..
OH.. FATHER...
STAY THERE.

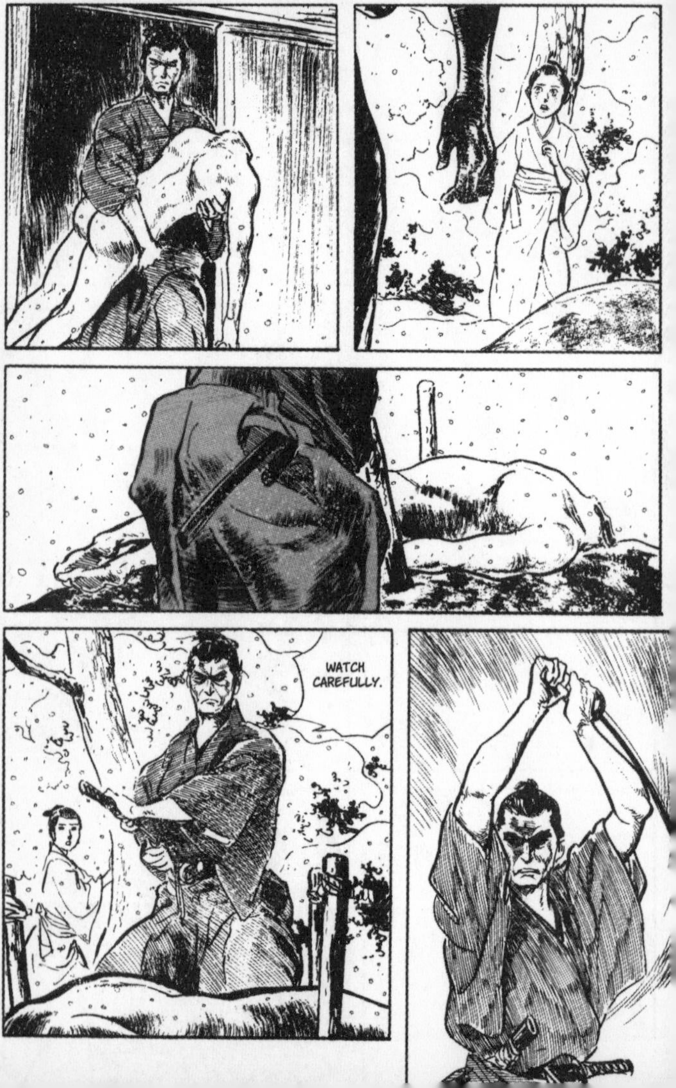
WATCH CAREFULLY.

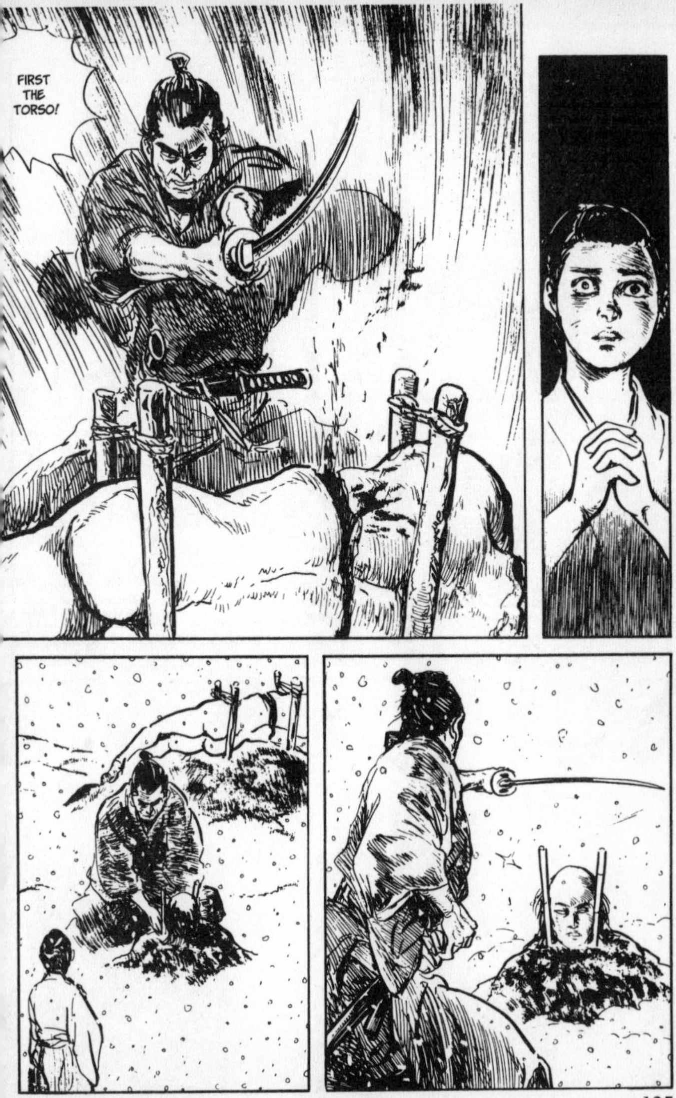
FIRST THE TORSO!

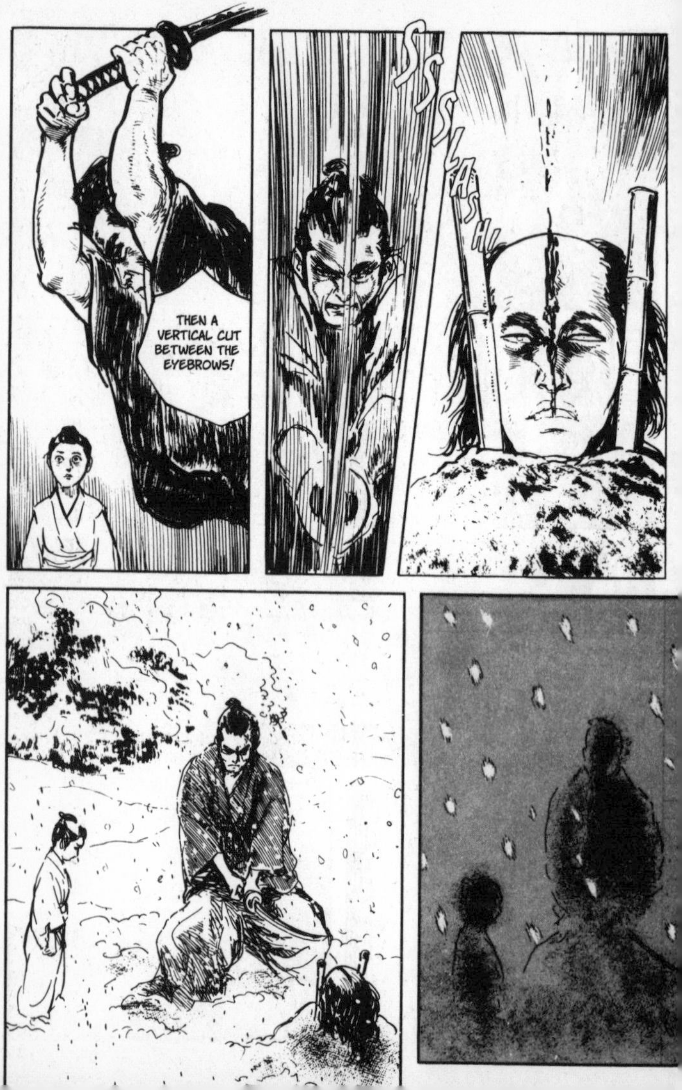
THEN A VERTICAL CUT BETWEEN THE EYEBROWS!
SSSLASH!

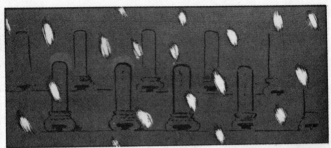

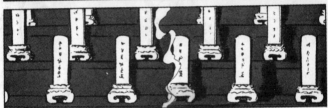

...

I WAS AFRAID OF THE CORPSE. BUT WHEN MY FATHER CUT IT IN TWO, MY FEAR DISAPPEARED.

127

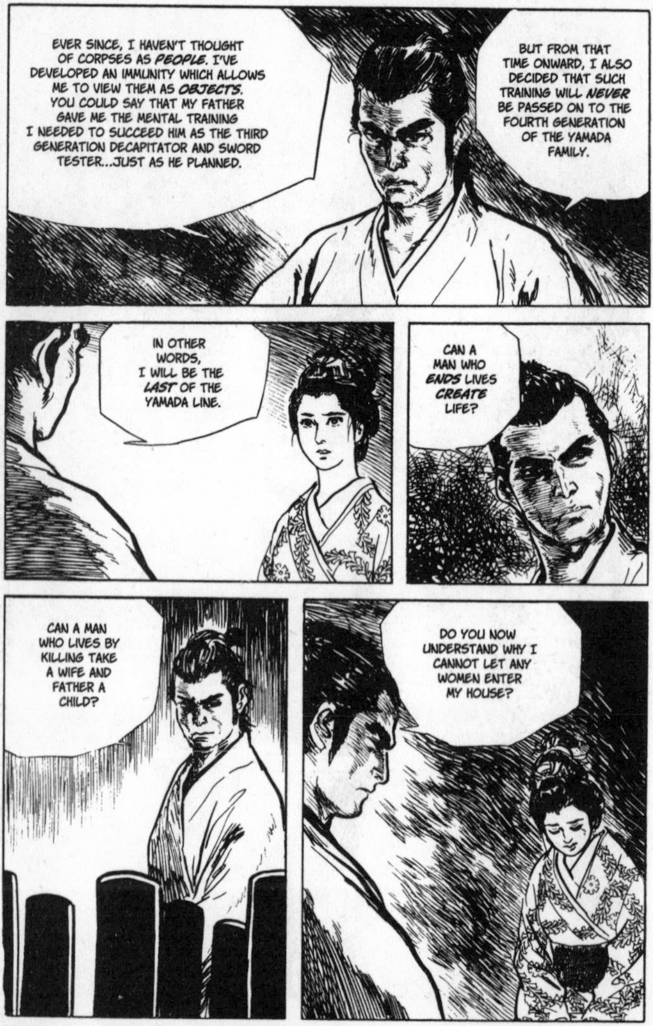
EVER SINCE, I HAVEN'T THOUGHT OF CORPSES AS *PEOPLE*. I'VE DEVELOPED AN IMMUNITY WHICH ALLOWS ME TO VIEW THEM AS *OBJECTS*. YOU COULD SAY THAT MY FATHER GAVE ME THE MENTAL TRAINING I NEEDED TO SUCCEED HIM AS THE THIRD GENERATION DECAPITATOR AND SWORD TESTER...JUST AS HE PLANNED.
BUT FROM THAT TIME ONWARD, I ALSO DECIDED THAT SUCH TRAINING WILL *NEVER* BE PASSED ON TO THE FOURTH GENERATION OF THE YAMADA FAMILY.
IN OTHER WORDS, I WILL BE THE *LAST* OF THE YAMADA LINE.
CAN A MAN WHO *ENDS* LIVES *CREATE* LIFE?
CAN A MAN WHO LIVES BY KILLING TAKE A WIFE AND FATHER A CHILD?
DO YOU NOW UNDERSTAND WHY I CANNOT LET ANY WOMEN ENTER MY HOUSE?

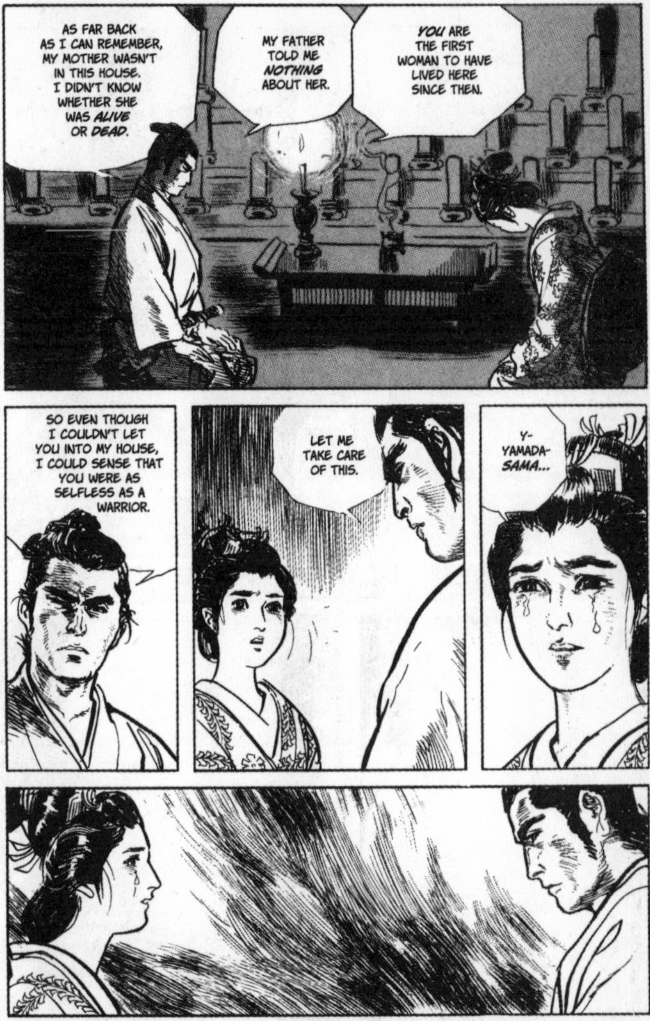
AS FAR BACK AS I CAN REMEMBER, MY MOTHER WASN'T IN THIS HOUSE. I DIDN'T KNOW WHETHER SHE WAS *ALIVE* OR *DEAD*.
MY FATHER TOLD ME *NOTHING* ABOUT HER.
YOU ARE THE FIRST WOMAN TO HAVE LIVED HERE SINCE THEN.
SO EVEN THOUGH I COULDN'T LET YOU INTO MY HOUSE, I COULD SENSE THAT YOU WERE AS SELFLESS AS A WARRIOR.
LET ME TAKE CARE OF THIS.
Y-YAMADA-*SAMA*...

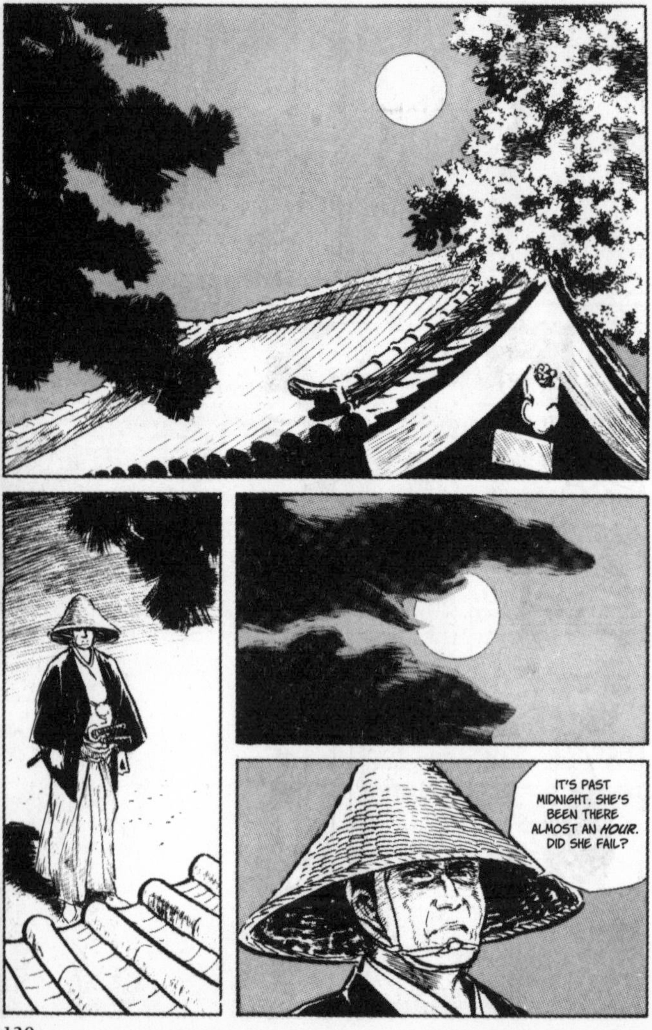
IT'S PAST MIDNIGHT. SHE'S BEEN THERE ALMOST AN *HOUR*. DID SHE FAIL?

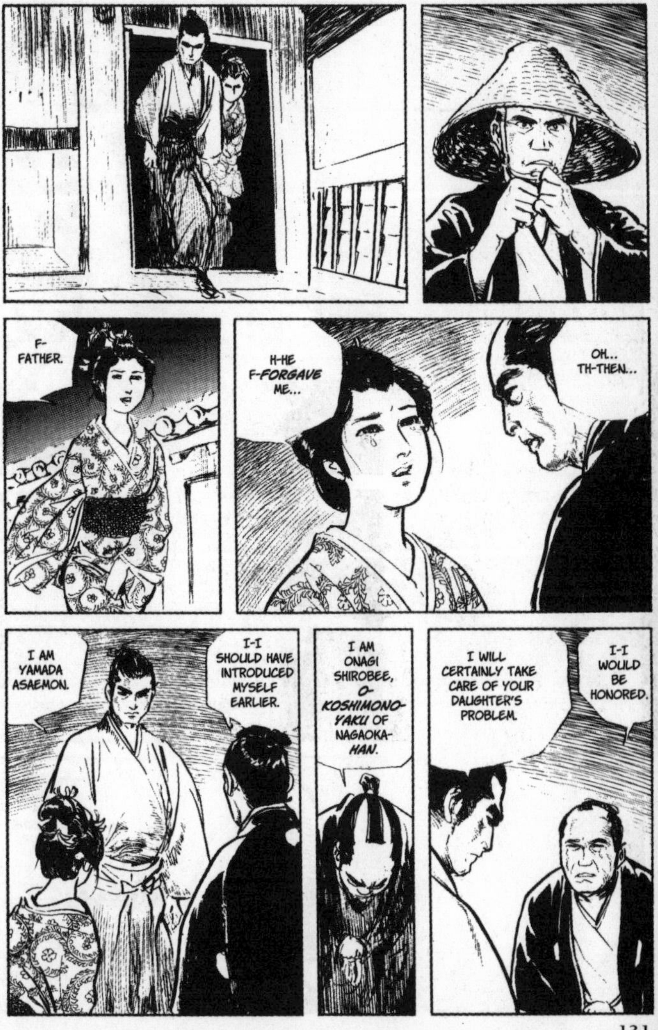
F-FATHER.
H-HE F-FORGAVE ME...
OH... TH-THEN...
I AM YAMADA ASAEMON.
I-I SHOULD HAVE INTRODUCED MYSELF EARLIER.
I AM ONAGI SHIROBEE, O-KOSHIMONO-YAKU OF NAGAOKA-HAN.
I WILL CERTAINLY TAKE CARE OF YOUR DAUGHTER'S PROBLEM.
I-I WOULD BE HONORED.

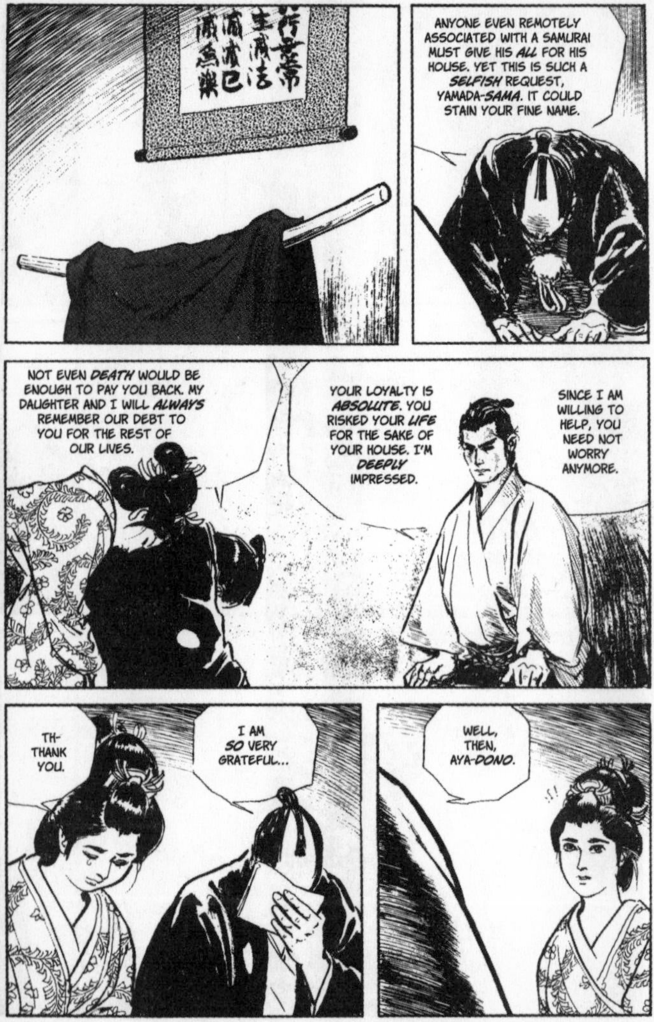
ANYONE EVEN REMOTELY ASSOCIATED WITH A SAMURAI MUST GIVE HIS *ALL* FOR HIS HOUSE. YET THIS IS SUCH A *SELFISH* REQUEST, YAMADA-*SAMA*. IT COULD STAIN YOUR FINE NAME.
NOT EVEN *DEATH* WOULD BE ENOUGH TO PAY YOU BACK. MY DAUGHTER AND I WILL *ALWAYS* REMEMBER OUR DEBT TO YOU FOR THE REST OF OUR LIVES.
YOUR LOYALTY IS *ABSOLUTE*. YOU RISKED YOUR *LIFE* FOR THE SAKE OF YOUR HOUSE. I'M *DEEPLY* IMPRESSED.
SINCE I AM WILLING TO HELP, YOU NEED NOT WORRY ANYMORE.
TH-THANK YOU.
I AM *SO* VERY GRATEFUL...
WELL, THEN, AYA-*DONO*.

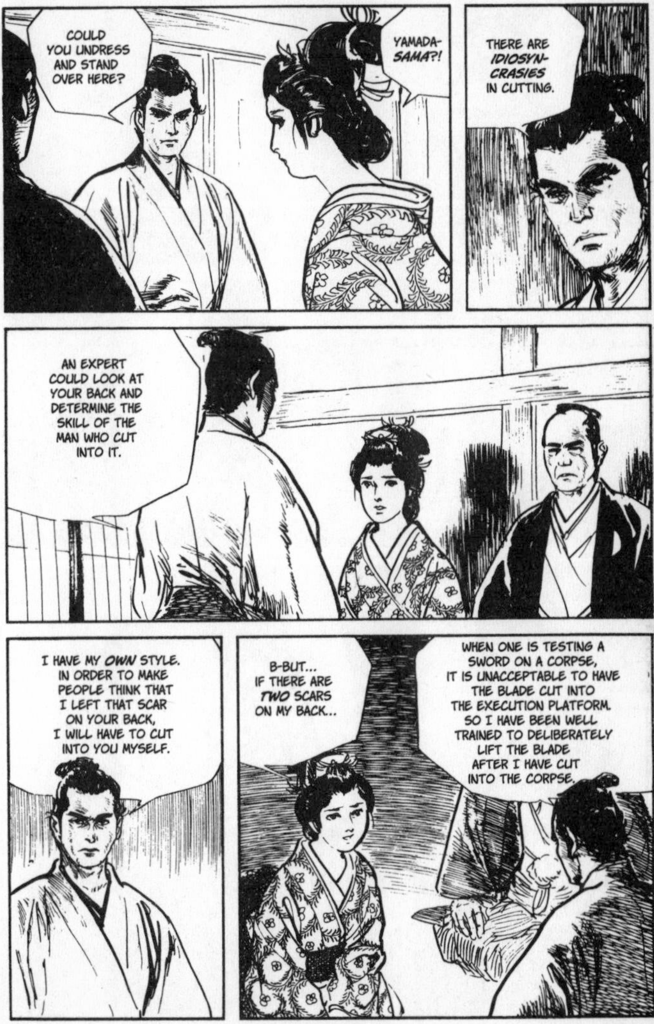
COULD YOU UNDRESS AND STAND OVER HERE?
YAMADA-SAMA?!
THERE ARE IDIOSYN-CRASIES IN CUTTING.
AN EXPERT COULD LOOK AT YOUR BACK AND DETERMINE THE SKILL OF THE MAN WHO CUT INTO IT.
I HAVE MY OWN STYLE. IN ORDER TO MAKE PEOPLE THINK THAT I LEFT THAT SCAR ON YOUR BACK, I WILL HAVE TO CUT INTO YOU MYSELF.
B-BUT... IF THERE ARE TWO SCARS ON MY BACK...
WHEN ONE IS TESTING A SWORD ON A CORPSE, IT IS UNACCEPTABLE TO HAVE THE BLADE CUT INTO THE EXECUTION PLATFORM. SO I HAVE BEEN WELL TRAINED TO DELIBERATELY LIFT THE BLADE AFTER I HAVE CUT INTO THE CORPSE.

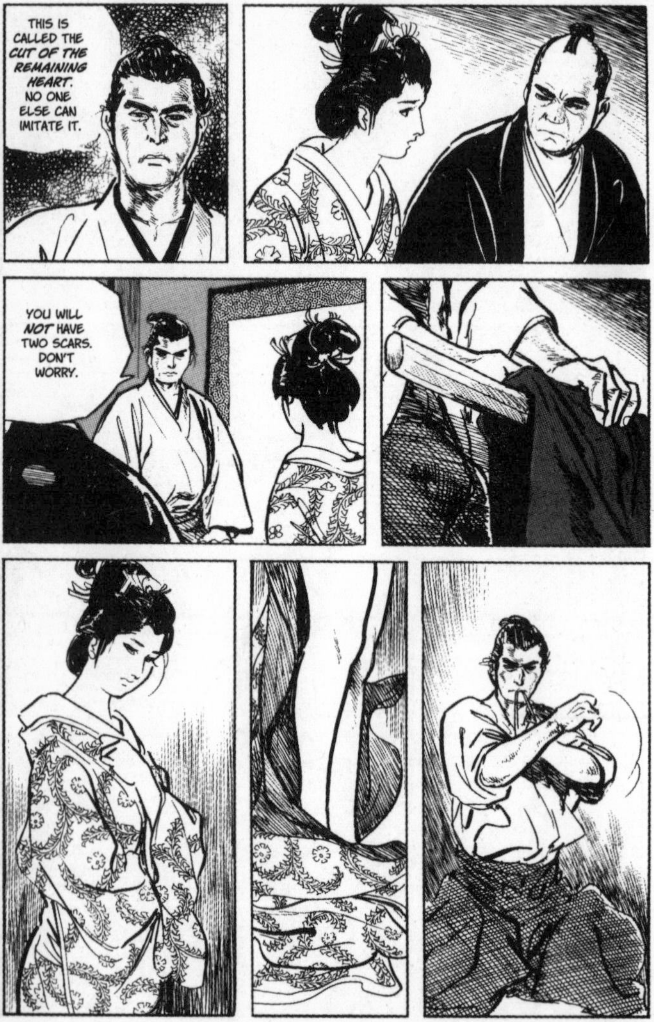
THIS IS CALLED THE *CUT OF THE REMAINING HEART*. NO ONE ELSE CAN IMITATE IT.
YOU WILL *NOT* HAVE TWO SCARS. DON'T WORRY.

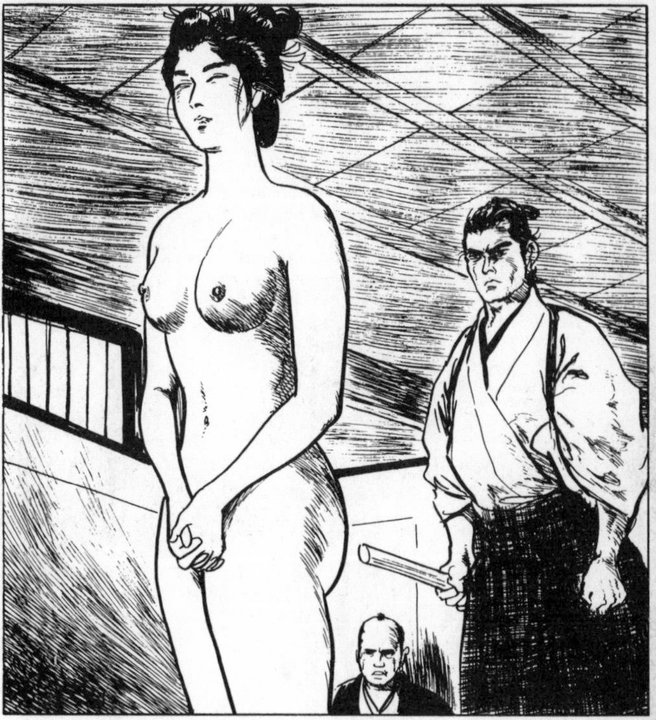
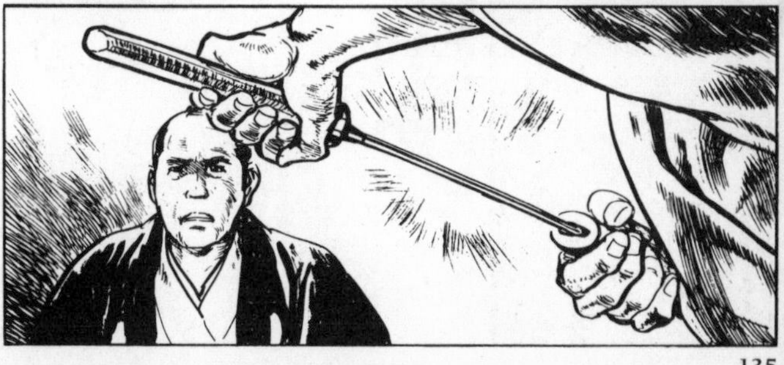

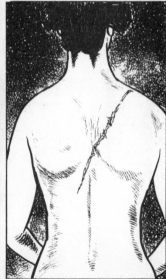

136

URGH!

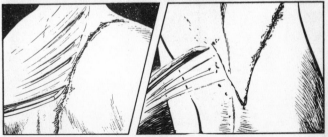

137

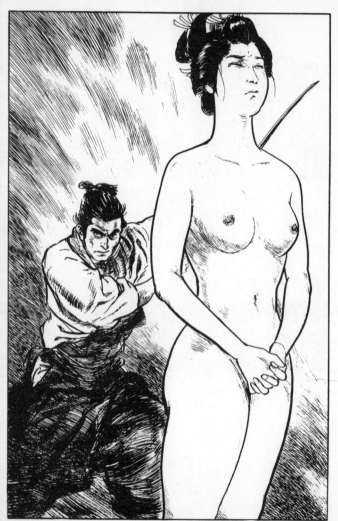

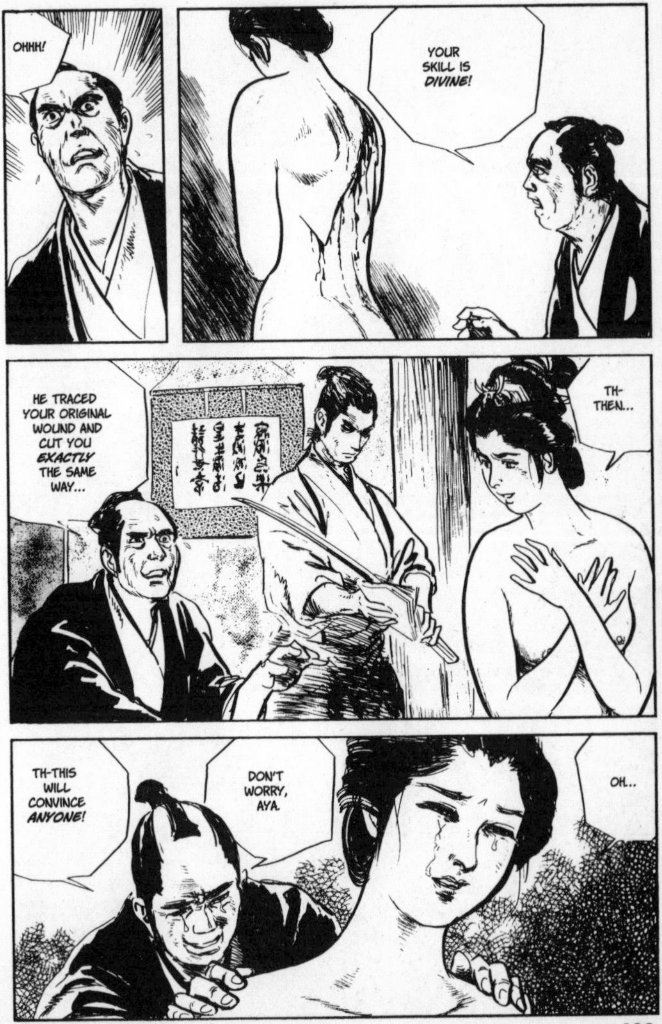
OHHH!
YOUR SKILL IS *DIVINE!*
HE TRACED YOUR ORIGINAL WOUND AND CUT YOU *EXACTLY* THE SAME WAY...
TH- THEN...
TH-THIS WILL CONVINCE *ANYONE!*
DON'T WORRY, AYA.
OH...

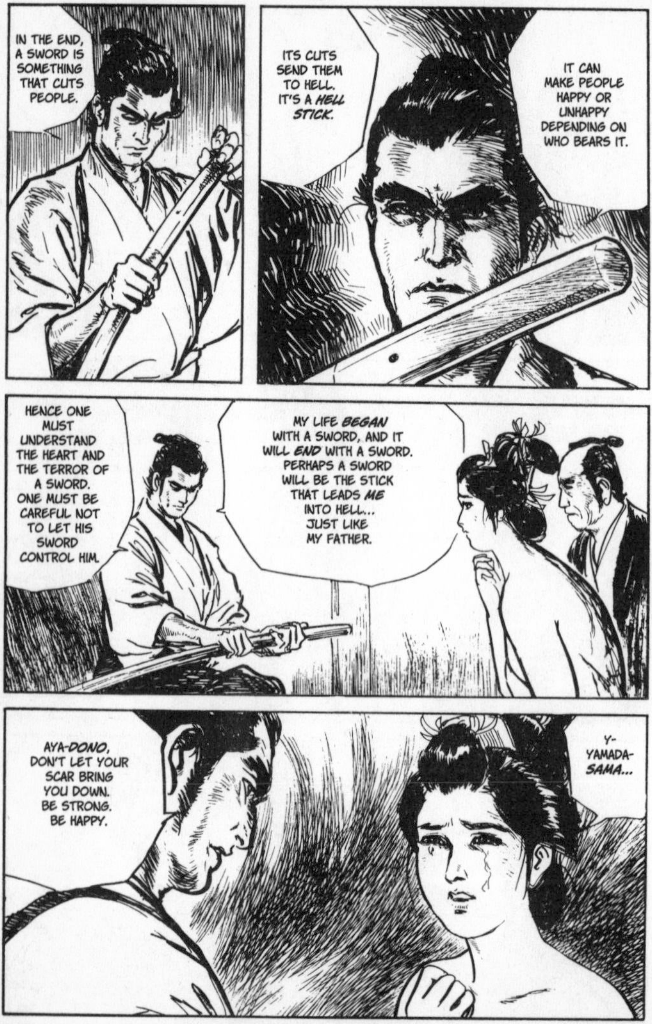
IN THE END, A SWORD IS SOMETHING THAT CUTS PEOPLE.
ITS CUTS SEND THEM TO HELL. IT'S A *HELL STICK.*
IT CAN MAKE PEOPLE HAPPY OR UNHAPPY DEPENDING ON WHO BEARS IT.
HENCE ONE MUST UNDERSTAND THE HEART AND THE TERROR OF A SWORD. ONE MUST BE CAREFUL NOT TO LET HIS SWORD CONTROL HIM.
MY LIFE *BEGAN* WITH A SWORD, AND IT WILL *END* WITH A SWORD. PERHAPS A SWORD WILL BE THE STICK THAT LEADS *ME* INTO HELL... JUST LIKE MY FATHER.
AYA-*DONO,* DON'T LET YOUR SCAR BRING YOU DOWN. BE STRONG. BE HAPPY.
Y-YAMADA-*SAMA...*

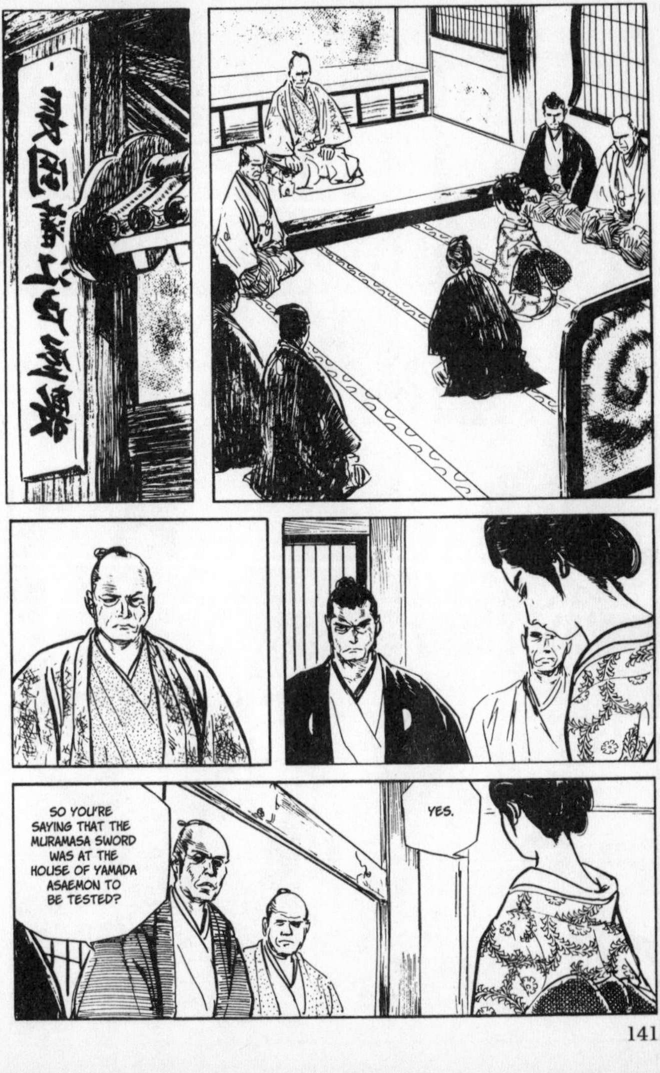
SO YOU'RE SAYING THAT THE MURAMASA SWORD WAS AT THE HOUSE OF YAMADA ASAEMON TO BE TESTED?
YES.

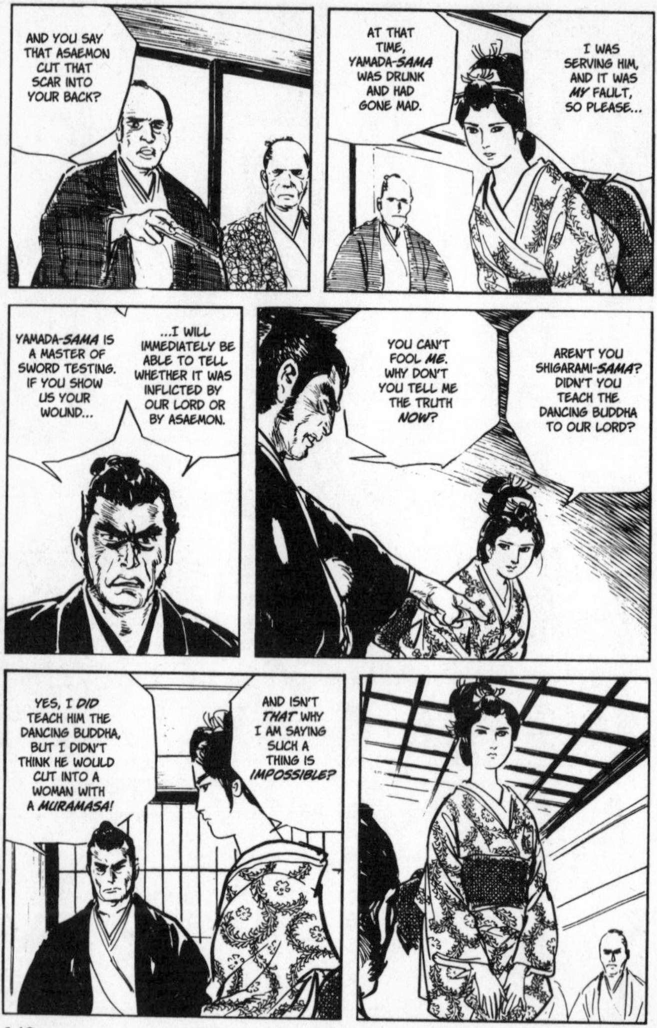
AND YOU SAY THAT ASAEMON CUT THAT SCAR INTO YOUR BACK?
AT THAT TIME, YAMADA-*SAMA* WAS DRUNK AND HAD GONE MAD.
I WAS SERVING HIM, AND IT WAS *MY* FAULT, SO PLEASE...
YAMADA-*SAMA* IS A MASTER OF SWORD TESTING. IF YOU SHOW US YOUR WOUND...
...I WILL IMMEDIATELY BE ABLE TO TELL WHETHER IT WAS INFLICTED BY OUR LORD OR BY ASAEMON.
YOU CAN'T FOOL *ME*. WHY DON'T YOU TELL ME THE TRUTH *NOW*?
AREN'T YOU SHIGARAMI-*SAMA*? DIDN'T YOU TEACH THE DANCING BUDDHA TO OUR LORD?
YES, I *DID* TEACH HIM THE DANCING BUDDHA, BUT I DIDN'T THINK HE WOULD CUT INTO A WOMAN WITH A *MURAMASA*!
AND ISN'T *THAT* WHY I AM SAYING SUCH A THING IS *IMPOSSIBLE*?

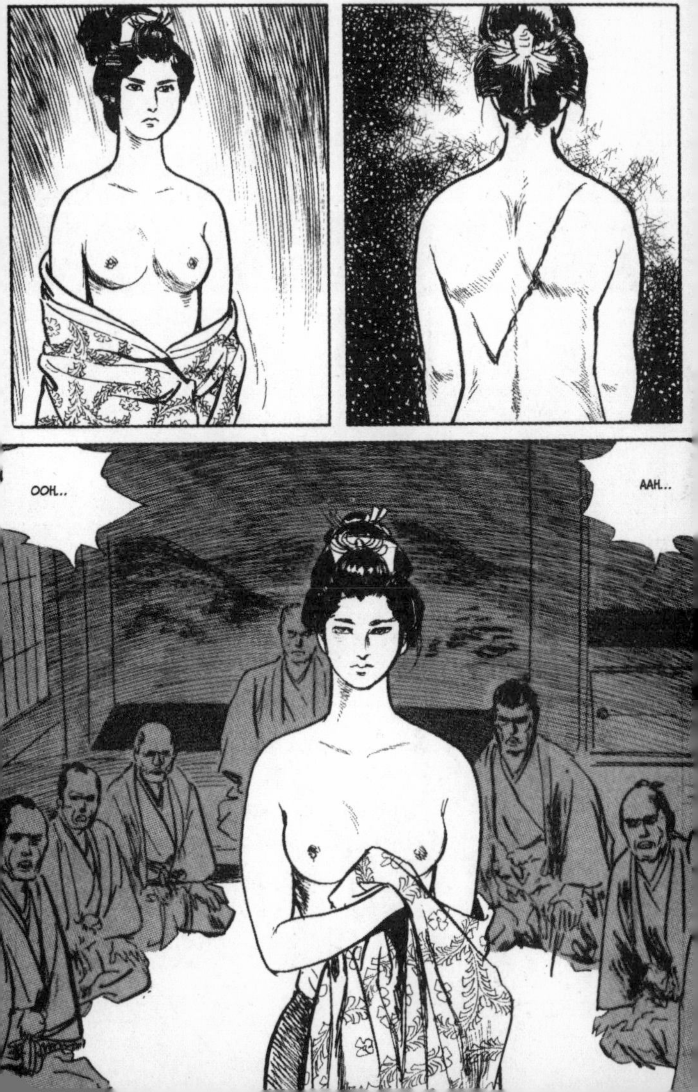
OOH..
AAH..

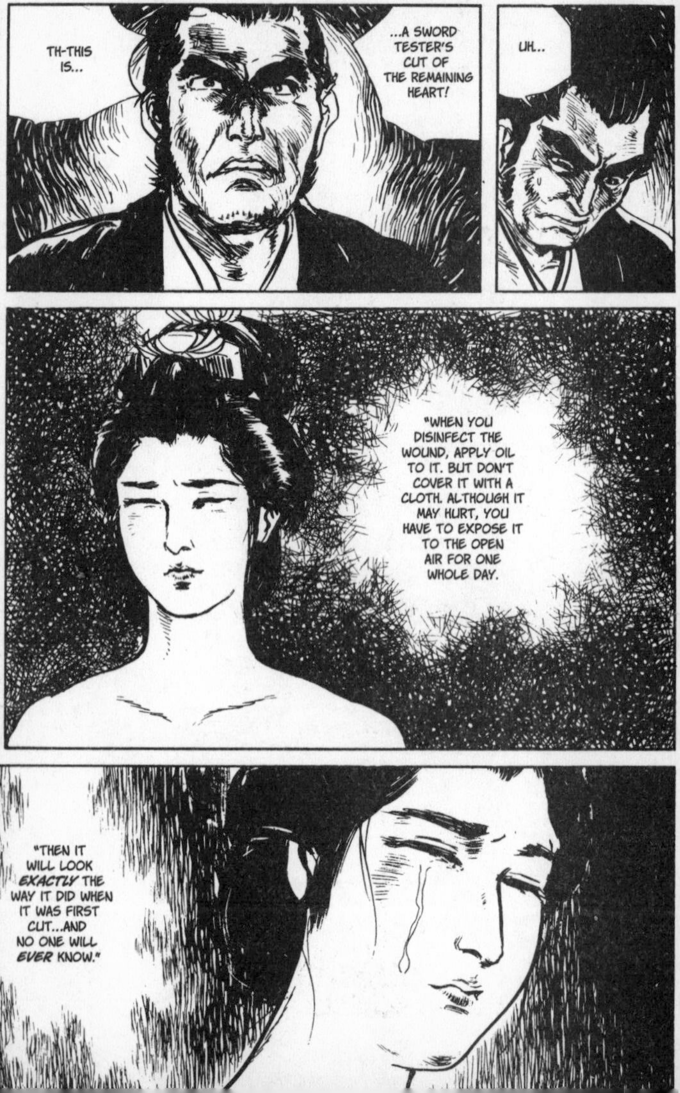
TH-THIS IS...
...A SWORD TESTER'S CUT OF THE REMAINING HEART!
UH...
"WHEN YOU DISINFECT THE WOUND, APPLY OIL TO IT. BUT DON'T COVER IT WITH A CLOTH. ALTHOUGH IT MAY HURT, YOU HAVE TO EXPOSE IT TO THE OPEN AIR FOR ONE WHOLE DAY.
"THEN IT WILL LOOK *EXACTLY* THE WAY IT DID WHEN IT WAS FIRST CUT...AND NO ONE WILL *EVER* KNOW."

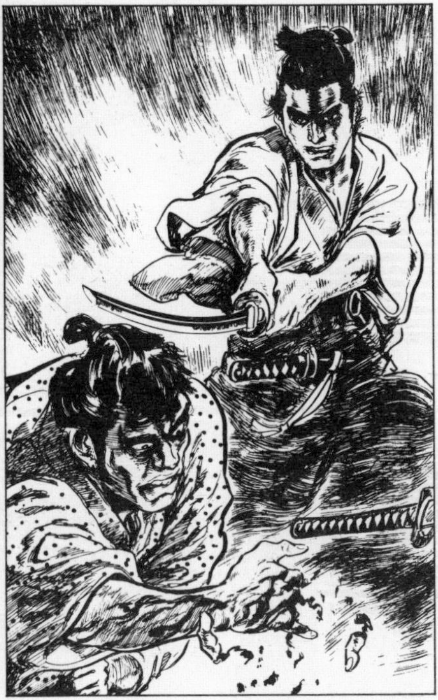

the tenth

The mad sword of Tsukuba Bakushū

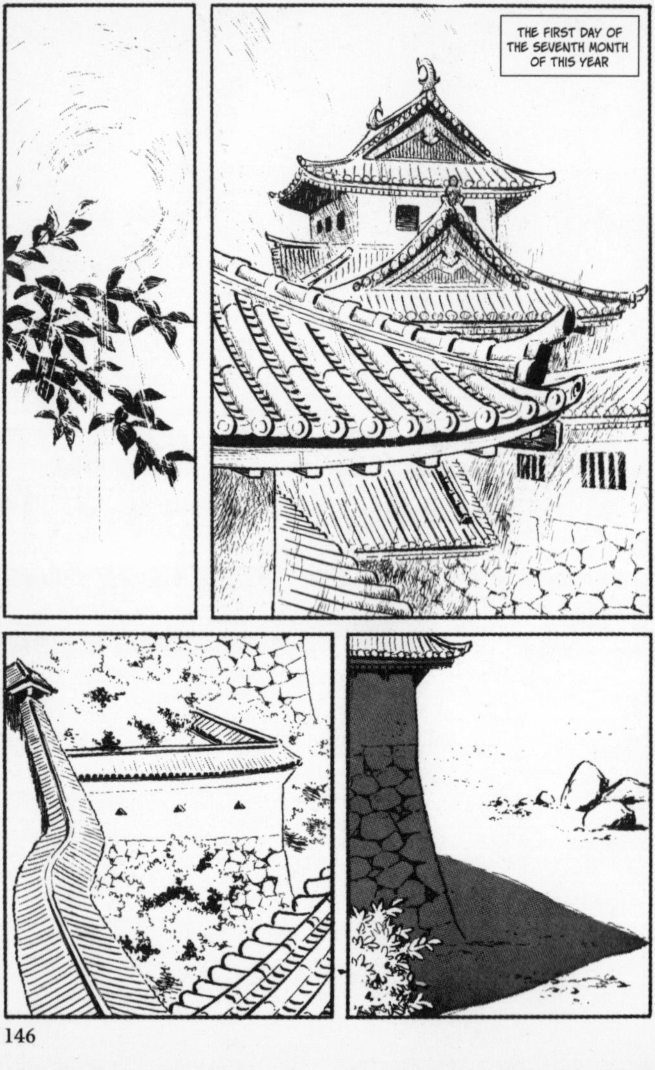
THE FIRST DAY OF THE SEVENTH MONTH OF THIS YEAR

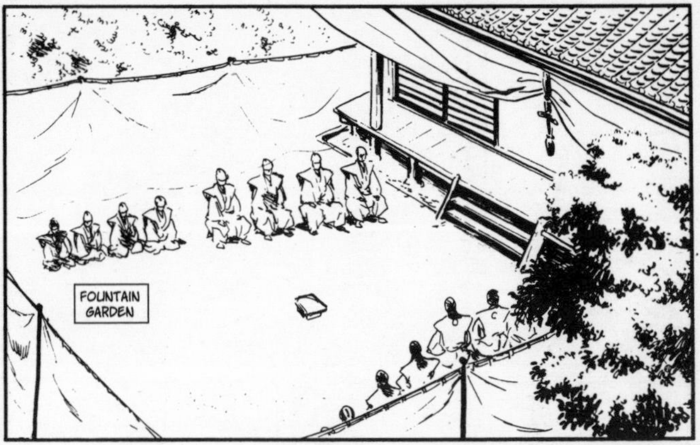
FOUNTAIN
GARDEN
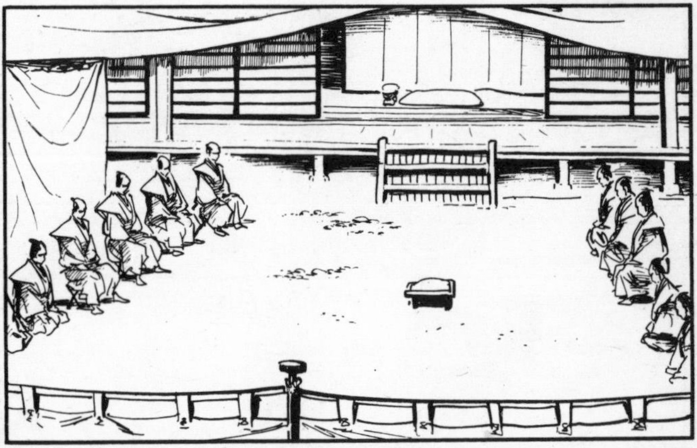
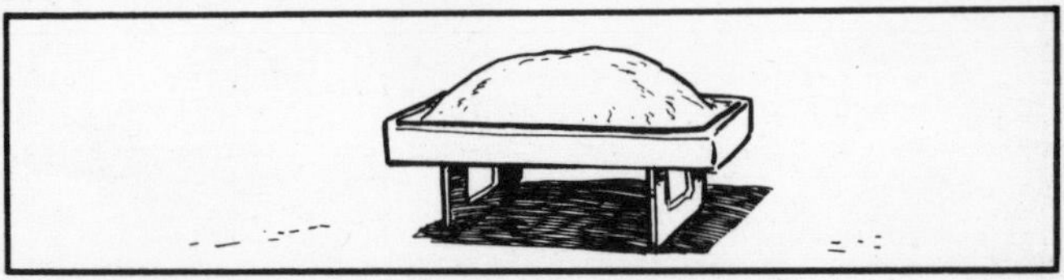

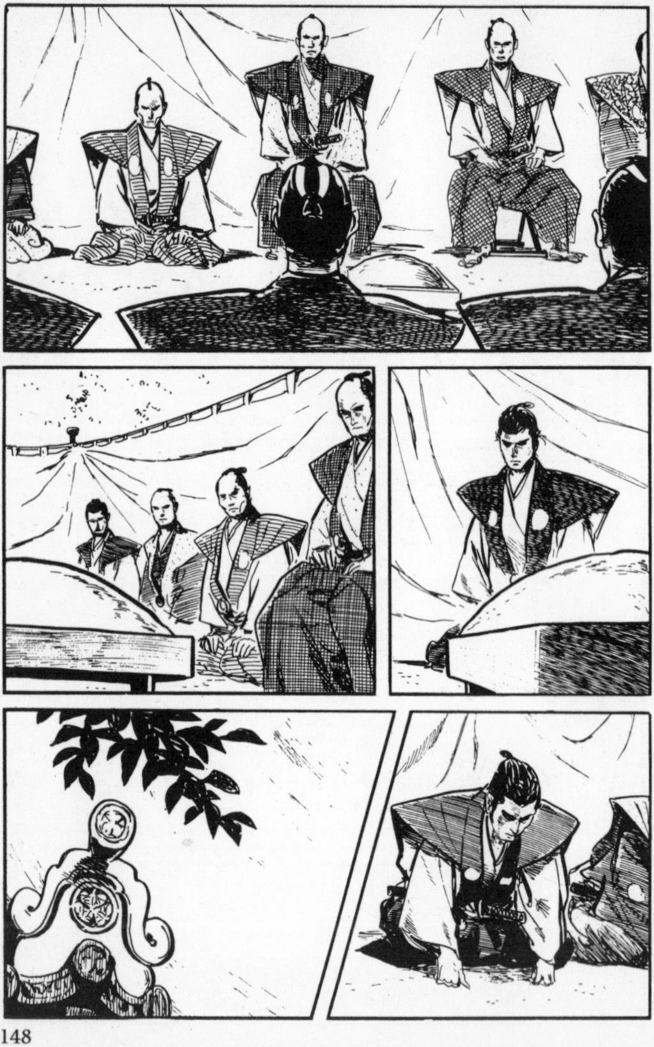

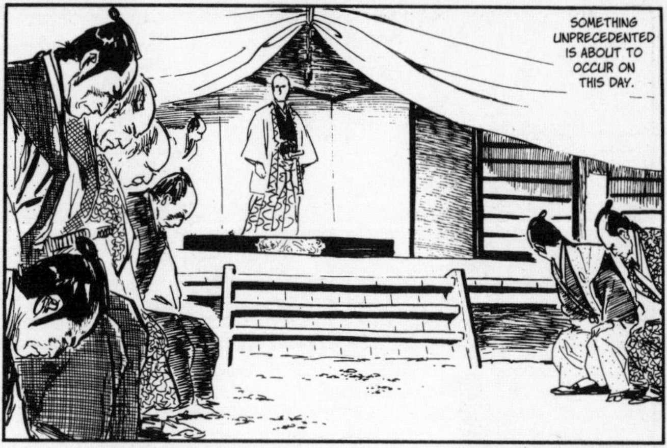
SOMETHING UNPRECEDENTED IS ABOUT TO OCCUR ON THIS DAY.

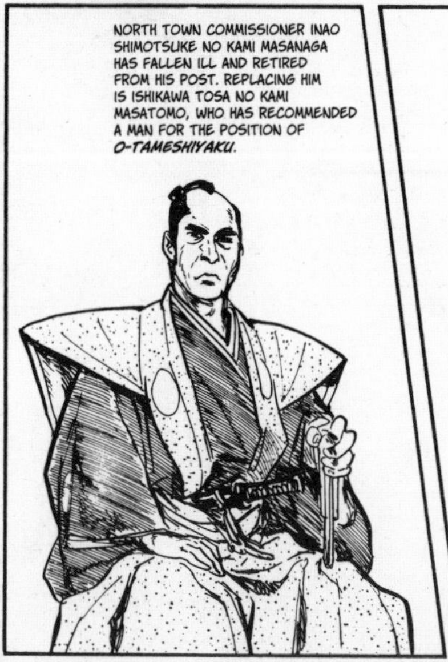
NORTH TOWN COMMISSIONER INAO SHIMOTSUKE NO KAMI MASANAGA HAS FALLEN ILL AND RETIRED FROM HIS POST. REPLACING HIM IS ISHIKAWA TOSA NO KAMI MASATOMO, WHO HAS RECOMMENDED A MAN FOR THE POSITION OF *O-TAMESHIYAKU*.

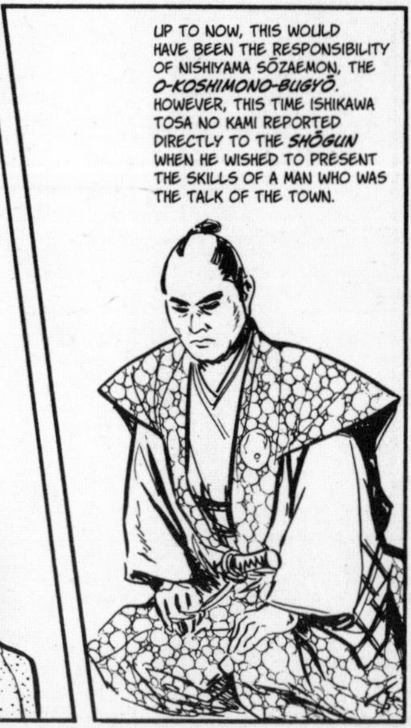
UP TO NOW, THIS WOULD HAVE BEEN THE RESPONSIBILITY OF NISHIYAMA SŌZAEMON, THE *O-KOSHIMONO-BUGYŌ*. HOWEVER, THIS TIME ISHIKAWA TOSA NO KAMI REPORTED DIRECTLY TO THE *SHŌGUN* WHEN HE WISHED TO PRESENT THE SKILLS OF A MAN WHO WAS THE TALK OF THE TOWN.

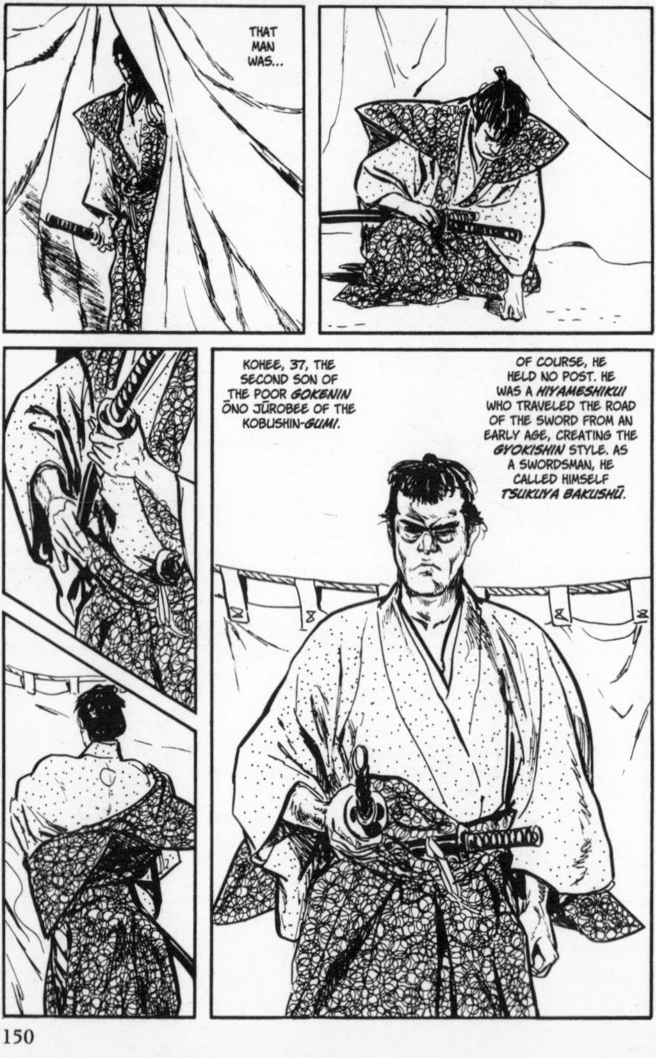
THAT MAN WAS...
KOHEE, 37, THE SECOND SON OF THE POOR *GOKENIN* ŌNO JŪROBEE OF THE KOBUSHIN-*GUMI*.
OF COURSE, HE HELD NO POST. HE WAS A *HIYAMESHIKUI* WHO TRAVELED THE ROAD OF THE SWORD FROM AN EARLY AGE, CREATING THE *GYOKISHIN* STYLE. AS A SWORDSMAN, HE CALLED HIMSELF *TSUKUYA BAKUSHŪ*.

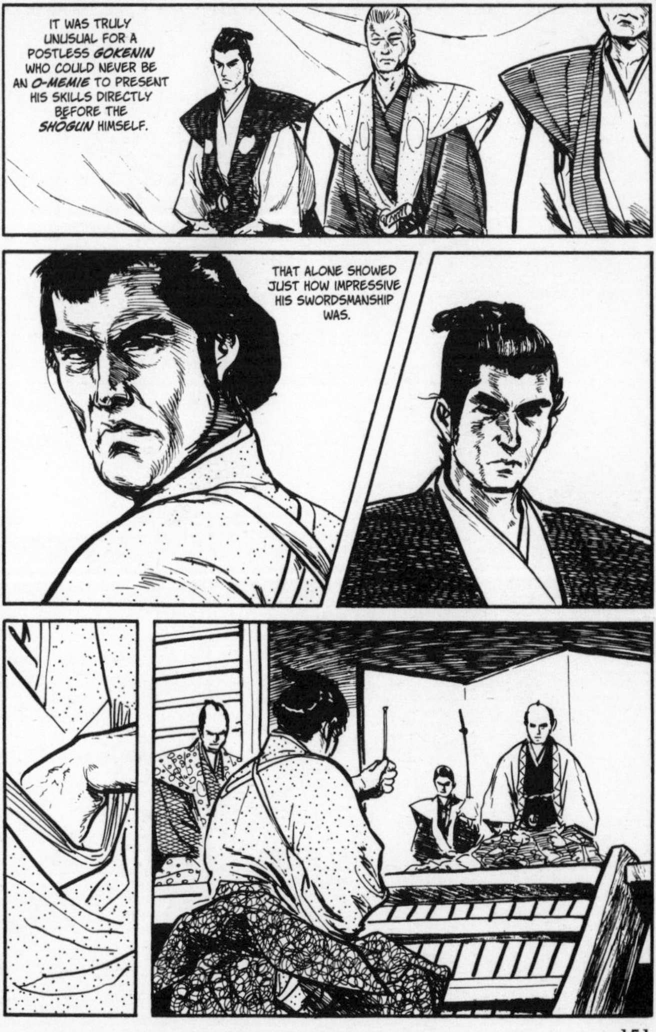
IT WAS TRULY UNUSUAL FOR A POSTLESS *GOKENIN* WHO COULD NEVER BE AN *O-MEMIE* TO PRESENT HIS SKILLS DIRECTLY BEFORE THE *SHŌGUN* HIMSELF.
THAT ALONE SHOWED JUST HOW IMPRESSIVE HIS SWORDSMANSHIP WAS.

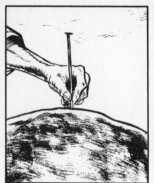

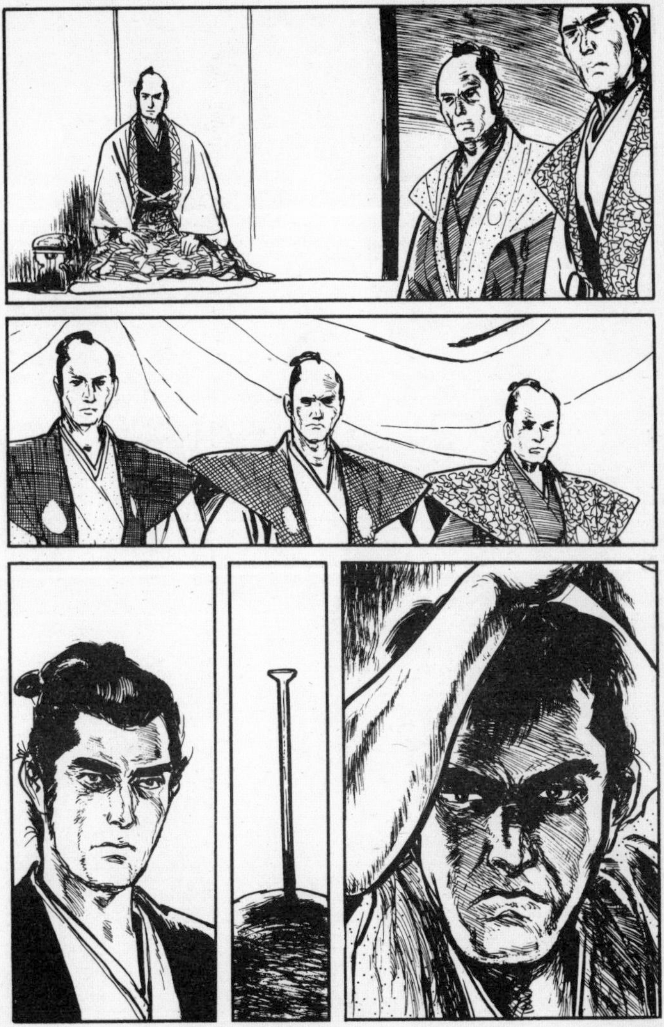

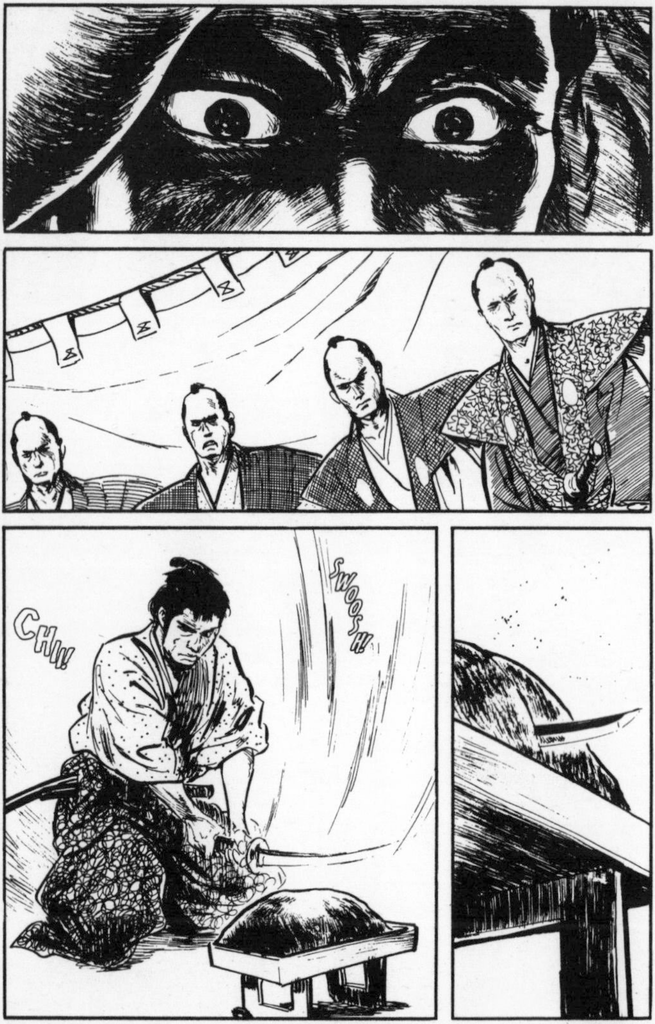
CHI!!
SWOOSH!

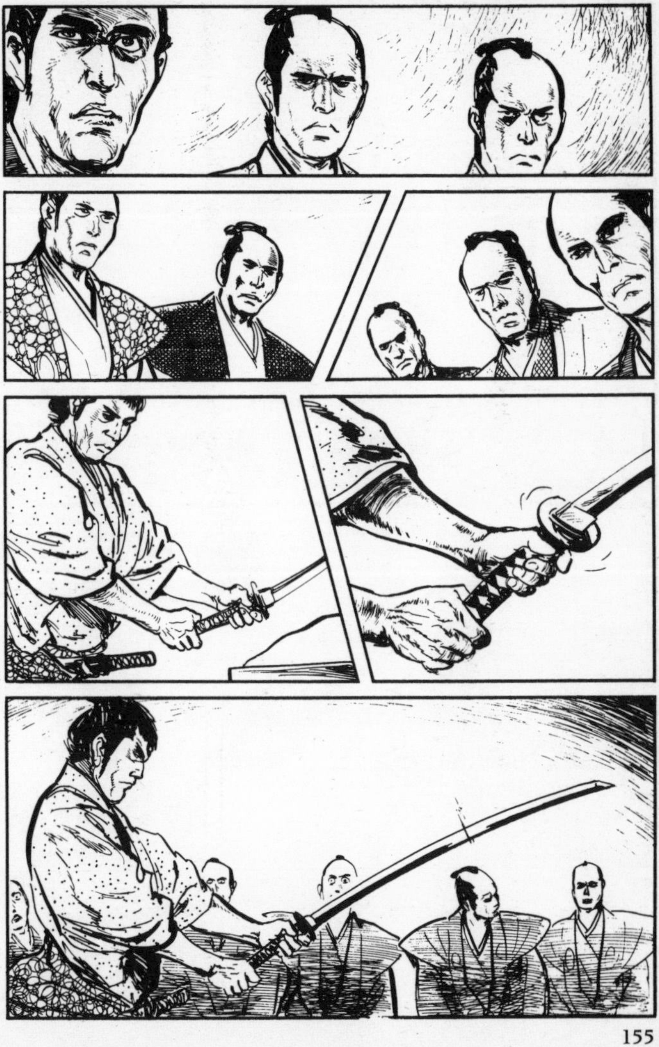

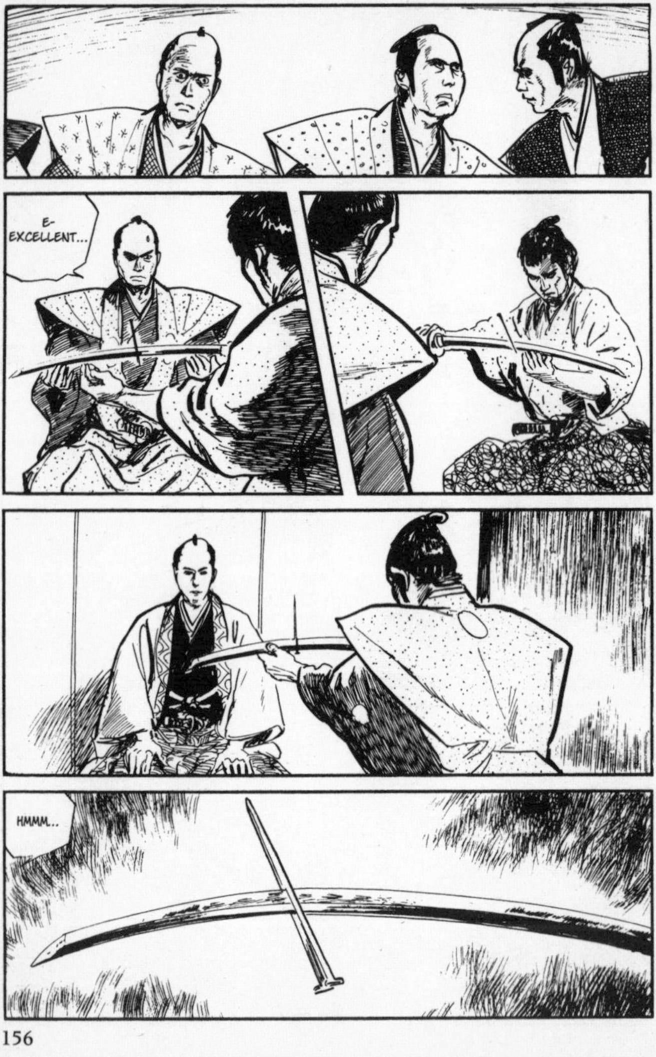
E-EXCELLENT...
HMMM...

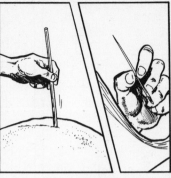

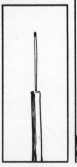

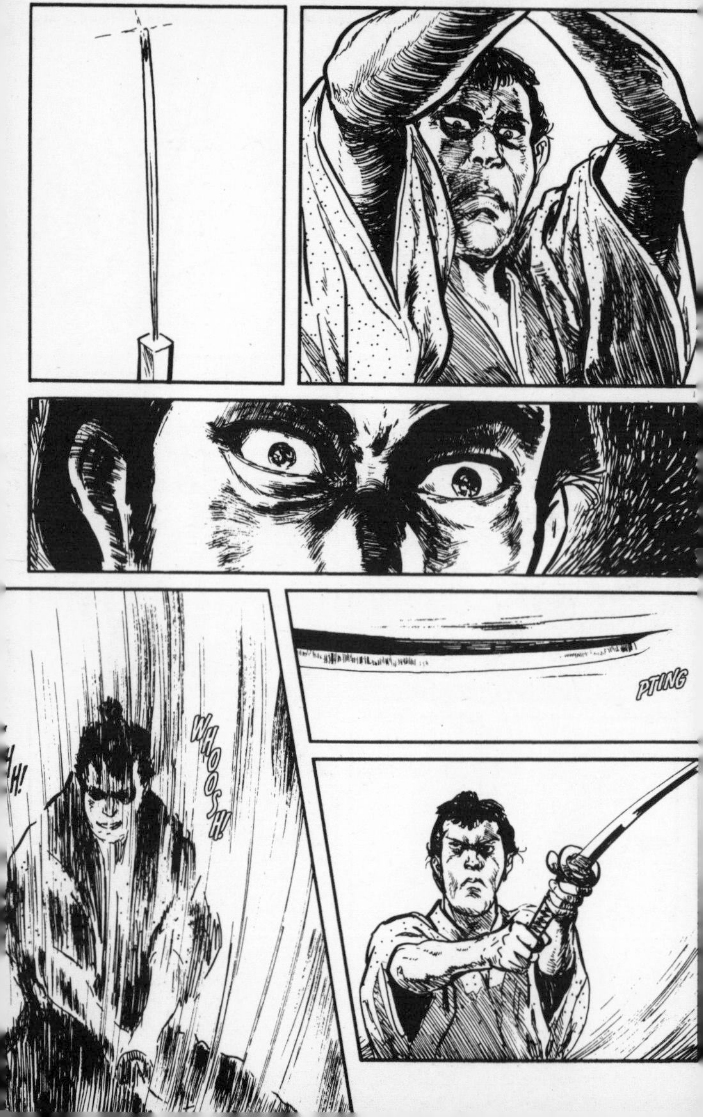
WHOOSH!
PTING

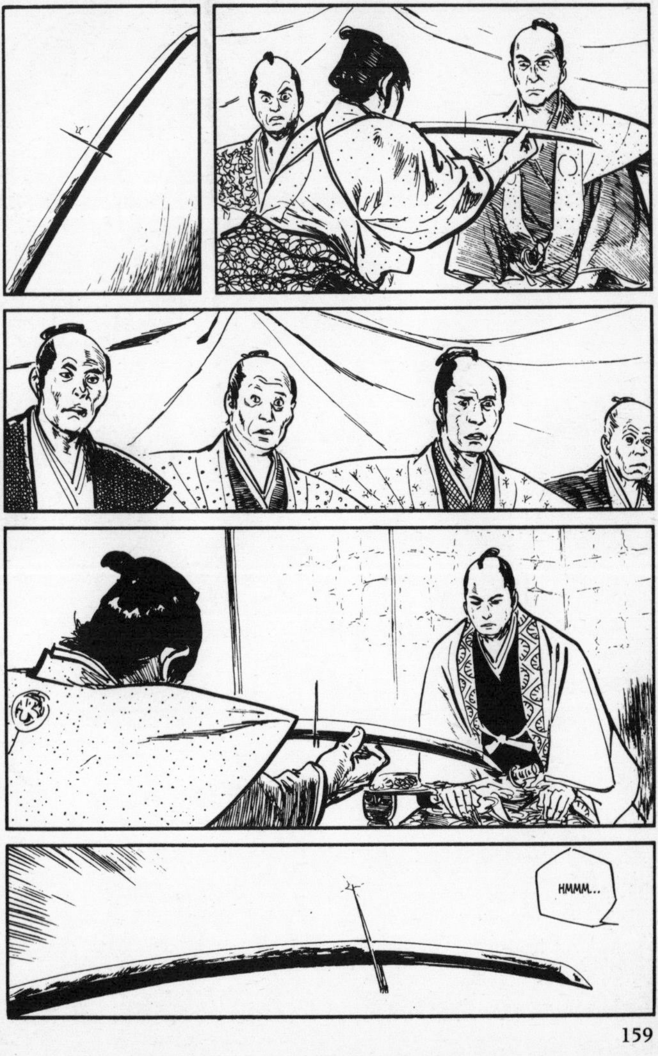
HMMM...

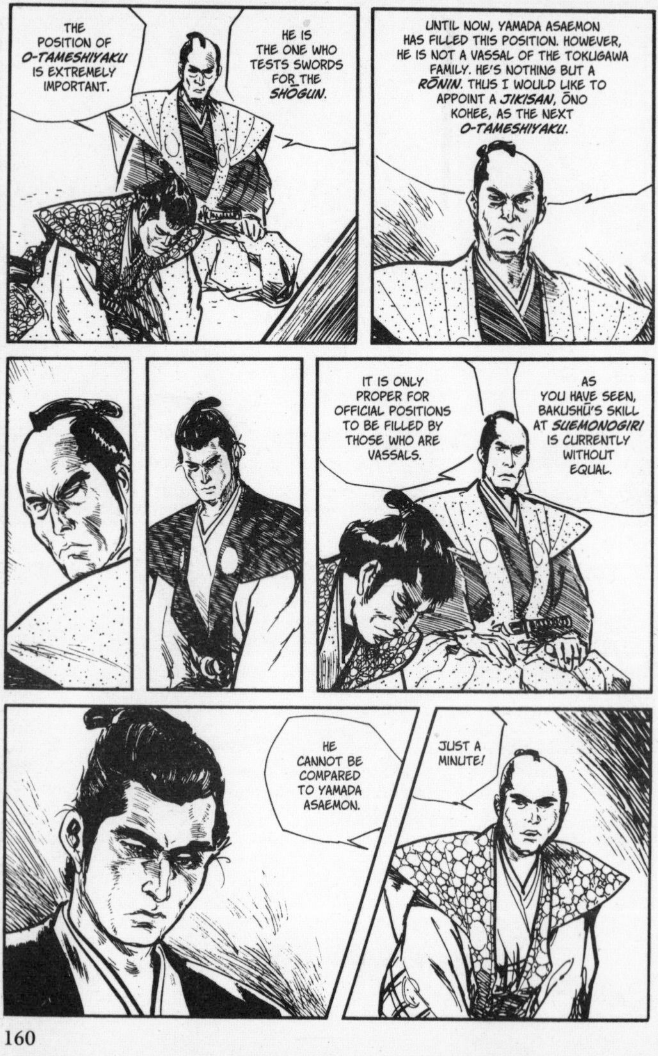
THE POSITION OF O-TAMESHIYAKU IS EXTREMELY IMPORTANT.
HE IS THE ONE WHO TESTS SWORDS FOR THE SHŌGUN.
UNTIL NOW, YAMADA ASAEMON HAS FILLED THIS POSITION. HOWEVER, HE IS NOT A VASSAL OF THE TOKUGAWA FAMILY. HE'S NOTHING BUT A RŌNIN. THUS I WOULD LIKE TO APPOINT A JIKISAN, ŌNO KOHEE, AS THE NEXT O-TAMESHIYAKU.
IT IS ONLY PROPER FOR OFFICIAL POSITIONS TO BE FILLED BY THOSE WHO ARE VASSALS.
AS YOU HAVE SEEN, BAKUSHŪ'S SKILL AT SUEMONOGIRI IS CURRENTLY WITHOUT EQUAL.
HE CANNOT BE COMPARED TO YAMADA ASAEMON.
JUST A MINUTE!

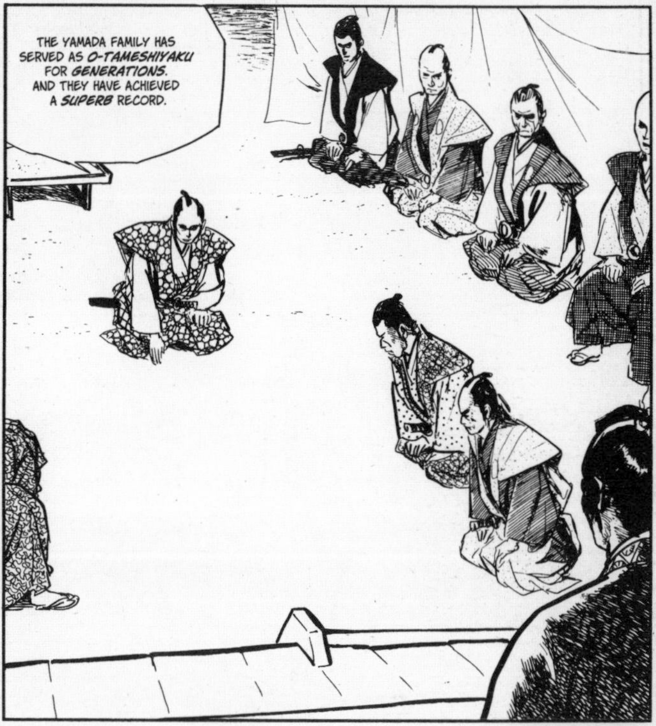
THE YAMADA FAMILY HAS SERVED AS O-TAMESHIYAKU FOR GENERATIONS. AND THEY HAVE ACHIEVED A SUPERB RECORD.

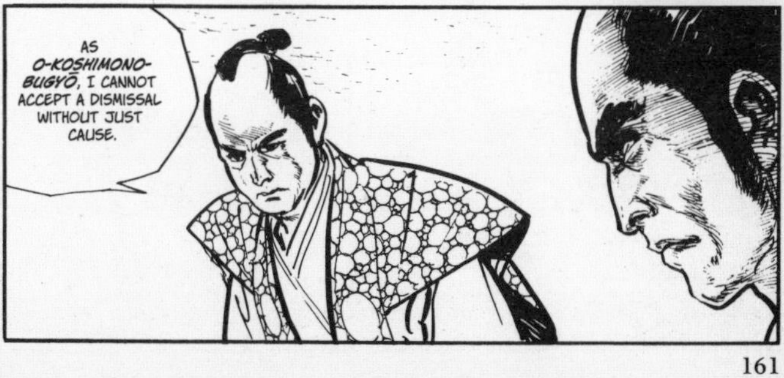
AS O-KOSHIMONO-BUGYŌ, I CANNOT ACCEPT A DISMISSAL WITHOUT JUST CAUSE.

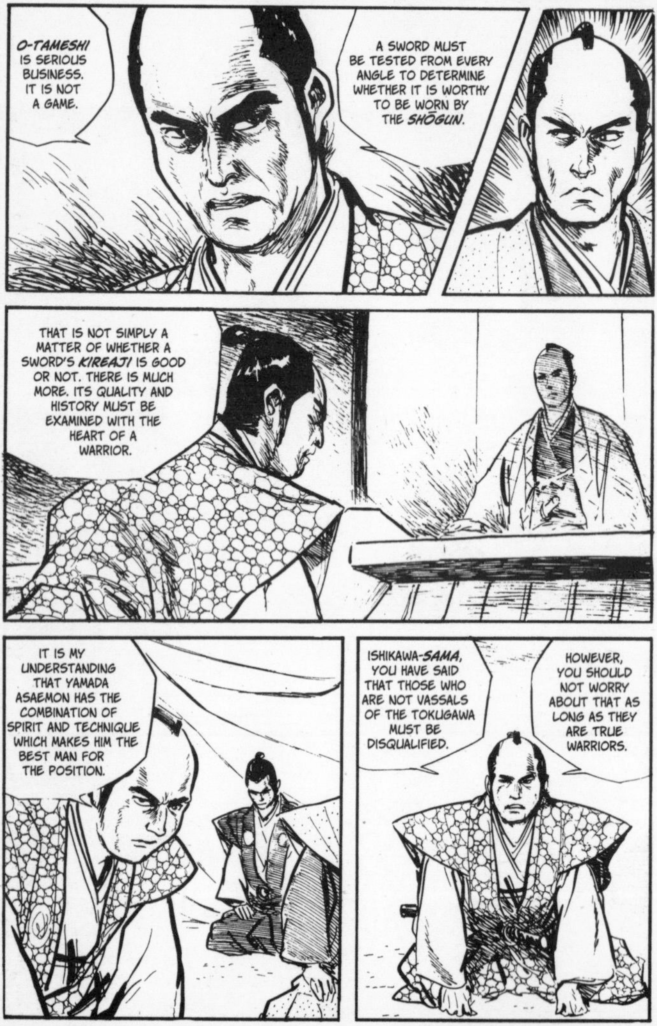
O-TAMESHI IS SERIOUS BUSINESS. IT IS NOT A GAME.
A SWORD MUST BE TESTED FROM EVERY ANGLE TO DETERMINE WHETHER IT IS WORTHY TO BE WORN BY THE SHŌGUN.
THAT IS NOT SIMPLY A MATTER OF WHETHER A SWORD'S KIREAJI IS GOOD OR NOT. THERE IS MUCH MORE. ITS QUALITY AND HISTORY MUST BE EXAMINED WITH THE HEART OF A WARRIOR.
IT IS MY UNDERSTANDING THAT YAMADA ASAEMON HAS THE COMBINATION OF SPIRIT AND TECHNIQUE WHICH MAKES HIM THE BEST MAN FOR THE POSITION.
ISHIKAWA-SAMA, YOU HAVE SAID THAT THOSE WHO ARE NOT VASSALS OF THE TOKUGAWA MUST BE DISQUALIFIED.
HOWEVER, YOU SHOULD NOT WORRY ABOUT THAT AS LONG AS THEY ARE TRUE WARRIORS.

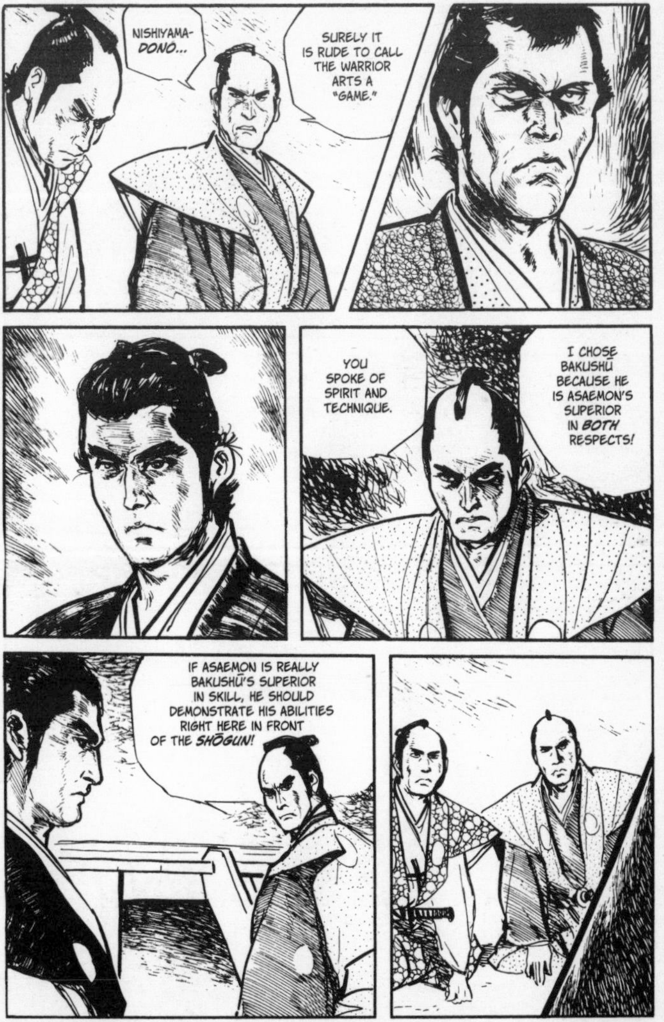
NISHIYAMA-DONO...
SURELY IT IS RUDE TO CALL THE WARRIOR ARTS A "GAME."
YOU SPOKE OF SPIRIT AND TECHNIQUE.
I CHOSE BAKUSHŪ BECAUSE HE IS ASAEMON'S SUPERIOR IN *BOTH* RESPECTS!
IF ASAEMON IS REALLY BAKUSHŪ'S SUPERIOR IN SKILL, HE SHOULD DEMONSTRATE HIS ABILITIES RIGHT HERE IN FRONT OF THE *SHŌGUN*!

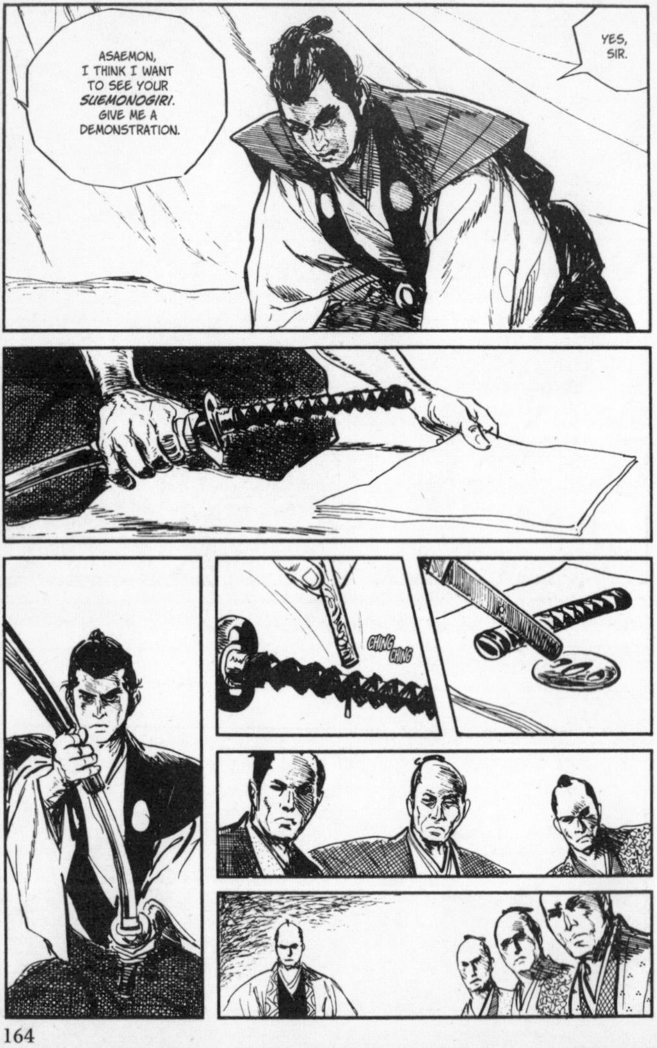
ASAEMON, I THINK I WANT TO SEE YOUR *SUEMONOGIRI*. GIVE ME A DEMONSTRATION.
YES, SIR.
CHING CHING

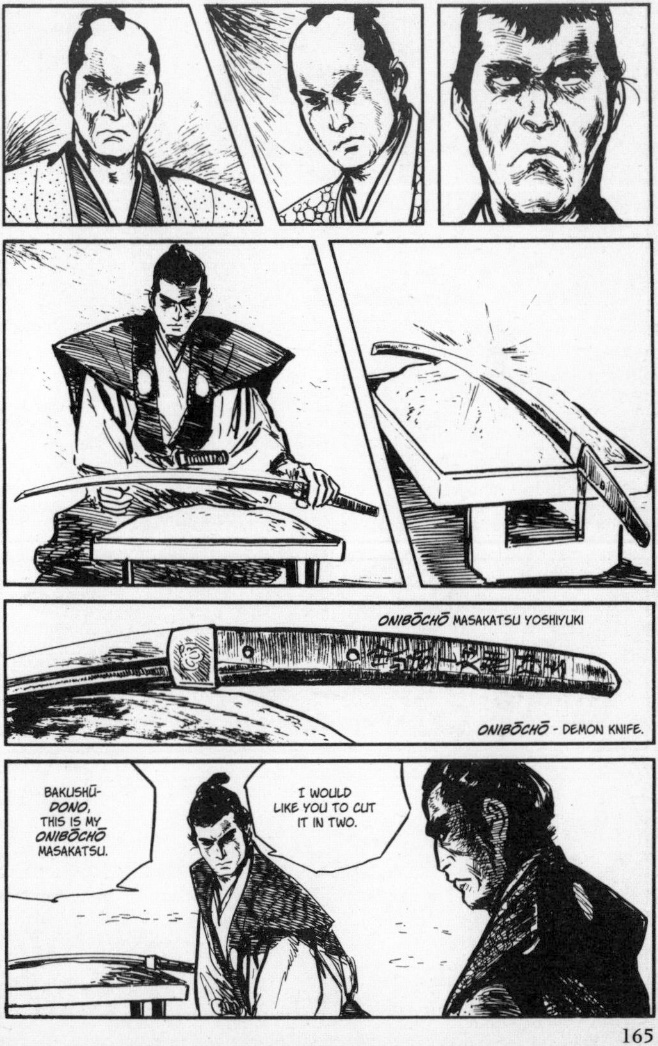
ONIBŌCHŌ MASAKATSU YOSHIYUKI
ONIBŌCHŌ - DEMON KNIFE.
BAKUSHŪ-DONO, THIS IS MY ONIBŌCHŌ MASAKATSU.
I WOULD LIKE YOU TO CUT IT IN TWO.

WELL?

I'LL DO IT!

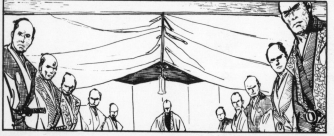

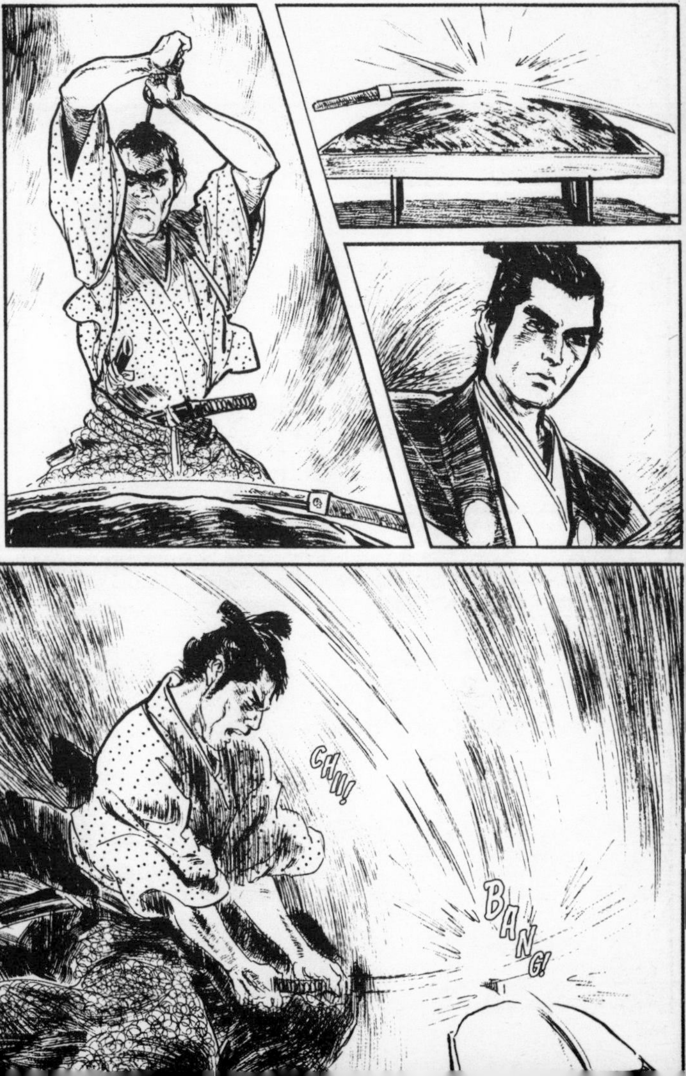
CHII!
BANG!

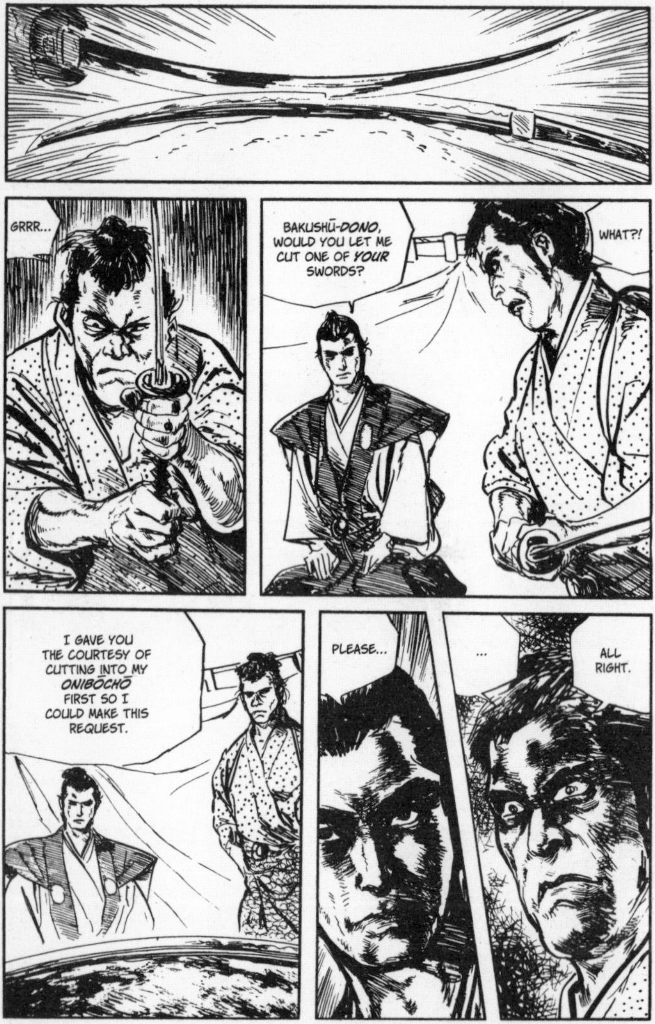
GRRR...
BAKUSHŪ-*DONO*, WOULD YOU LET ME CUT ONE OF *YOUR* SWORDS?
WHAT?!
I GAVE YOU THE COURTESY OF CUTTING INTO MY *ONIBŌCHŌ* FIRST SO I COULD MAKE THIS REQUEST.
PLEASE...
...
ALL RIGHT.

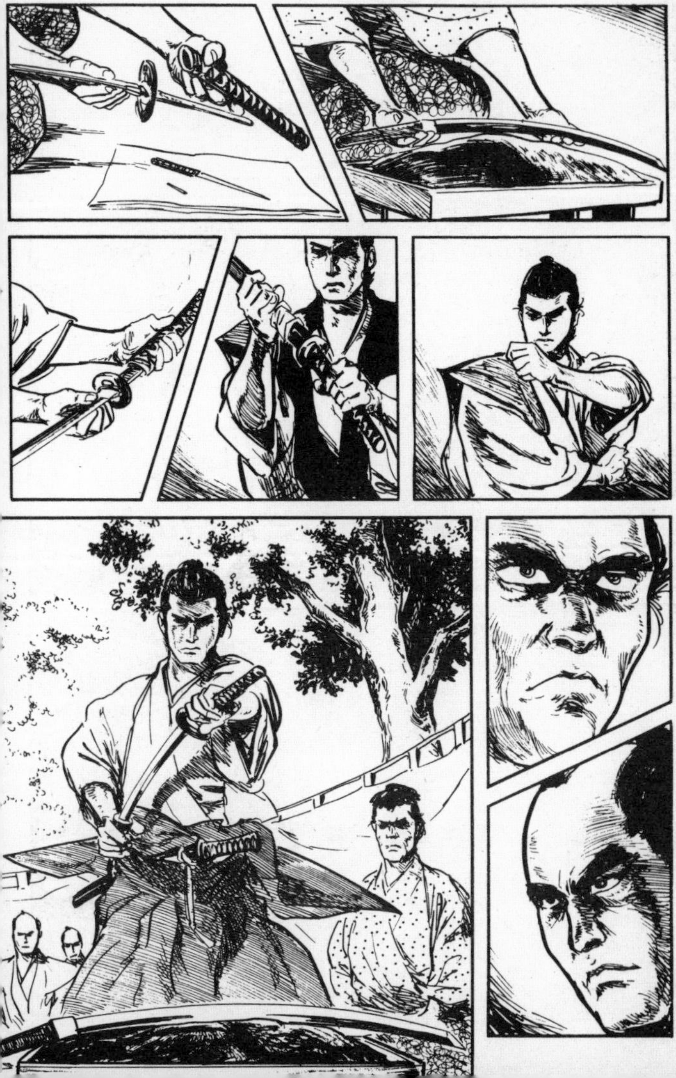

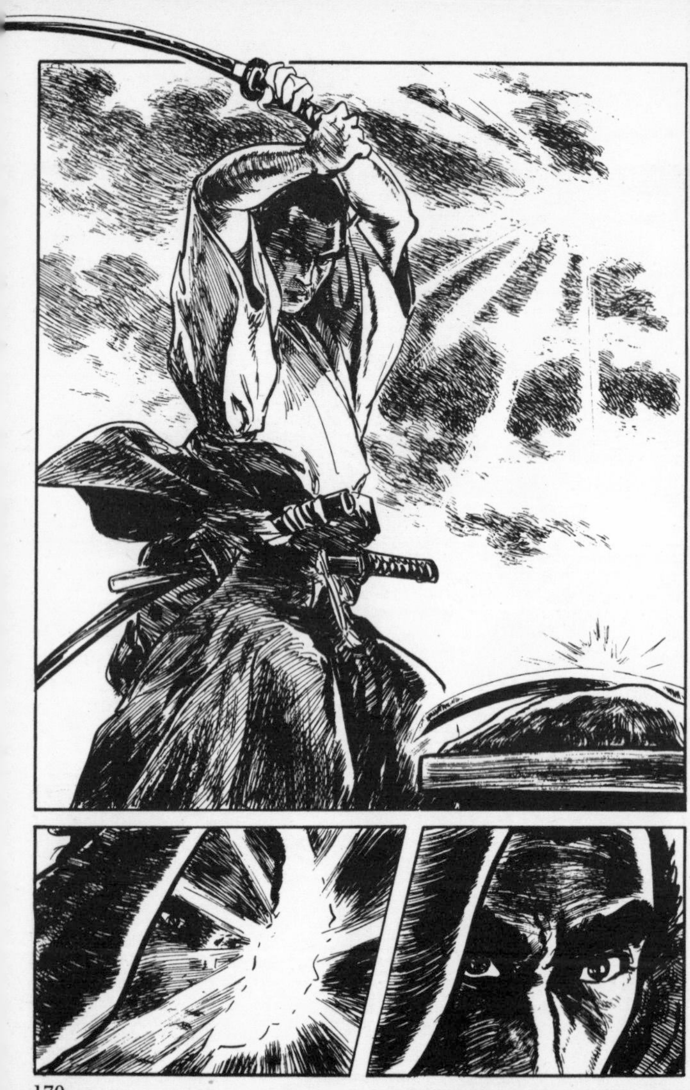

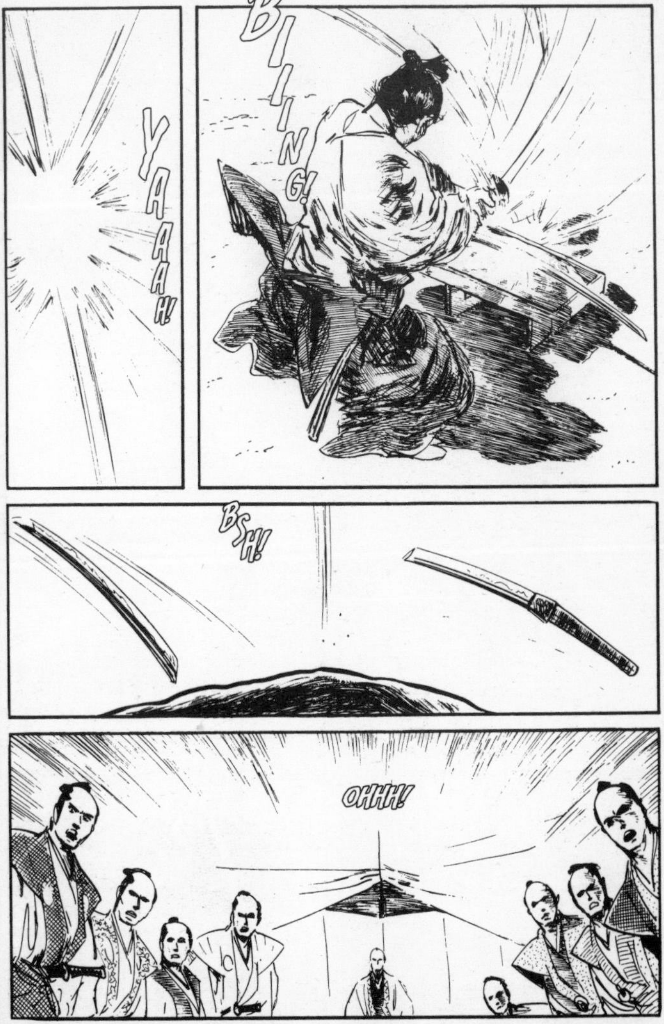
YAAAAH!
BIIING!
BSH!
OHHH!

E-
EXCELL-
ENT!

HMMM!

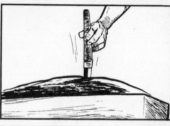

*MURAMASA

OOH...

NOTHING LESS THAN EXCELLENCE COULD BE EXPECTED FROM YAMADA ASAEMON!

YAMADA-*DONO*, THAT SWORD'S INSCRIPTION...

I NOTICED THAT BAKUSHŪ-*DONO*'S SWORD HAD AN EXTREME *TANAGOBARA*.

COULD IT BE A *MU*...?

NO.

IT'S A TAKAGI SADAMUNE FROM SŌSHŪ.

OH...

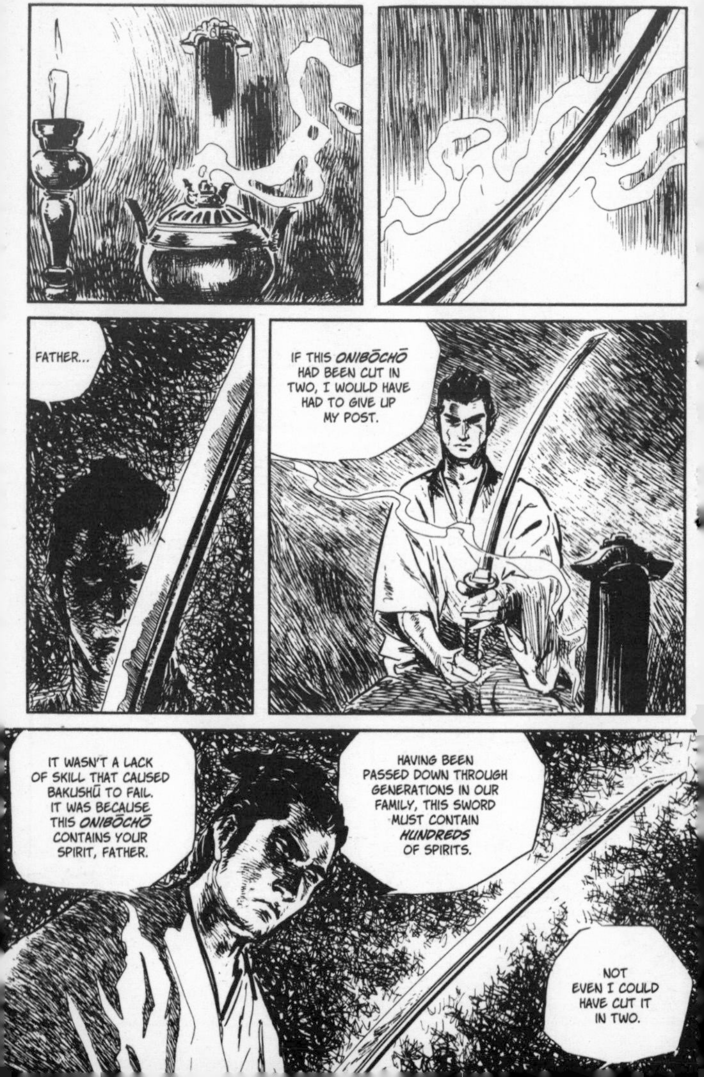
FATHER...
IF THIS *ONIBŌCHŌ* HAD BEEN CUT IN TWO, I WOULD HAVE HAD TO GIVE UP MY POST.
IT WASN'T A LACK OF SKILL THAT CAUSED BAKUSHŪ TO FAIL. IT WAS BECAUSE THIS *ONIBŌCHŌ* CONTAINS YOUR SPIRIT, FATHER.
HAVING BEEN PASSED DOWN THROUGH GENERATIONS IN OUR FAMILY, THIS SWORD MUST CONTAIN ***HUNDREDS*** OF SPIRITS.
NOT EVEN I COULD HAVE CUT IT IN TWO.

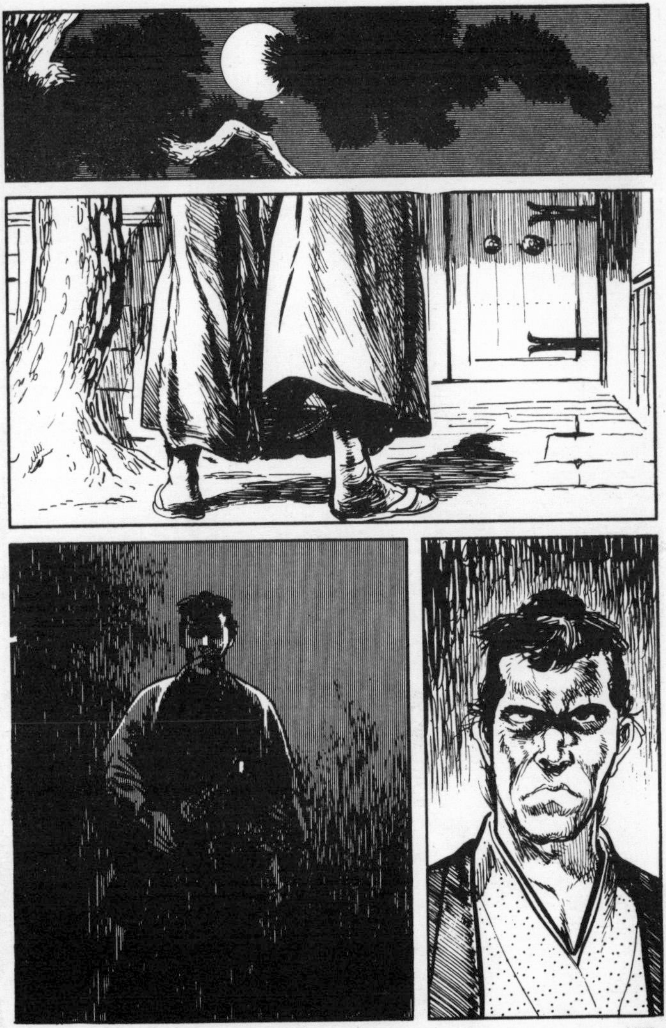

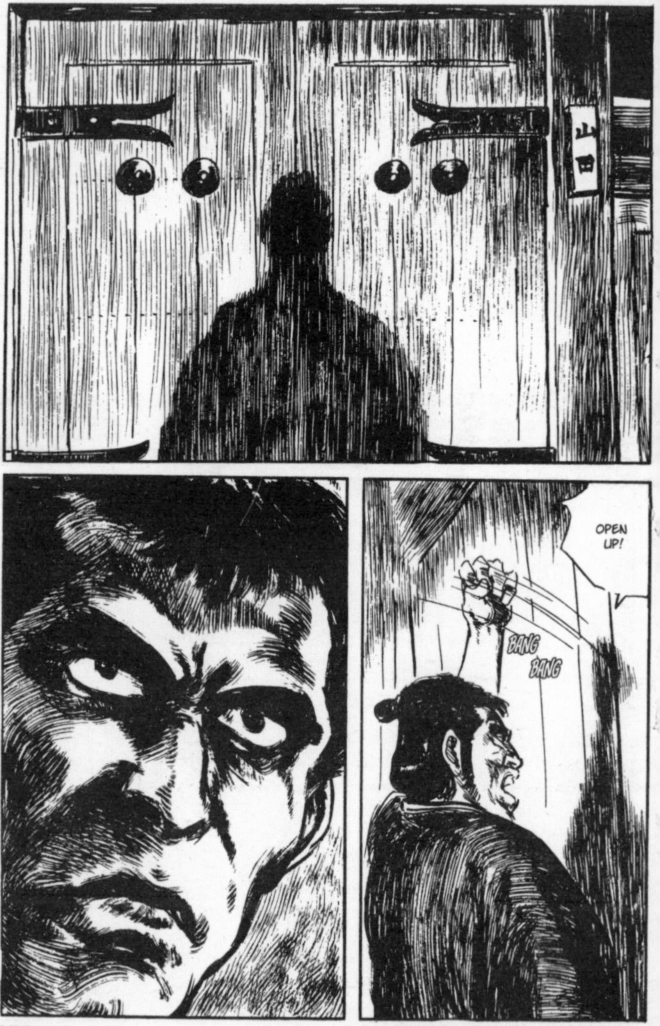
OPEN UP!
BANG
BANG

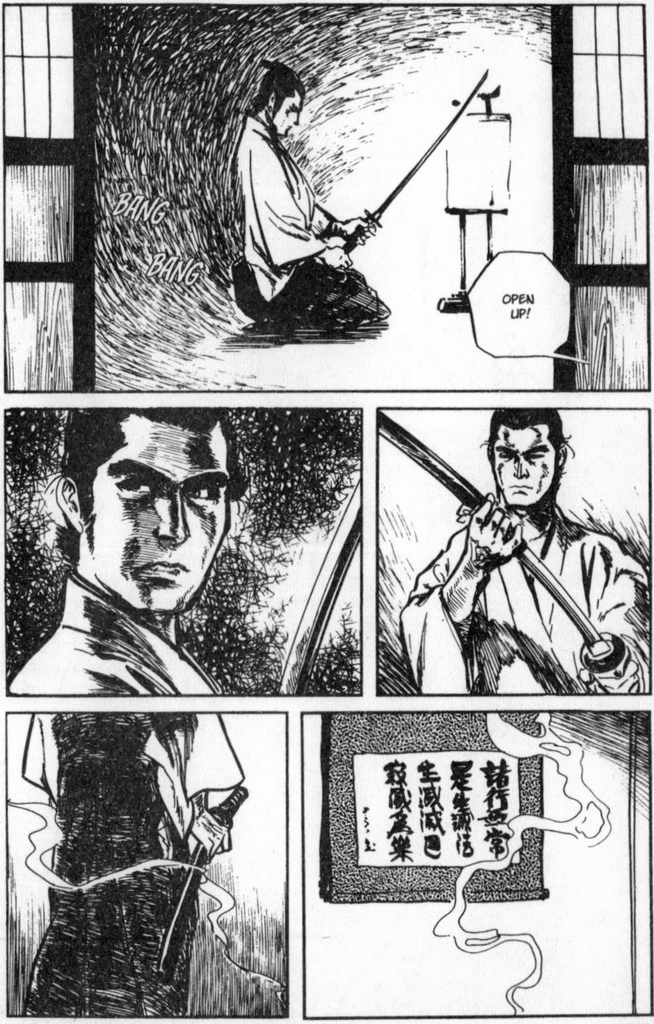
BANG
BANG
OPEN UP!
諸行無常
是生滅法
生滅滅已
寂滅為楽

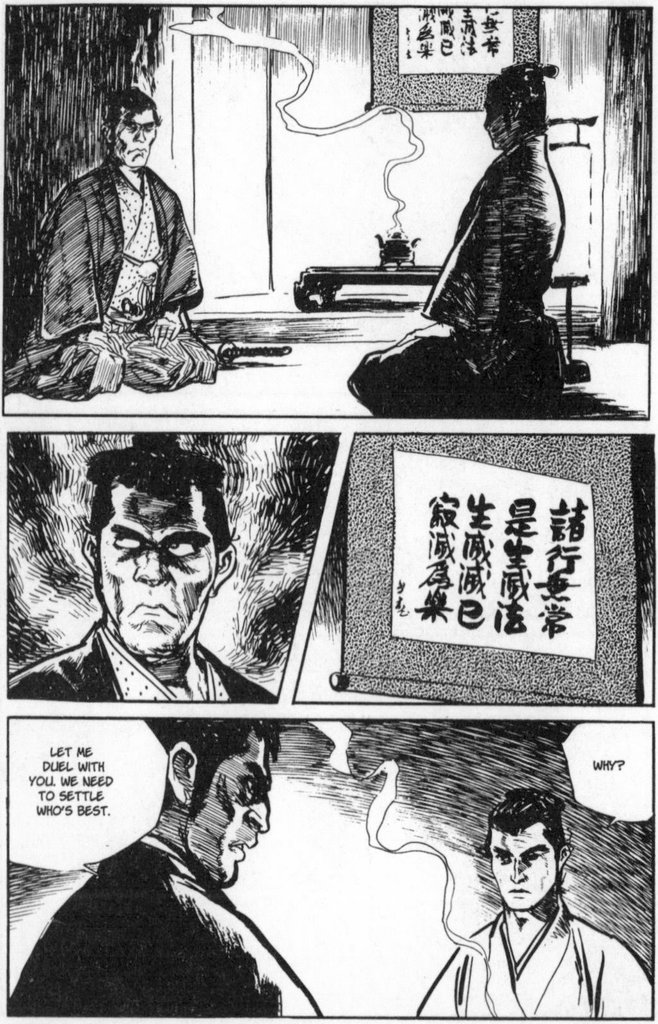
諸行無常
是生滅法
生滅滅已
寂滅為樂
LET ME DUEL WITH YOU. WE NEED TO SETTLE WHO'S BEST.
WHY?

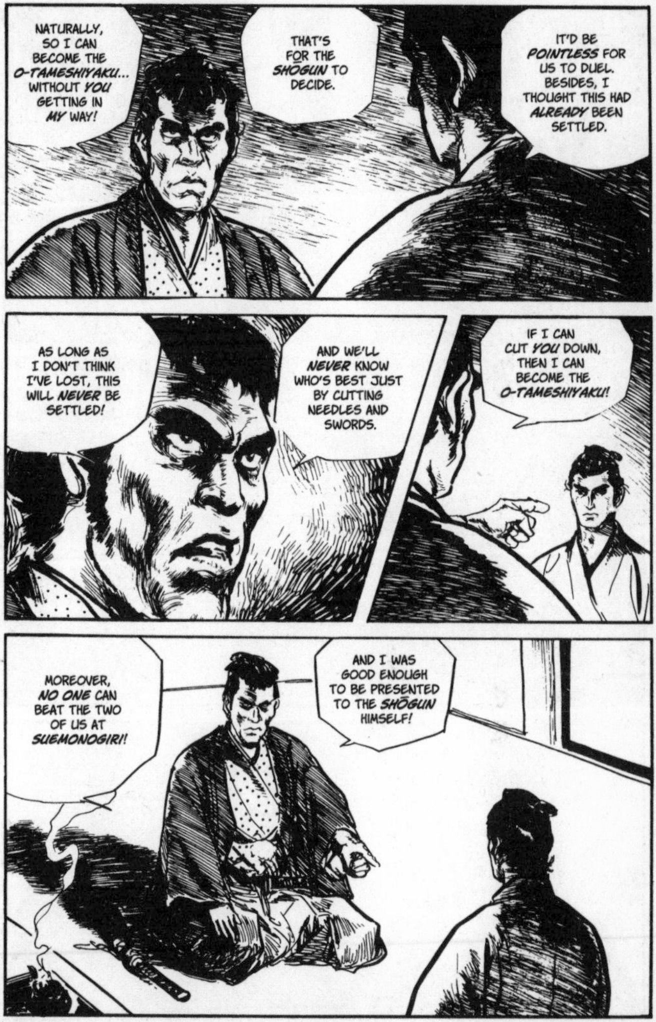
NATURALLY, SO I CAN BECOME THE *O-TAMESHIYAKU*... WITHOUT *YOU* GETTING IN *MY* WAY!
THAT'S FOR THE *SHŌGUN* TO DECIDE.
IT'D BE *POINTLESS* FOR US TO DUEL. BESIDES, I THOUGHT THIS HAD *ALREADY* BEEN SETTLED.
AS LONG AS I DON'T THINK I'VE LOST, THIS WILL *NEVER* BE SETTLED!
AND WE'LL *NEVER* KNOW WHO'S BEST JUST BY CUTTING NEEDLES AND SWORDS.
IF I CAN CUT *YOU* DOWN, THEN I CAN BECOME THE *O-TAMESHIYAKU*!
MOREOVER, *NO ONE* CAN BEAT THE TWO OF US AT *SUEMONOGIRI*!
AND I WAS GOOD ENOUGH TO BE PRESENTED TO THE *SHŌGUN* HIMSELF!

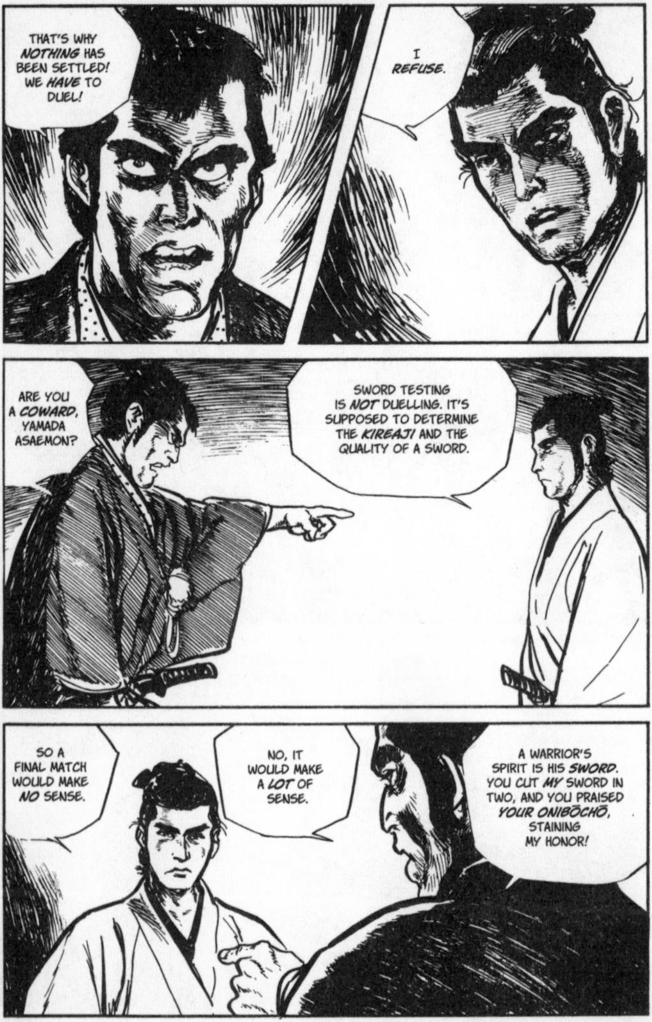
THAT'S WHY NOTHING HAS BEEN SETTLED! WE HAVE TO DUEL!
I REFUSE.
ARE YOU A COWARD, YAMADA ASAEMON?
SWORD TESTING IS NOT DUELLING. IT'S SUPPOSED TO DETERMINE THE KIREAJI AND THE QUALITY OF A SWORD.
SO A FINAL MATCH WOULD MAKE NO SENSE.
NO, IT WOULD MAKE A LOT OF SENSE.
A WARRIOR'S SPIRIT IS HIS SWORD. YOU CUT MY SWORD IN TWO, AND YOU PRAISED YOUR ONIBŌCHŌ, STAINING MY HONOR!

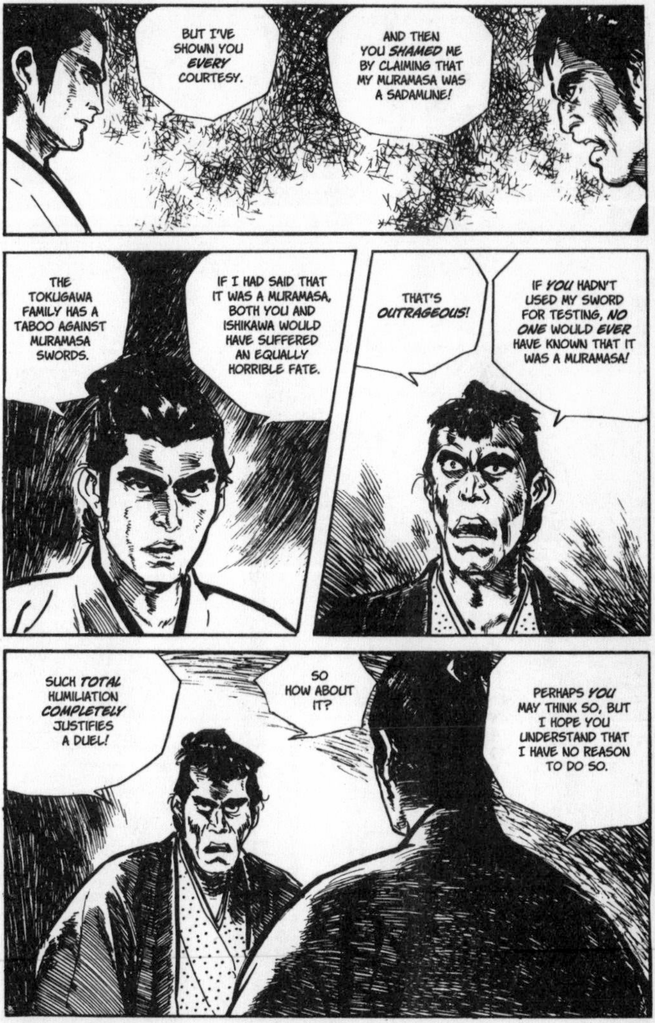
BUT I'VE SHOWN YOU *EVERY* COURTESY.
AND THEN YOU *SHAMED* ME BY CLAIMING THAT MY MURAMASA WAS A SADAMUNE!
THE TOKUGAWA FAMILY HAS A TABOO AGAINST MURAMASA SWORDS.
IF I HAD SAID THAT IT WAS A MURAMASA, BOTH YOU AND ISHIKAWA WOULD HAVE SUFFERED AN EQUALLY HORRIBLE FATE.
THAT'S *OUTRAGEOUS!*
IF *YOU* HADN'T USED MY SWORD FOR TESTING, *NO ONE* WOULD *EVER* HAVE KNOWN THAT IT WAS A MURAMASA!
SUCH *TOTAL* HUMILIATION *COMPLETELY* JUSTIFIES A DUEL!
SO HOW ABOUT IT?
PERHAPS *YOU* MAY THINK SO, BUT I HOPE YOU UNDERSTAND THAT I HAVE NO REASON TO DO SO.

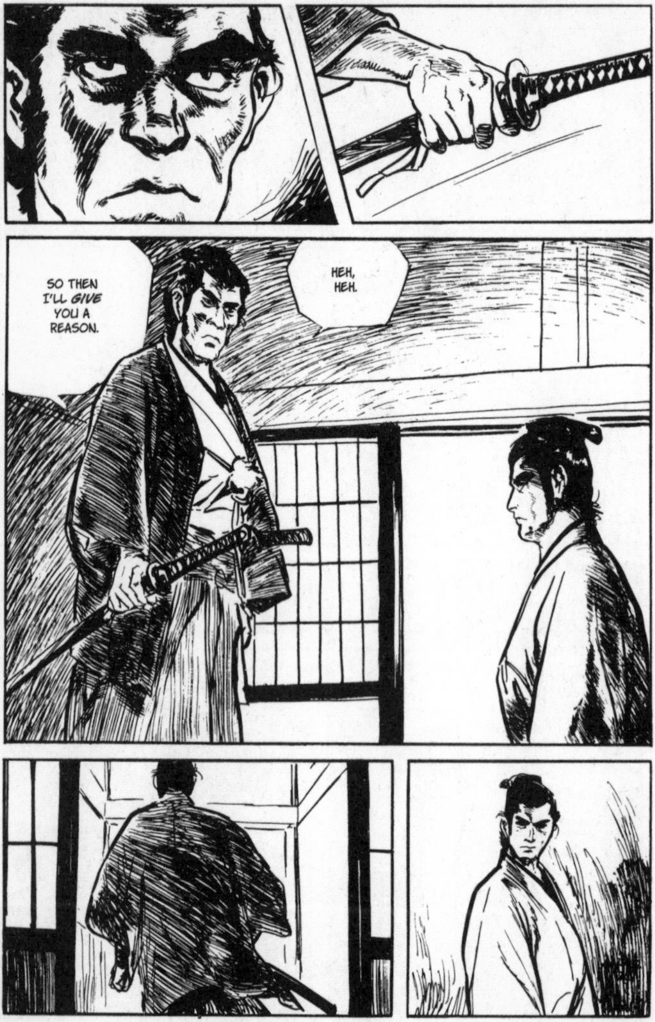
SO THEN I'LL *GIVE* YOU A REASON.
HEH, HEH.

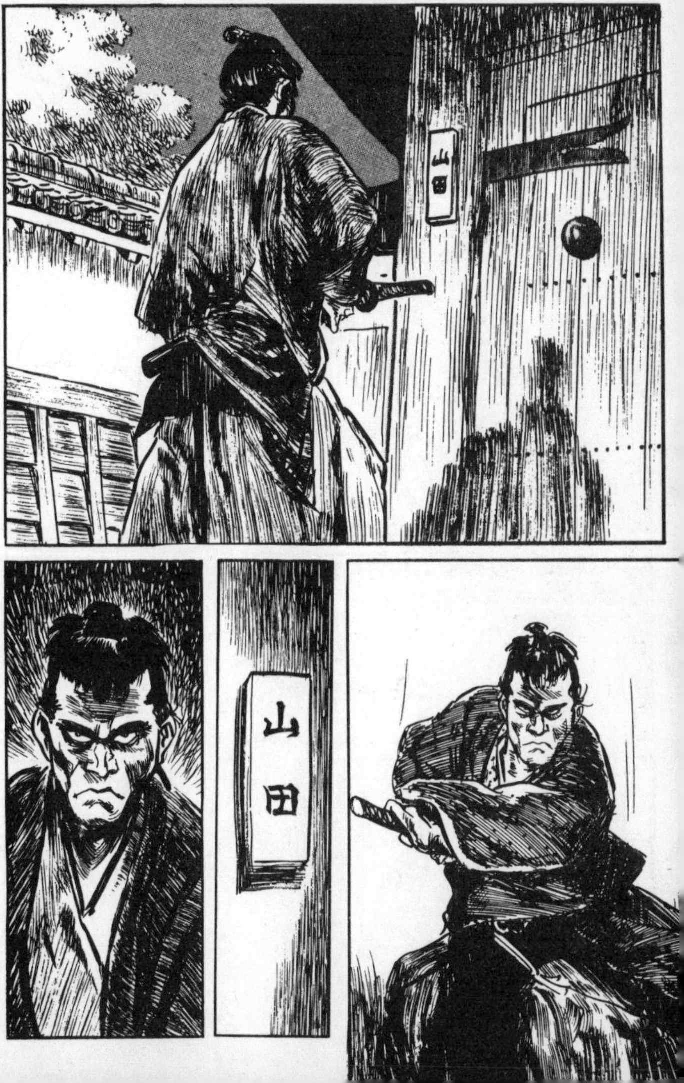
山田
山田

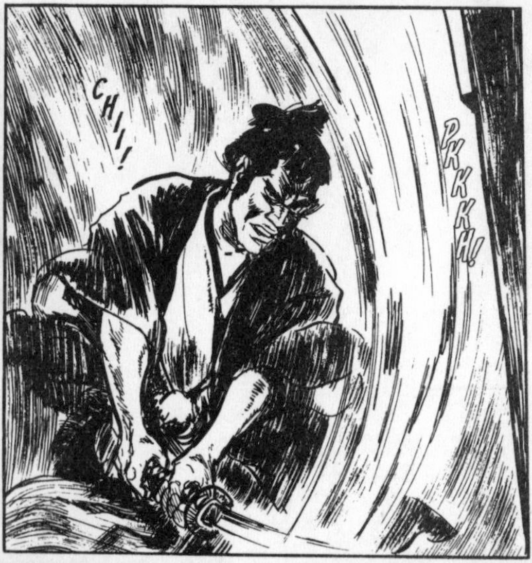
CHI!!
PKKKKH!
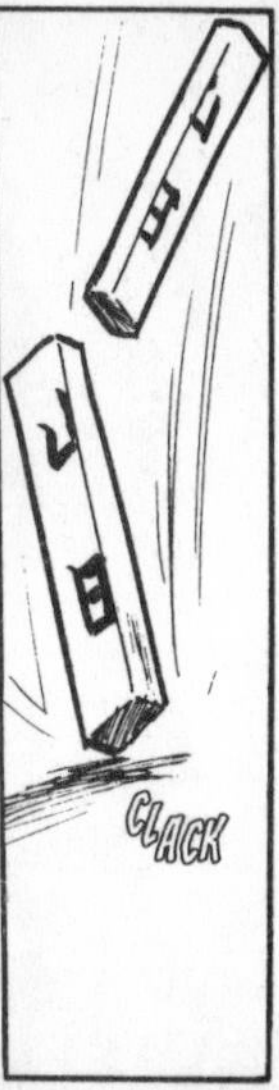
CLACK
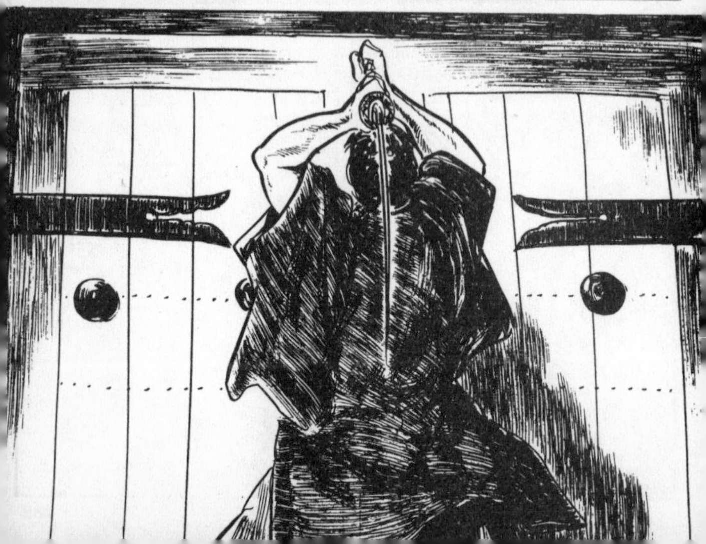

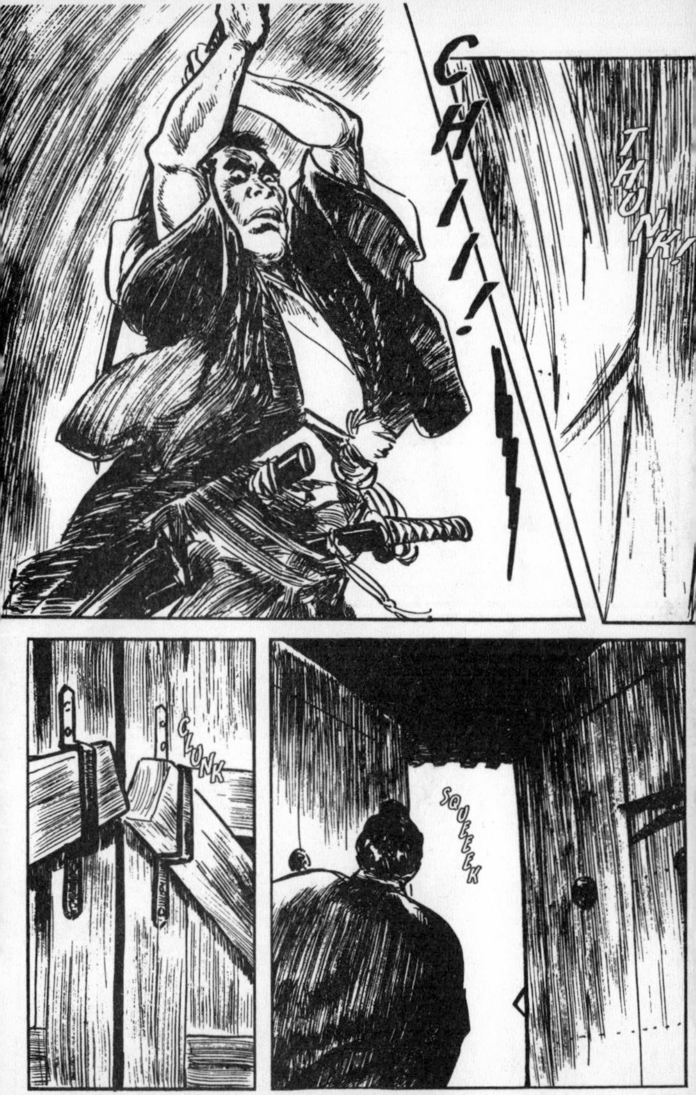
CHIIII!
THUNK!
CLUNK
SQUEEEK

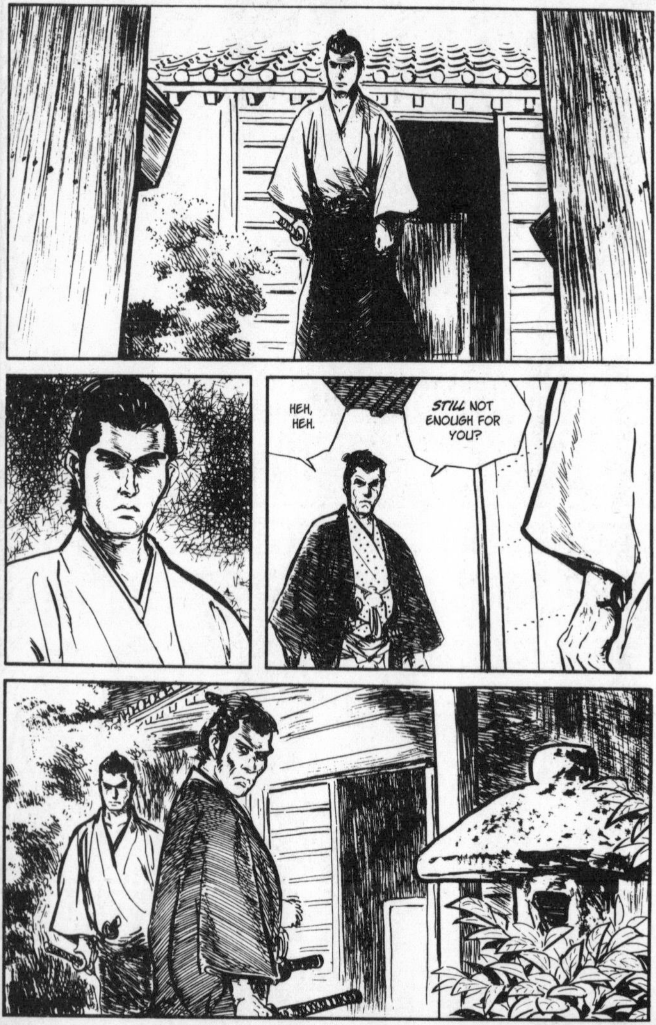
HEH, HEH.
STILL NOT ENOUGH FOR YOU?

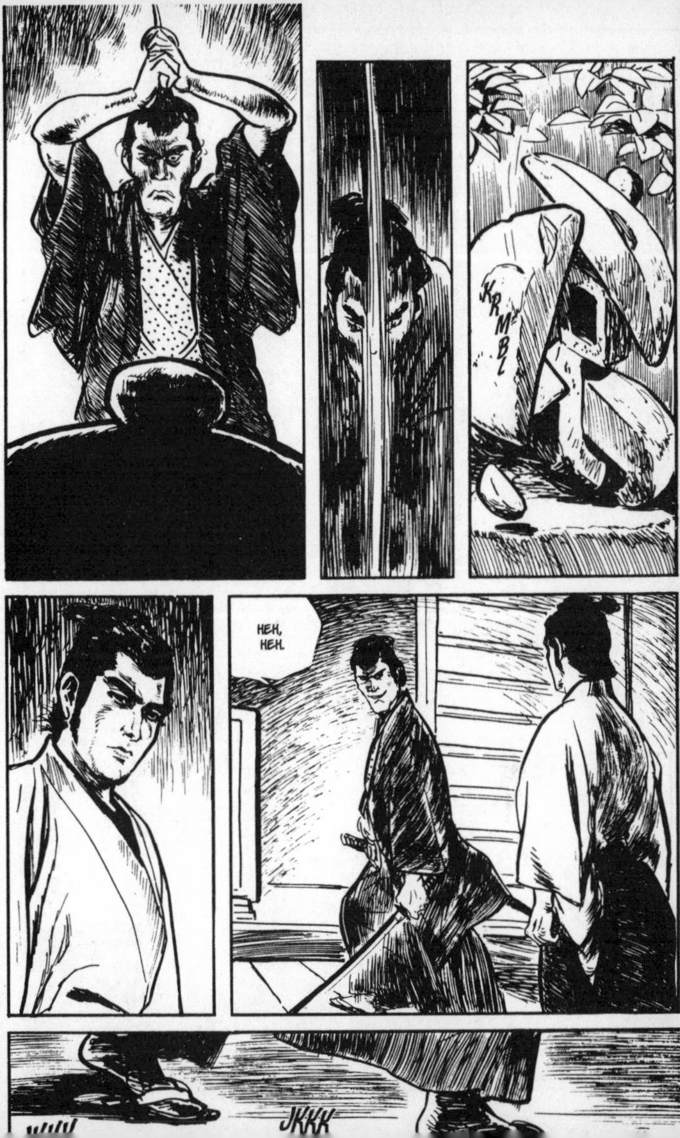
KRMBL
HEH, HEH.
JKKK

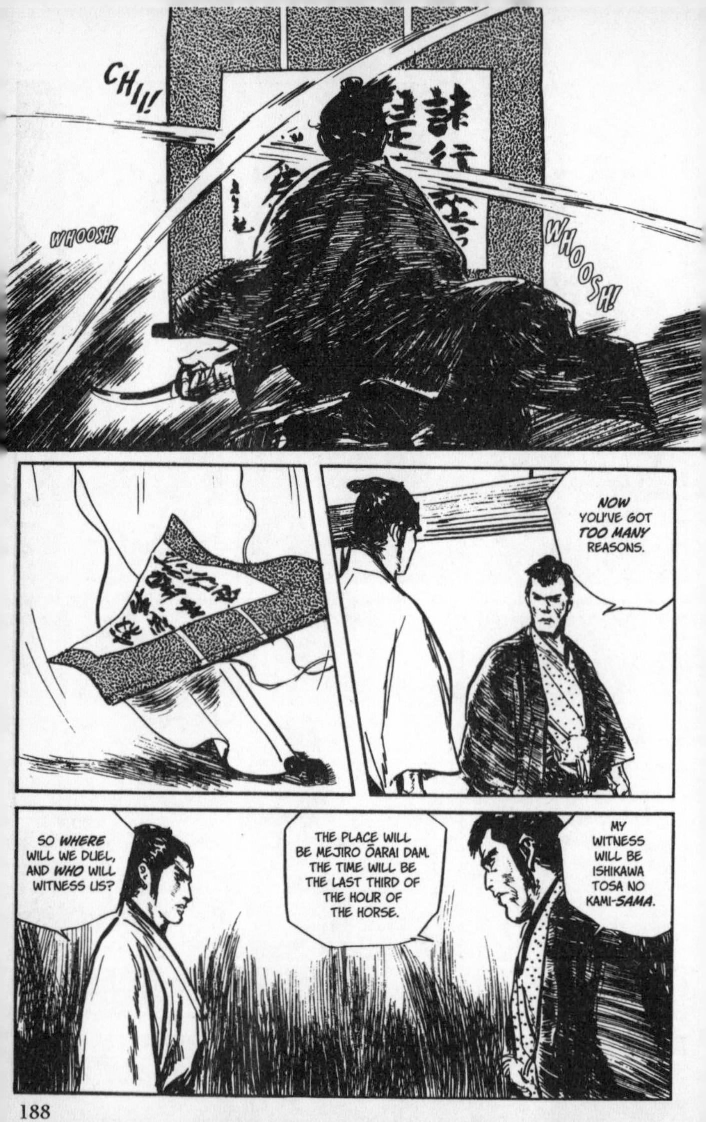
CHII!
WHOOSH!
WHOOSH!
NOW YOU'VE GOT TOO MANY REASONS.
SO WHERE WILL WE DUEL, AND WHO WILL WITNESS US?
THE PLACE WILL BE MEJIRO ŌARAI DAM. THE TIME WILL BE THE LAST THIRD OF THE HOUR OF THE HORSE.
MY WITNESS WILL BE ISHIKAWA TOSA NO KAMI-SAMA.

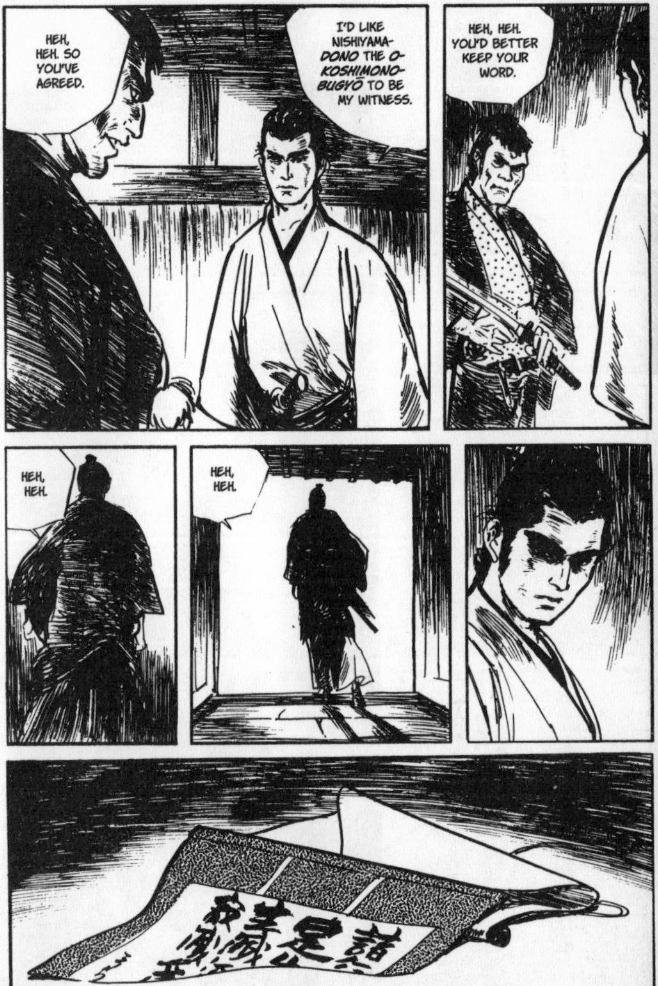
HEH, HEH. SO YOU'VE AGREED.
I'D LIKE NISHIYAMA-DONO THE O-KOSHIMONO-BUGYŌ TO BE MY WITNESS.
HEH, HEH. YOU'D BETTER KEEP YOUR WORD.
HEH, HEH.
HEH, HEH.

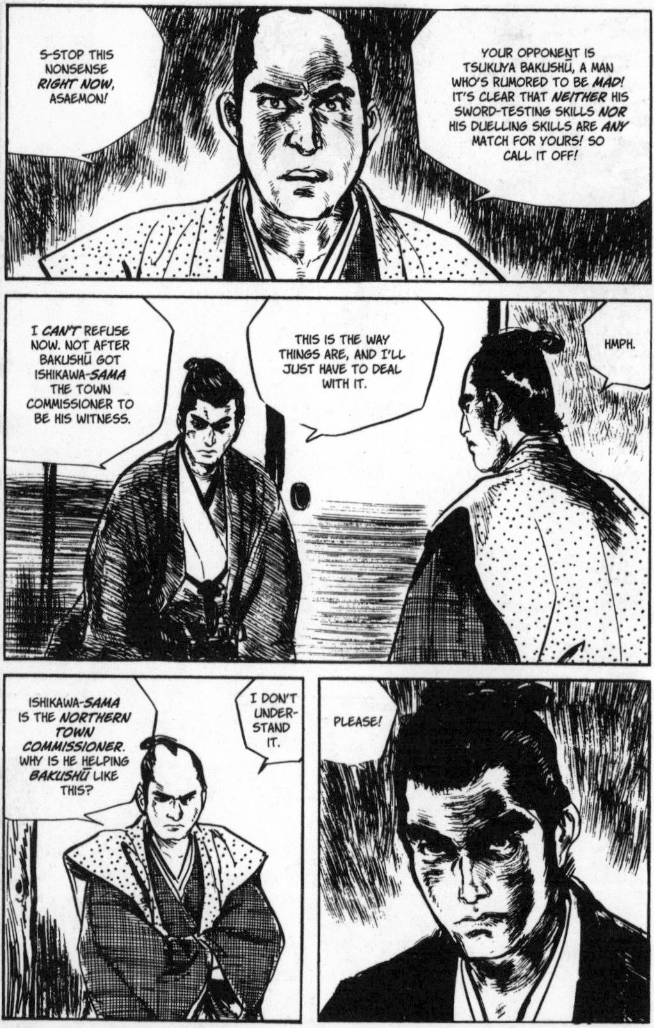
S-STOP THIS NONSENSE *RIGHT NOW*, ASAEMON!
YOUR OPPONENT IS TSUKUYA BAKUSHŪ, A MAN WHO'S RUMORED TO BE *MAD!* IT'S CLEAR THAT *NEITHER* HIS SWORD-TESTING SKILLS *NOR* HIS DUELLING SKILLS ARE *ANY* MATCH FOR YOURS! SO CALL IT OFF!
I *CAN'T* REFUSE NOW. NOT AFTER BAKUSHŪ GOT ISHIKAWA-*SAMA* THE TOWN COMMISSIONER TO BE HIS WITNESS.
THIS IS THE WAY THINGS ARE, AND I'LL JUST HAVE TO DEAL WITH IT.
HMPH.
ISHIKAWA-*SAMA* IS THE *NORTHERN TOWN COMMISSIONER*. WHY IS HE HELPING *BAKUSHŪ* LIKE THIS?
I DON'T UNDER-STAND IT.
PLEASE!

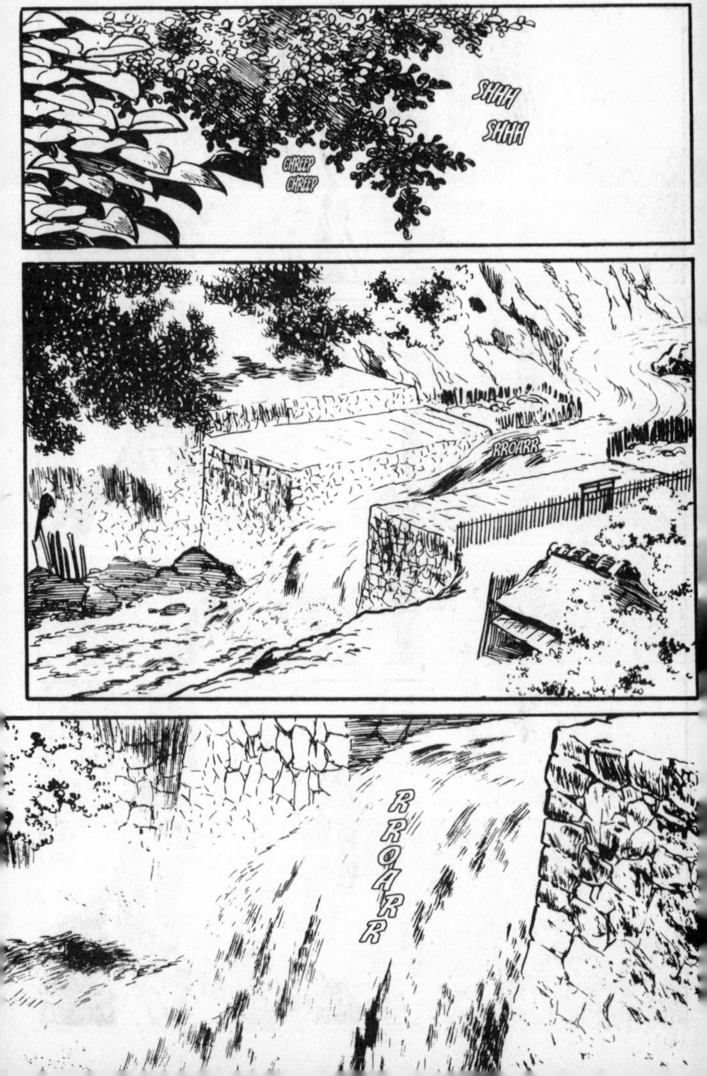
SHHH
SHHH
CHREEP
CHREEP
RROARR
RROARR

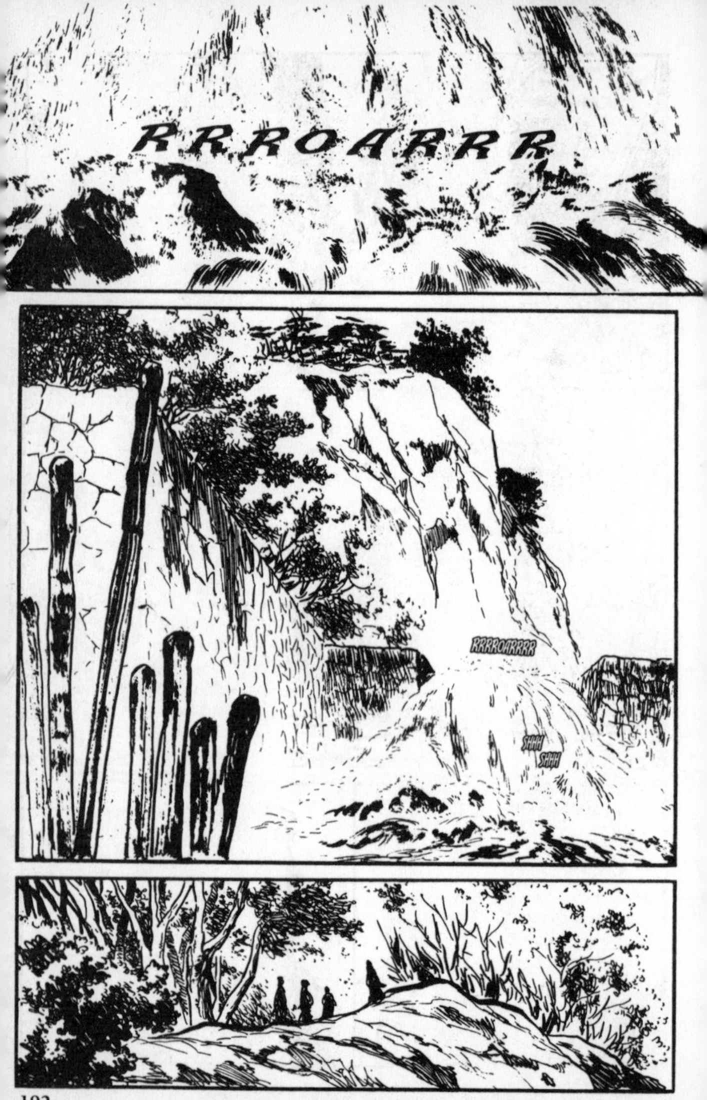
RRRROARRRR
RRRROARRRR
SHHH
SHHH

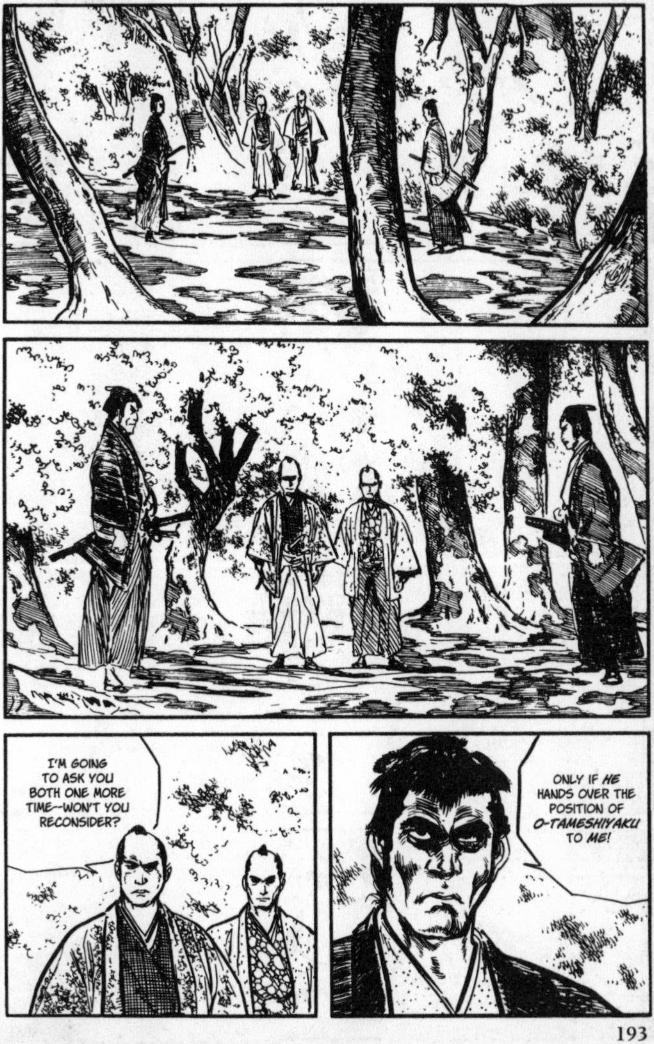
I'M GOING TO ASK YOU BOTH ONE MORE TIME--WON'T YOU RECONSIDER?
ONLY IF *HE* HANDS OVER THE POSITION OF *O-TAMESHIYAKU* TO *ME!*

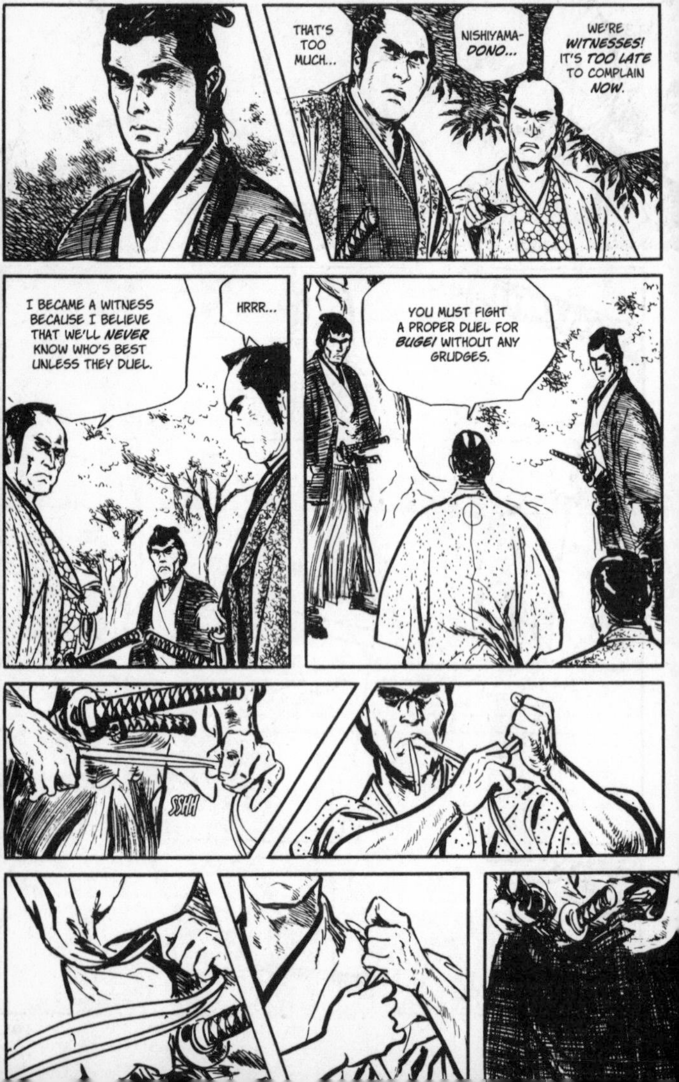
THAT'S TOO MUCH...
NISHIYAMA-DONO...
WE'RE WITNESSES! IT'S TOO LATE TO COMPLAIN NOW.
I BECAME A WITNESS BECAUSE I BELIEVE THAT WE'LL NEVER KNOW WHO'S BEST UNLESS THEY DUEL.
HRRR...
YOU MUST FIGHT A PROPER DUEL FOR BUGEI WITHOUT ANY GRUDGES.
SSHH

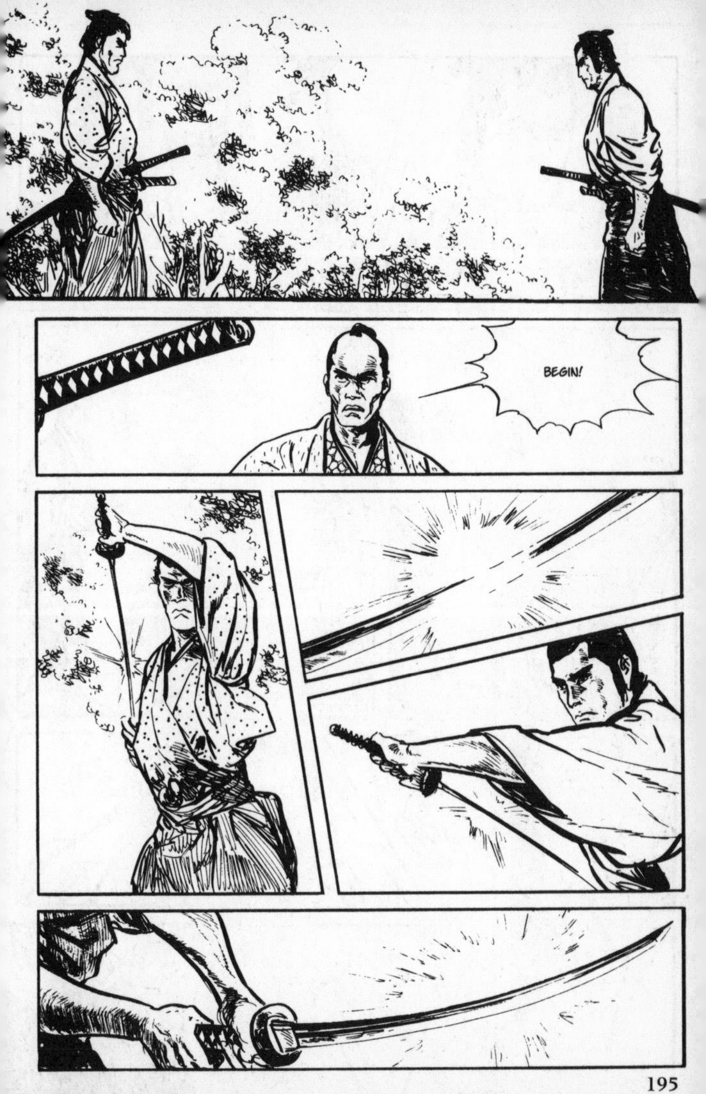
BEGIN!

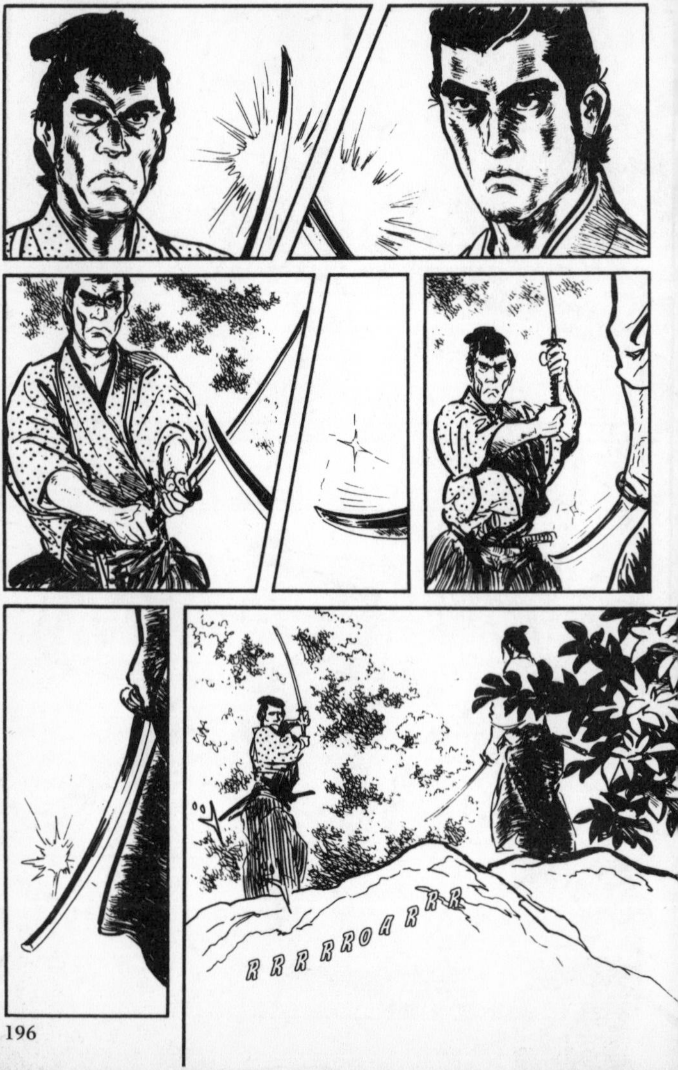
RRRRROARRR

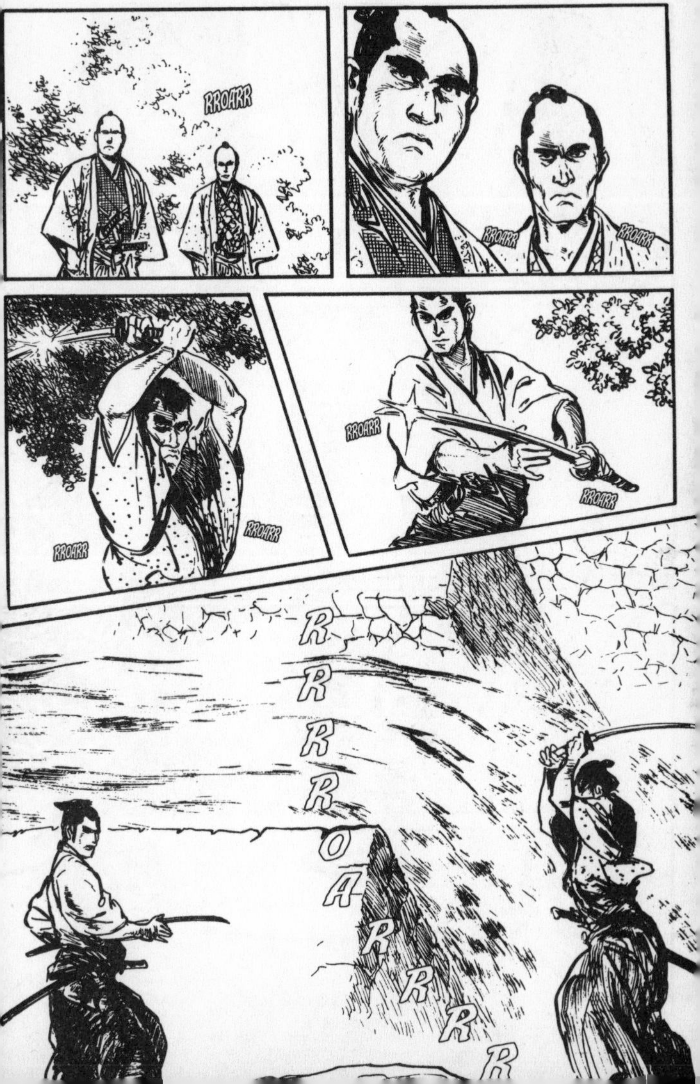
RROARR
RROARR
RROARR
RROARR
RROARR
RROARR
RROARR
RROARR
RRRROARRRRR

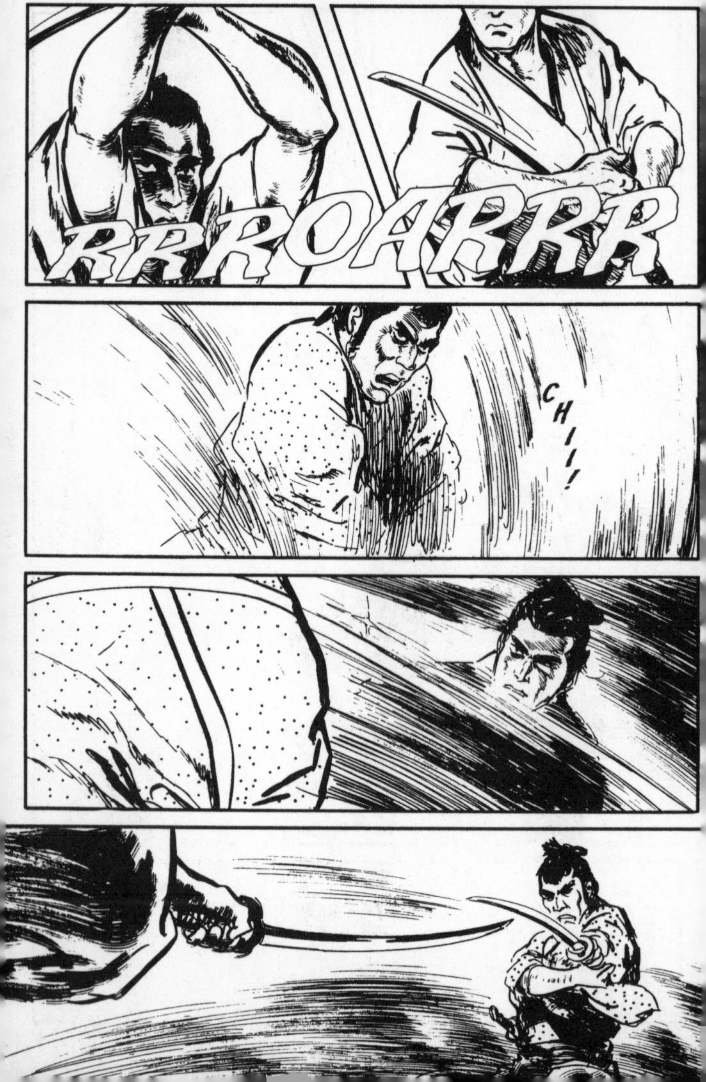
RRRROARRRR
CHIII!

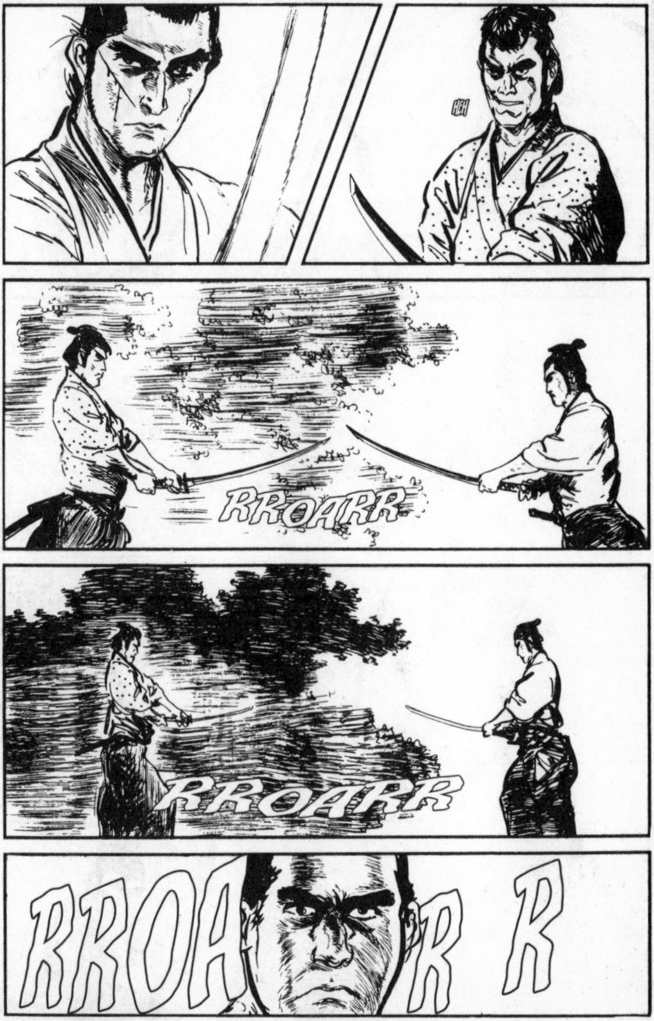
HEH
RROARR
RROARR
RROA R R

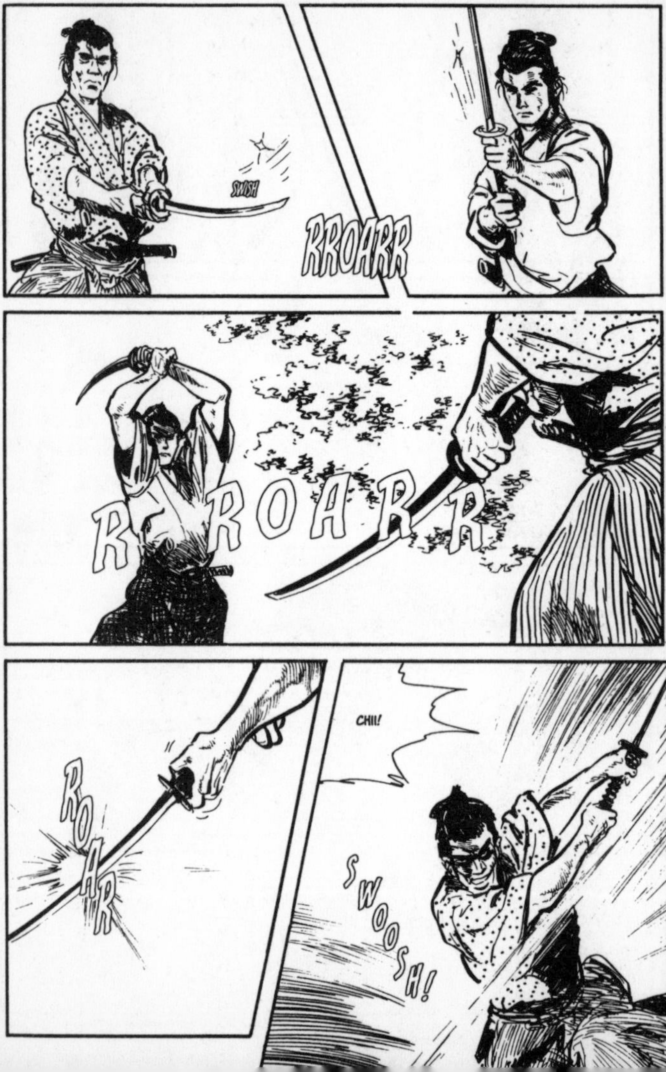
SWISH
RROARR
R ROARR
ROAR
CHII!
SWOOSH!

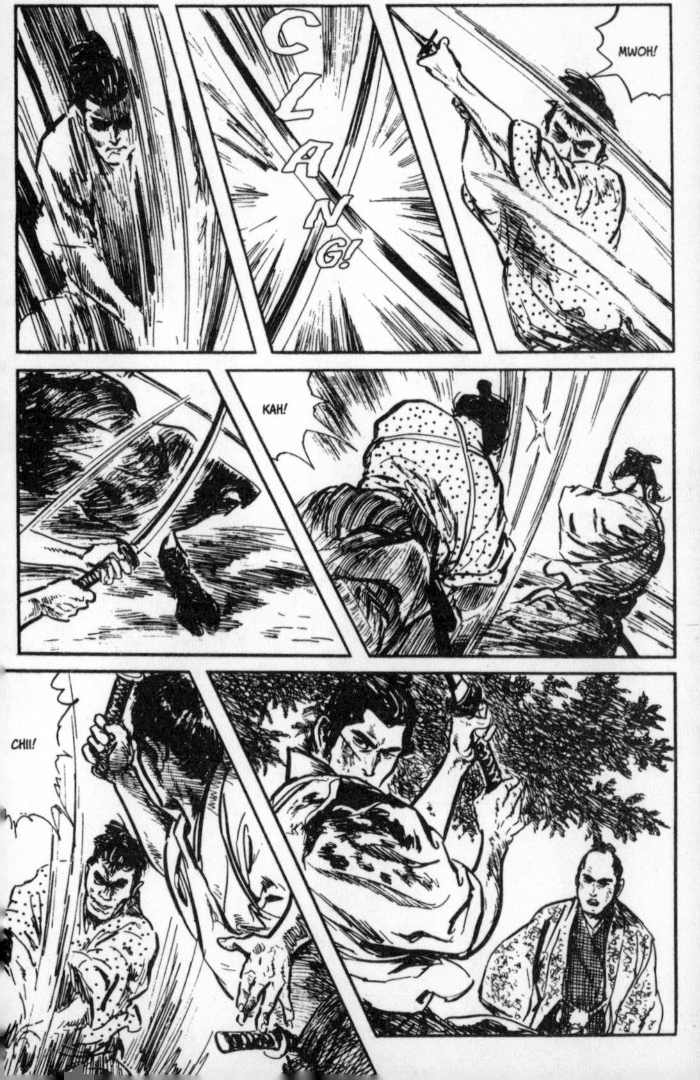
CLANG!
MWOH!
KAH!
CHII!

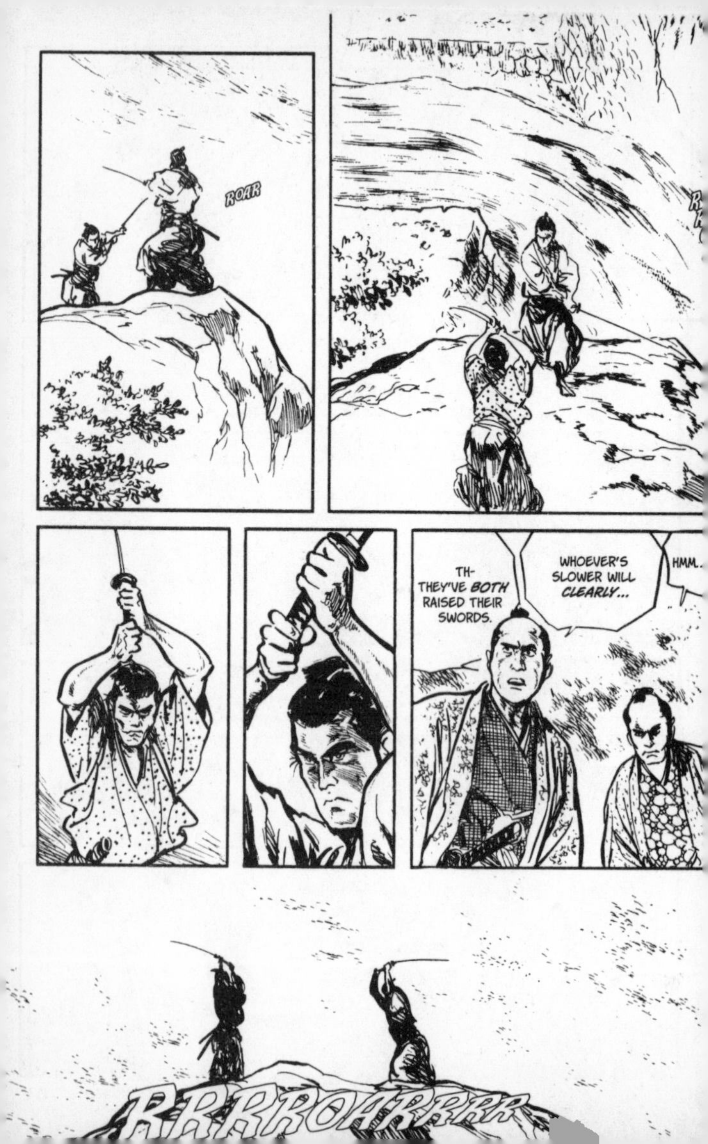
ROAR
TH- THEY'VE *BOTH* RAISED THEIR SWORDS.
WHOEVER'S SLOWER WILL *CLEARLY*...
HMM..
RRRROARRRRR

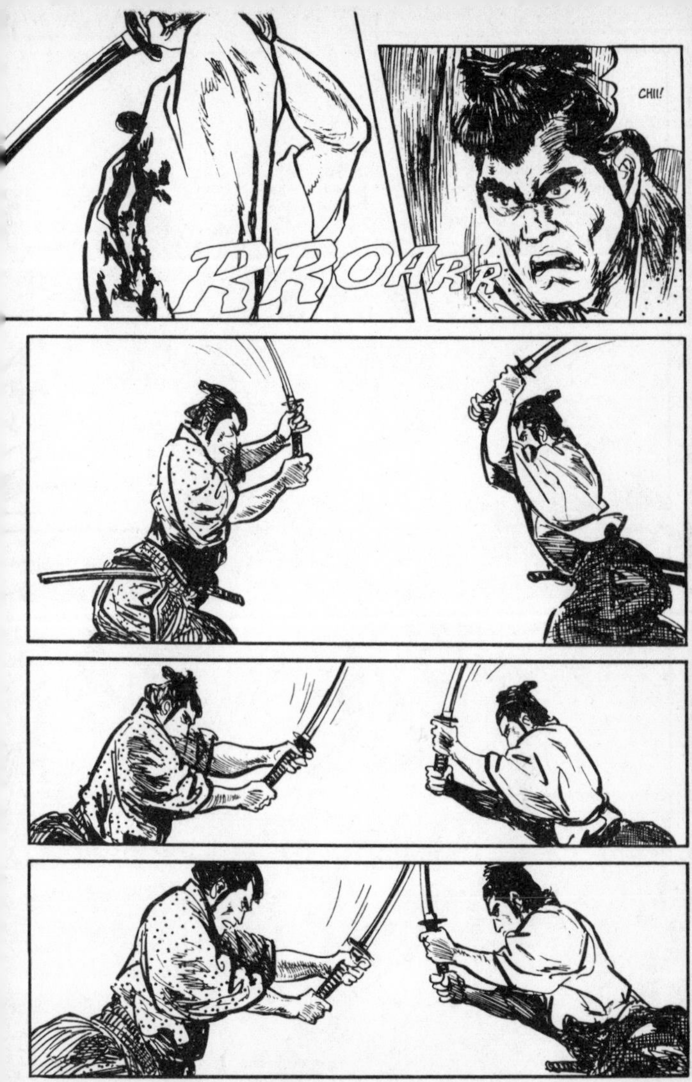
RROARR
CHII!

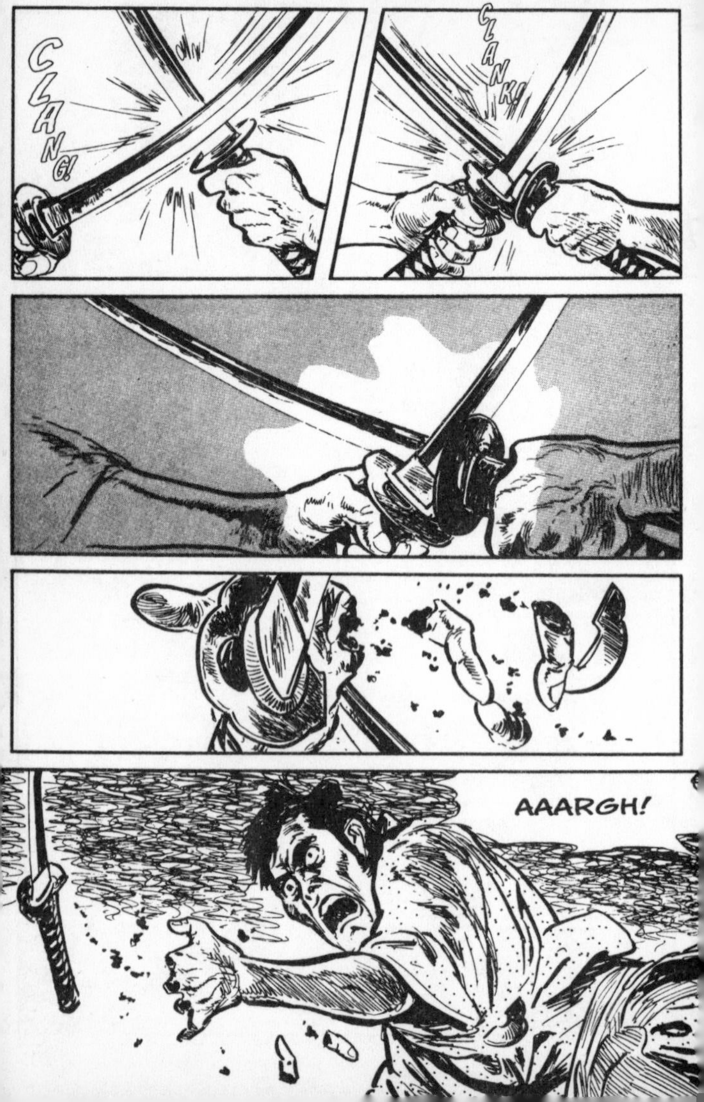
CLANG!
CLANK!
AAARGH!

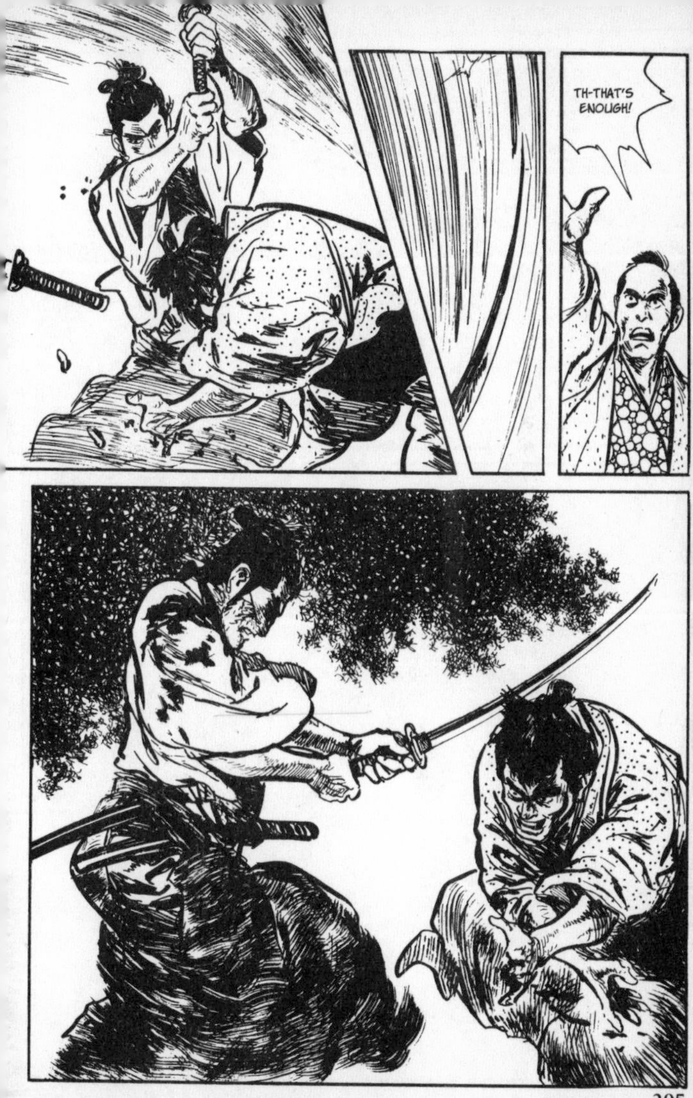
TH-THAT'S ENOUGH!

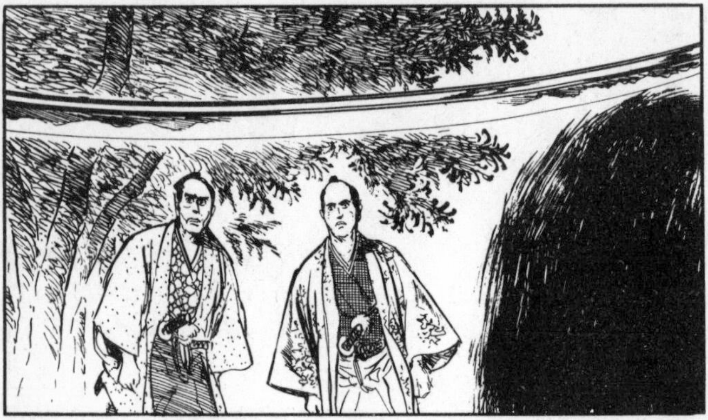

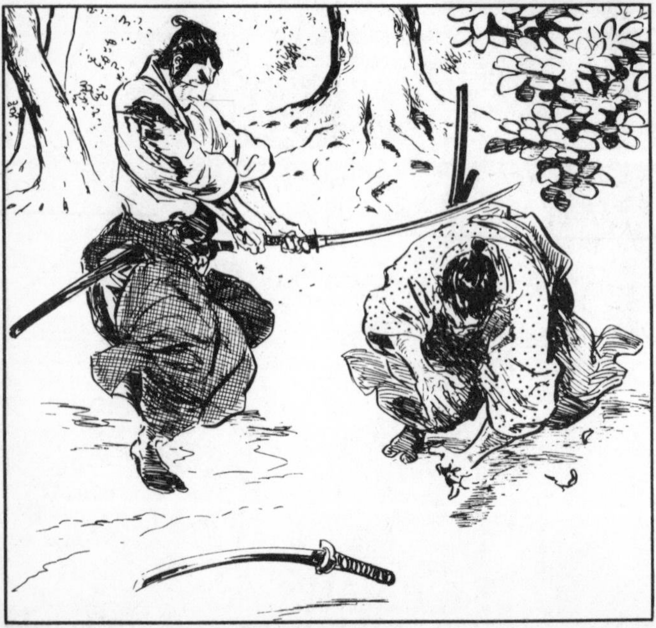

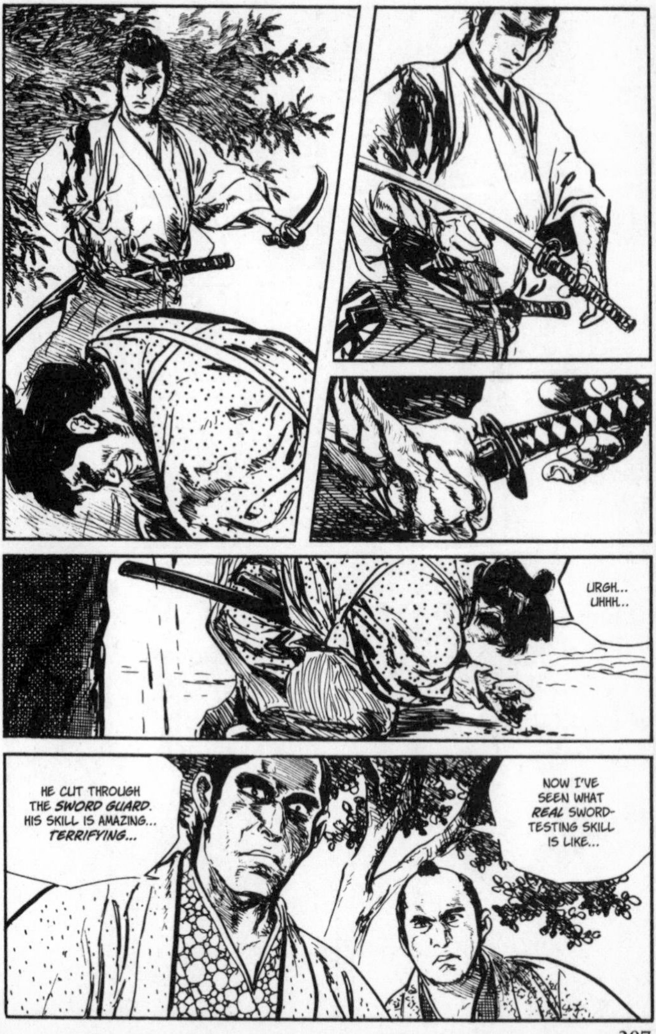
URGH... UHHH...
HE CUT THROUGH THE *SWORD GUARD.* HIS SKILL IS AMAZING... *TERRIFYING...*
NOW I'VE SEEN WHAT *REAL* SWORD-TESTING SKILL IS LIKE...

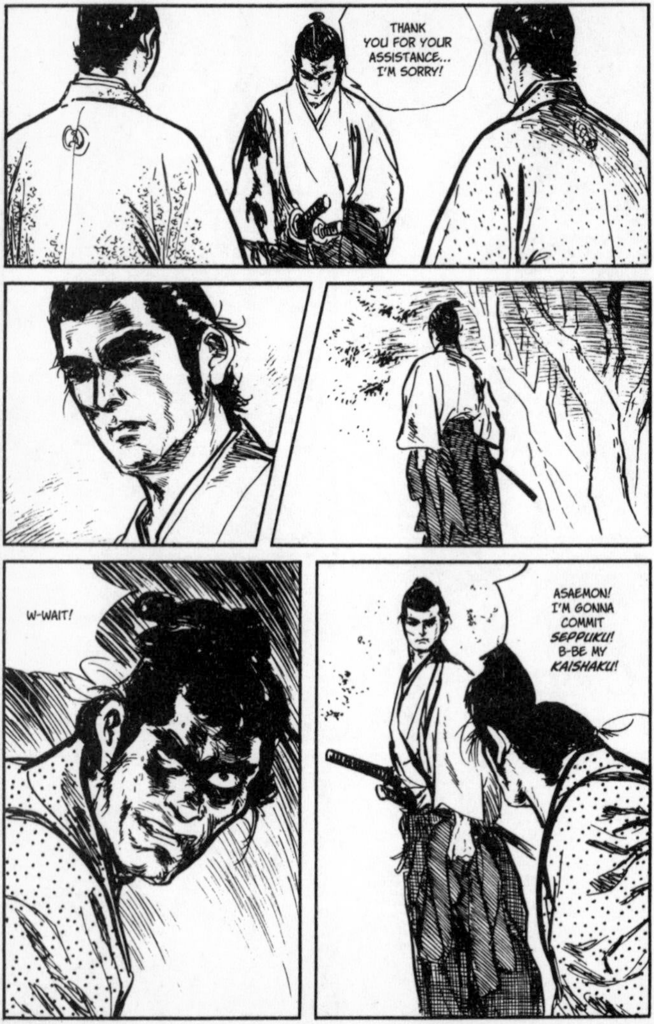
THANK YOU FOR YOUR ASSISTANCE... I'M SORRY!
W-WAIT!
ASAEMON! I'M GONNA COMMIT *SEPPUKU!* B-BE MY *KAISHAKU!*

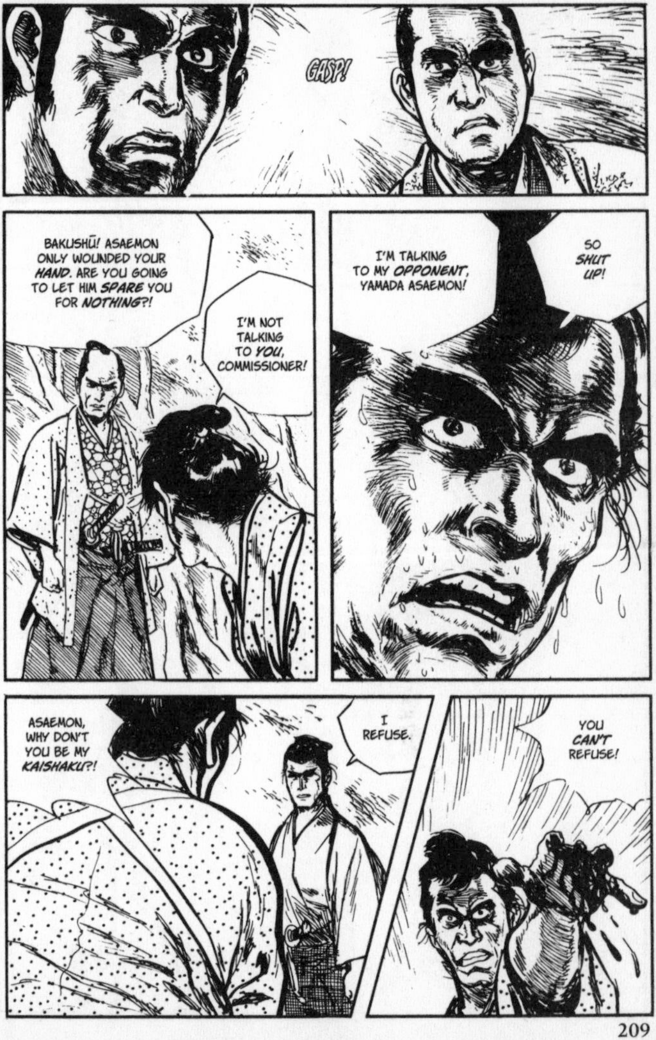
GASP!
BAKUSHŪ! ASAEMON ONLY WOUNDED YOUR *HAND*. ARE YOU GOING TO LET HIM *SPARE* YOU FOR *NOTHING*?!
I'M NOT TALKING TO *YOU*, COMMISSIONER!
I'M TALKING TO MY *OPPONENT*, YAMADA ASAEMON!
SO *SHUT UP*!
ASAEMON, WHY DON'T YOU BE MY *KAISHAKU*?!
I REFUSE.
YOU *CAN'T* REFUSE!

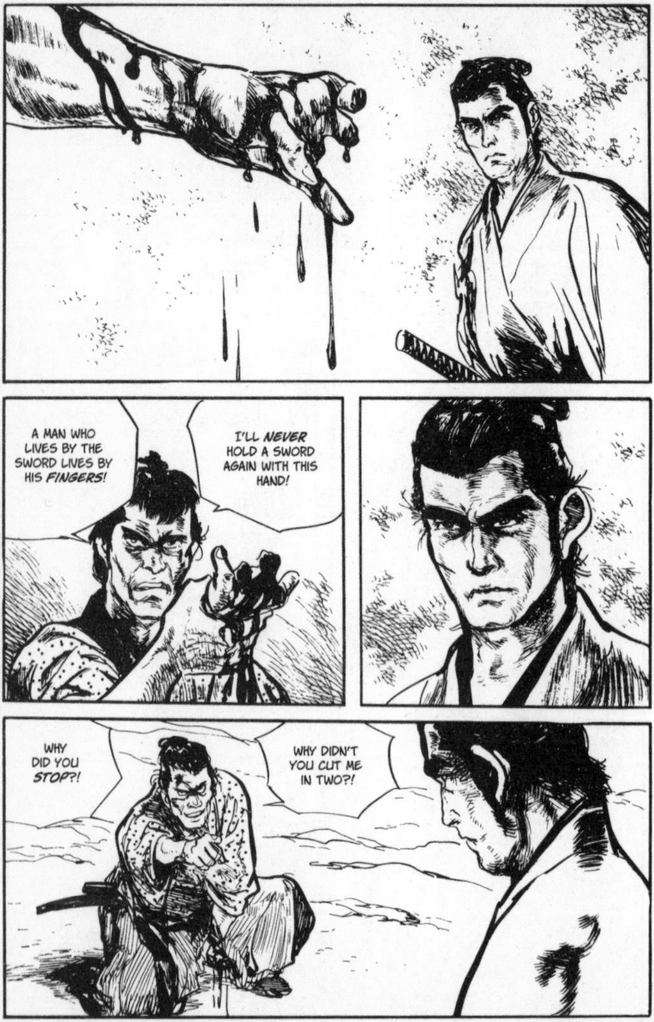
A MAN WHO LIVES BY THE SWORD LIVES BY HIS *FINGERS!*
I'LL *NEVER* HOLD A SWORD AGAIN WITH THIS HAND!
WHY DID YOU *STOP?!*
WHY DIDN'T YOU CUT ME IN TWO?!

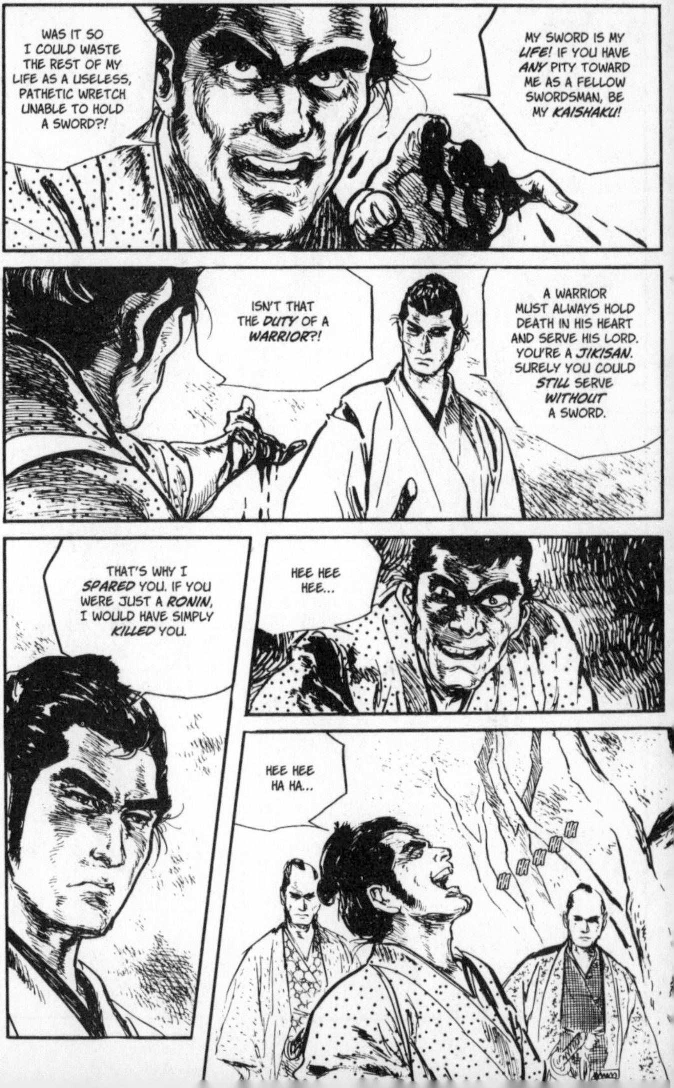
WAS IT SO I COULD WASTE THE REST OF MY LIFE AS A USELESS, PATHETIC WRETCH UNABLE TO HOLD A SWORD?!
MY SWORD IS MY *LIFE!* IF YOU HAVE *ANY* PITY TOWARD ME AS A FELLOW SWORDSMAN, BE MY *KAISHAKU!*
ISN'T THAT THE *DUTY* OF A *WARRIOR?!*
A WARRIOR MUST ALWAYS HOLD DEATH IN HIS HEART AND SERVE HIS LORD. YOU'RE A *JIKISAN.* SURELY YOU COULD *STILL* SERVE *WITHOUT* A SWORD.
THAT'S WHY I *SPARED* YOU. IF YOU WERE JUST A *RONIN,* I WOULD HAVE SIMPLY *KILLED* YOU.
HEE HEE HEE...
HEE HEE HA HA...
HA HA HA HA HA

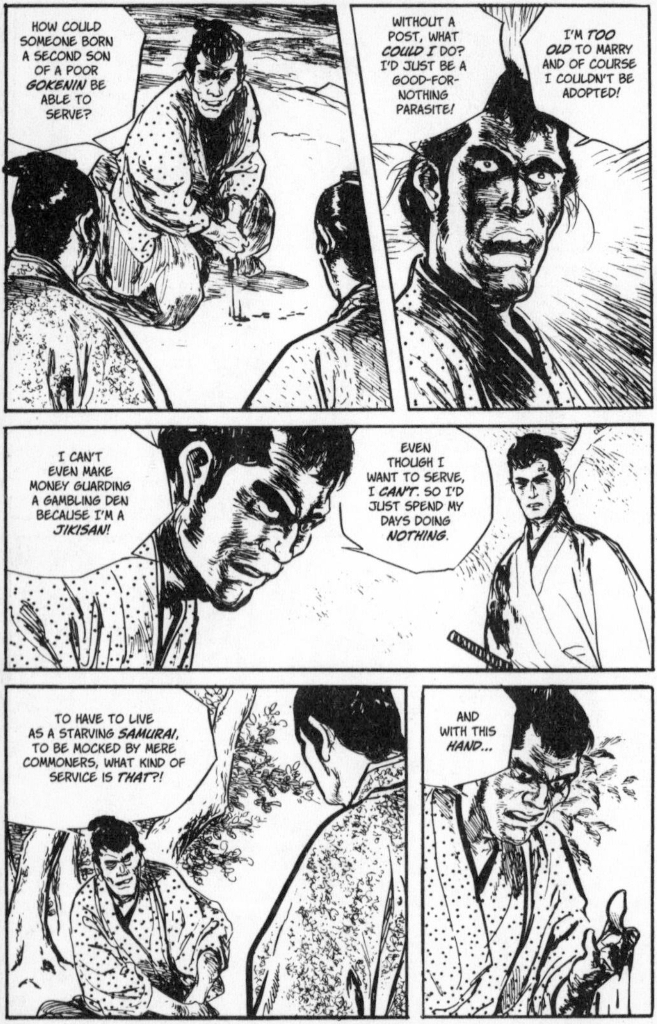
HOW COULD SOMEONE BORN A SECOND SON OF A POOR *GOKENIN* BE ABLE TO SERVE?
WITHOUT A POST, WHAT *COULD I* DO? I'D JUST BE A GOOD-FOR-NOTHING PARASITE!
I'M *TOO OLD* TO MARRY AND OF COURSE I COULDN'T BE ADOPTED!
I CAN'T EVEN MAKE MONEY GUARDING A GAMBLING DEN BECAUSE I'M A *JIKISAN*!
EVEN THOUGH I WANT TO SERVE, I *CAN'T*. SO I'D JUST SPEND MY DAYS DOING *NOTHING*.
TO HAVE TO LIVE AS A STARVING *SAMURAI*, TO BE MOCKED BY MERE COMMONERS, WHAT KIND OF SERVICE IS *THAT*?!
AND WITH THIS *HAND*...

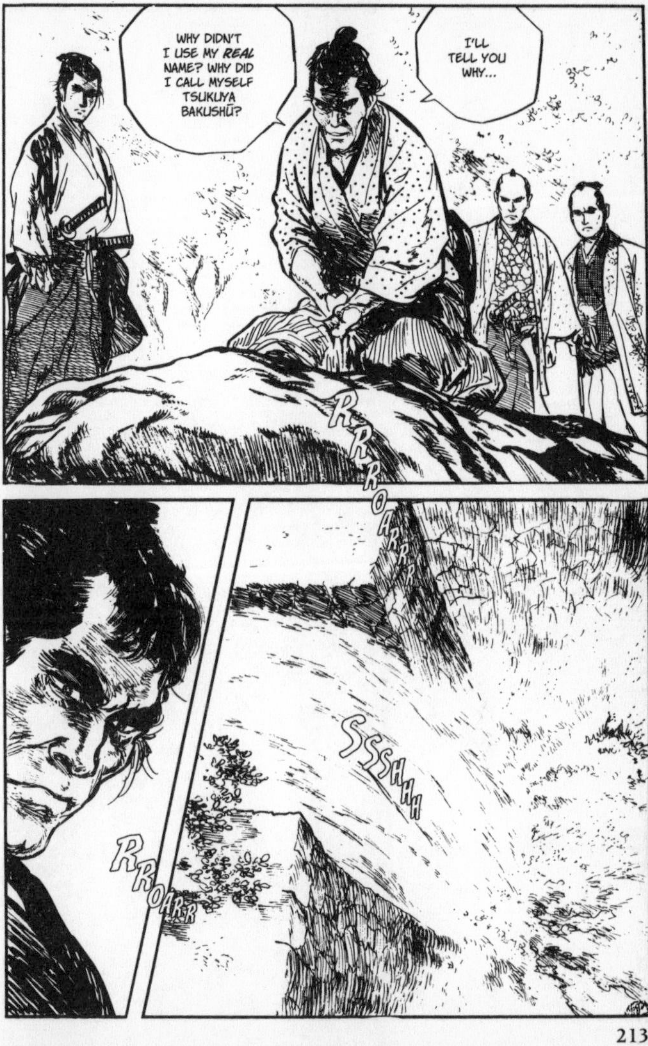
WHY DIDN'T I USE MY REAL NAME? WHY DID I CALL MYSELF TSUKUYA BAKUSHŪ?
I'LL TELL YOU WHY...
RRROARRR
SSSHHH
RROARR

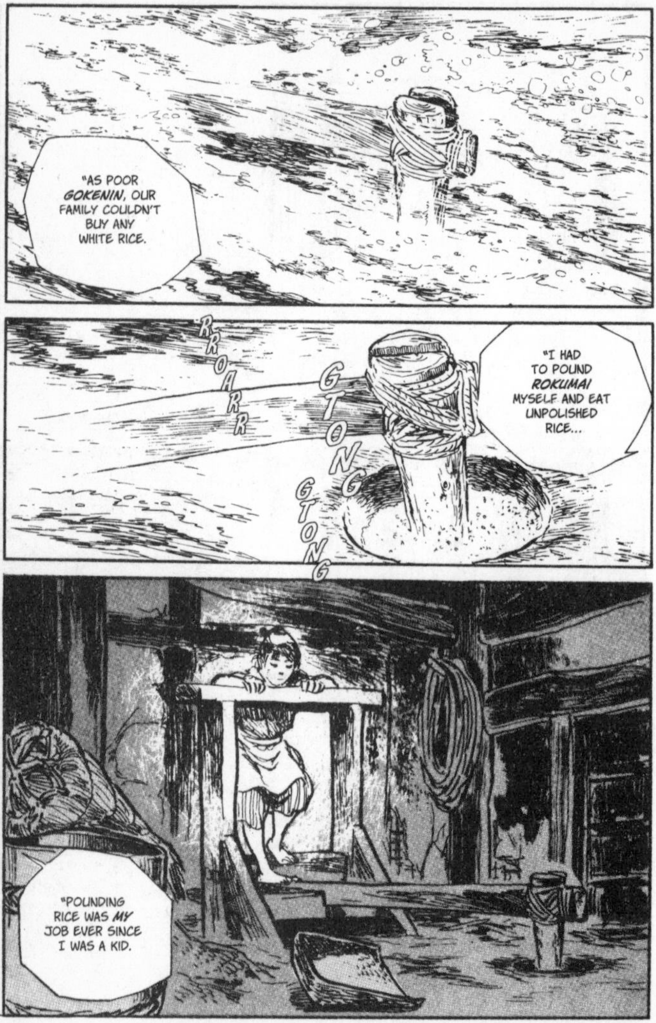

"AS POOR GOKENIN, OUR FAMILY COULDN'T BUY ANY WHITE RICE.
RROARRR
GTONG
GTONG
"I HAD TO POUND ROKUMAI MYSELF AND EAT UNPOLISHED RICE...
"POUNDING RICE WAS MY JOB EVER SINCE I WAS A KID.

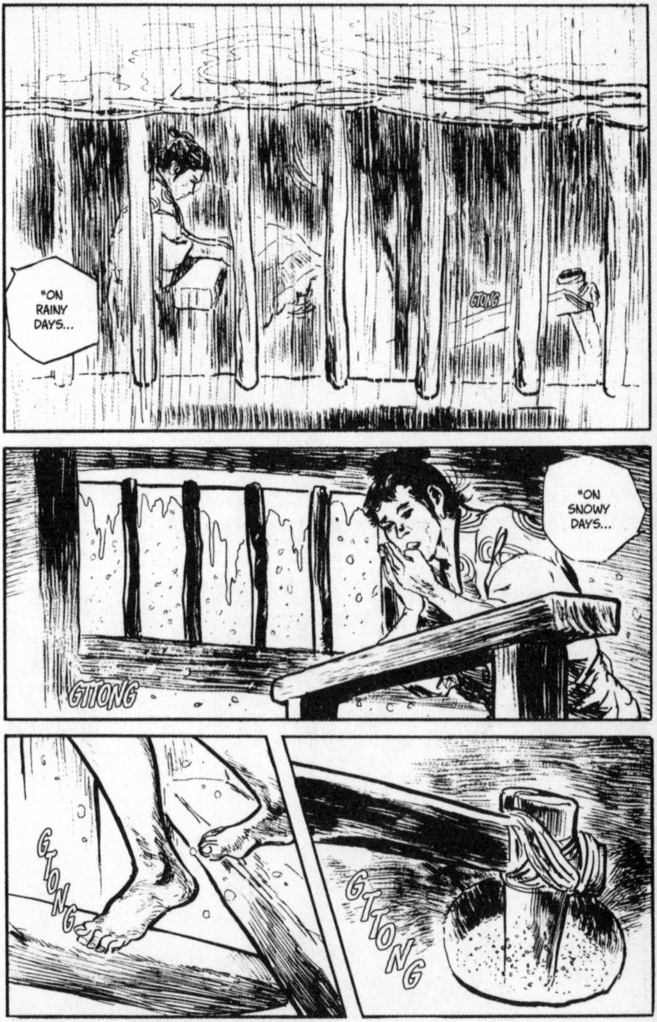

"ON RAINY DAYS...
GTONG
"ON SNOWY DAYS...
GTTONG
GTONG
GTTONG

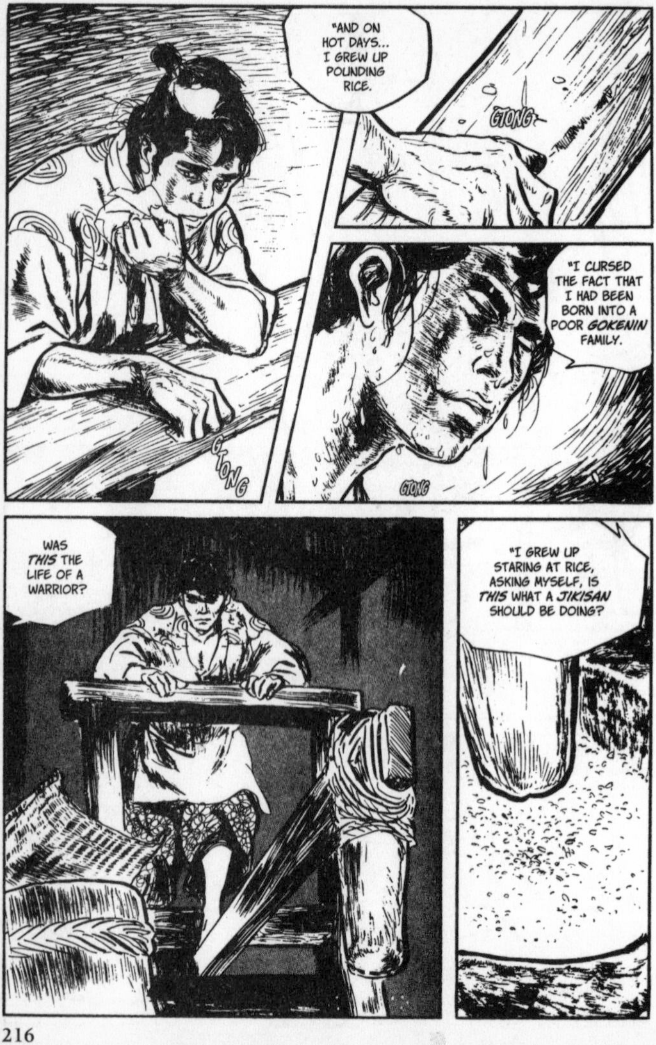

"AND ON HOT DAYS... I GREW UP POUNDING RICE.
GTONG
GTONG
"I CURSED THE FACT THAT I HAD BEEN BORN INTO A POOR *GOKENIN* FAMILY.
GTONG
WAS *THIS* THE LIFE OF A WARRIOR?
"I GREW UP STARING AT RICE, ASKING MYSELF, IS *THIS* WHAT A *JIKISAN* SHOULD BE DOING?

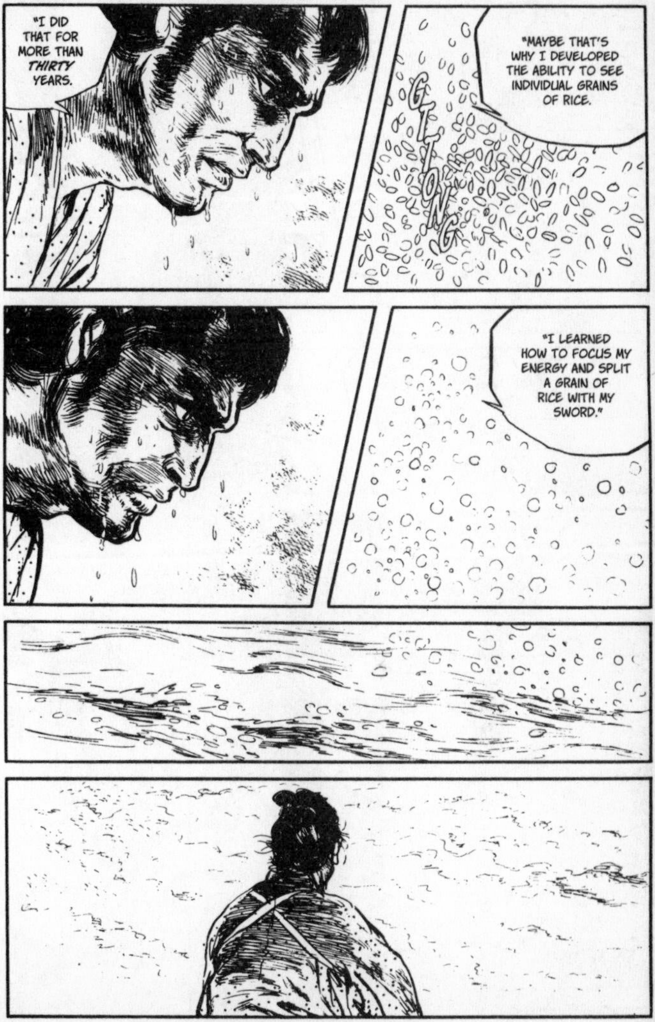
"I DID THAT FOR MORE THAN *THIRTY* YEARS.
"MAYBE THAT'S WHY I DEVELOPED THE ABILITY TO SEE INDIVIDUAL GRAINS OF RICE.
GLING
"I LEARNED HOW TO FOCUS MY ENERGY AND SPLIT A GRAIN OF RICE WITH MY SWORD."

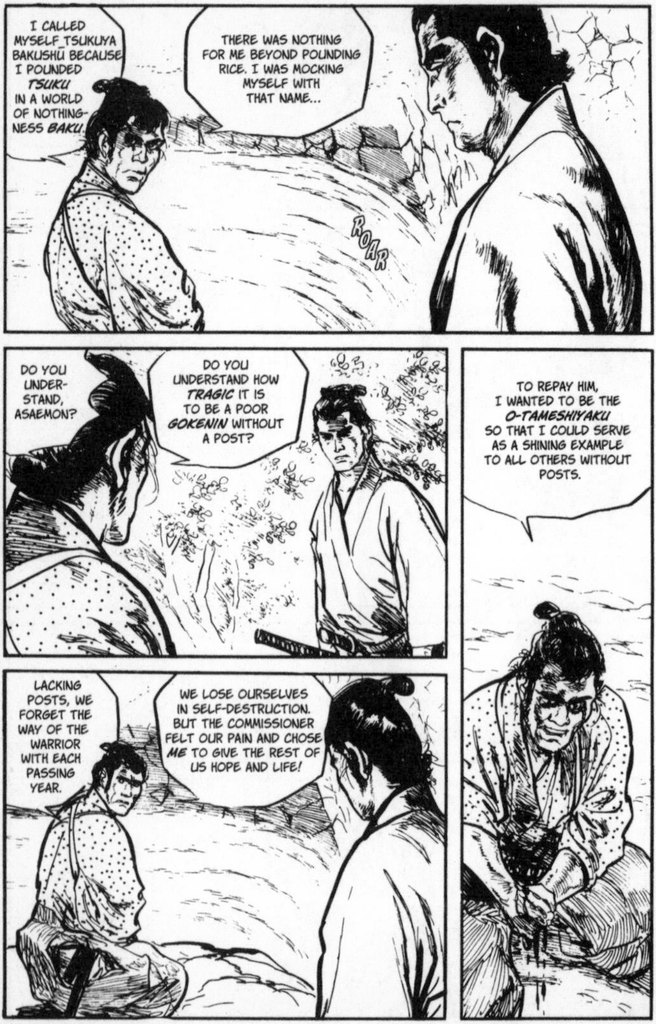
I CALLED MYSELF TSUKUYA BAKUSHŪ BECAUSE I POUNDED *TSUKU* IN A WORLD OF NOTHINGNESS *BAKU*.
THERE WAS NOTHING FOR ME BEYOND POUNDING RICE. I WAS MOCKING MYSELF WITH THAT NAME...
ROAR
DO YOU UNDERSTAND, ASAEMON?
DO YOU UNDERSTAND HOW *TRAGIC* IT IS TO BE A POOR *GOKENIN* WITHOUT A POST?
LACKING POSTS, WE FORGET THE WAY OF THE WARRIOR WITH EACH PASSING YEAR.
WE LOSE OURSELVES IN SELF-DESTRUCTION. BUT THE COMMISSIONER FELT OUR PAIN AND CHOSE *ME* TO GIVE THE REST OF US HOPE AND LIFE!
TO REPAY HIM, I WANTED TO BE THE *O-TAMESHIYAKU* SO THAT I COULD SERVE AS A SHINING EXAMPLE TO ALL OTHERS WITHOUT POSTS.

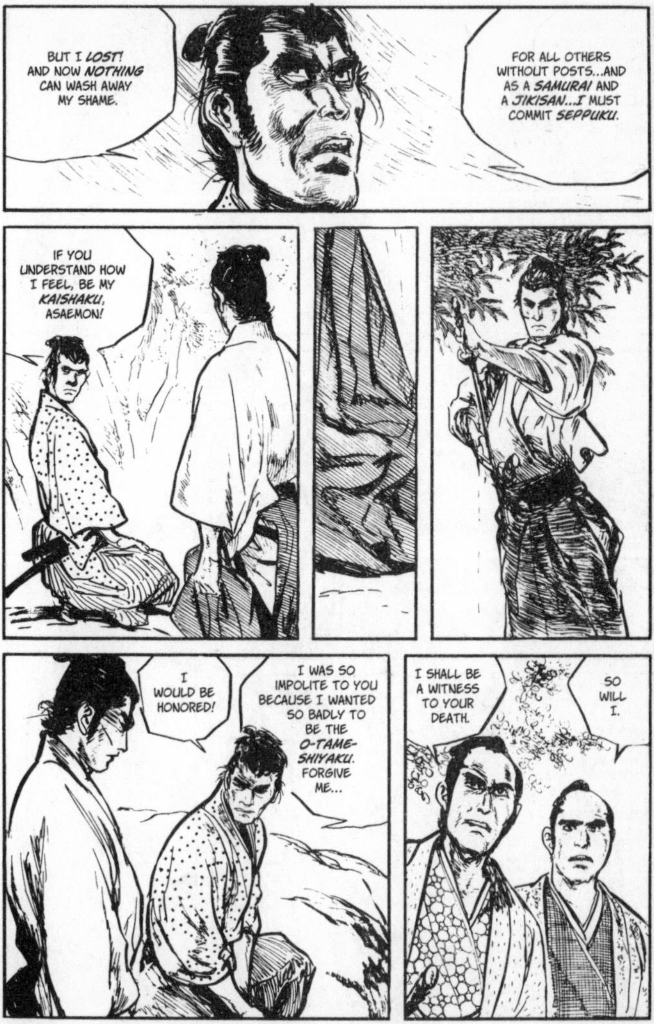
BUT I *LOST!* AND NOW *NOTHING* CAN WASH AWAY MY SHAME.
FOR ALL OTHERS WITHOUT POSTS...AND AS A *SAMURAI* AND A *JIKISAN*...I MUST COMMIT *SEPPUKU*.
IF YOU UNDERSTAND HOW I FEEL, BE MY *KAISHAKU*, ASAEMON!
I WOULD BE HONORED!
I WAS SO IMPOLITE TO YOU BECAUSE I WANTED SO BADLY TO BE THE *O-TAME-SHIYAKU*. FORGIVE ME...
I SHALL BE A WITNESS TO YOUR DEATH.
SO WILL I.

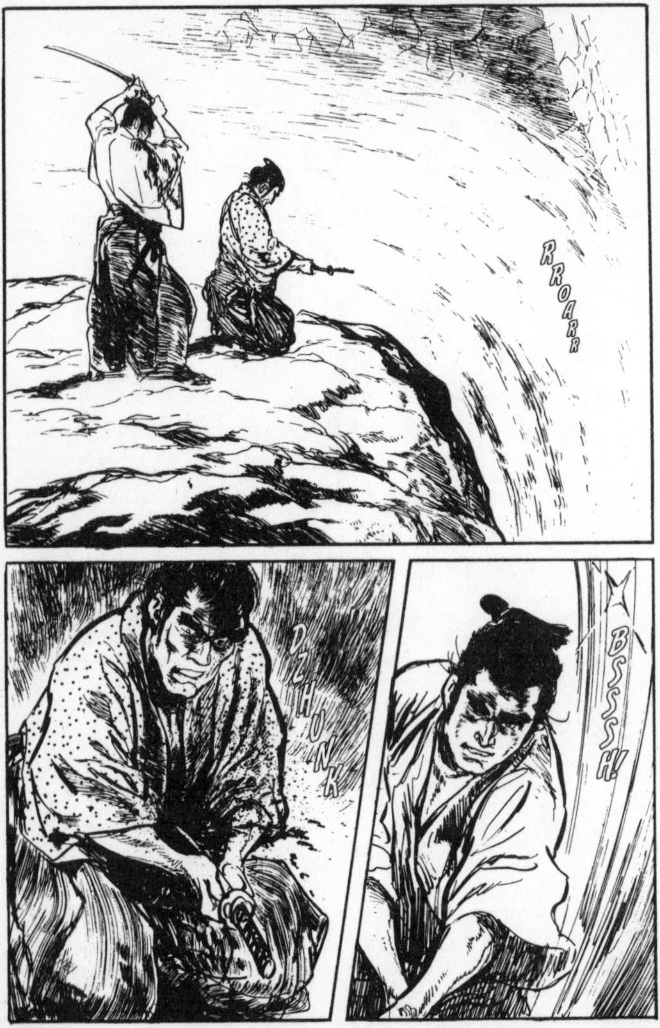
RROARR
DZHUNK
BSSSH!

the eleventh

Catcher Kasajiro

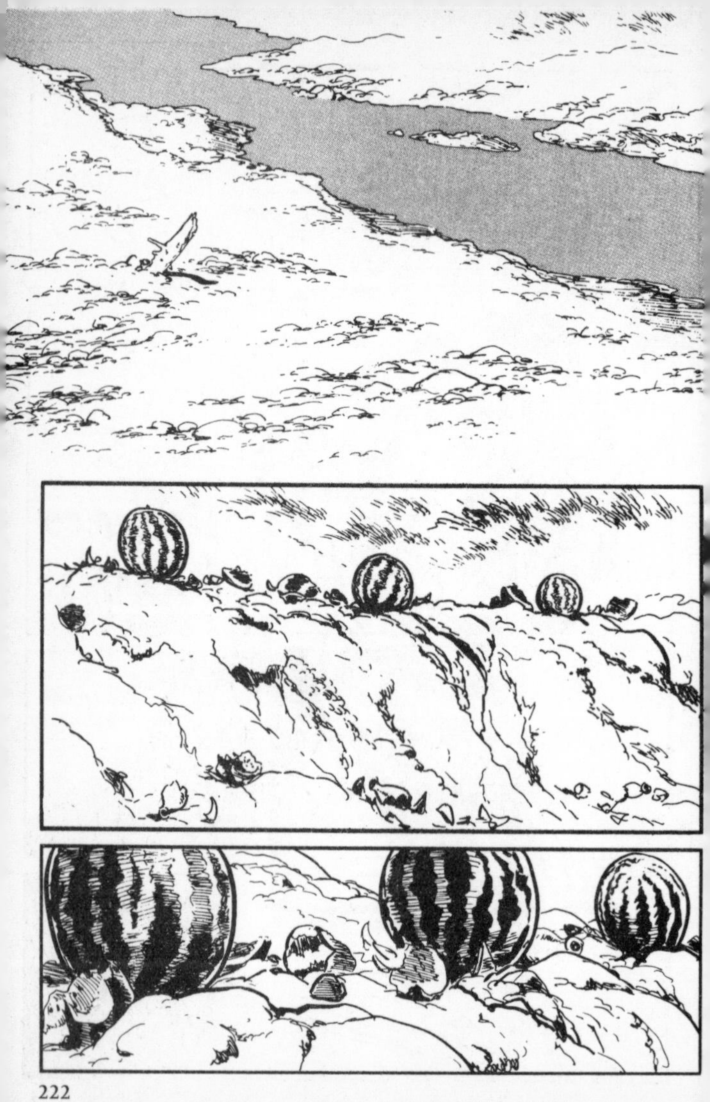

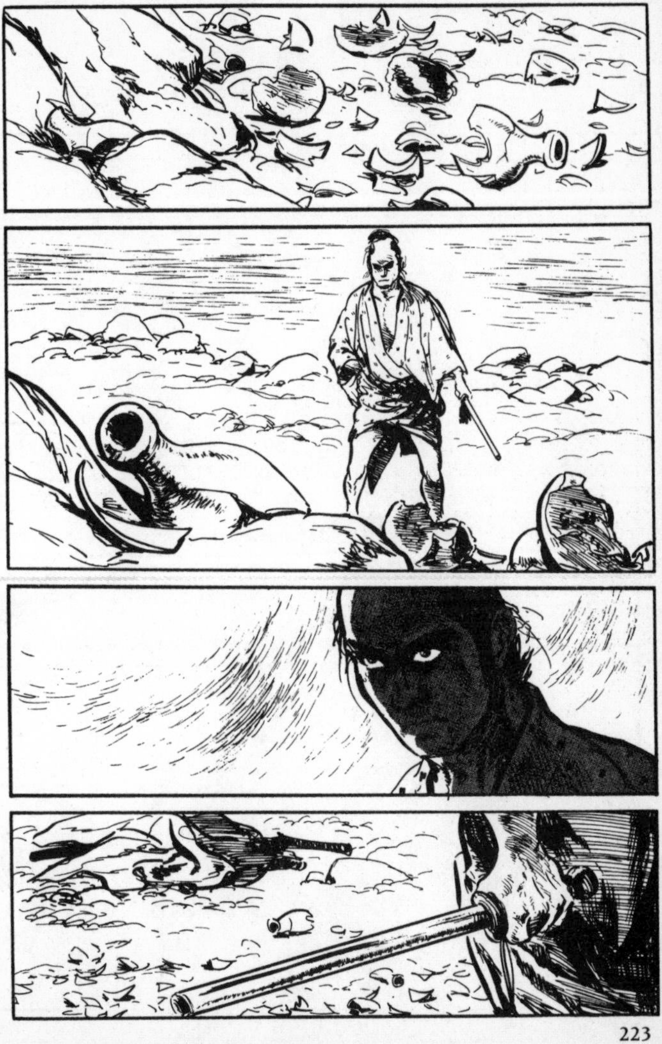

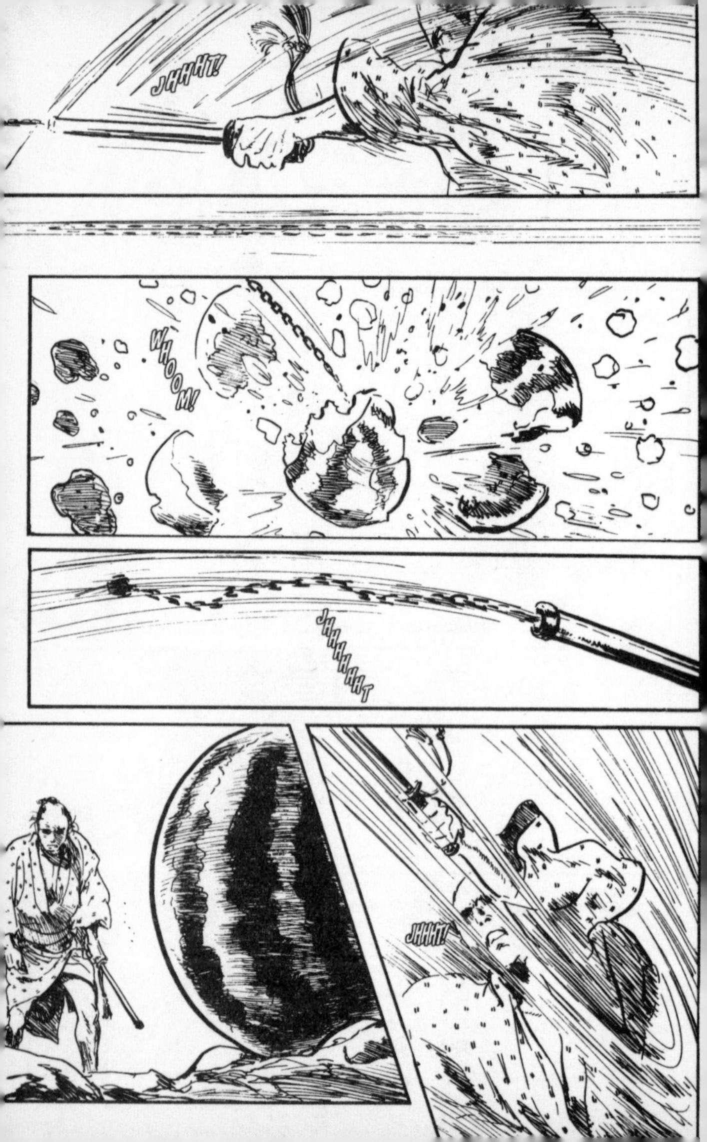
JHHHT!
WHOOM!
JHHHHHHT
JHHHT!

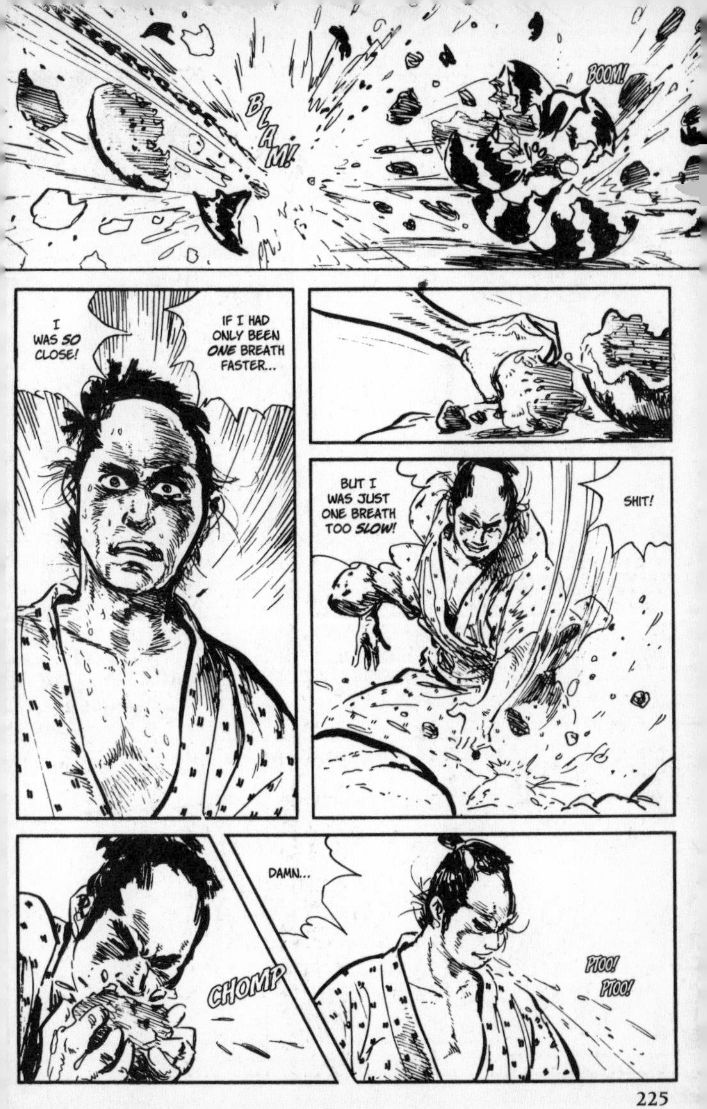
BLAM!
BOOM!
I WAS *SO* CLOSE!
IF I HAD ONLY BEEN *ONE* BREATH FASTER...
BUT I WAS JUST ONE BREATH TOO *SLOW*!
SHIT!
CHOMP
DAMN...
PTOO! PTOO!

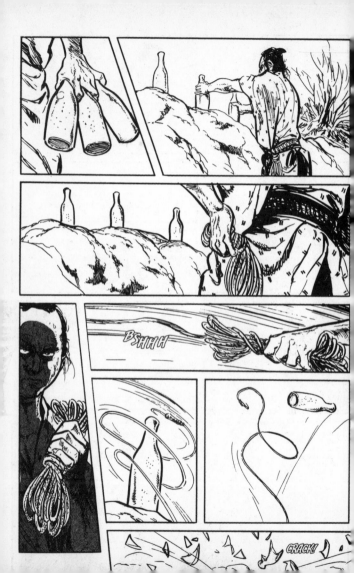

BSHHH

CRACK!

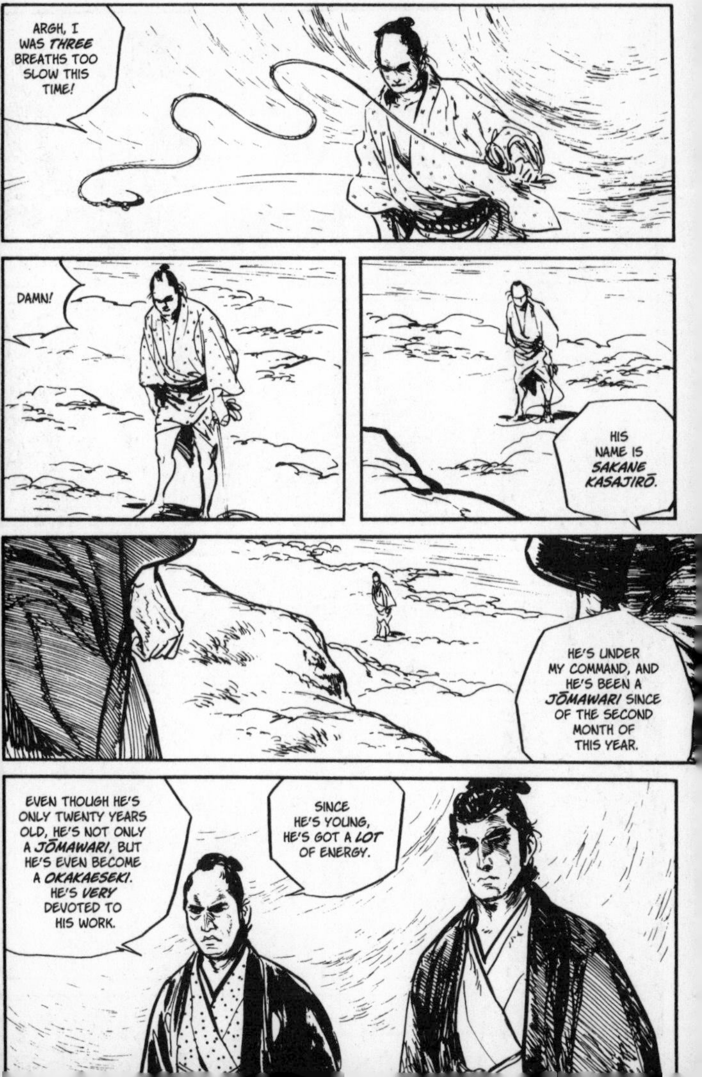
ARGH, I WAS *THREE* BREATHS TOO SLOW THIS TIME!
DAMN!
HIS NAME IS *SAKANE KASAJIRŌ*.
HE'S UNDER MY COMMAND, AND HE'S BEEN A *JŌMAWARI* SINCE OF THE SECOND MONTH OF THIS YEAR.
EVEN THOUGH HE'S ONLY TWENTY YEARS OLD, HE'S NOT ONLY A *JŌMAWARI*, BUT HE'S EVEN BECOME A *OKAKAESEKI*. HE'S *VERY* DEVOTED TO HIS WORK.
SINCE HE'S YOUNG, HE'S GOT A *LOT* OF ENERGY.

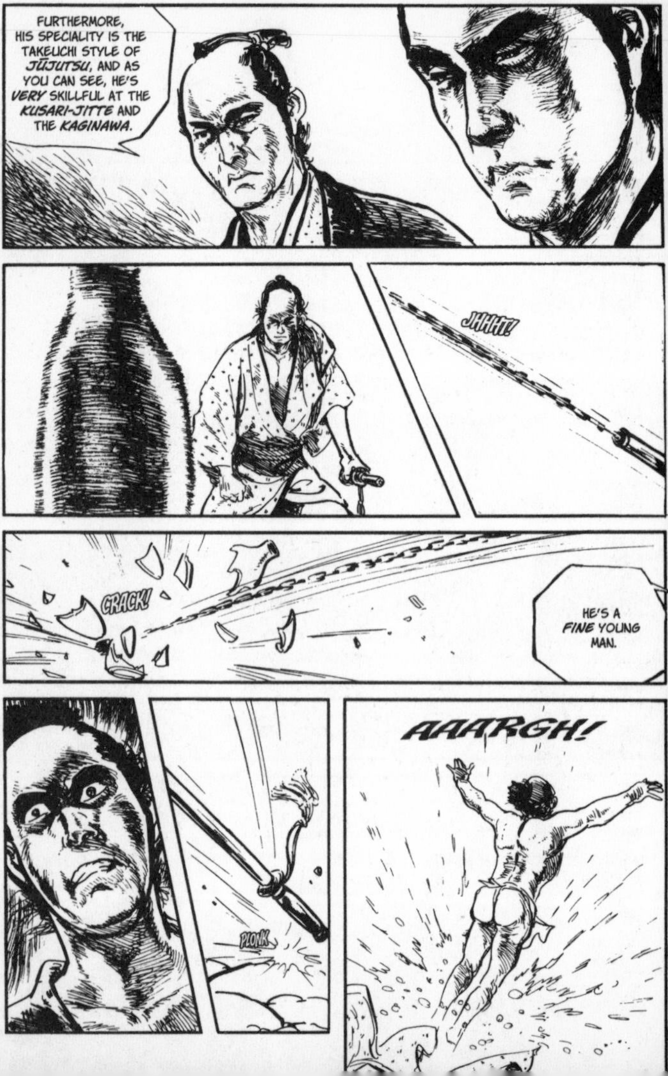
FURTHERMORE, HIS SPECIALITY IS THE TAKEUCHI STYLE OF JŪJUTSU, AND AS YOU CAN SEE, HE'S VERY SKILLFUL AT THE KUSARI-JITTE AND THE KAGINAWA.
JHHHT!
CRACK!
HE'S A FINE YOUNG MAN.
PLONK
AAARGH!

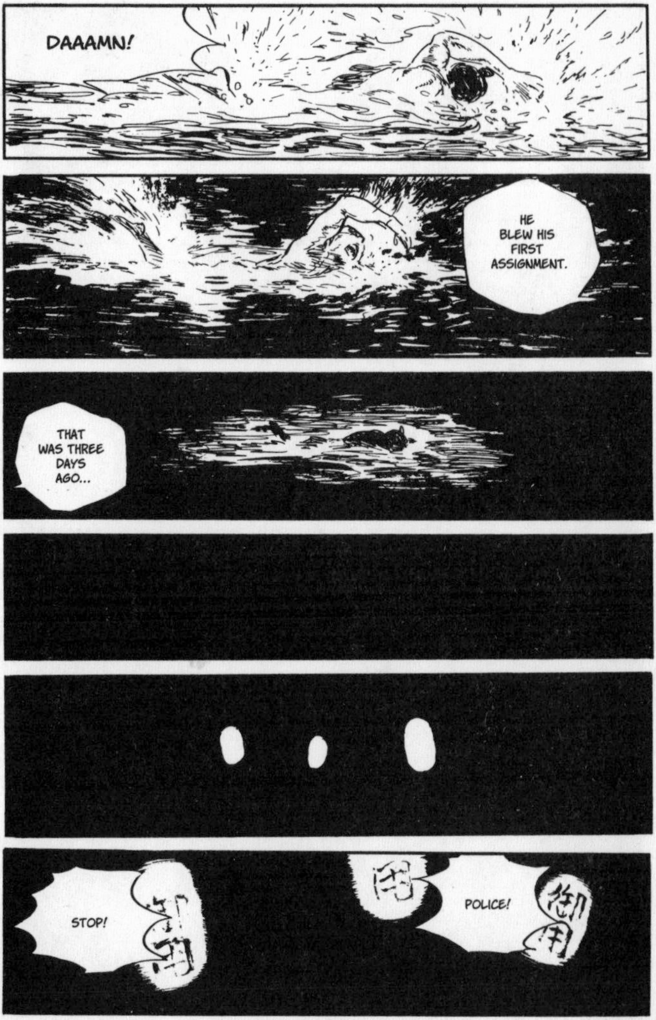
DAAAMN!
HE BLEW HIS FIRST ASSIGNMENT.
THAT WAS THREE DAYS AGO...
STOP!
POLICE!

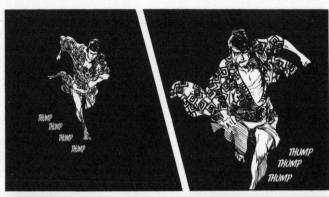

THUMP
THUMP
THUMP
THUMP

THUMP
THUMP

THUMP

230

"WE HAD A TIP THAT NIGHT, SO WE LAID A DRAGNET OVER ALL OF EDO.

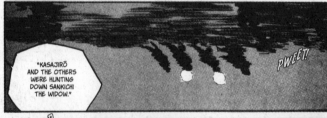

"KASAJIRŌ AND THE OTHERS WERE HUNTING DOWN SANKICHI THE WIDOW."

PWEET!

PWEET!

PWEET!

231

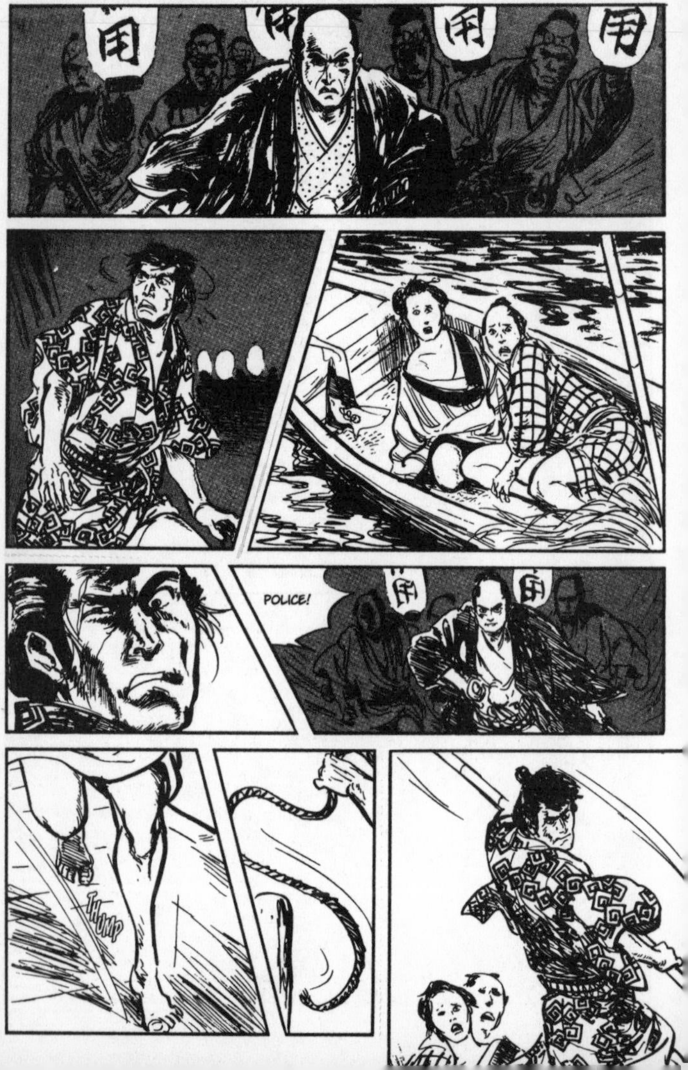
POLICE!
THUMP

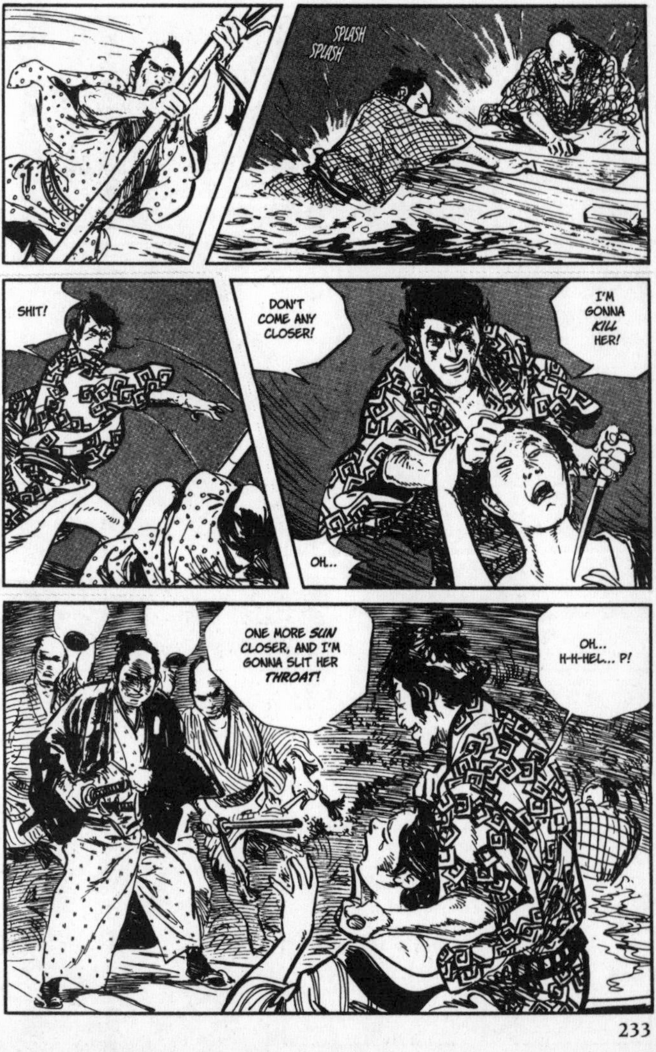
SPLASH
SPLASH
SHIT!
DON'T COME ANY CLOSER!
I'M GONNA *KILL* HER!
OH..
ONE MORE *SUN* CLOSER, AND I'M GONNA SLIT HER *THROAT!*
OH.. H-H-HEL... P!

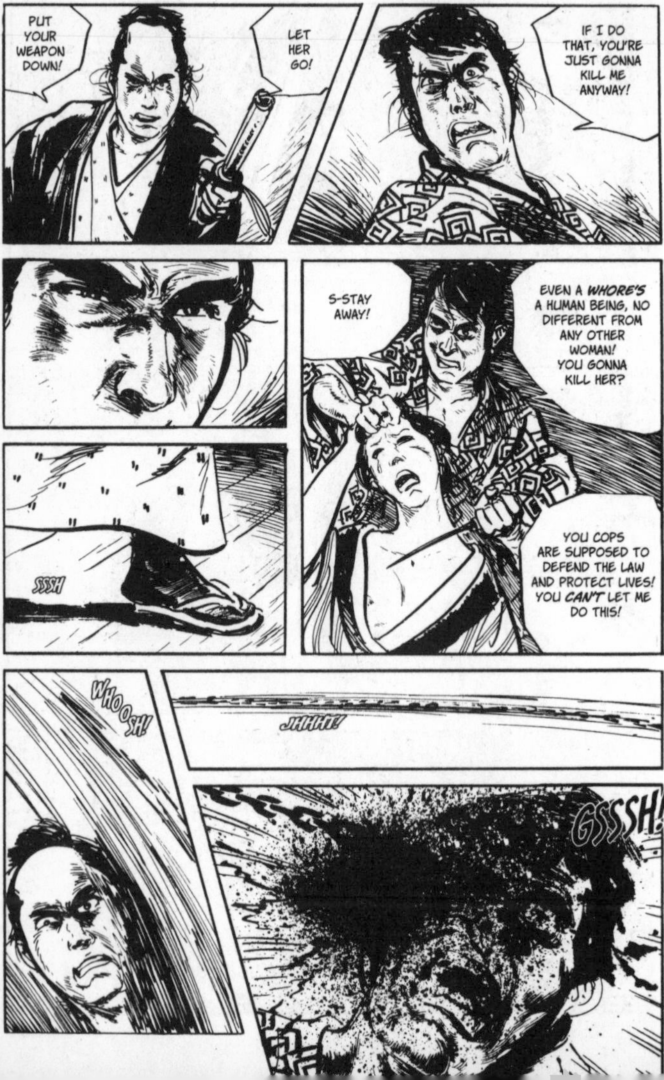
PUT YOUR WEAPON DOWN!
LET HER GO!
IF I DO THAT, YOU'RE JUST GONNA KILL ME ANYWAY!
S-STAY AWAY!
EVEN A *WHORE'S* A HUMAN BEING, NO DIFFERENT FROM ANY OTHER WOMAN! YOU GONNA KILL HER?
YOU COPS ARE SUPPOSED TO DEFEND THE LAW AND PROTECT LIVES! YOU *CAN'T* LET ME DO THIS!
SSSH
WHOOSH!
JHHHT!
GSSSH!

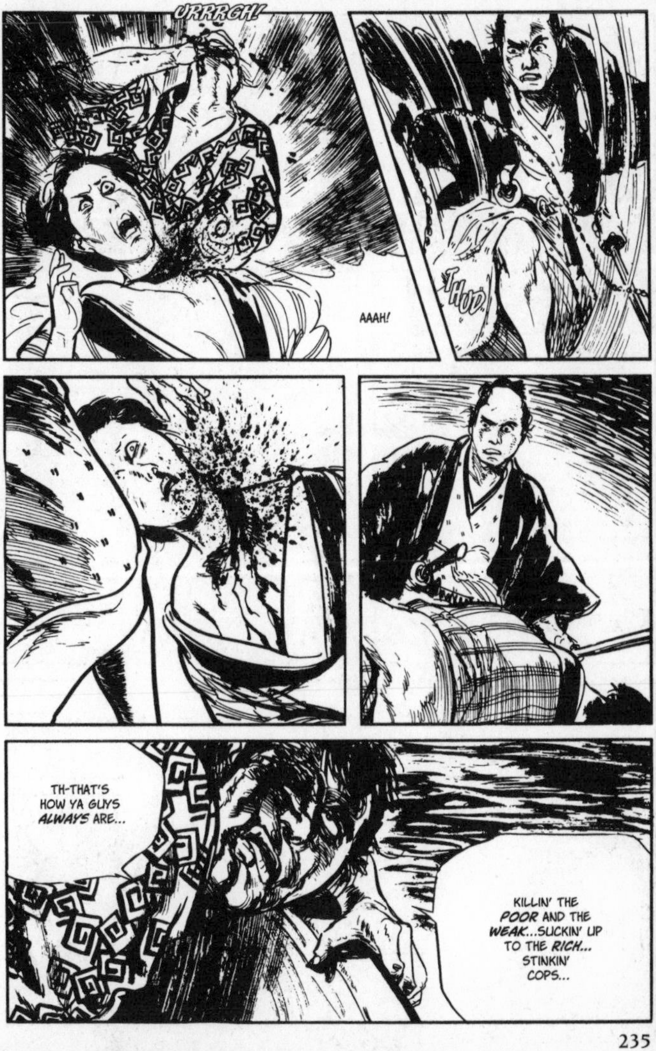
URRRGH!
AAAH!
THUD
TH-THAT'S HOW YA GUYS *ALWAYS* ARE...
KILLIN' THE *POOR* AND THE *WEAK*...SUCKIN' UP TO THE *RICH*... STINKIN' COPS...

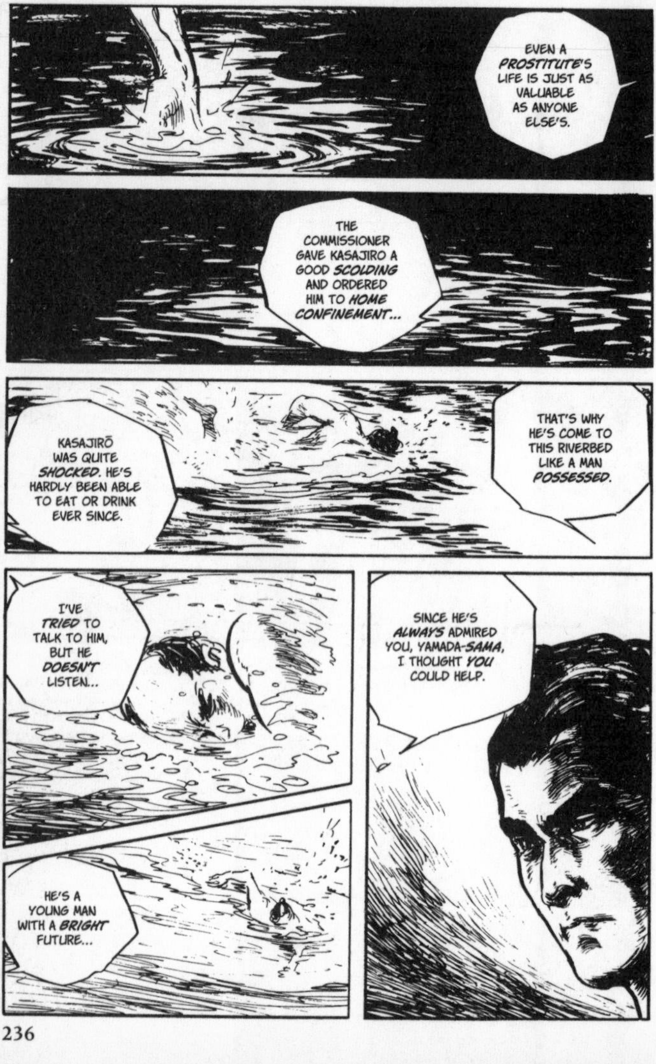
EVEN A PROSTITUTE'S LIFE IS JUST AS VALUABLE AS ANYONE ELSE'S.
THE COMMISSIONER GAVE KASAJIRO A GOOD SCOLDING AND ORDERED HIM TO HOME CONFINEMENT...
KASAJIRŌ WAS QUITE SHOCKED. HE'S HARDLY BEEN ABLE TO EAT OR DRINK EVER SINCE.
THAT'S WHY HE'S COME TO THIS RIVERBED LIKE A MAN POSSESSED.
I'VE TRIED TO TALK TO HIM, BUT HE DOESN'T LISTEN...
HE'S A YOUNG MAN WITH A BRIGHT FUTURE...
SINCE HE'S ALWAYS ADMIRED YOU, YAMADA-SAMA, I THOUGHT YOU COULD HELP.

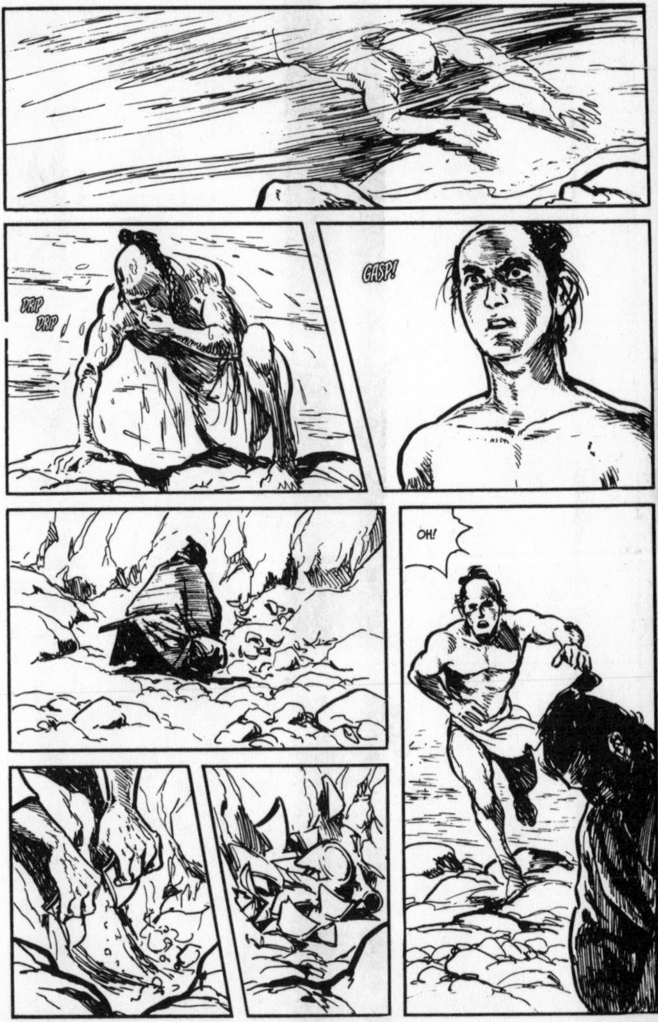
DRIP
DRIP
GASP!
OH!

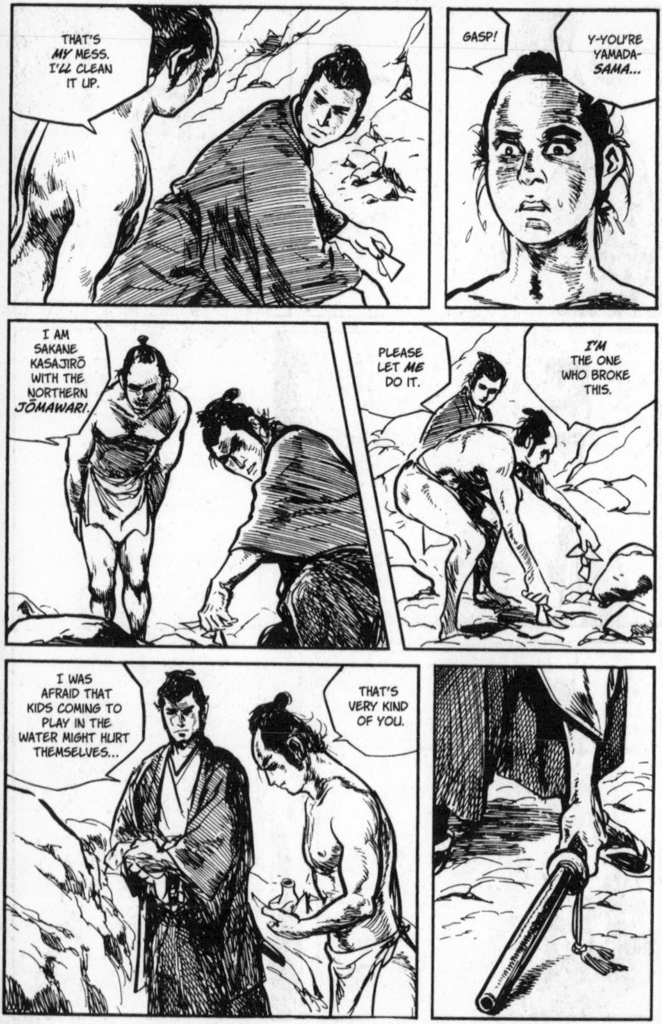
THAT'S *MY* MESS. I'LL CLEAN IT UP.
GASP!
Y-YOU'RE YAMADA-*SAMA*...
I AM SAKANE KASAJIRŌ WITH THE NORTHERN *JŌMAWARI*.
PLEASE LET *ME* DO IT.
I'M THE ONE WHO BROKE THIS.
I WAS AFRAID THAT KIDS COMING TO PLAY IN THE WATER MIGHT HURT THEMSELVES...
THAT'S VERY KIND OF YOU.

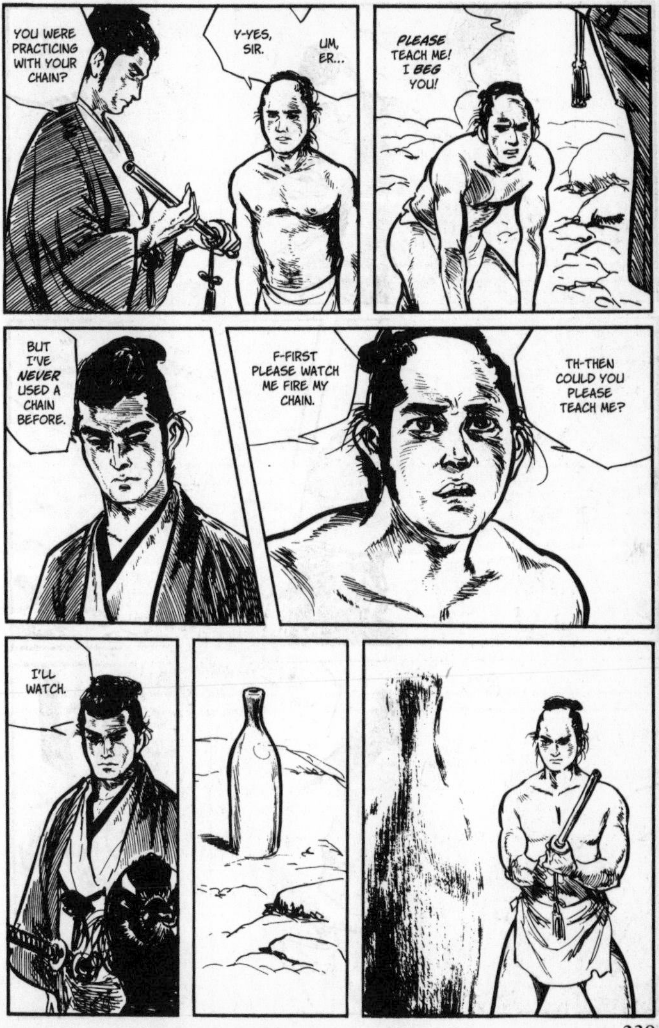
YOU WERE PRACTICING WITH YOUR CHAIN?
Y-YES, SIR.
UM, ER...
PLEASE TEACH ME! I BEG YOU!
BUT I'VE NEVER USED A CHAIN BEFORE.
F-FIRST PLEASE WATCH ME FIRE MY CHAIN.
TH-THEN COULD YOU PLEASE TEACH ME?
I'LL WATCH.

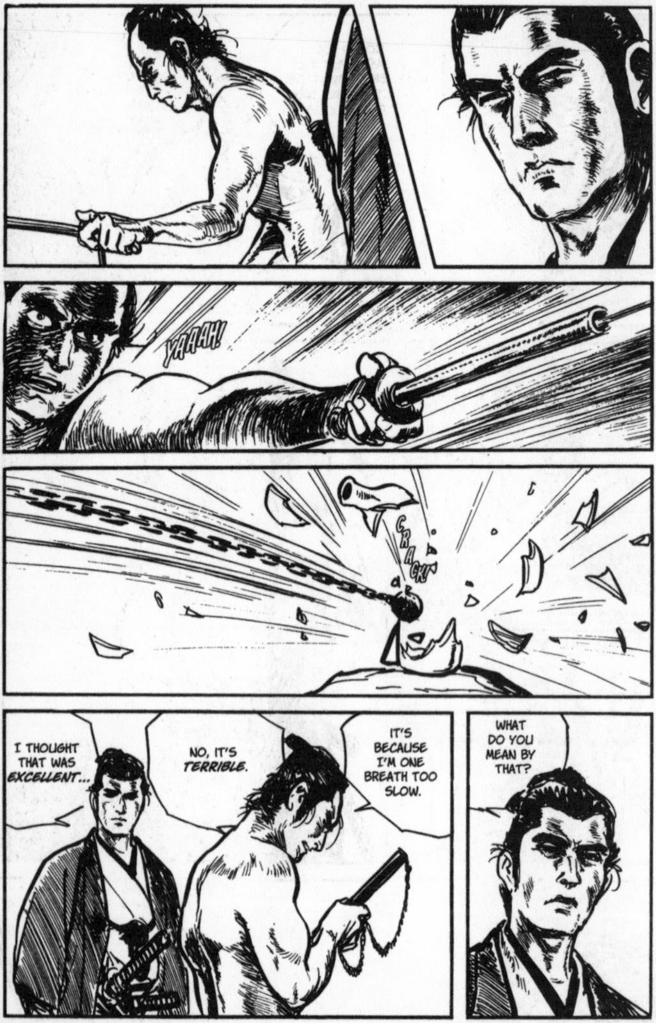
YAAAH!
CRACK!
I THOUGHT THAT WAS EXCELLENT...
NO, IT'S TERRIBLE.
IT'S BECAUSE I'M ONE BREATH TOO SLOW.
WHAT DO YOU MEAN BY THAT?

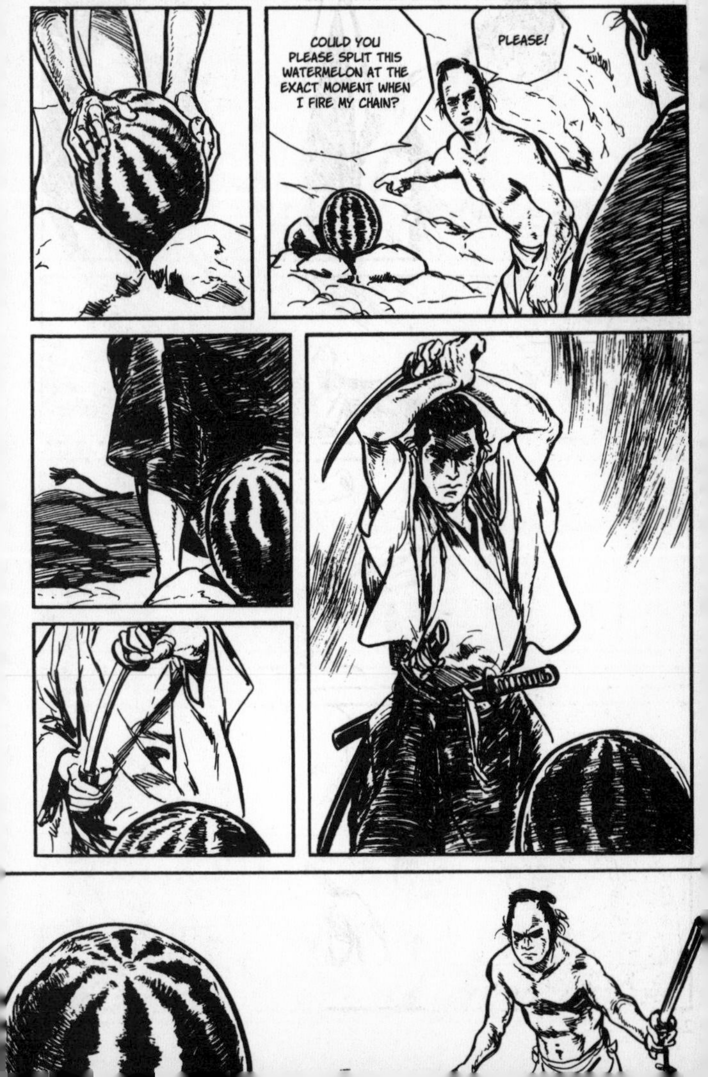
COULD YOU PLEASE SPLIT THIS WATERMELON AT THE EXACT MOMENT WHEN I FIRE MY CHAIN?
PLEASE!

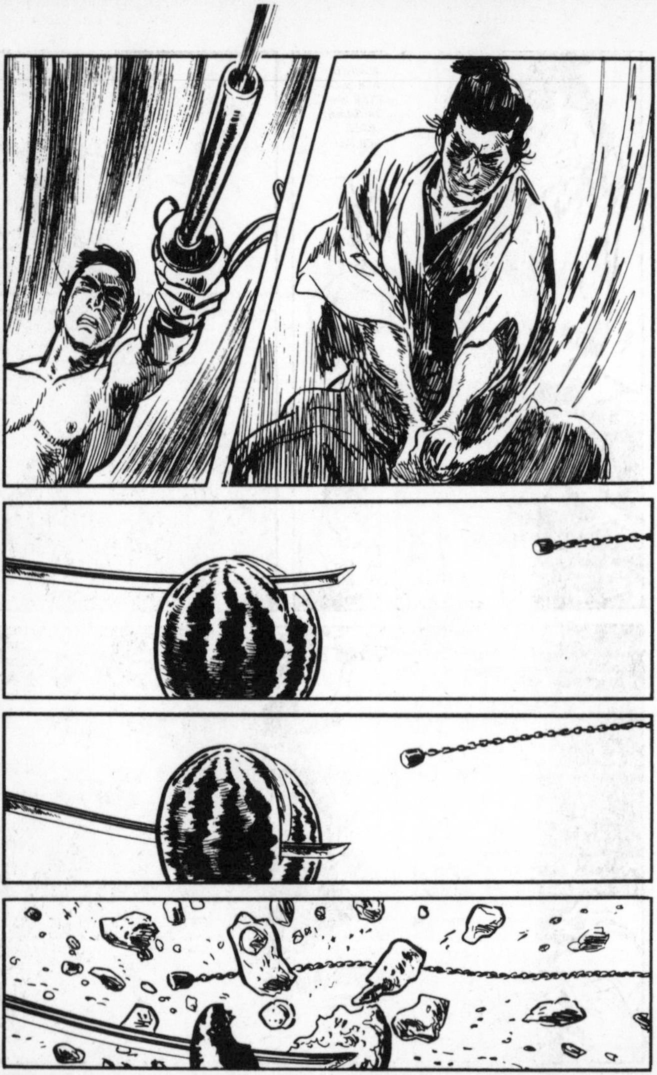

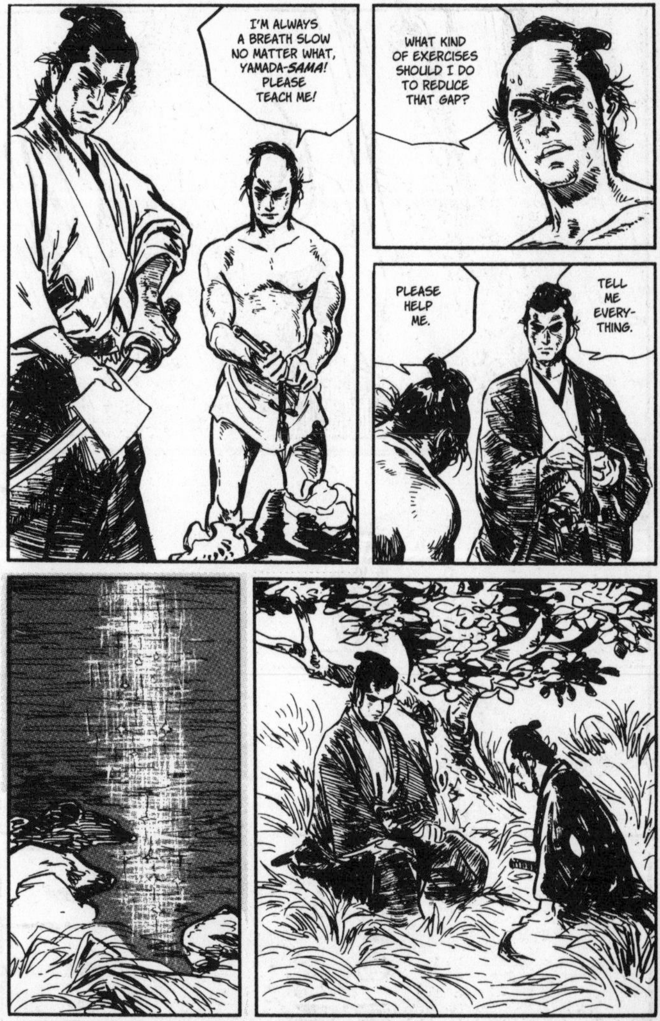
I'M ALWAYS A BREATH SLOW NO MATTER WHAT, YAMADA-*SAMA*! PLEASE TEACH ME!
WHAT KIND OF EXERCISES SHOULD I DO TO REDUCE THAT GAP?
PLEASE HELP ME.
TELL ME EVERY-THING.

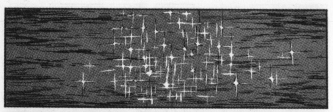

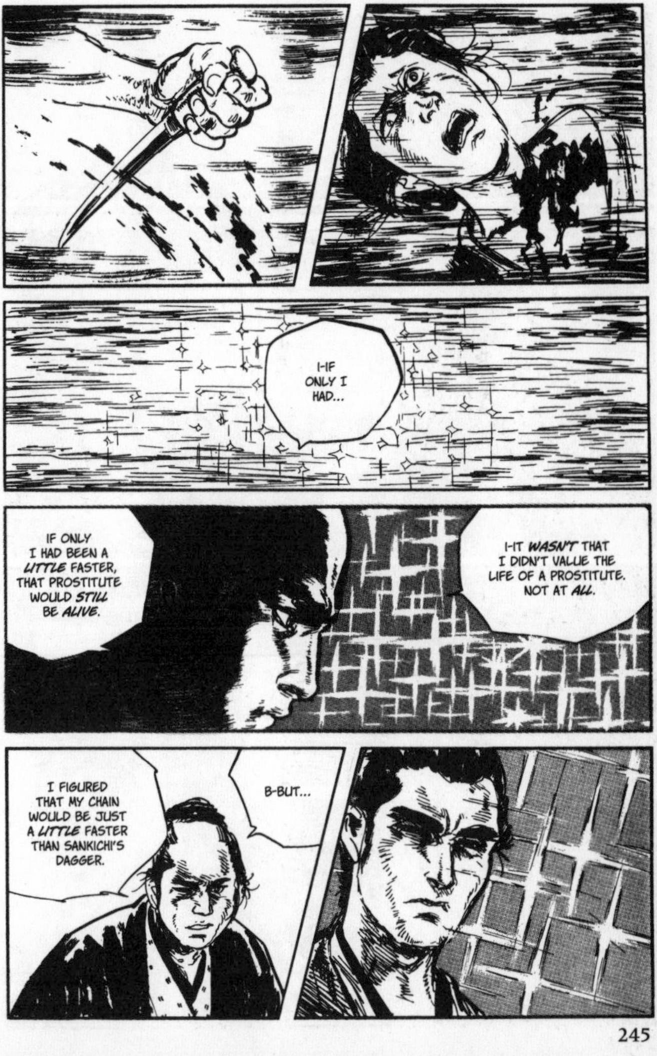
I-IF ONLY I HAD...
IF ONLY I HAD BEEN A LITTLE FASTER, THAT PROSTITUTE WOULD STILL BE ALIVE.
I-IT WASN'T THAT I DIDN'T VALUE THE LIFE OF A PROSTITUTE. NOT AT ALL.
I FIGURED THAT MY CHAIN WOULD BE JUST A LITTLE FASTER THAN SANKICHI'S DAGGER.
B-BUT...

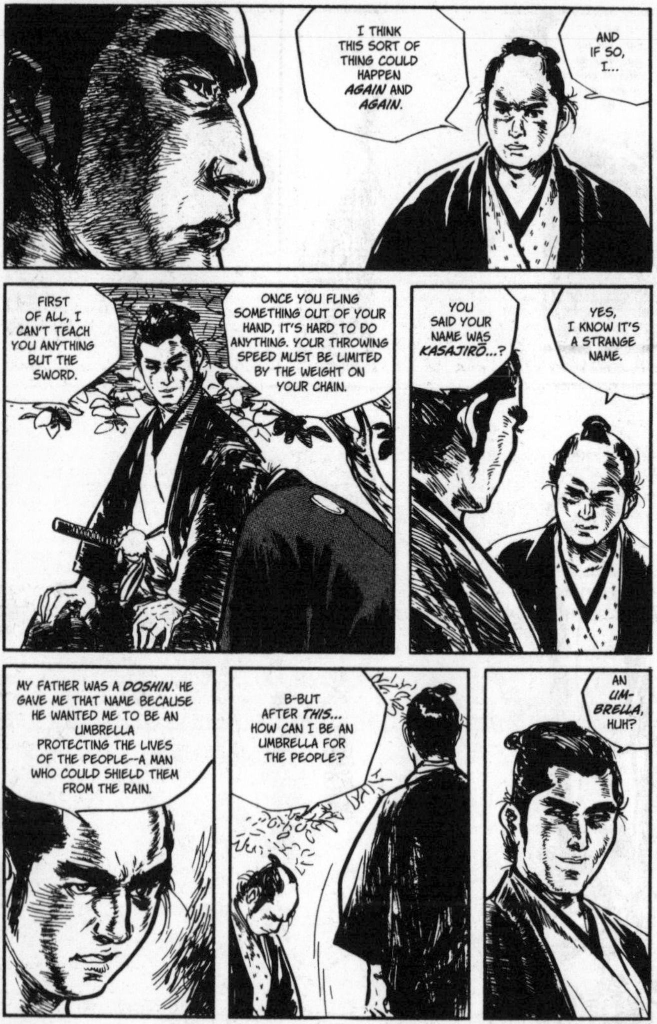

I THINK THIS SORT OF THING COULD HAPPEN *AGAIN* AND *AGAIN*.
AND IF SO, I...
FIRST OF ALL, I CAN'T TEACH YOU ANYTHING BUT THE SWORD.
ONCE YOU FLING SOMETHING OUT OF YOUR HAND, IT'S HARD TO DO ANYTHING. YOUR THROWING SPEED MUST BE LIMITED BY THE WEIGHT ON YOUR CHAIN.
YOU SAID YOUR NAME WAS *KASAJIRŌ*...?
YES, I KNOW IT'S A STRANGE NAME.
MY FATHER WAS A *DOSHIN*. HE GAVE ME THAT NAME BECAUSE HE WANTED ME TO BE AN UMBRELLA PROTECTING THE LIVES OF THE PEOPLE--A MAN WHO COULD SHIELD THEM FROM THE RAIN.
B-BUT AFTER *THIS*... HOW CAN I BE AN UMBRELLA FOR THE PEOPLE?
AN *UMBRELLA*, HUH?

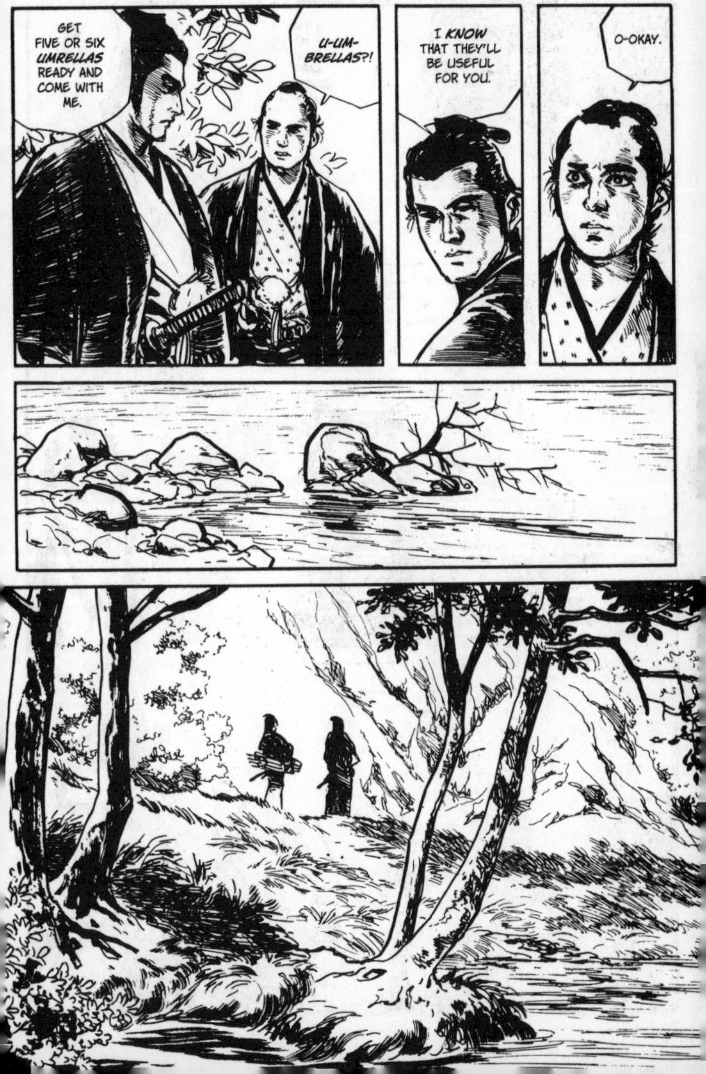
GET FIVE OR SIX UMRELLAS READY AND COME WITH ME.
U-UM-BRELLAS?!
I KNOW THAT THEY'LL BE USEFUL FOR YOU.
O-OKAY.

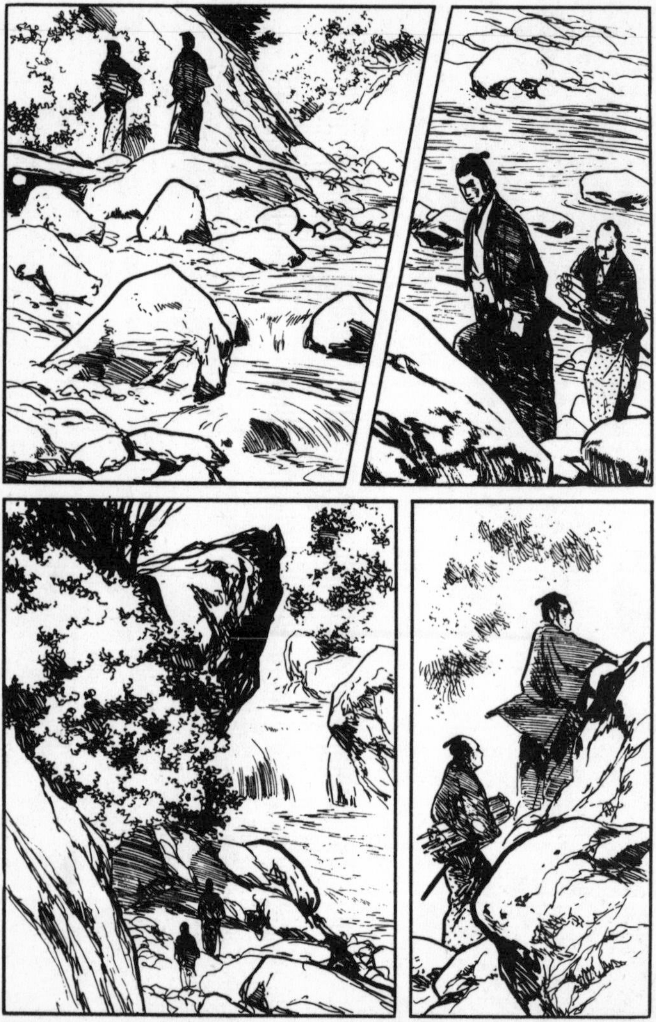

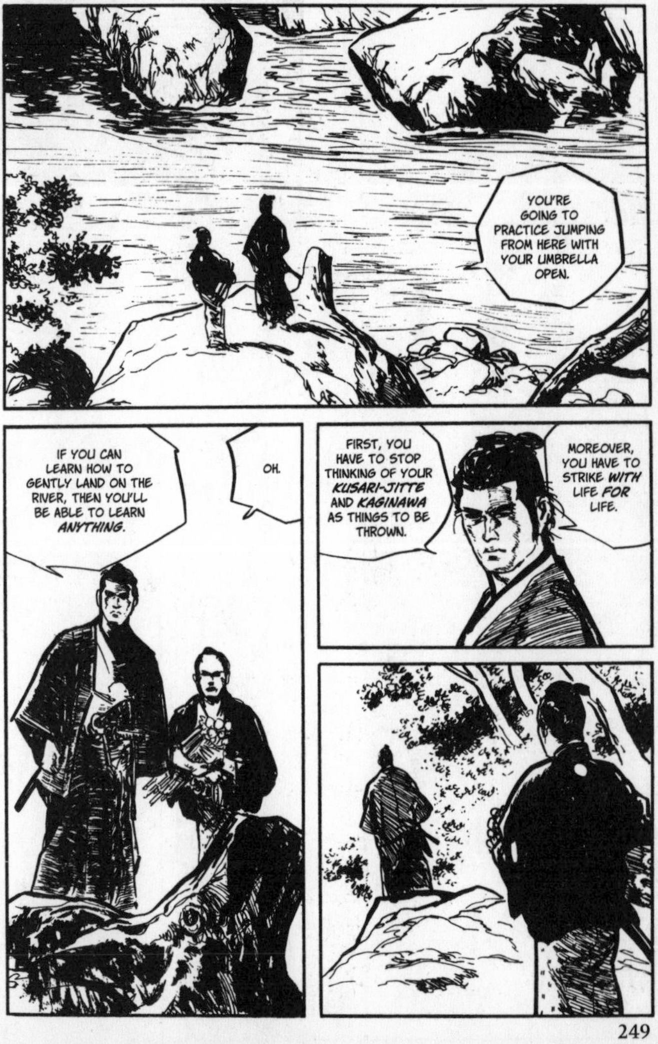
YOU'RE GOING TO PRACTICE JUMPING FROM HERE WITH YOUR UMBRELLA OPEN.
IF YOU CAN LEARN HOW TO GENTLY LAND ON THE RIVER, THEN YOU'LL BE ABLE TO LEARN *ANYTHING*.
OH.
FIRST, YOU HAVE TO STOP THINKING OF YOUR *KUSARI-JITTE* AND *KAGINAWA* AS THINGS TO BE THROWN.
MOREOVER, YOU HAVE TO STRIKE *WITH* LIFE *FOR* LIFE.

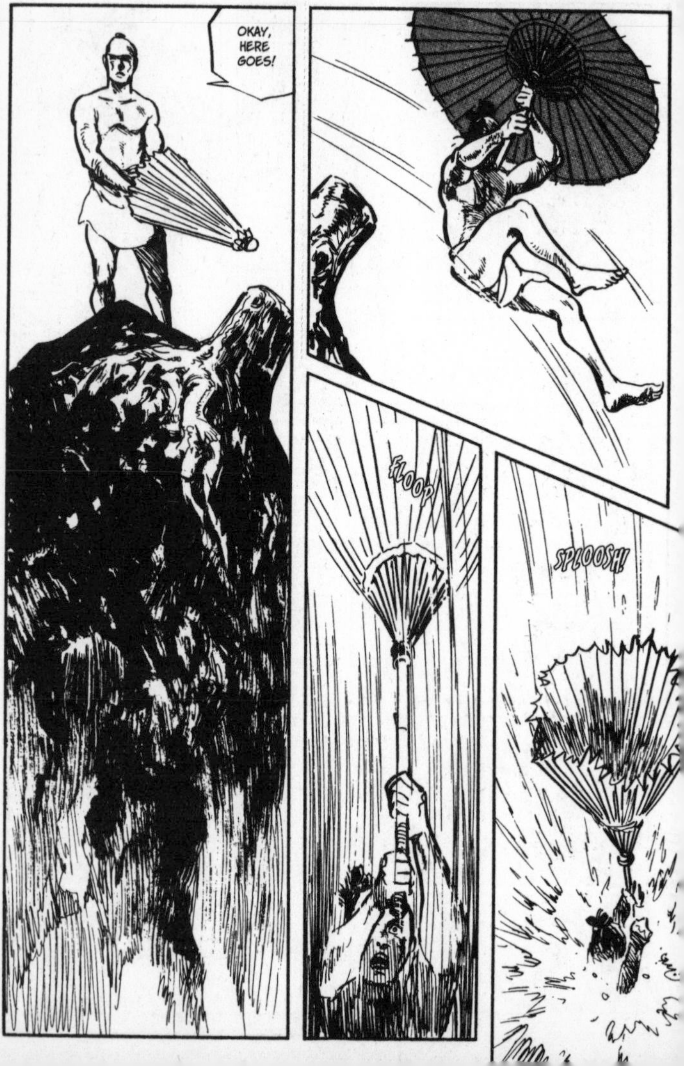
OKAY, HERE GOES!
FLOOP
SPLOOSH!

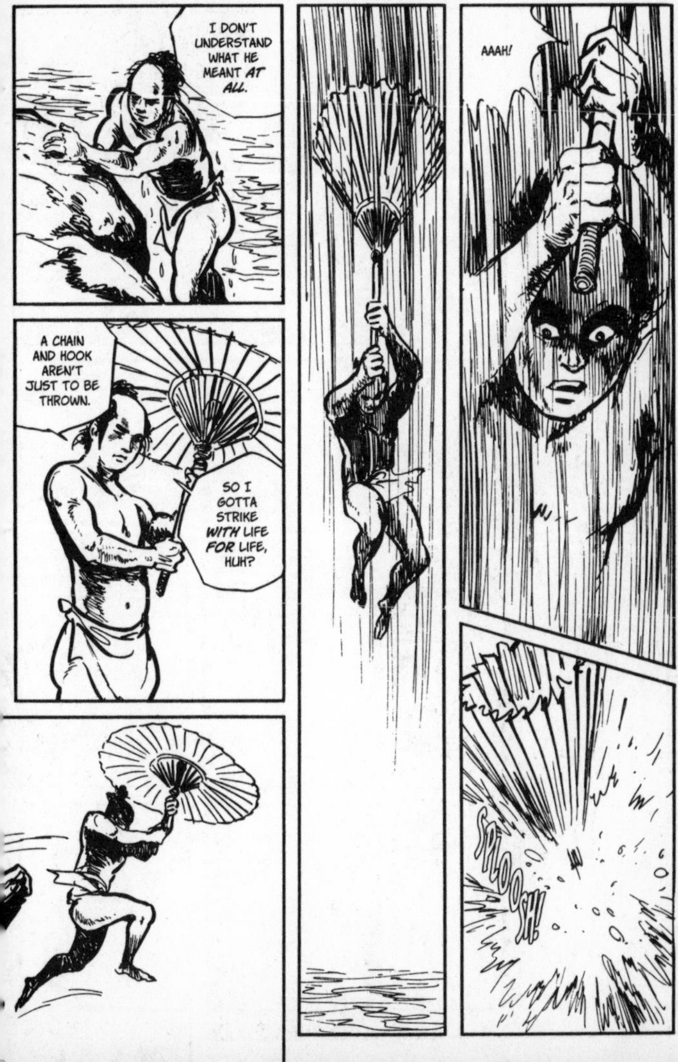
I DON'T UNDERSTAND WHAT HE MEANT AT ALL.
A CHAIN AND HOOK AREN'T JUST TO BE THROWN.
SO I GOTTA STRIKE WITH LIFE FOR LIFE, HUH?
AAAH!
SPLOOSH!

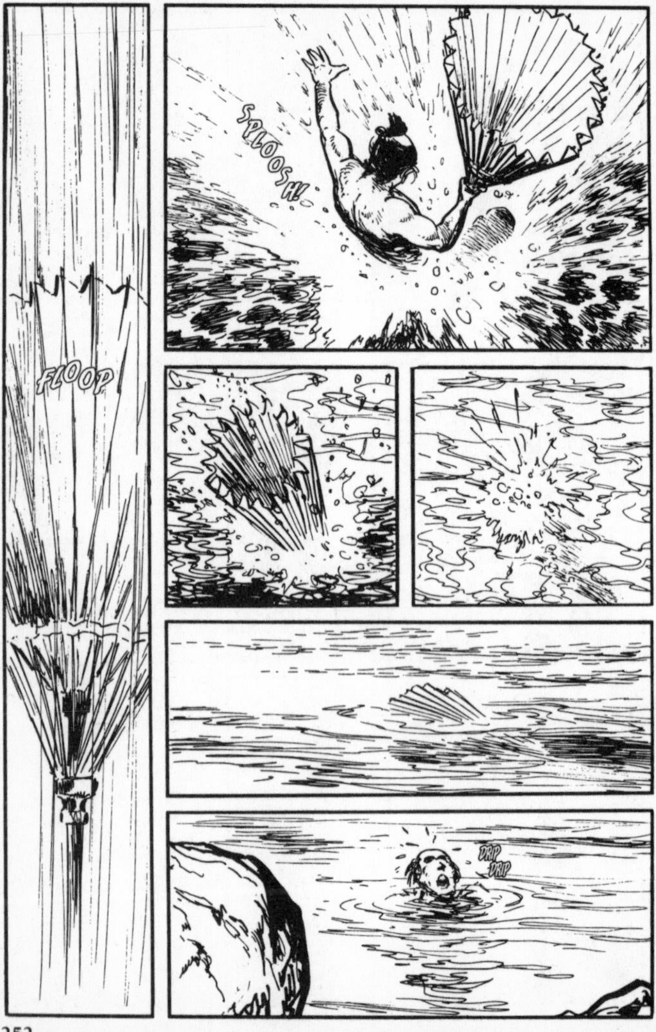
FLOOP
SPLOOSH!
DRIP
DRIP

NOW I GET IT!
NOW I GET IT!
THAT'S WHAT YAMADA-SAMA MEANT...
WHEN HE SAID THAT A CHAIN AND HOOK AREN'T JUST TO BE THROWN...
...THAT I HAVE TO STRIKE WITH LIFE FOR LIFE.
NOW I GET IT...

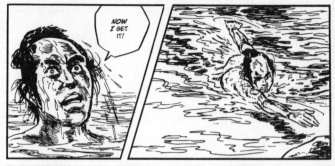

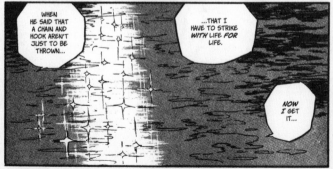

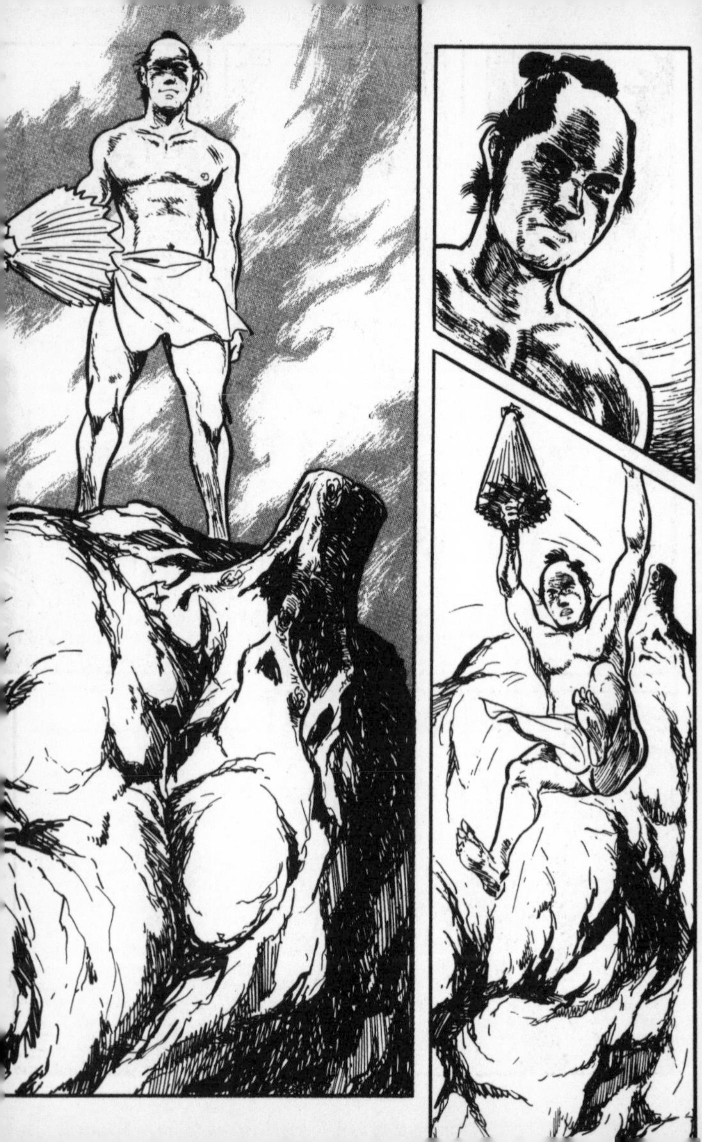

FLOOP

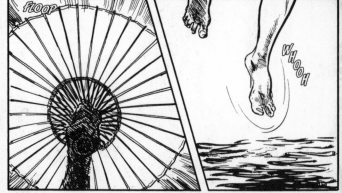

WHOOH

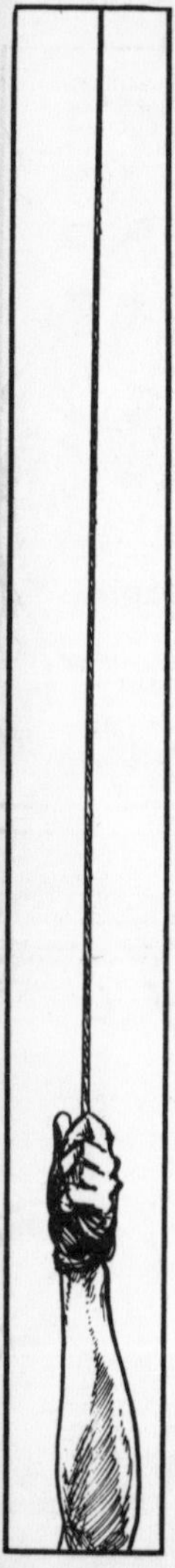

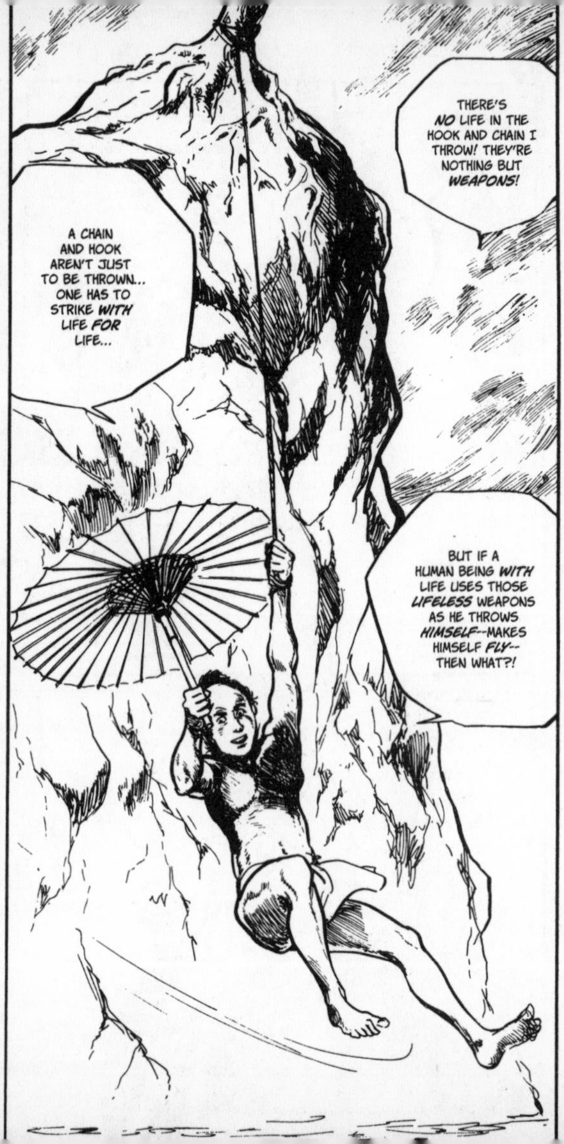
A CHAIN AND HOOK AREN'T JUST TO BE THROWN... ONE HAS TO STRIKE *WITH* LIFE *FOR* LIFE...
THERE'S *NO* LIFE IN THE HOOK AND CHAIN I THROW! THEY'RE NOTHING BUT *WEAPONS!*
BUT IF A HUMAN BEING *WITH* LIFE USES THOSE *LIFELESS* WEAPONS AS HE THROWS *HIMSELF*--MAKES HIMSELF *FLY*-- THEN WHAT?!

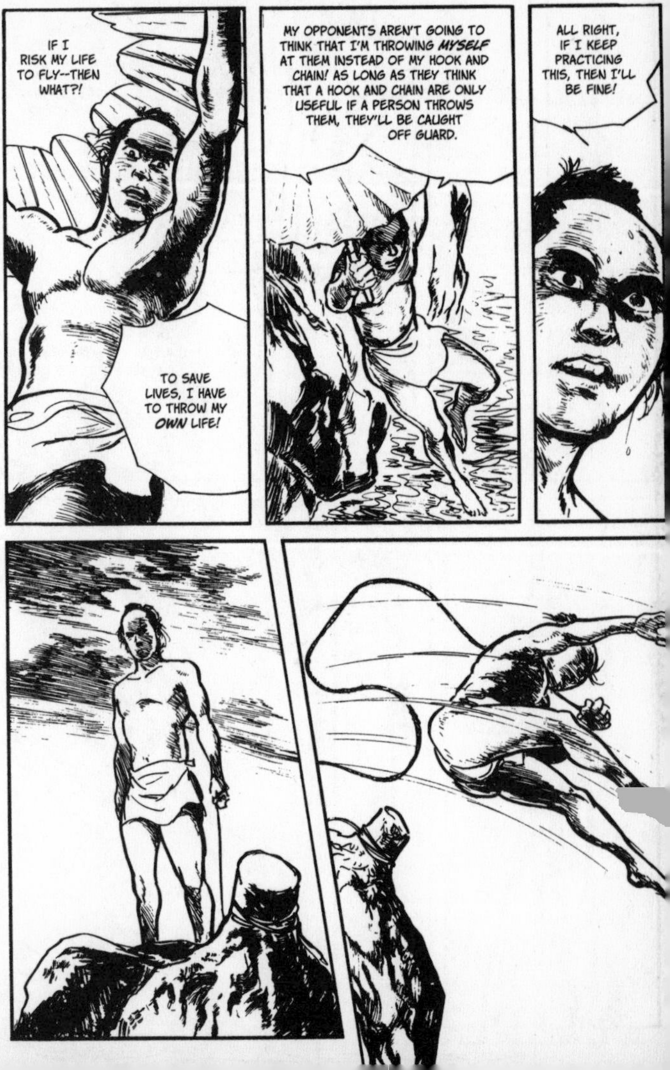
IF I RISK MY LIFE TO FLY--THEN WHAT?!
TO SAVE LIVES, I HAVE TO THROW MY *OWN* LIFE!
MY OPPONENTS AREN'T GOING TO THINK THAT I'M THROWING ***MYSELF*** AT THEM INSTEAD OF MY HOOK AND CHAIN! AS LONG AS THEY THINK THAT A HOOK AND CHAIN ARE ONLY USEFUL IF A PERSON THROWS THEM, THEY'LL BE CAUGHT OFF GUARD.
ALL RIGHT, IF I KEEP PRACTICING THIS, THEN I'LL BE FINE!

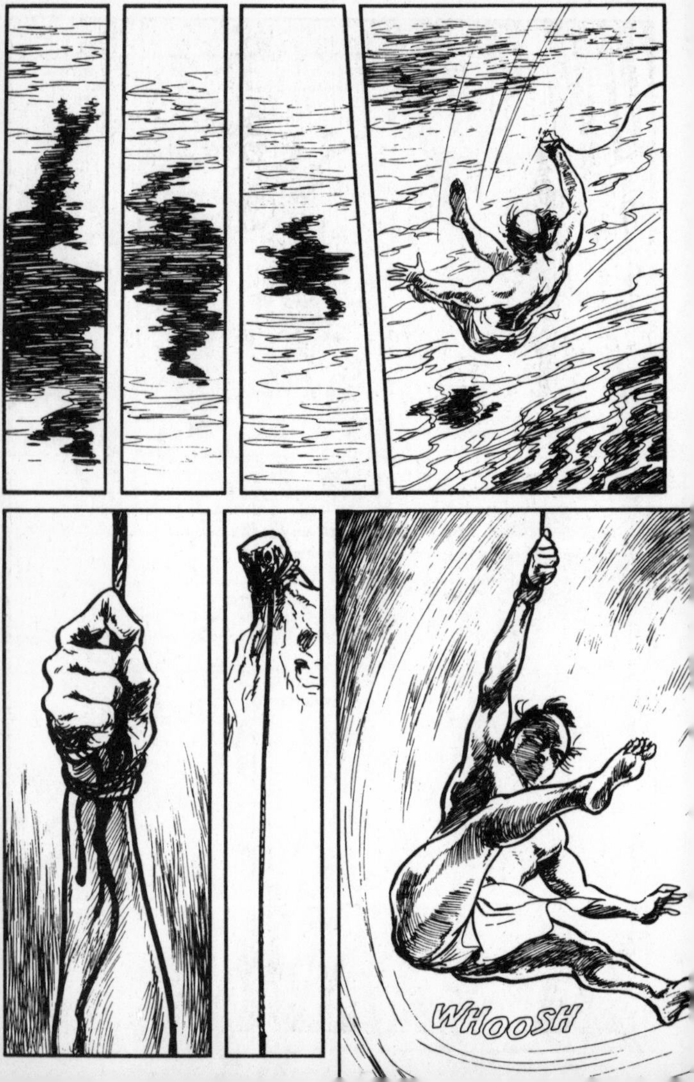
WHOOSH

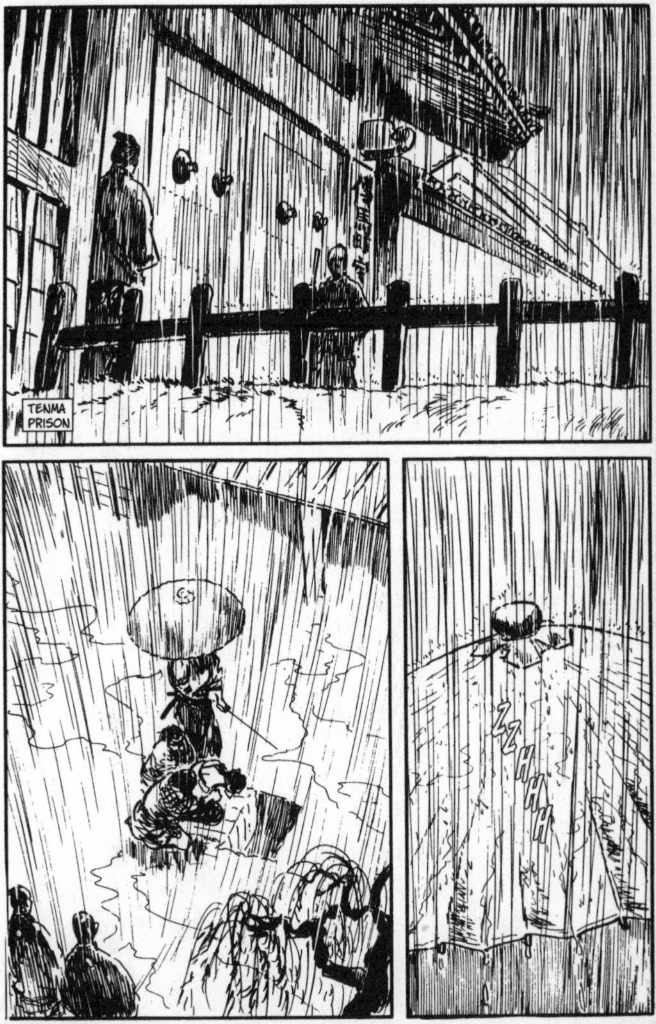
TENMA PRISON
ZZHHHH

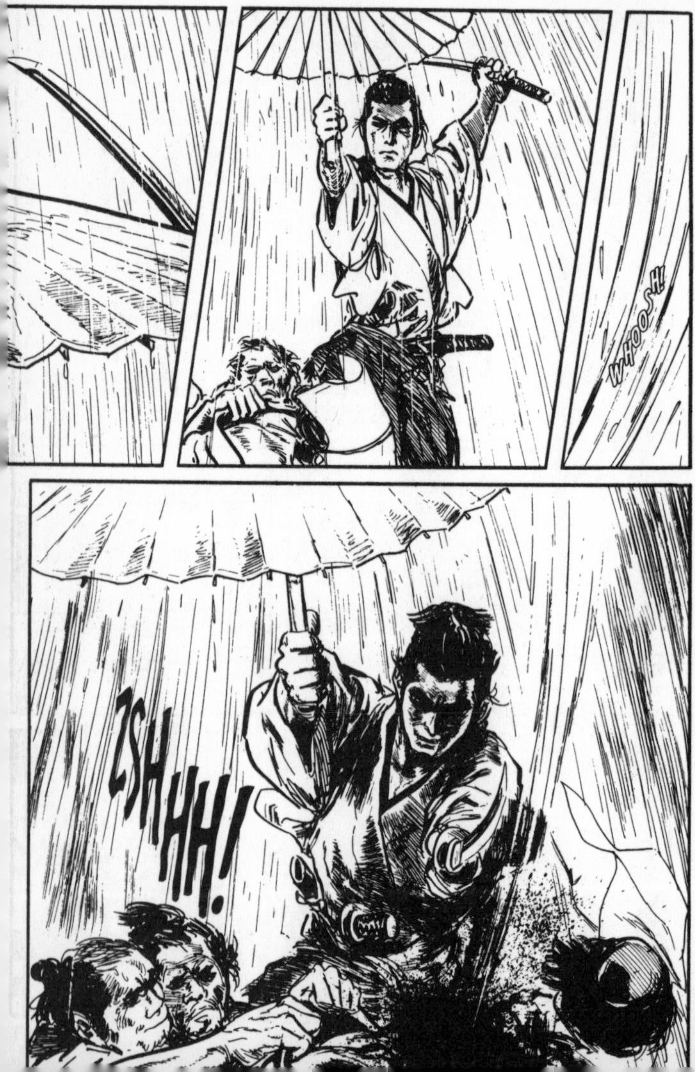
WHOOSH!
ZSHHH!

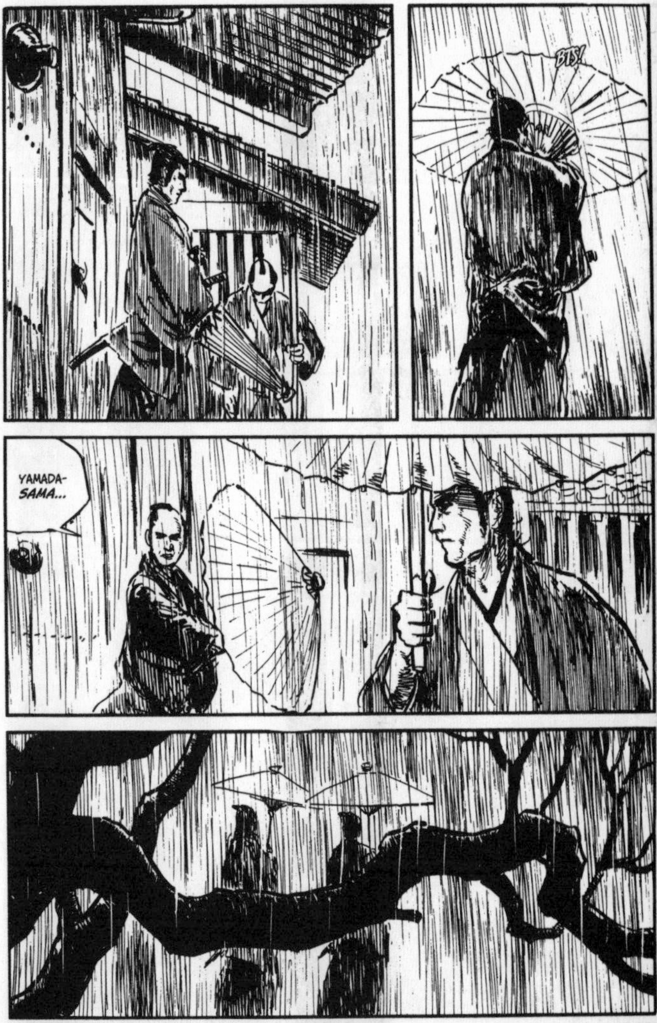
BTS!
YAMADA-SAMA...

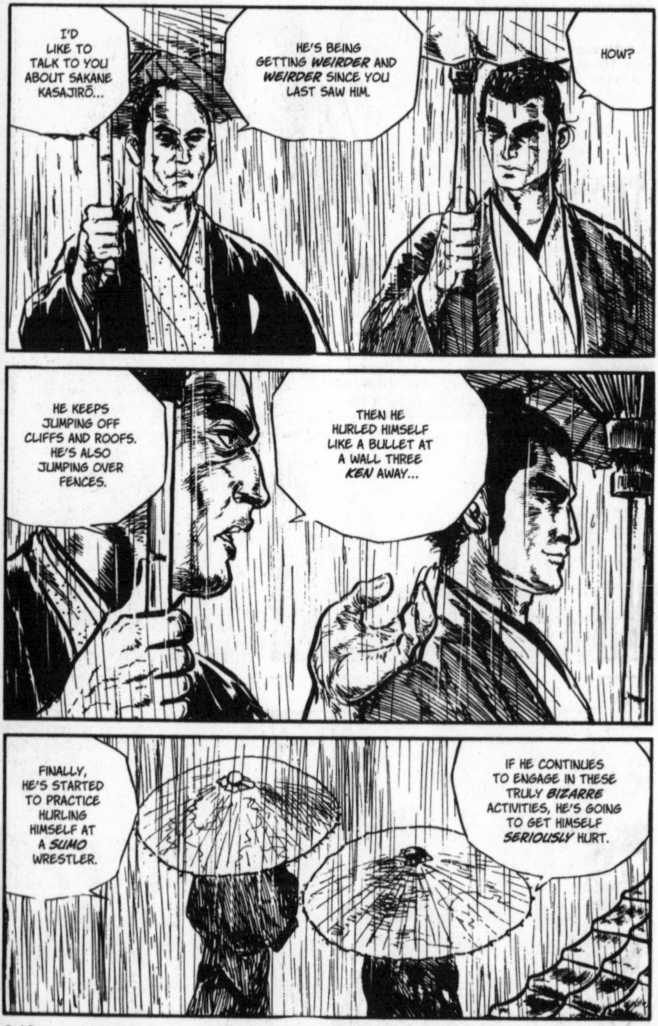

I'D LIKE TO TALK TO YOU ABOUT SAKANE KASAJIRŌ...
HE'S BEING GETTING *WEIRDER* AND *WEIRDER* SINCE YOU LAST SAW HIM.
HOW?
HE KEEPS JUMPING OFF CLIFFS AND ROOFS. HE'S ALSO JUMPING OVER FENCES.
THEN HE HURLED HIMSELF LIKE A BULLET AT A WALL THREE *KEN* AWAY...
FINALLY, HE'S STARTED TO PRACTICE HURLING HIMSELF AT A *SUMO* WRESTLER.
IF HE CONTINUES TO ENGAGE IN THESE TRULY *BIZARRE* ACTIVITIES, HE'S GOING TO GET HIMSELF *SERIOUSLY* HURT.

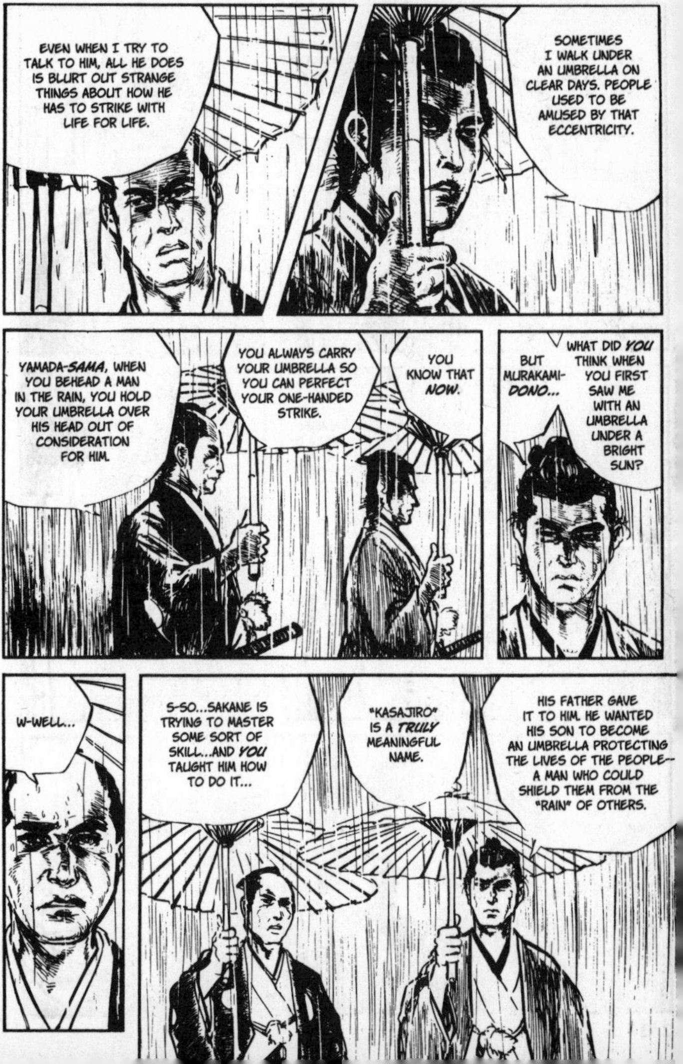
EVEN WHEN I TRY TO TALK TO HIM, ALL HE DOES IS BLURT OUT STRANGE THINGS ABOUT HOW HE HAS TO STRIKE WITH LIFE FOR LIFE.
SOMETIMES I WALK UNDER AN UMBRELLA ON CLEAR DAYS. PEOPLE USED TO BE AMUSED BY THAT ECCENTRICITY.
YAMADA-*SAMA*, WHEN YOU BEHEAD A MAN IN THE RAIN, YOU HOLD YOUR UMBRELLA OVER HIS HEAD OUT OF CONSIDERATION FOR HIM.
YOU ALWAYS CARRY YOUR UMBRELLA SO YOU CAN PERFECT YOUR ONE-HANDED STRIKE.
YOU KNOW THAT *NOW*.
BUT MURAKAMI-*DONO*...
WHAT DID *YOU* THINK WHEN YOU FIRST SAW ME WITH AN UMBRELLA UNDER A BRIGHT SUN?
W-WELL...
S-SO...SAKANE IS TRYING TO MASTER SOME SORT OF SKILL...AND *YOU* TAUGHT HIM HOW TO DO IT...
"KASAJIRO" IS A *TRULY* MEANINGFUL NAME.
HIS FATHER GAVE IT TO HIM. HE WANTED HIS SON TO BECOME AN UMBRELLA PROTECTING THE LIVES OF THE PEOPLE-- A MAN WHO COULD SHIELD THEM FROM THE "RAIN" OF OTHERS.

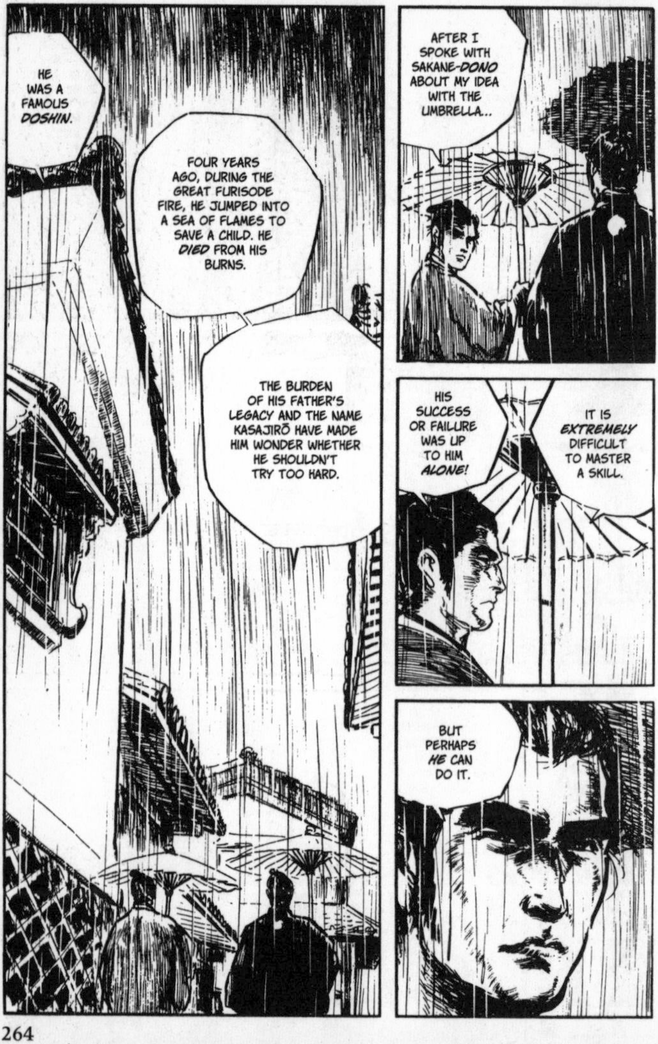
HE WAS A FAMOUS *DOSHIN*.
FOUR YEARS AGO, DURING THE GREAT FURISODE FIRE, HE JUMPED INTO A SEA OF FLAMES TO SAVE A CHILD. HE *DIED* FROM HIS BURNS.
THE BURDEN OF HIS FATHER'S LEGACY AND THE NAME KASAJIRŌ HAVE MADE HIM WONDER WHETHER HE SHOULDN'T TRY TOO HARD.
AFTER I SPOKE WITH SAKANE-*DONO* ABOUT MY IDEA WITH THE UMBRELLA...
HIS SUCCESS OR FAILURE WAS UP TO HIM *ALONE!*
IT IS *EXTREMELY* DIFFICULT TO MASTER A SKILL.
BUT PERHAPS *HE* CAN DO IT.

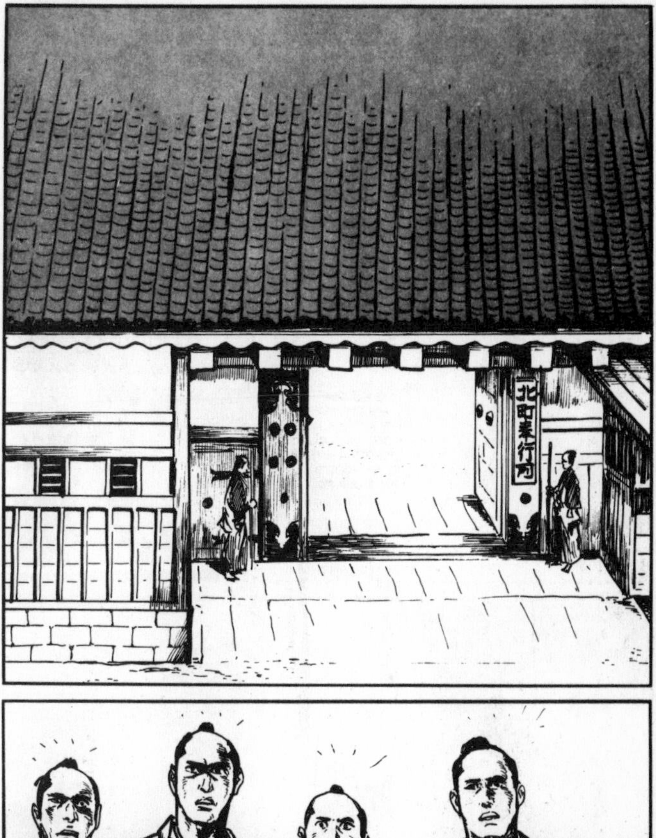
北町奉行所
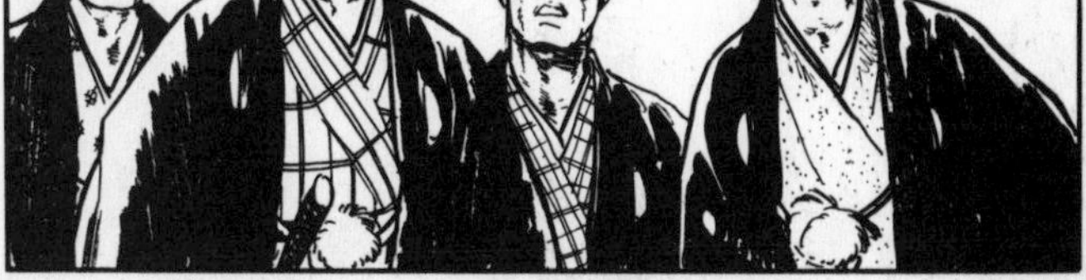

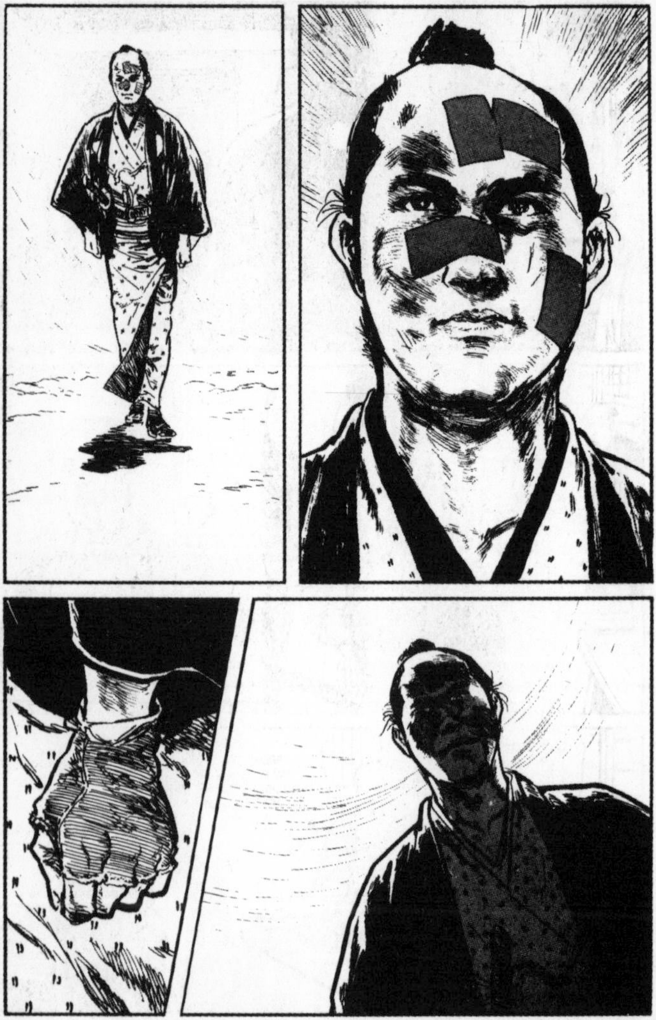

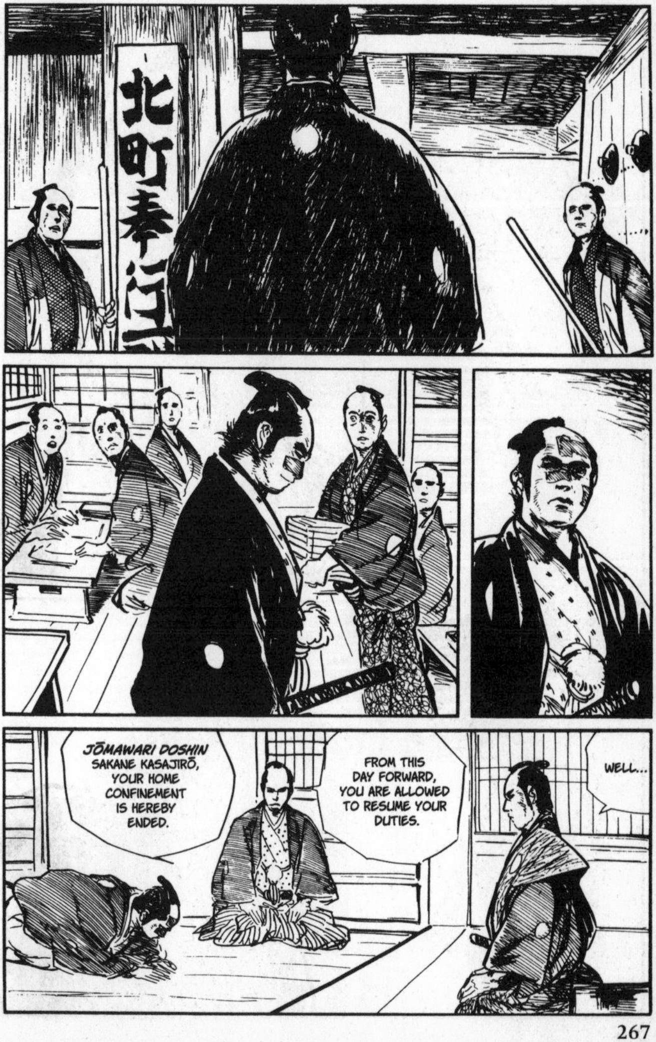
北町奉行
JŌMAWARI DOSHIN SAKANE KASAJIRŌ, YOUR HOME CONFINEMENT IS HEREBY ENDED.
FROM THIS DAY FORWARD, YOU ARE ALLOWED TO RESUME YOUR DUTIES.
WELL...

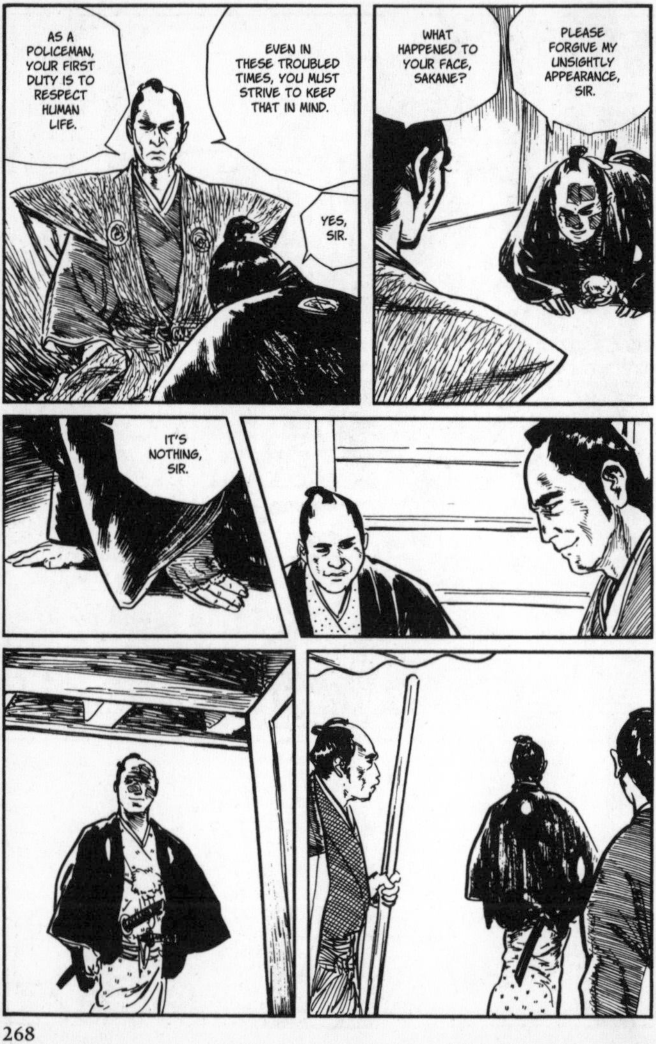
AS A POLICEMAN, YOUR FIRST DUTY IS TO RESPECT HUMAN LIFE.
EVEN IN THESE TROUBLED TIMES, YOU MUST STRIVE TO KEEP THAT IN MIND.
YES, SIR.
WHAT HAPPENED TO YOUR FACE, SAKANE?
PLEASE FORGIVE MY UNSIGHTLY APPEARANCE, SIR.
IT'S NOTHING, SIR.

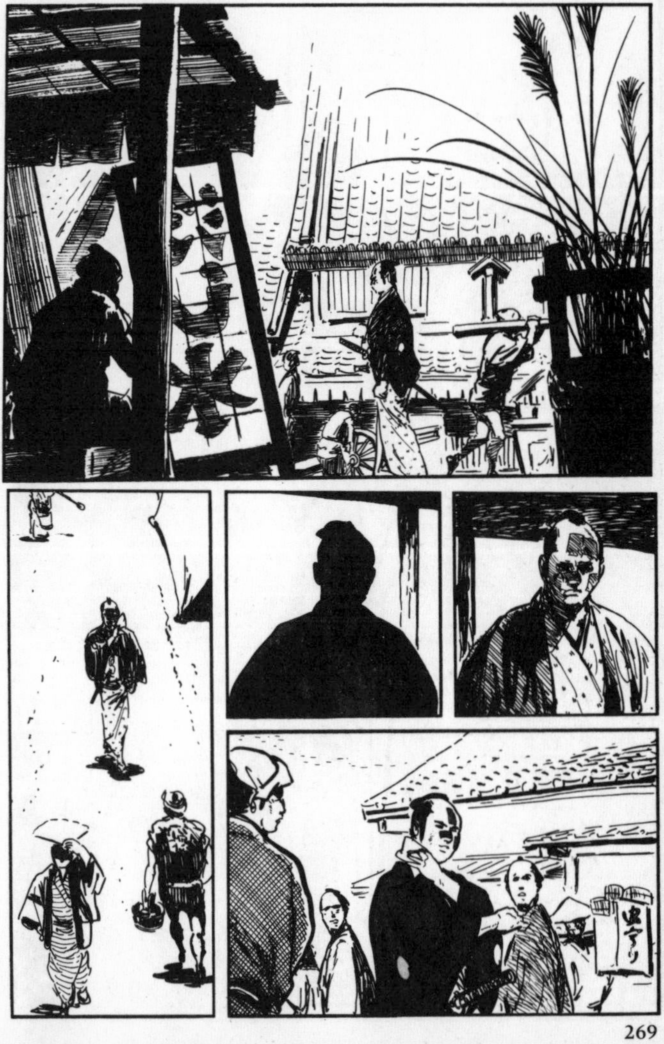

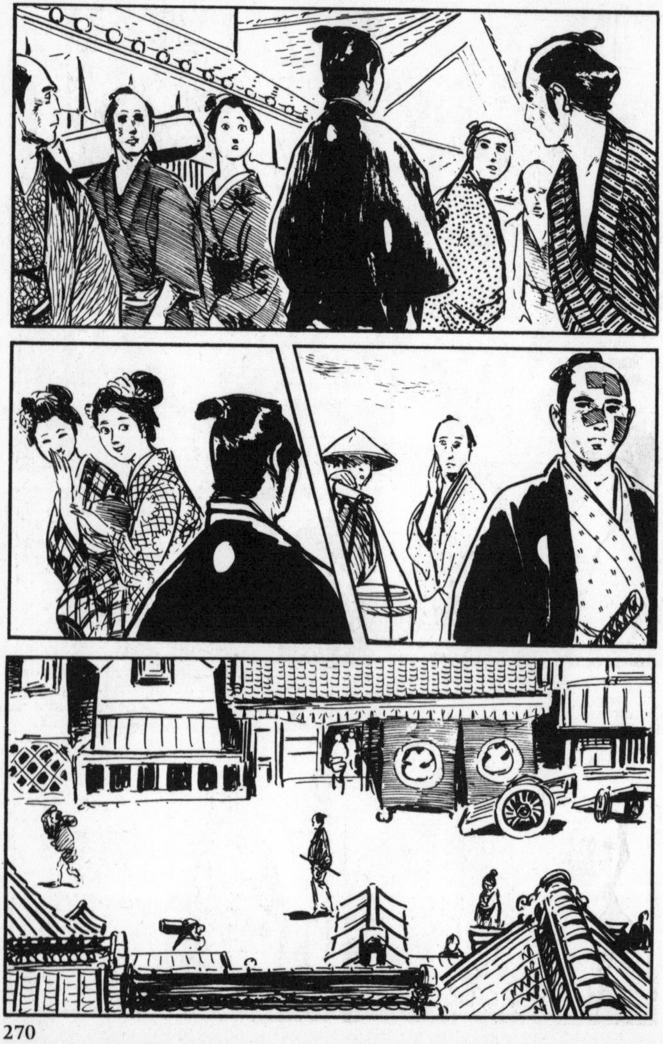

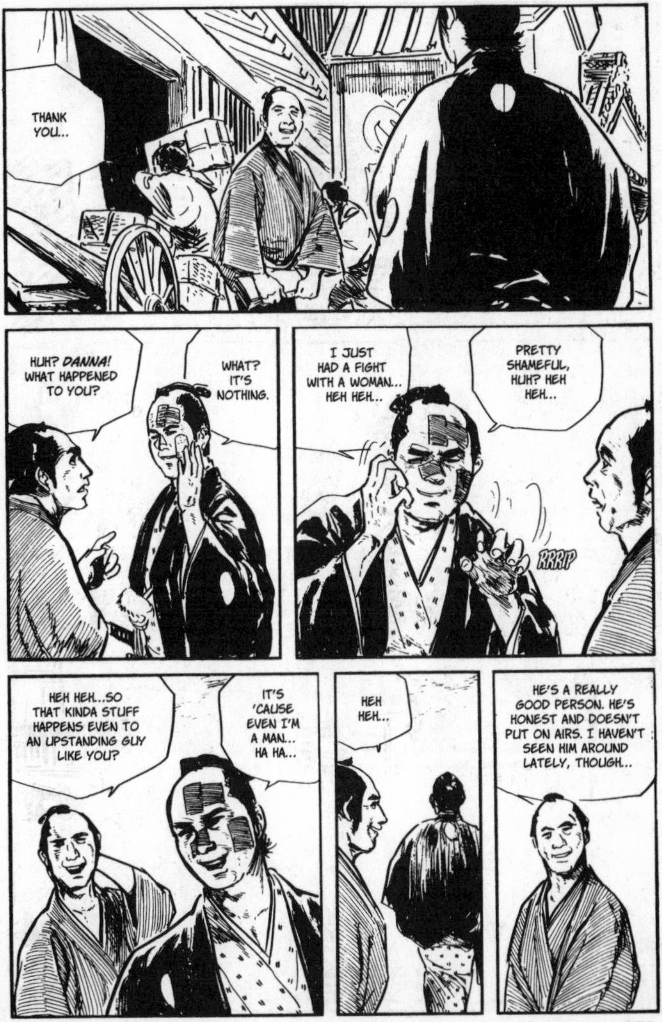

THANK YOU...
HUH? *DANNA!* WHAT HAPPENED TO YOU?
WHAT? IT'S NOTHING.
I JUST HAD A FIGHT WITH A WOMAN... HEH HEH...
PRETTY SHAMEFUL, HUH? HEH HEH...
RRRIP
HEH HEH...SO THAT KINDA STUFF HAPPENS EVEN TO AN UPSTANDING GUY LIKE YOU?
IT'S 'CAUSE EVEN I'M A MAN... HA HA...
HEH HEH...
HE'S A REALLY GOOD PERSON. HE'S HONEST AND DOESN'T PUT ON AIRS. I HAVEN'T SEEN HIM AROUND LATELY, THOUGH...

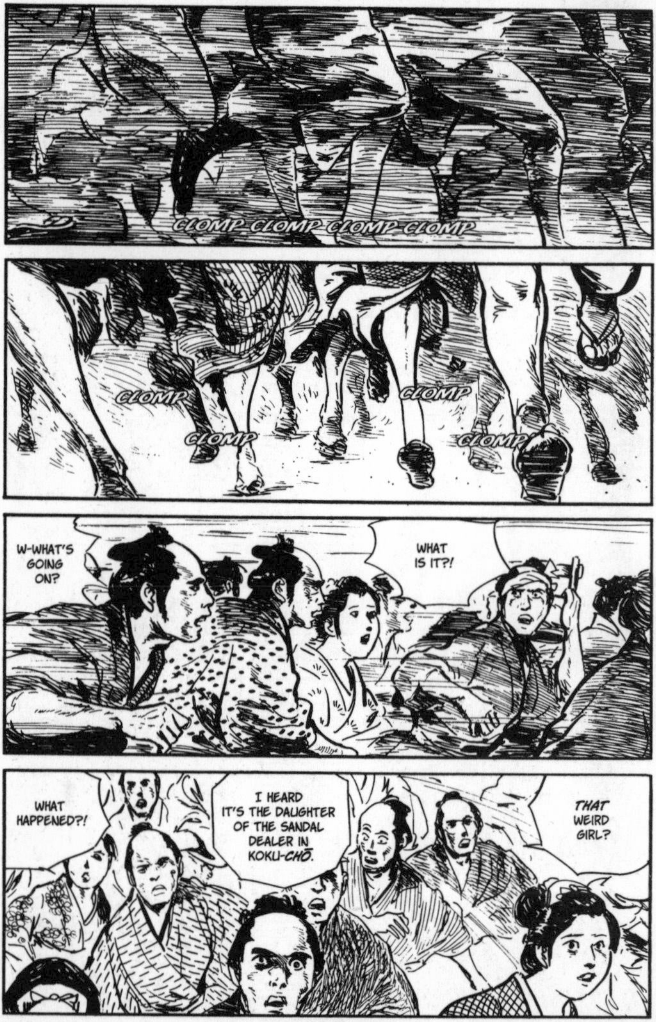
CLOMP CLOMP CLOMP CLOMP
CLOMP
CLOMP
CLOMP
CLOMP
W-WHAT'S GOING ON?
WHAT IS IT?!
WHAT HAPPENED?!
I HEARD IT'S THE DAUGHTER OF THE SANDAL DEALER IN KOKU-*CHŌ*.
THAT WEIRD GIRL?

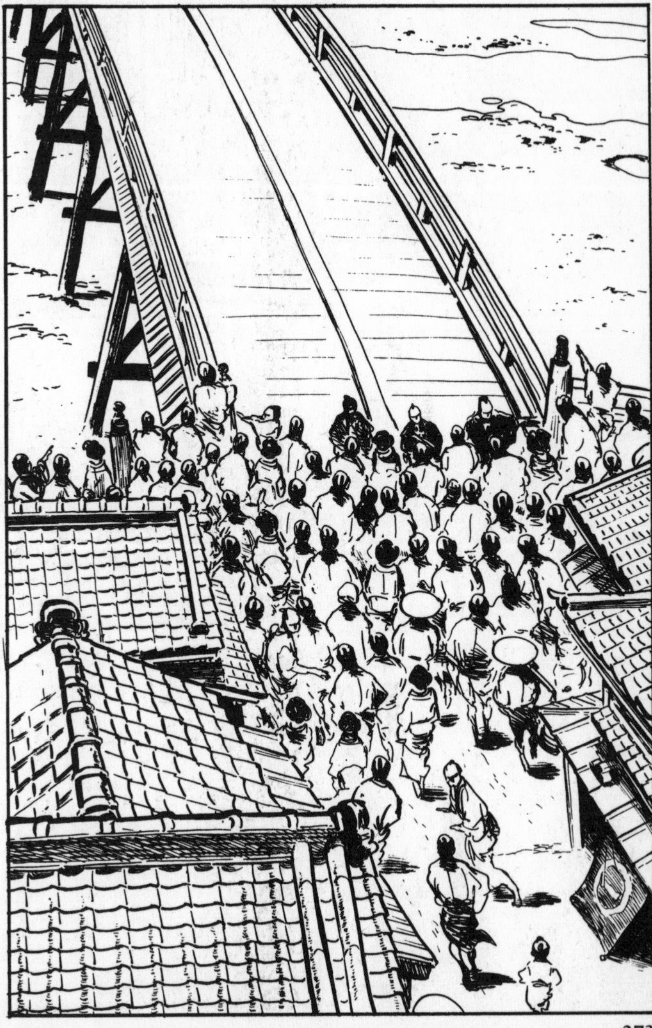

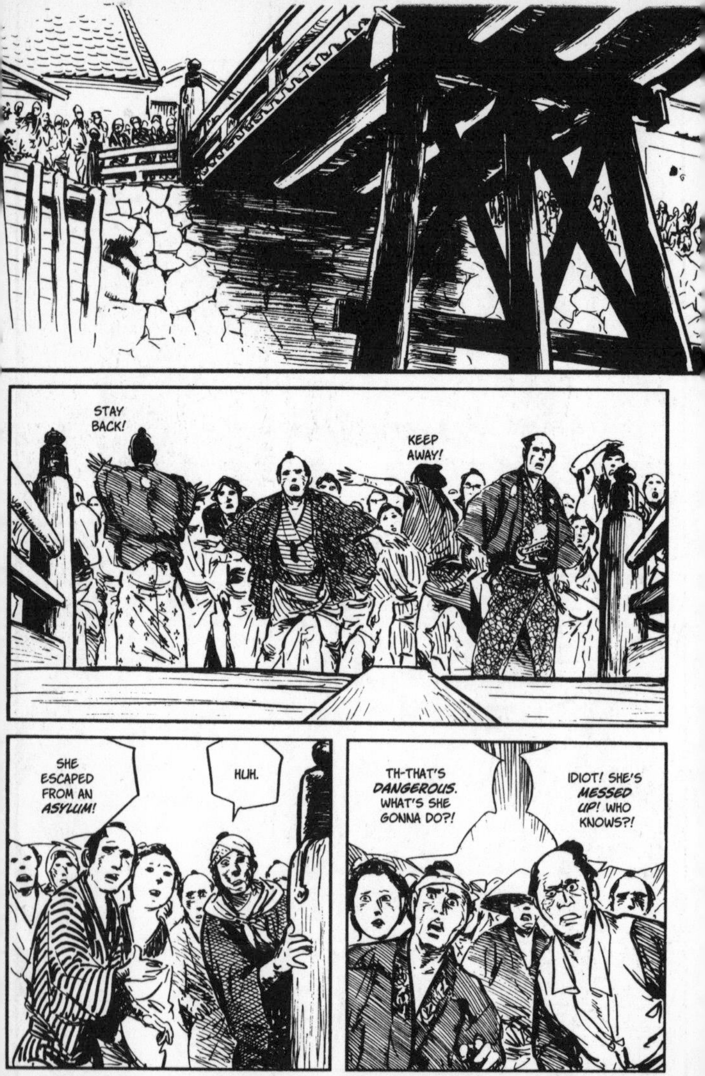

STAY BACK!
KEEP AWAY!
SHE ESCAPED FROM AN *ASYLUM!*
HUH.
TH-THAT'S *DANGEROUS.* WHAT'S SHE GONNA DO?!
IDIOT! SHE'S *MESSED UP!* WHO KNOWS?!

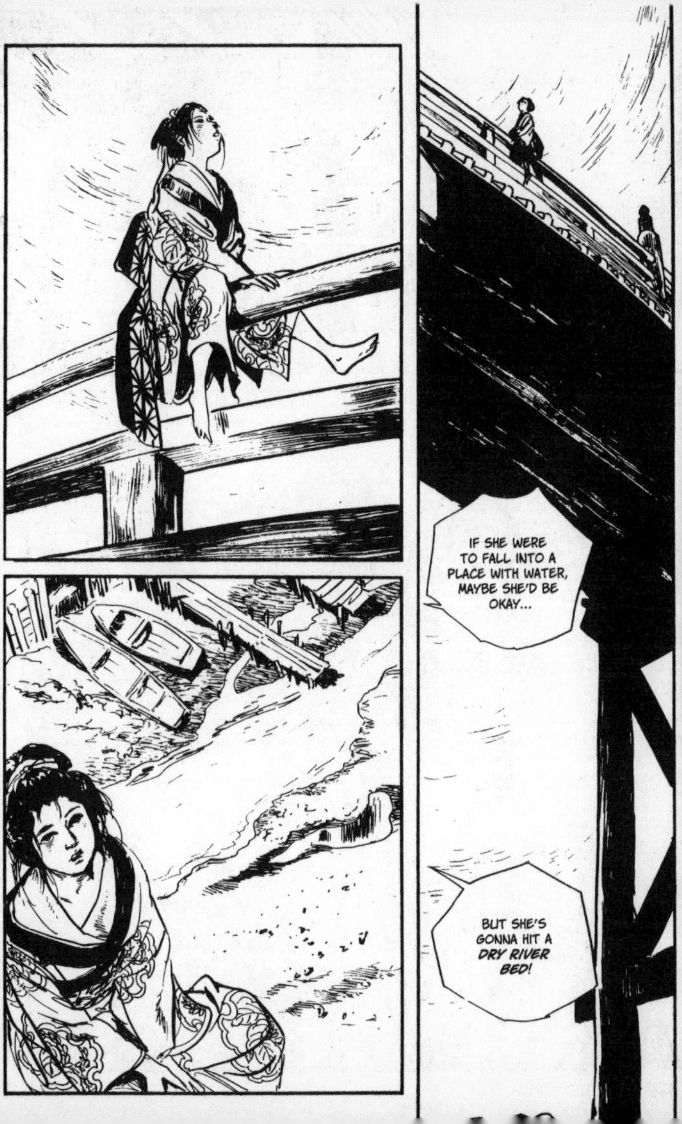
IF SHE WERE TO FALL INTO A PLACE WITH WATER, MAYBE SHE'D BE OKAY...
BUT SHE'S GONNA HIT A *DRY RIVER BED!*

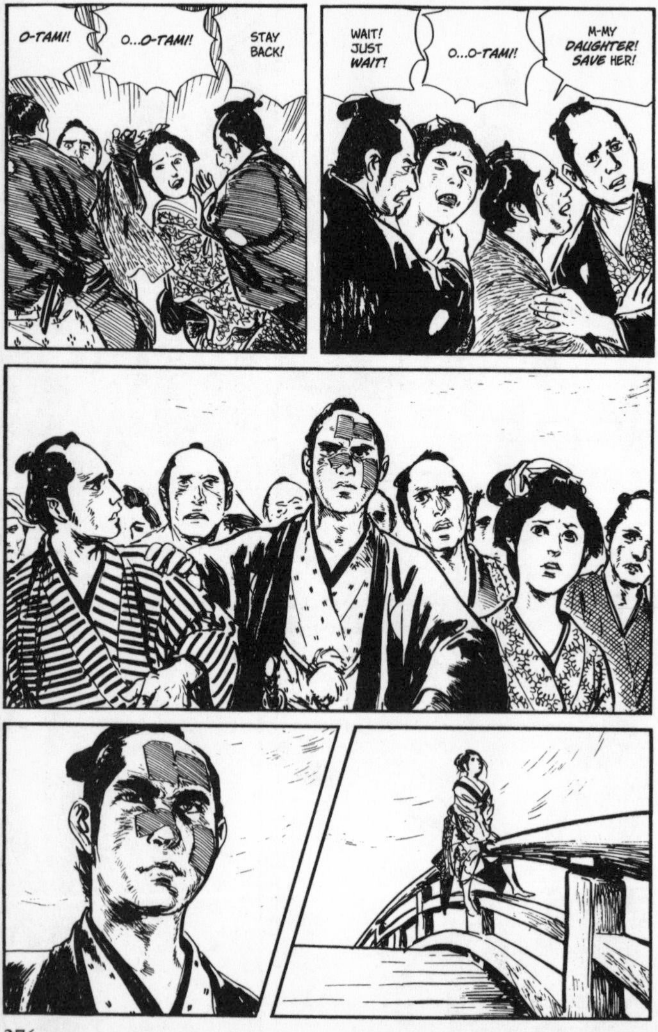
O-TAMI!
O...O-TAMI!
STAY BACK!
WAIT! JUST WAIT!
O...O-TAMI!
M-MY DAUGHTER! SAVE HER!

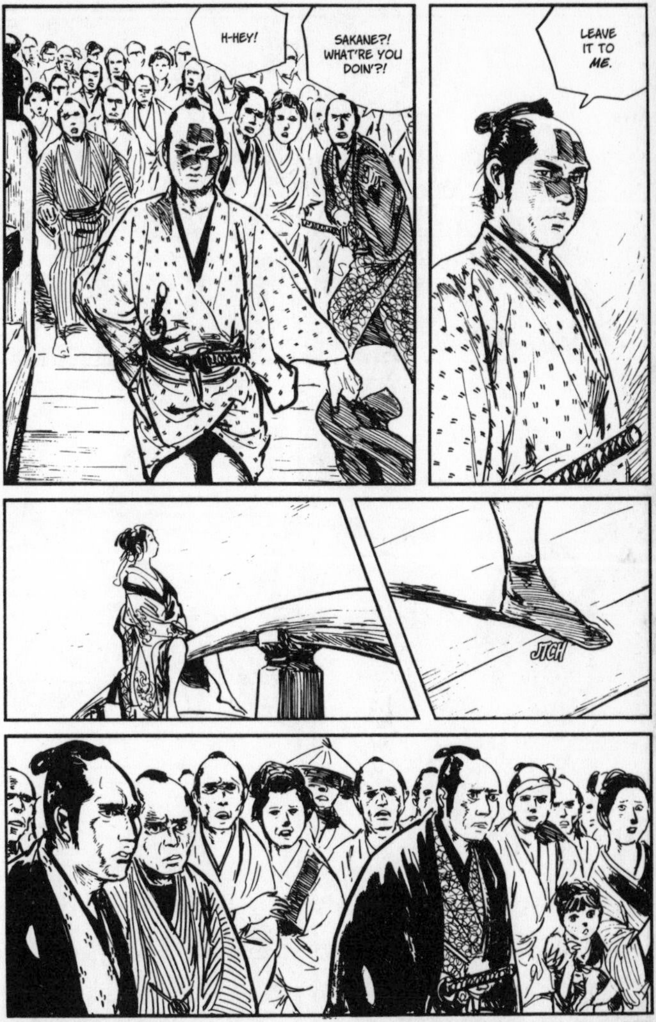
H-HEY!
SAKANE?! WHAT'RE YOU DOIN'?!
LEAVE IT TO ME.
JTCH

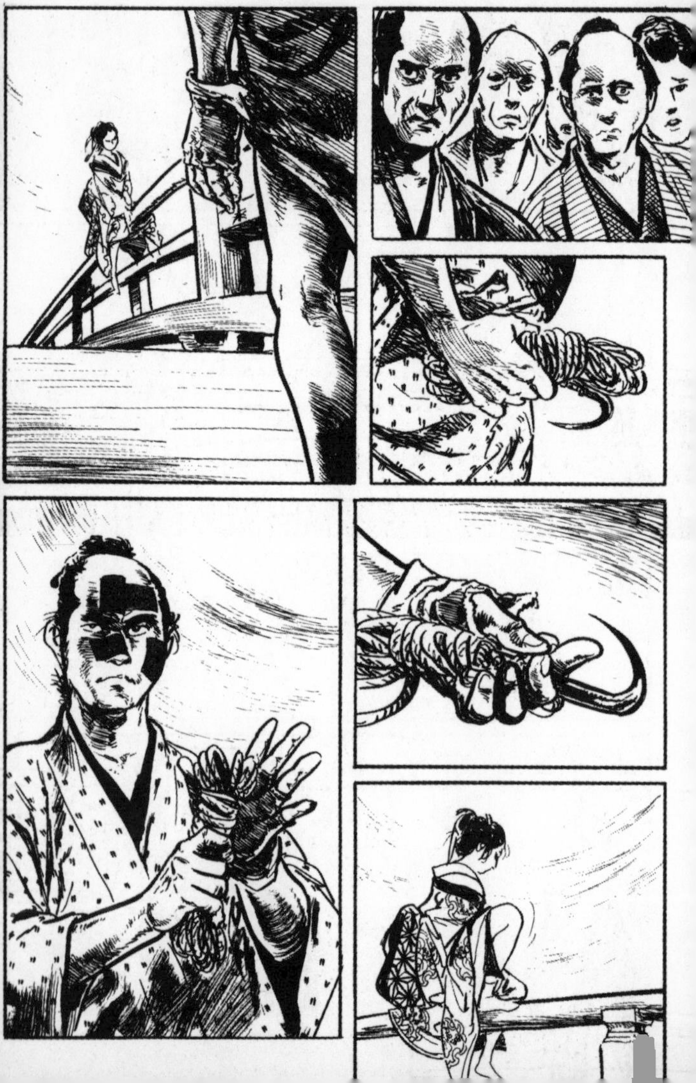

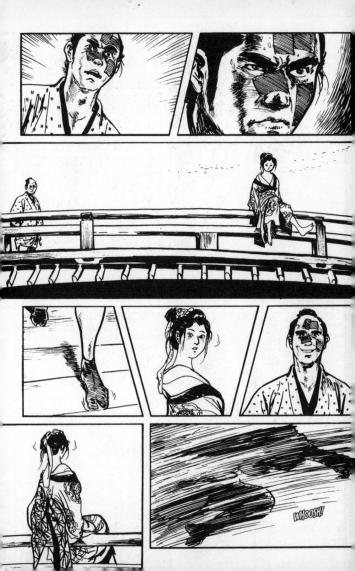

WHOOSH!

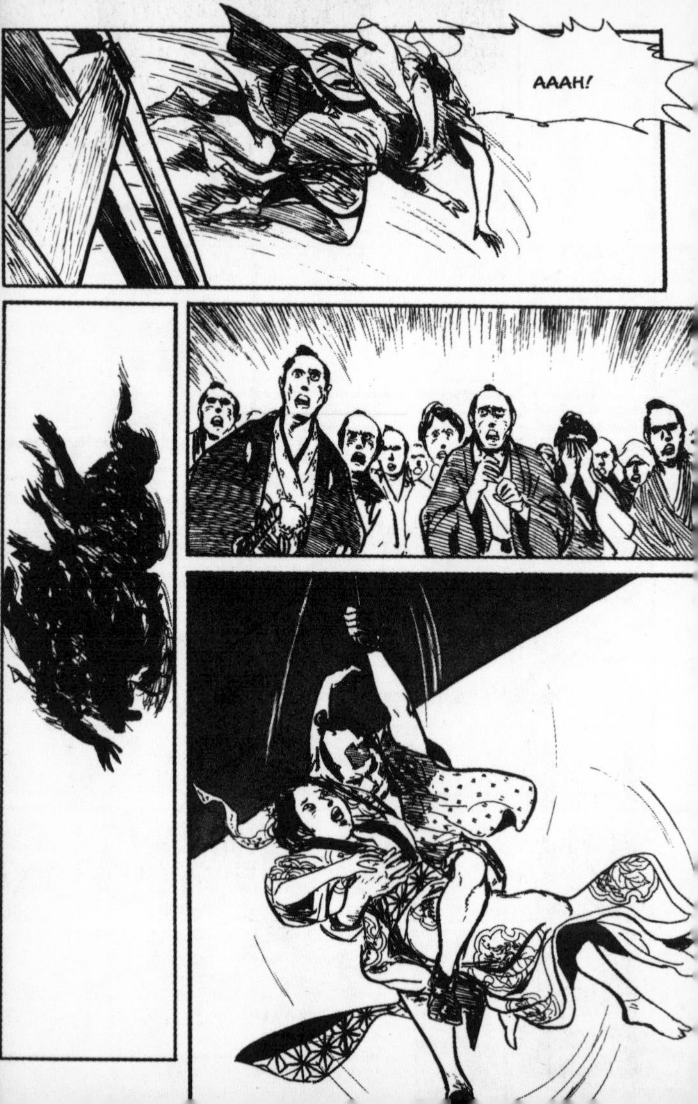
AAAH!

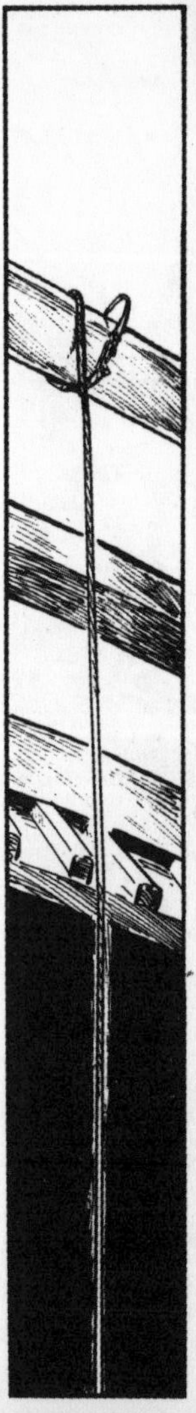

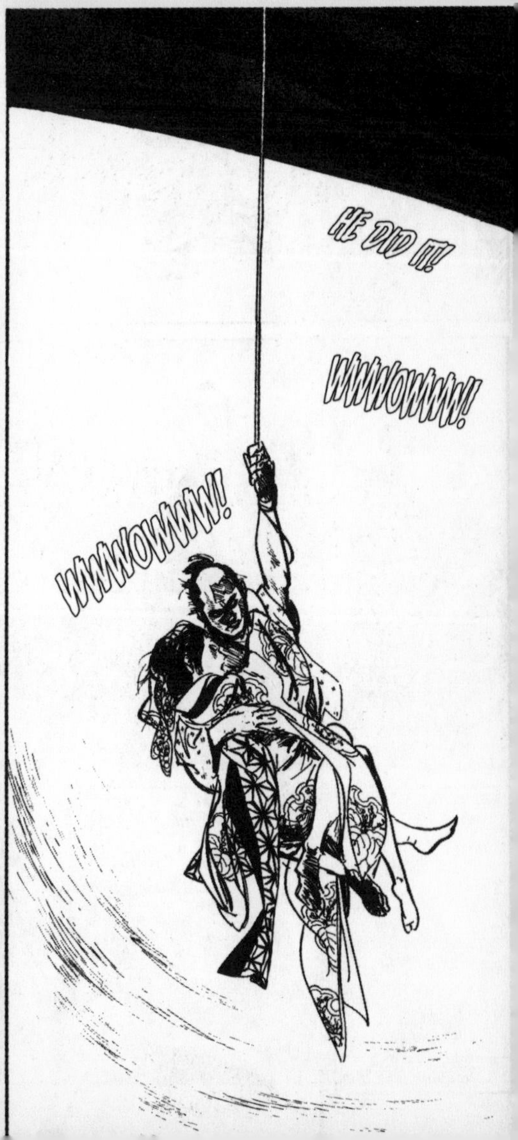
HE DID IT!
WWWOWWWW!
WWWOWWWW!

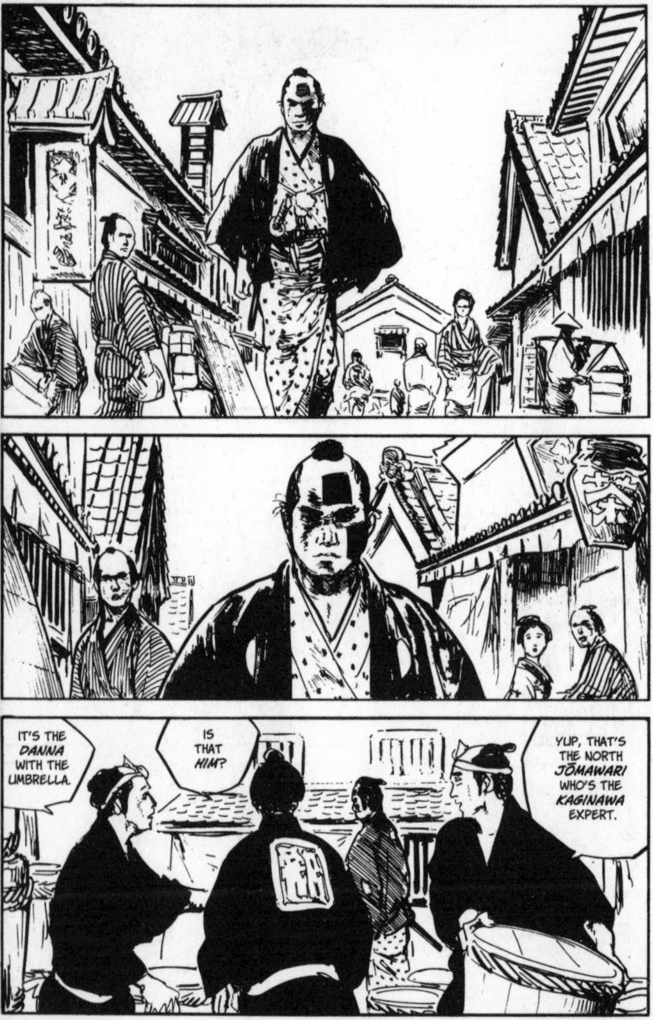
IT'S THE *DANNA* WITH THE UMBRELLA.
IS THAT *HIM?*
YUP, THAT'S THE NORTH *JŌMAWARI* WHO'S THE *KAGINAWA* EXPERT.

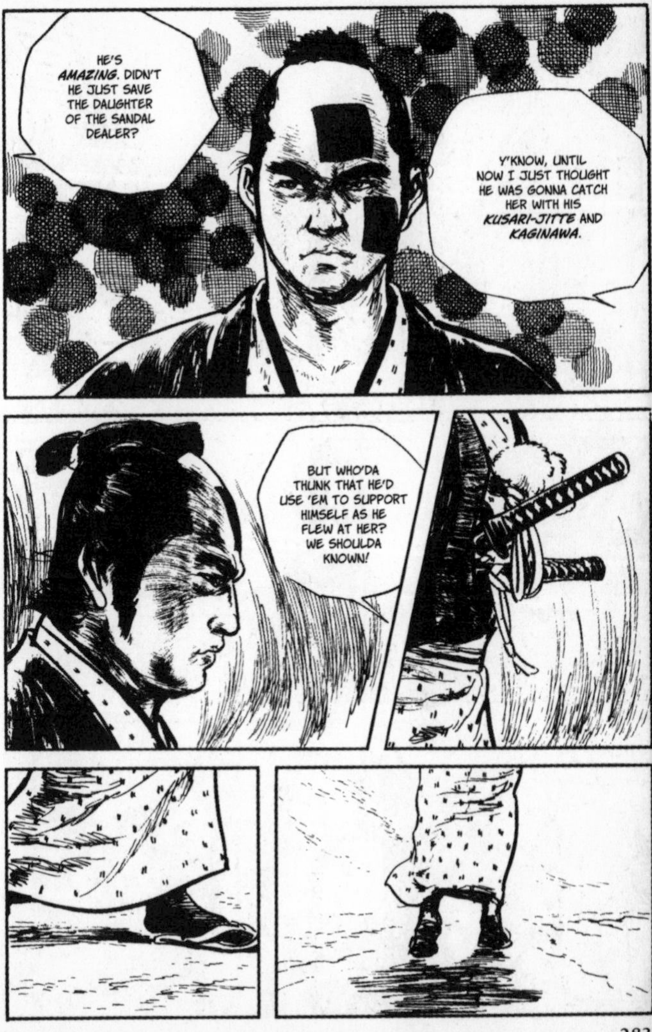
HE'S *AMAZING*. DIDN'T HE JUST SAVE THE DAUGHTER OF THE SANDAL DEALER?
Y'KNOW, UNTIL NOW I JUST THOUGHT HE WAS GONNA CATCH HER WITH HIS *KUSARI-JITTE* AND *KAGINAWA*.
BUT WHO'DA THUNK THAT HE'D USE 'EM TO SUPPORT HIMSELF AS HE FLEW AT HER? WE SHOULDA KNOWN!

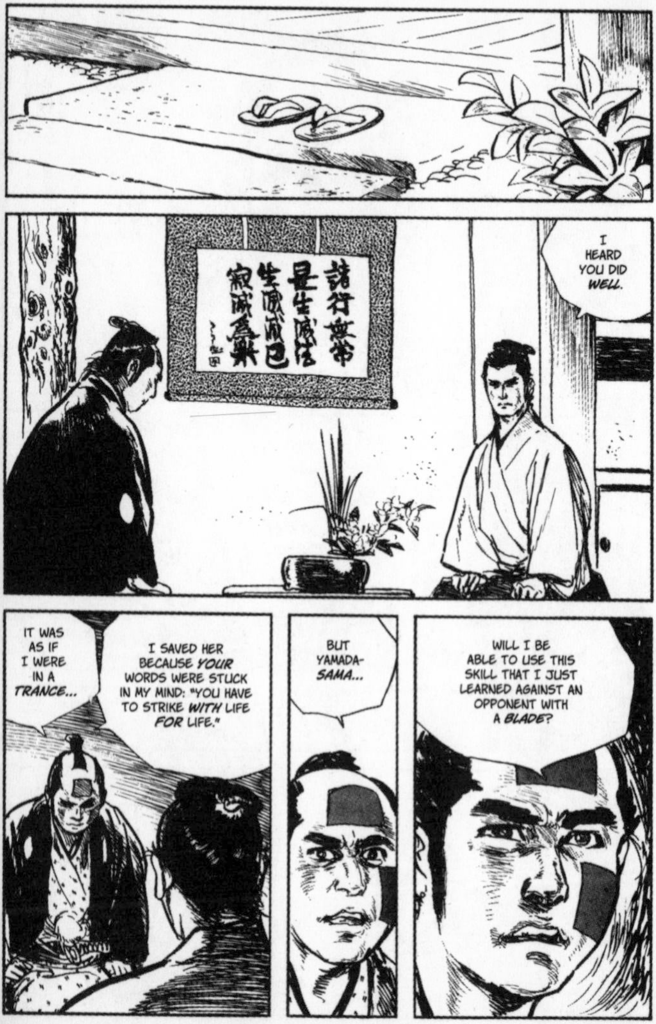
諸行無常
是生滅法
生滅滅已
寂滅爲樂
I HEARD YOU DID *WELL.*
IT WAS AS IF I WERE IN A *TRANCE...*
I SAVED HER BECAUSE *YOUR* WORDS WERE STUCK IN MY MIND: "YOU HAVE TO STRIKE *WITH* LIFE *FOR* LIFE."
BUT YAMADA-*SAMA...*
WILL I BE ABLE TO USE THIS SKILL THAT I JUST LEARNED AGAINST AN OPPONENT WITH A *BLADE?*

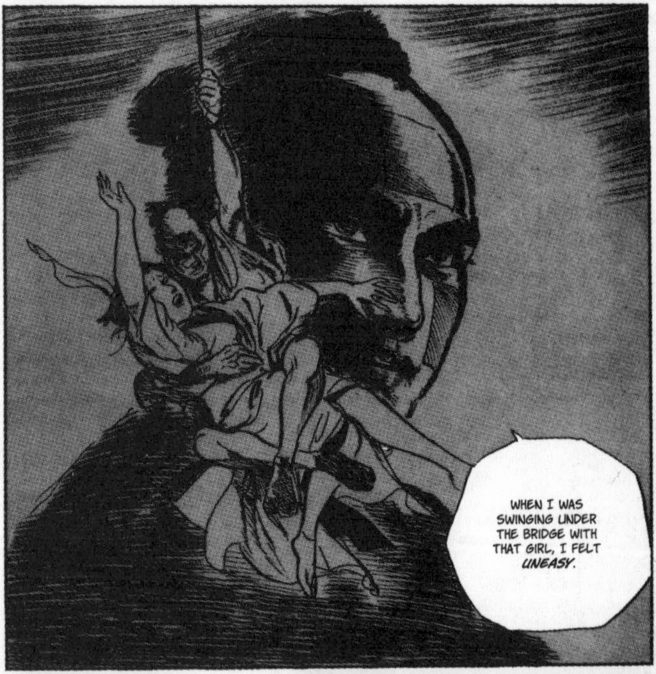
WHEN I WAS SWINGING UNDER THE BRIDGE WITH THAT GIRL, I FELT *UNEASY*.

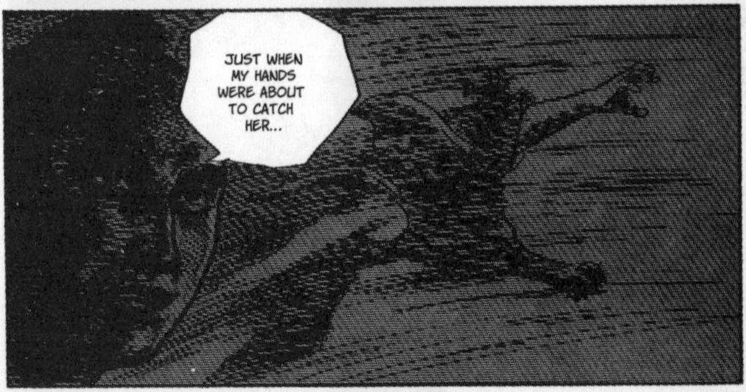
JUST WHEN MY HANDS WERE ABOUT TO CATCH HER...

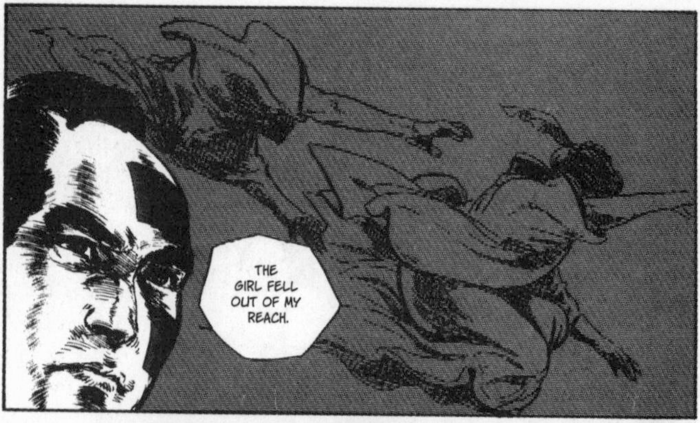
THE GIRL FELL OUT OF MY REACH.
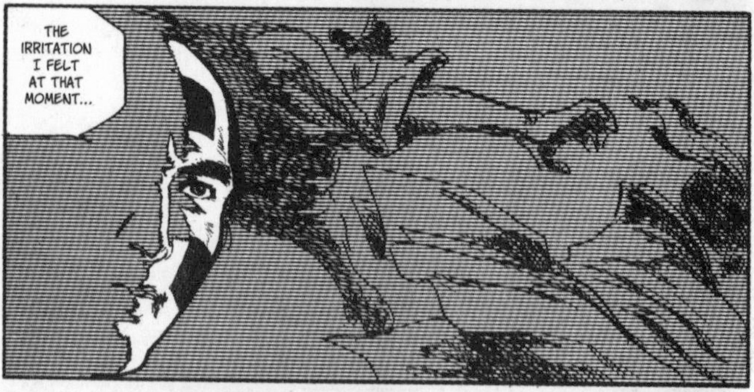
THE IRRITATION I FELT AT THAT MOMENT...
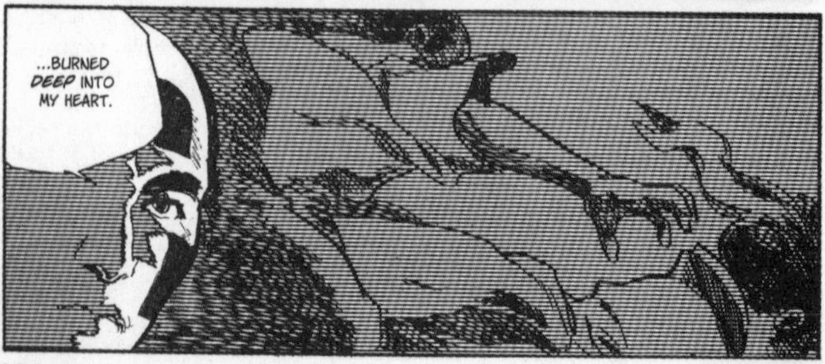
...BURNED *DEEP* INTO MY HEART.

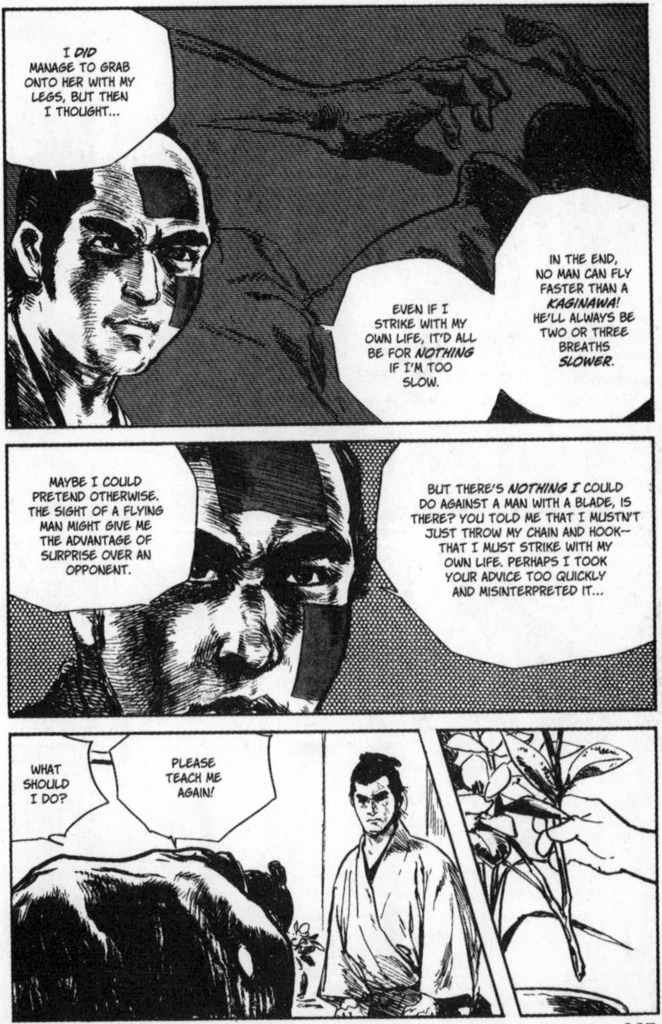
I DID MANAGE TO GRAB ONTO HER WITH MY LEGS, BUT THEN I THOUGHT...
EVEN IF I STRIKE WITH MY OWN LIFE, IT'D ALL BE FOR NOTHING IF I'M TOO SLOW.
IN THE END, NO MAN CAN FLY FASTER THAN A KAGINAWA! HE'LL ALWAYS BE TWO OR THREE BREATHS SLOWER.
MAYBE I COULD PRETEND OTHERWISE. THE SIGHT OF A FLYING MAN MIGHT GIVE ME THE ADVANTAGE OF SURPRISE OVER AN OPPONENT.
BUT THERE'S NOTHING I COULD DO AGAINST A MAN WITH A BLADE, IS THERE? YOU TOLD ME THAT I MUSTN'T JUST THROW MY CHAIN AND HOOK-- THAT I MUST STRIKE WITH MY OWN LIFE. PERHAPS I TOOK YOUR ADVICE TOO QUICKLY AND MISINTERPRETED IT...
WHAT SHOULD I DO?
PLEASE TEACH ME AGAIN!

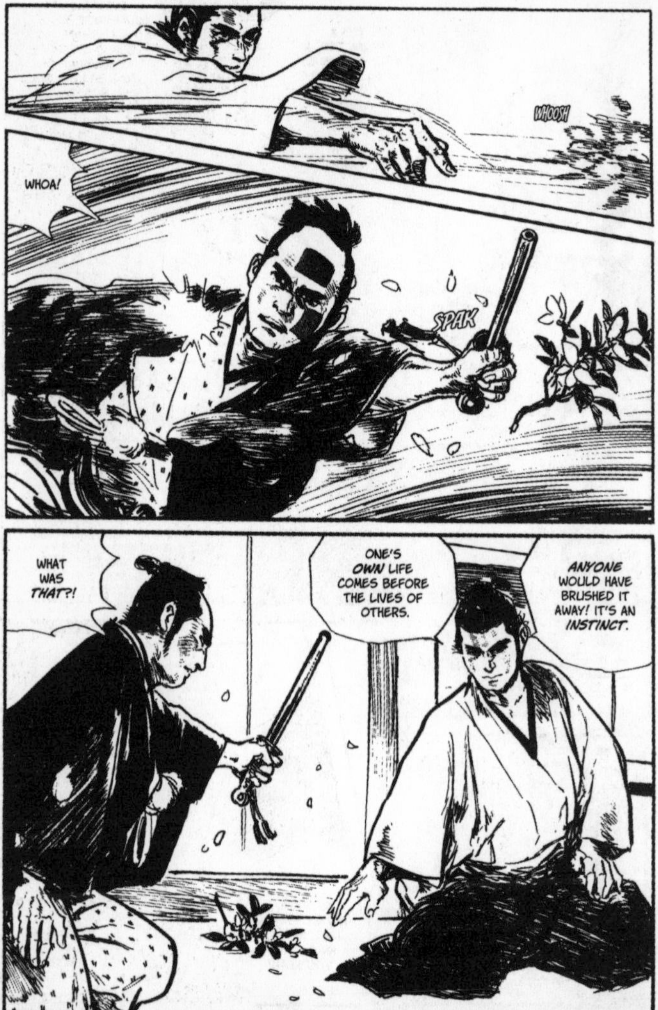
WHOOSH
WHOA!
SPAK
WHAT WAS *THAT?!*
ONE'S *OWN* LIFE COMES BEFORE THE LIVES OF OTHERS.
ANYONE WOULD HAVE BRUSHED IT AWAY! IT'S AN *INSTINCT*.

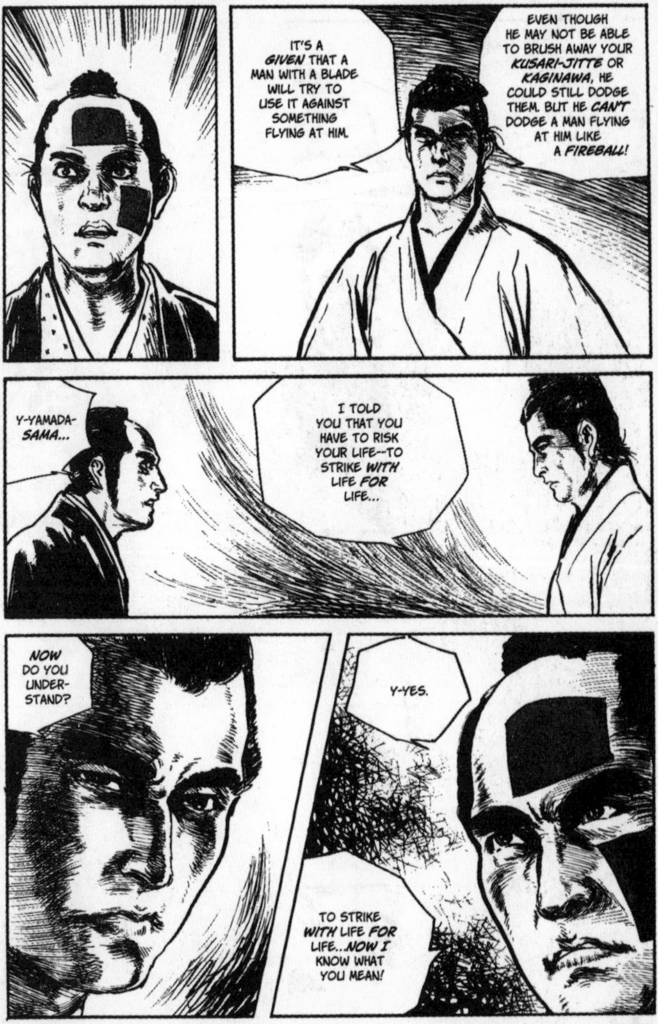
IT'S A *GIVEN* THAT A MAN WITH A BLADE WILL TRY TO USE IT AGAINST SOMETHING FLYING AT HIM.
EVEN THOUGH HE MAY NOT BE ABLE TO BRUSH AWAY YOUR *KUSARI-JITTE* OR *KAGINAWA*, HE COULD STILL DODGE THEM. BUT HE *CAN'T* DODGE A MAN FLYING AT HIM LIKE A *FIREBALL!*
Y-YAMADA-*SAMA*...
I TOLD YOU THAT YOU HAVE TO RISK YOUR LIFE--TO STRIKE *WITH* LIFE *FOR* LIFE...
NOW DO YOU UNDER-STAND?
Y-YES.
TO STRIKE *WITH* LIFE *FOR* LIFE... *NOW I* KNOW WHAT YOU MEAN!

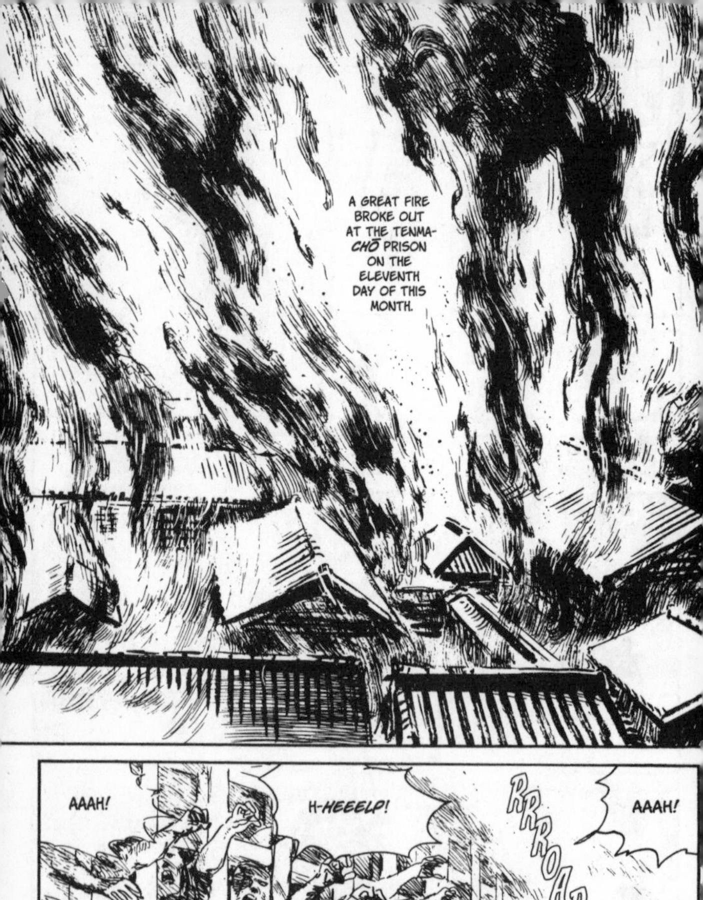
A GREAT FIRE BROKE OUT AT THE TENMA-CHŌ PRISON ON THE ELEVENTH DAY OF THIS MONTH.

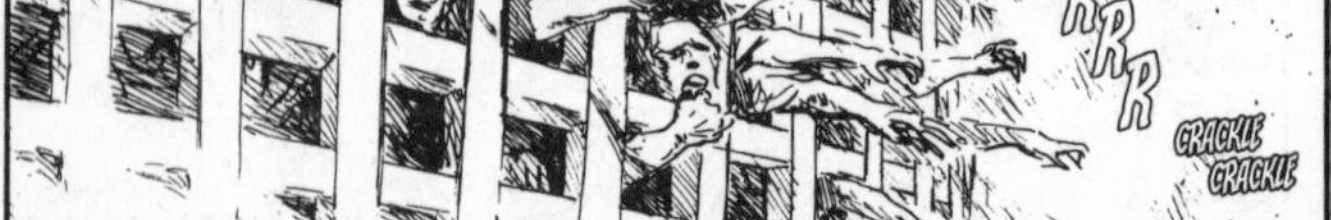
AAAH!
H-HEEELP!
RRROARRRR
AAAH!
CRACKLE CRACKLE

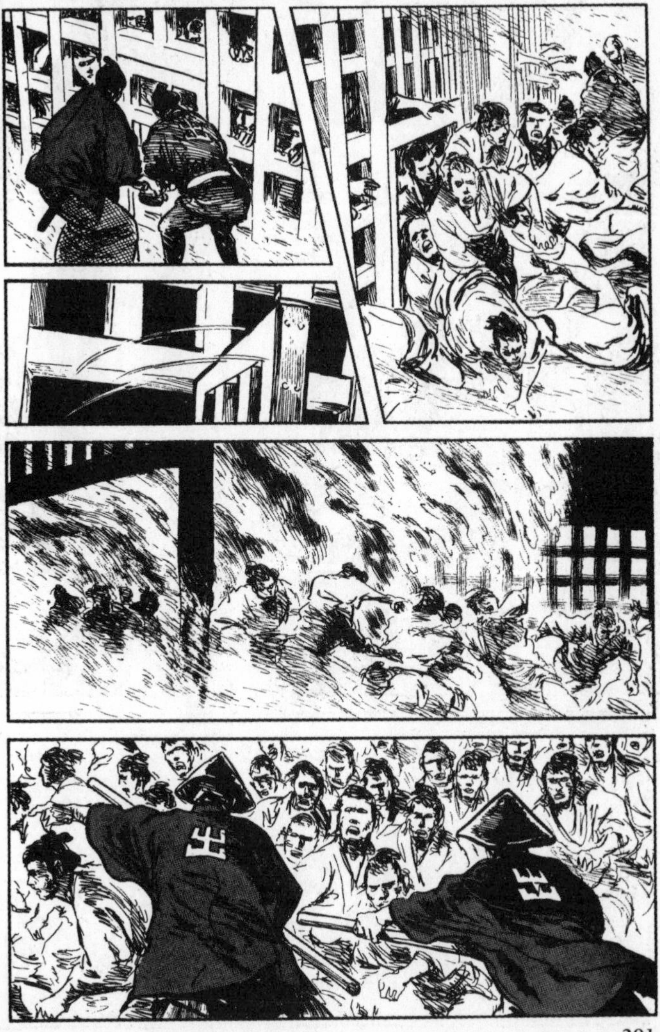

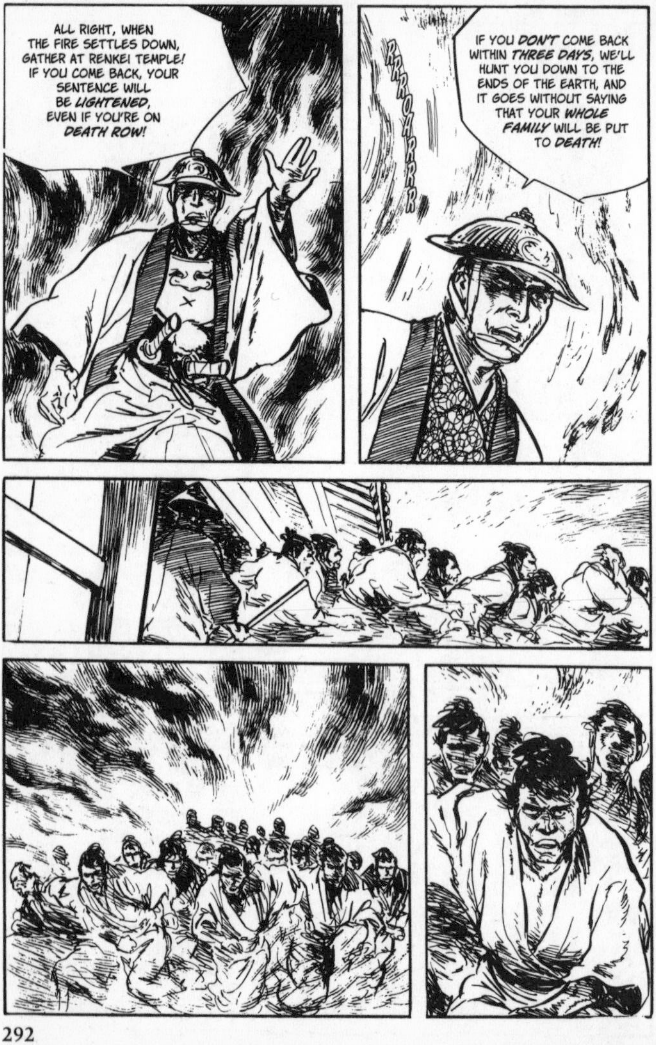
ALL RIGHT, WHEN THE FIRE SETTLES DOWN, GATHER AT RENKEI TEMPLE! IF YOU COME BACK, YOUR SENTENCE WILL BE *LIGHTENED*, EVEN IF YOU'RE ON *DEATH ROW!*
RRRROARRRR
IF YOU *DON'T* COME BACK WITHIN *THREE DAYS*, WE'LL HUNT YOU DOWN TO THE ENDS OF THE EARTH, AND IT GOES WITHOUT SAYING THAT YOUR *WHOLE FAMILY* WILL BE PUT TO *DEATH!*

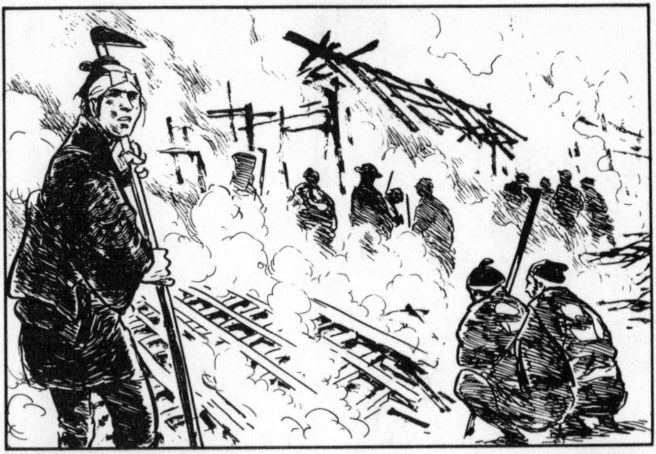

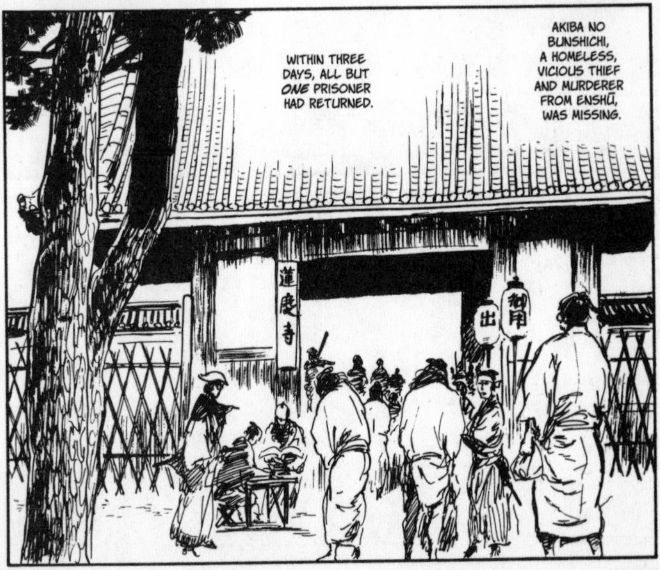
WITHIN THREE DAYS, ALL BUT *ONE* PRISONER HAD RETURNED.
AKIBA NO BUNSHICHI, A HOMELESS, VICIOUS THIEF AND MURDERER FROM ENSHŪ, WAS MISSING.
蓮慶寺
出
御用

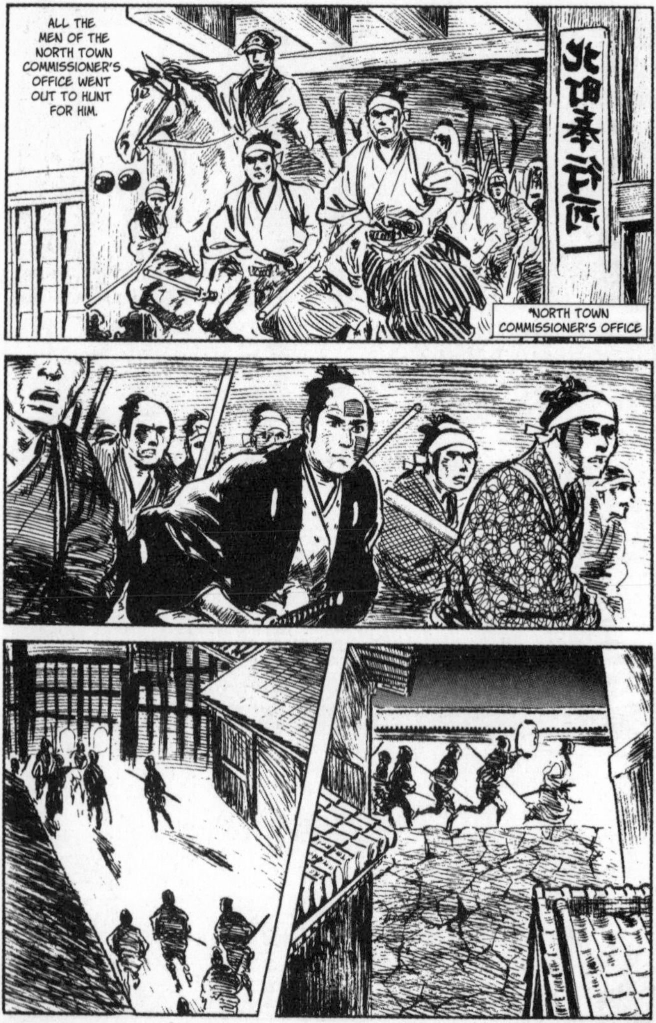
ALL THE MEN OF THE NORTH TOWN COMMISSIONER'S OFFICE WENT OUT TO HUNT FOR HIM.
北町奉行所
*NORTH TOWN COMMISSIONER'S OFFICE

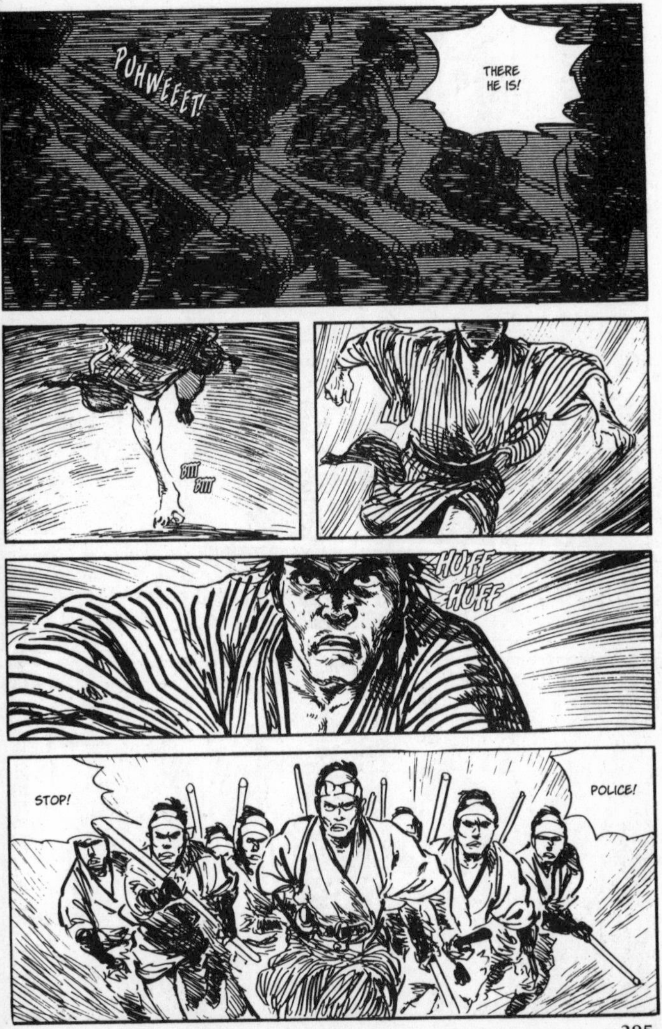
PUHWEEEET!
THERE HE IS!
BTTT
BTTT
HUFF
HUFF
STOP!
POLICE!

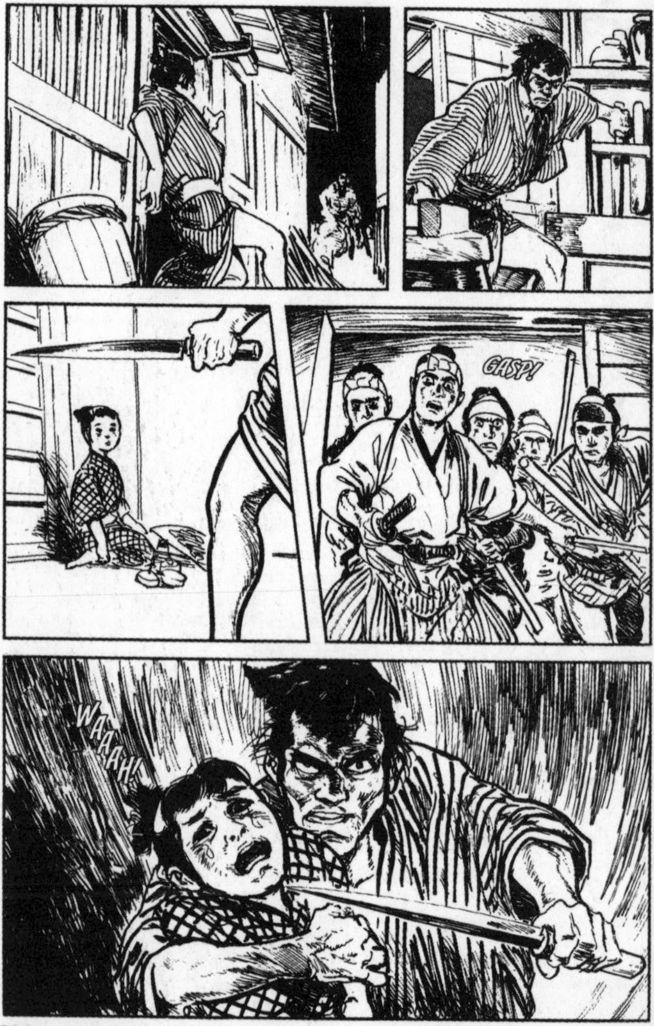
GASP!
WAAAAH!

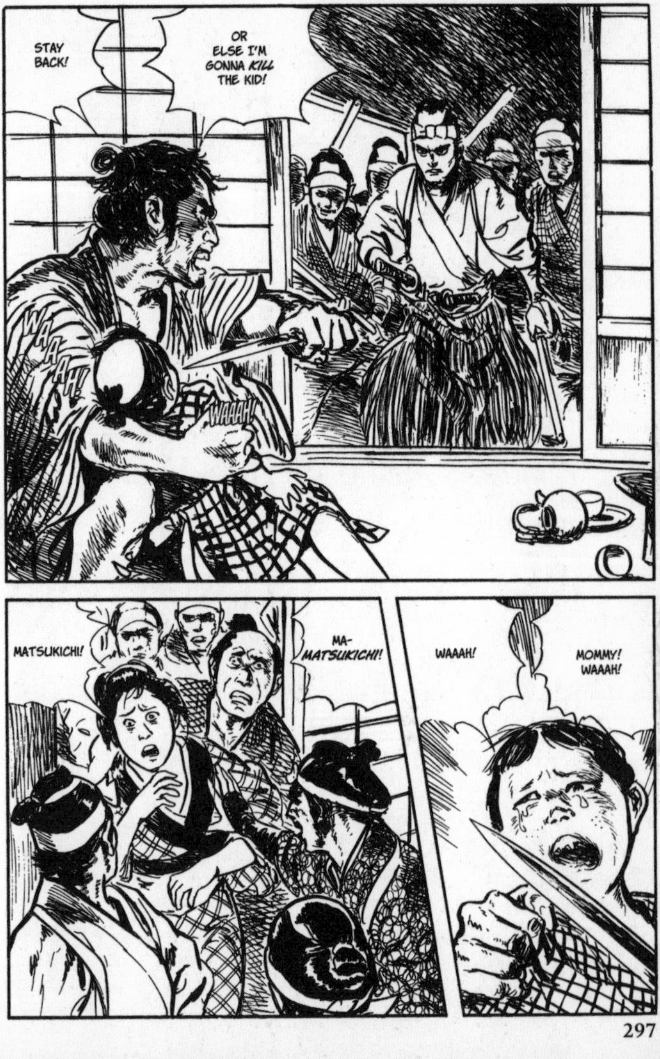
STAY BACK!
OR ELSE I'M GONNA *KILL* THE KID!
WAAAH!
WAAAH!
MATSUKICHI!
MA- MATSUKICHI!
WAAAH!
MOMMY! WAAAH!

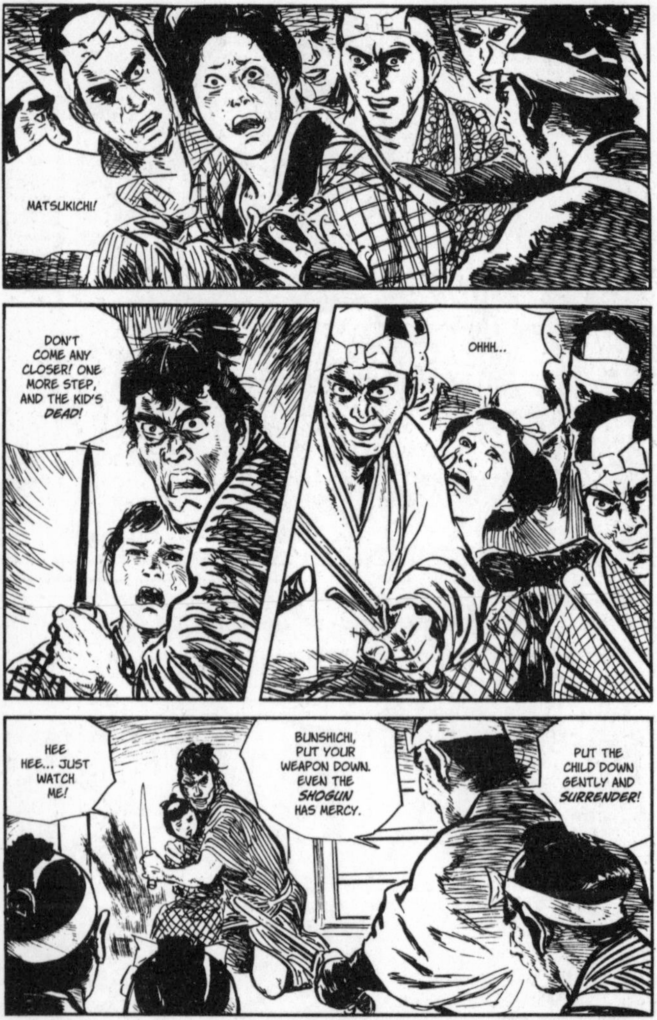
MATSUKICHI!
DON'T COME ANY CLOSER! ONE MORE STEP, AND THE KID'S *DEAD!*
OHHH...
HEE HEE... JUST WATCH ME!
BUNSHICHI, PUT YOUR WEAPON DOWN. EVEN THE *SHOGUN* HAS MERCY.
PUT THE CHILD DOWN GENTLY AND *SURRENDER!*

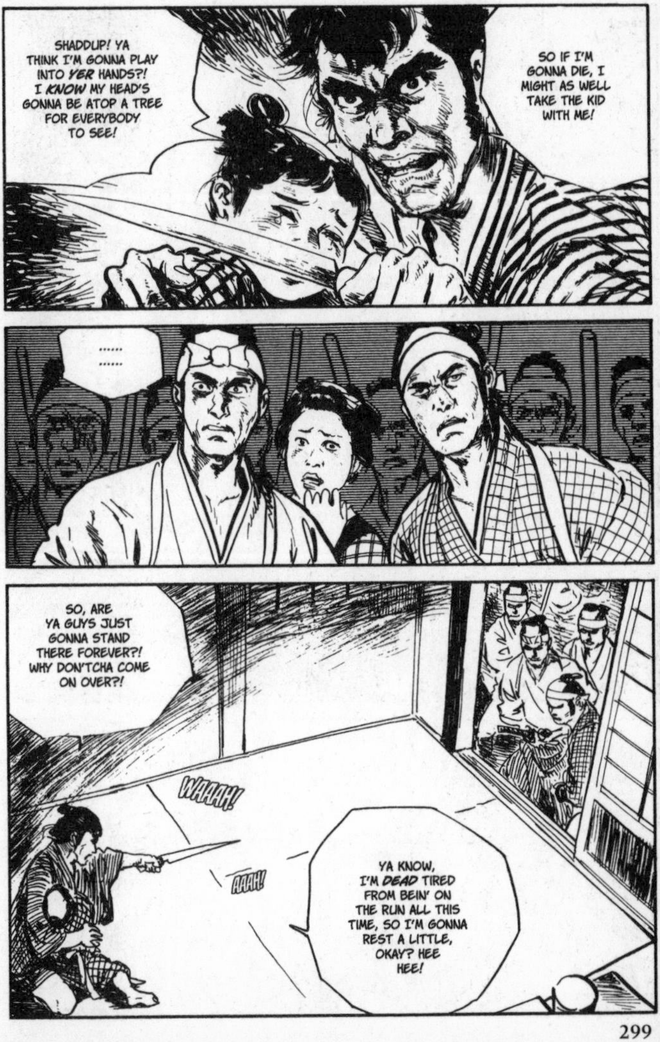
SHADDUP! YA THINK I'M GONNA PLAY INTO *YER* HANDS?! I *KNOW* MY HEAD'S GONNA BE ATOP A TREE FOR EVERYBODY TO SEE!
SO IF I'M GONNA DIE, I MIGHT AS WELL TAKE THE KID WITH ME!
......
......
SO, ARE YA GUYS JUST GONNA STAND THERE FOREVER?! WHY DON'TCHA COME ON OVER?!
WAAAH!
AAAH!
YA KNOW, I'M *DEAD* TIRED FROM BEIN' ON THE RUN ALL THIS TIME, SO I'M GONNA REST A LITTLE, OKAY? HEE HEE!

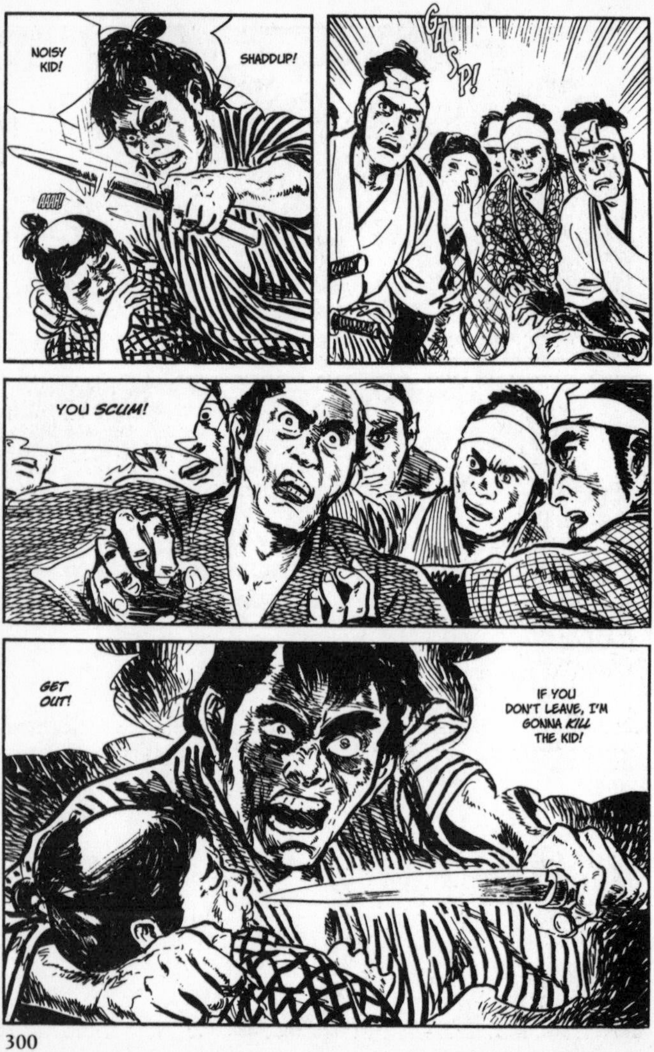
NOISY KID!
SHADDUP!
AAAH!
GASP!
YOU SCUM!
GET OUT!
IF YOU DON'T LEAVE, I'M GONNA KILL THE KID!

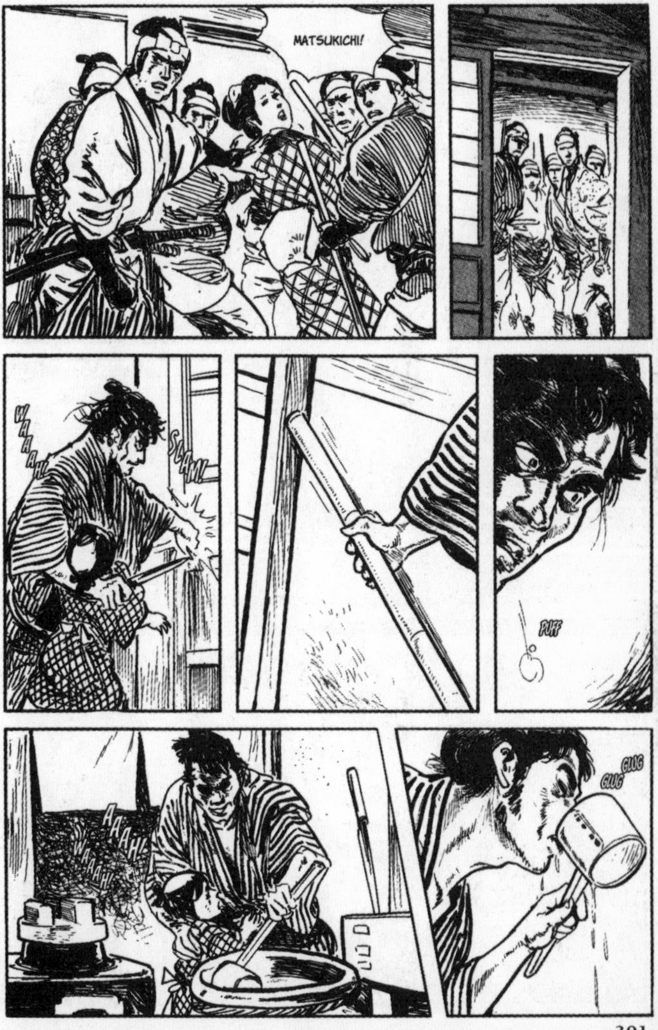
MATSUKICHI!
WAAAAH!
SLAM!
PUFF
AAAAH!
WAAAAH!
GLUG
GLUG

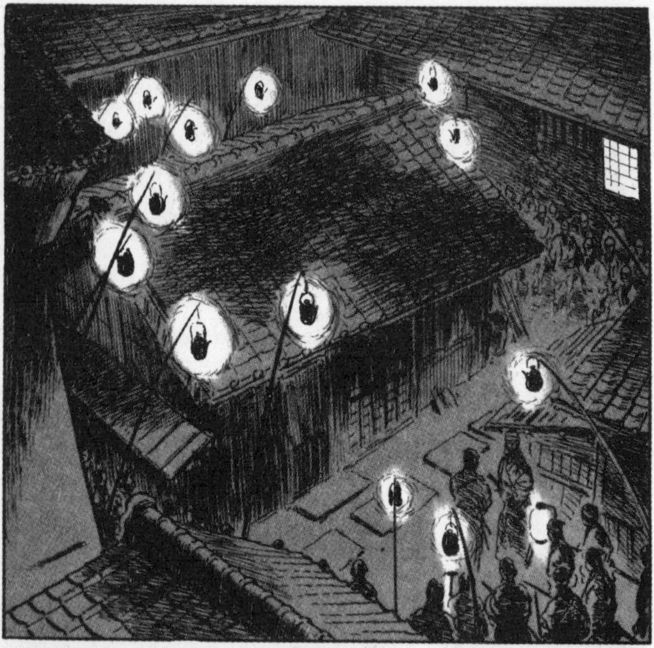

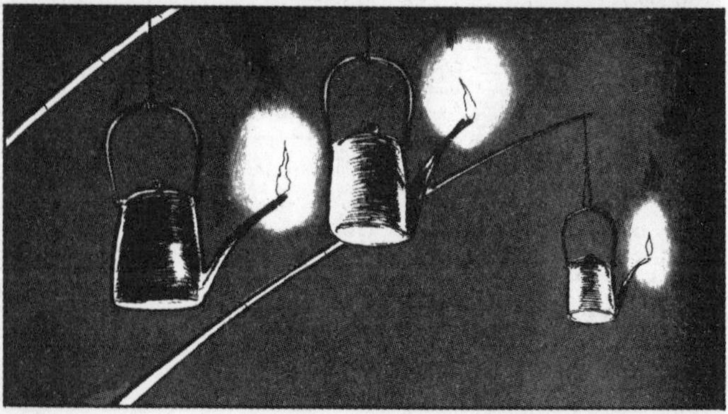

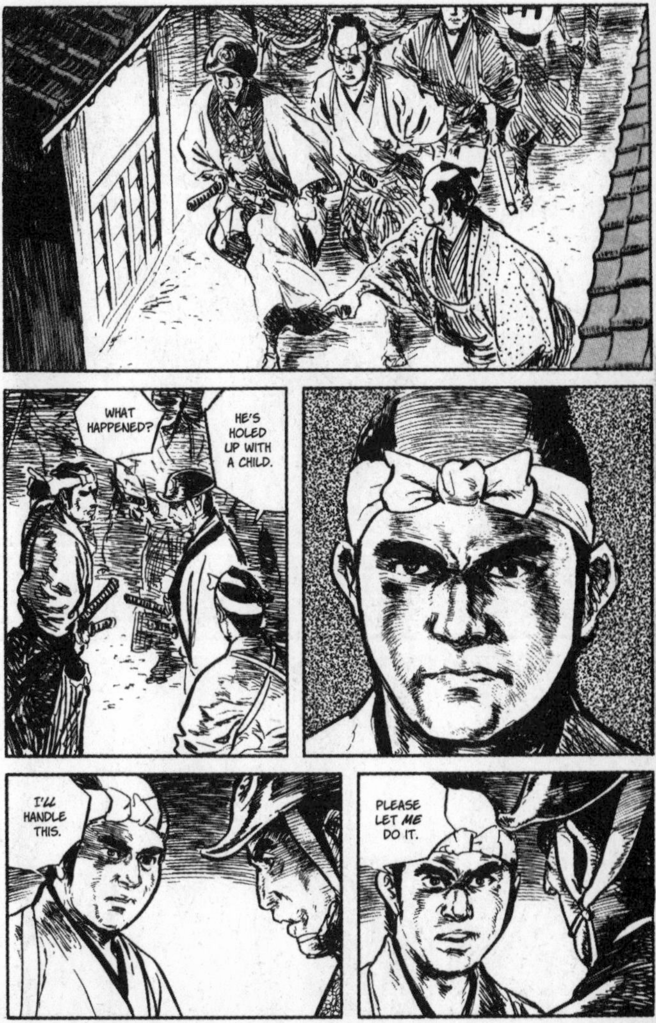
WHAT HAPPENED?
HE'S HOLED UP WITH A CHILD.
I'LL HANDLE THIS.
PLEASE LET *ME* DO IT.

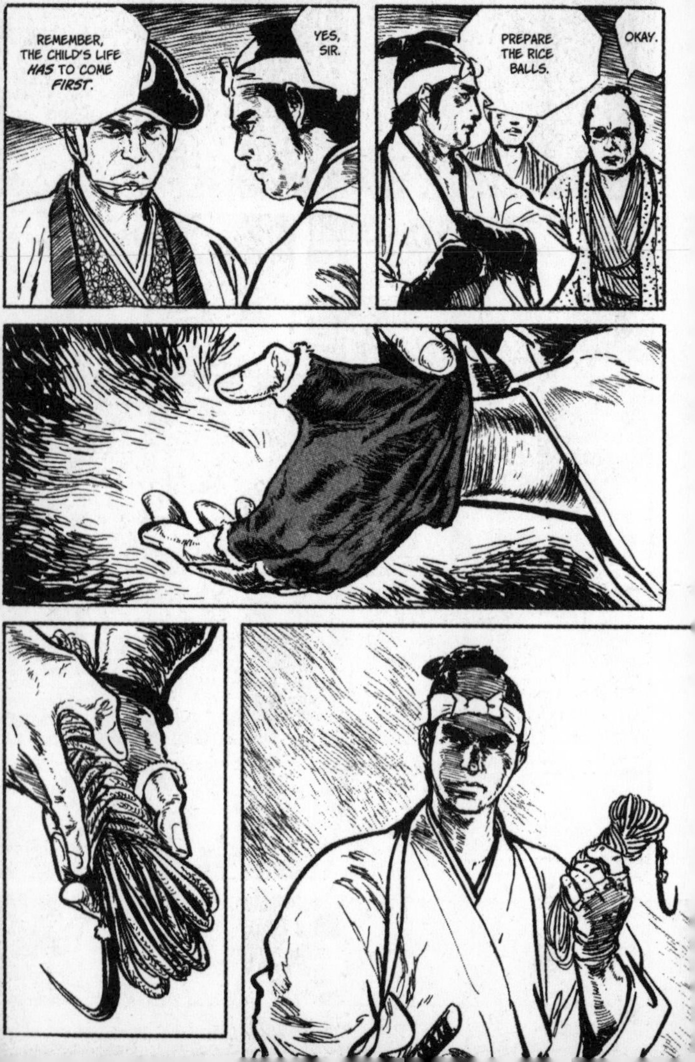
REMEMBER, THE CHILD'S LIFE *HAS* TO COME *FIRST*.
YES, SIR.
PREPARE THE RICE BALLS.
OKAY.

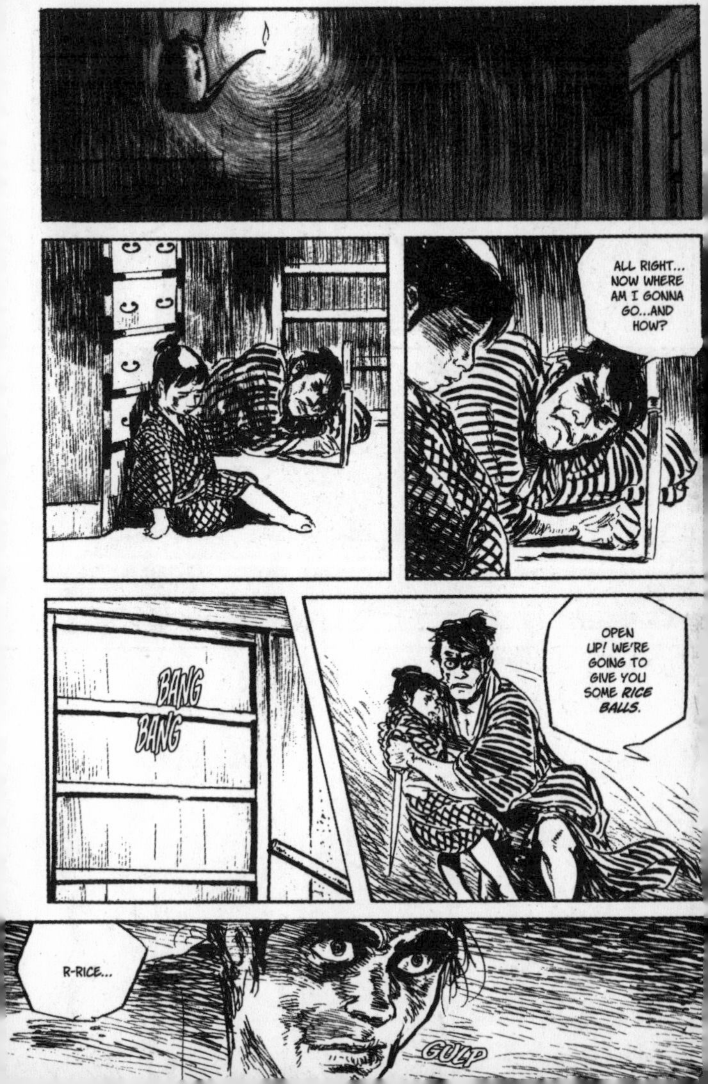
ALL RIGHT... NOW WHERE AM I GONNA GO...AND HOW?
BANG
BANG
OPEN UP! WE'RE GOING TO GIVE YOU SOME *RICE BALLS.*
R-RICE...
GULP

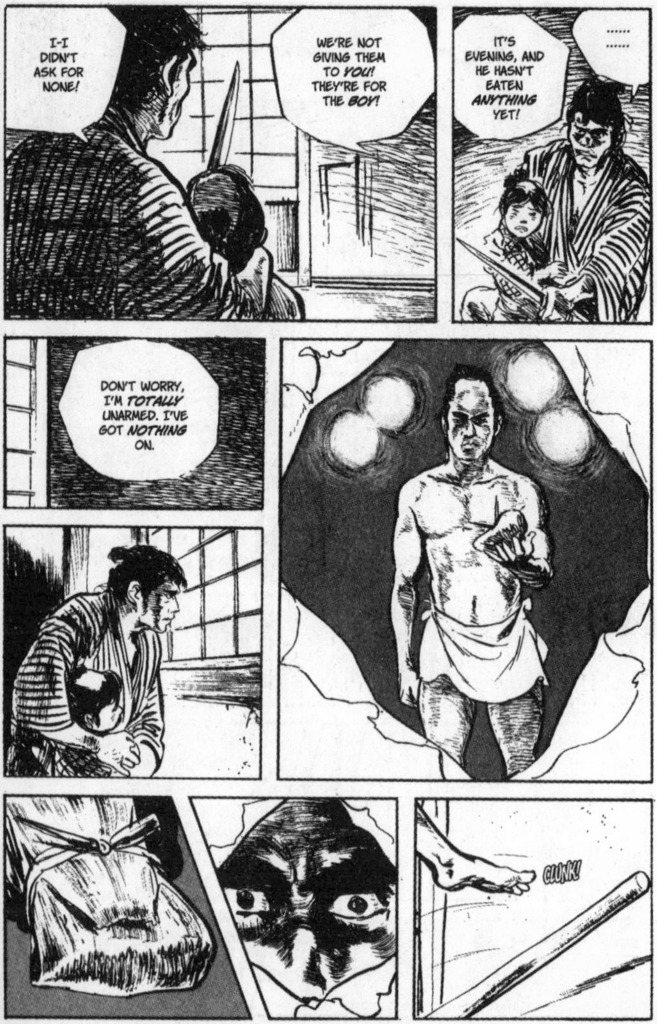
I-I DIDN'T ASK FOR NONE!
WE'RE NOT GIVING THEM TO *YOU!* THEY'RE FOR THE *BOY!*
IT'S EVENING, AND HE HASN'T EATEN *ANYTHING* YET!
......
......
DON'T WORRY, I'M *TOTALLY* UNARMED. I'VE GOT *NOTHING* ON.
CLUNK!

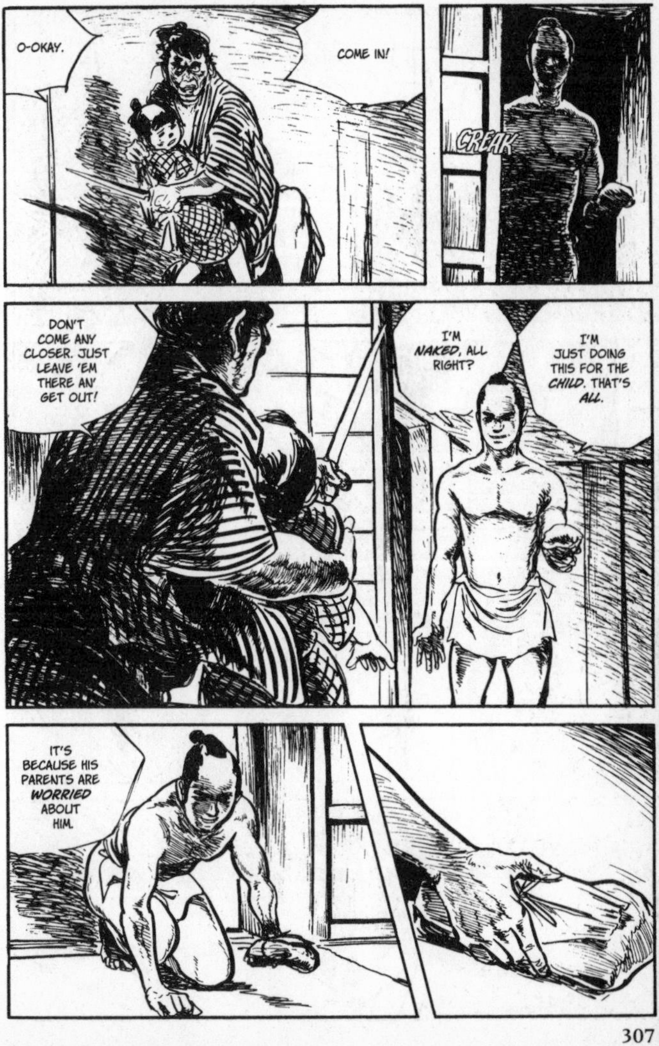
O-OKAY.
COME IN!
CREAK
DON'T COME ANY CLOSER. JUST LEAVE 'EM THERE AN' GET OUT!
I'M *NAKED*, ALL RIGHT?
I'M JUST DOING THIS FOR THE *CHILD*. THAT'S *ALL*.
IT'S BECAUSE HIS PARENTS ARE *WORRIED* ABOUT HIM.

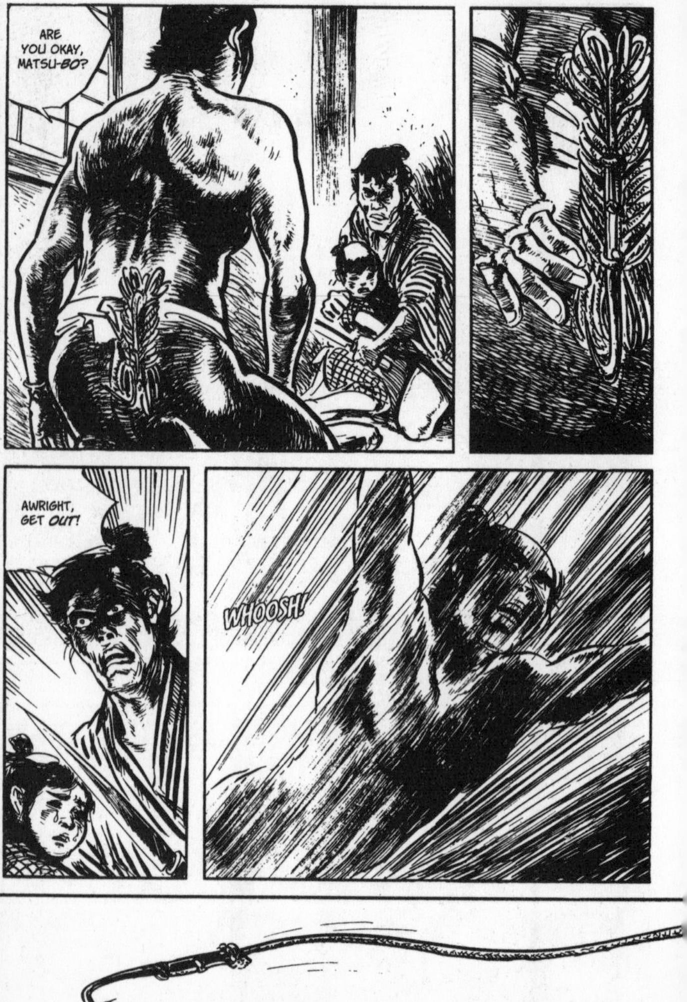
ARE YOU OKAY, MATSU-BO?
AWRIGHT, GET OUT!
WHOOSH!

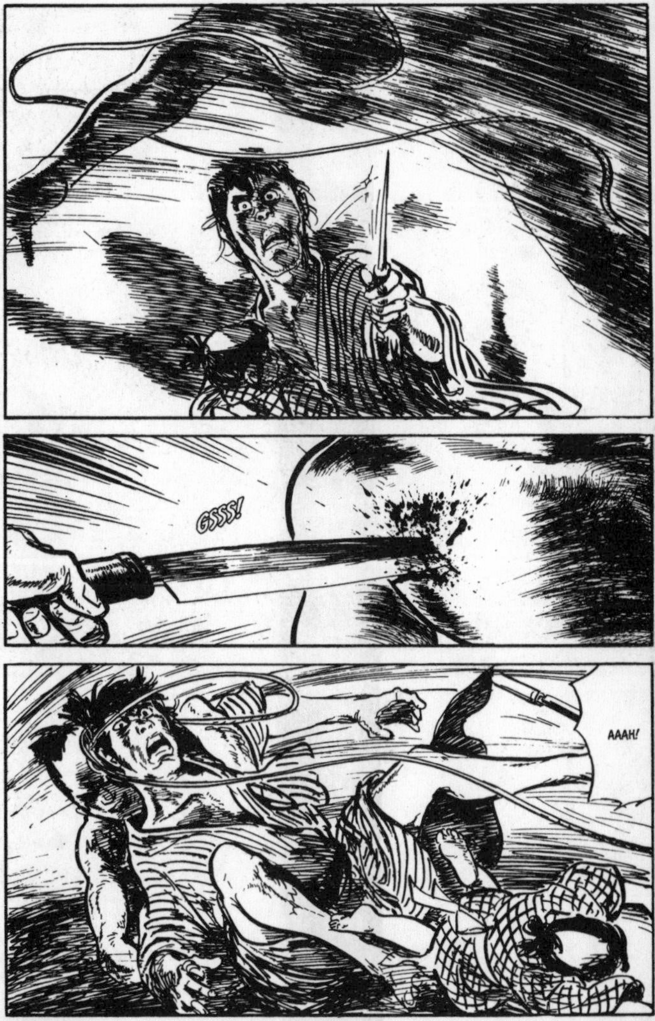
GSSS!
AAAH!

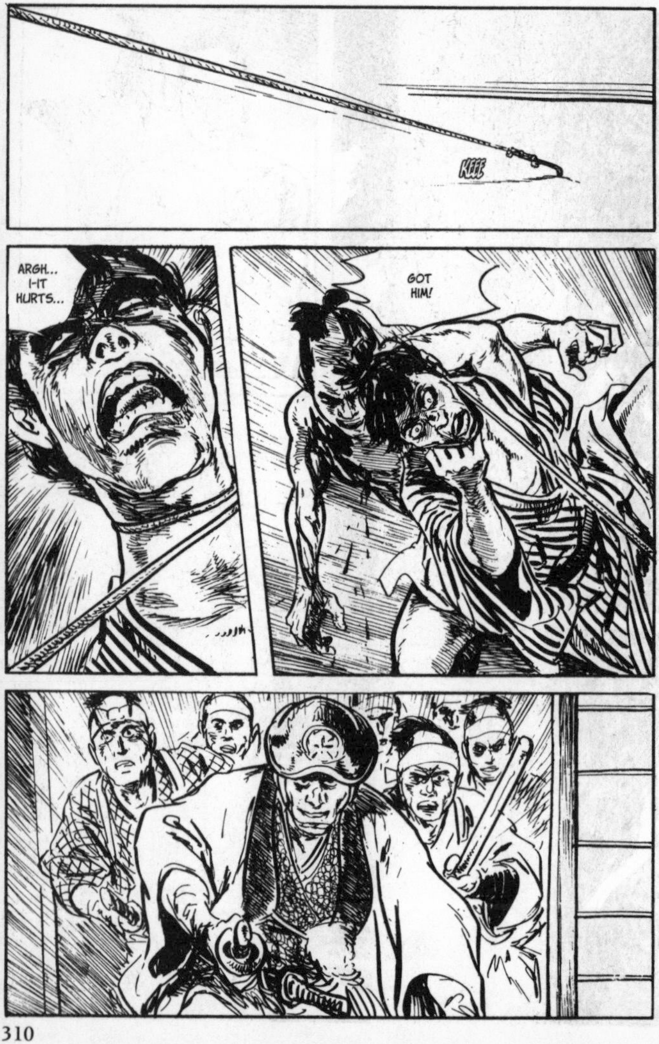
KEEE
ARGH... I-IT HURTS...
GOT HIM!

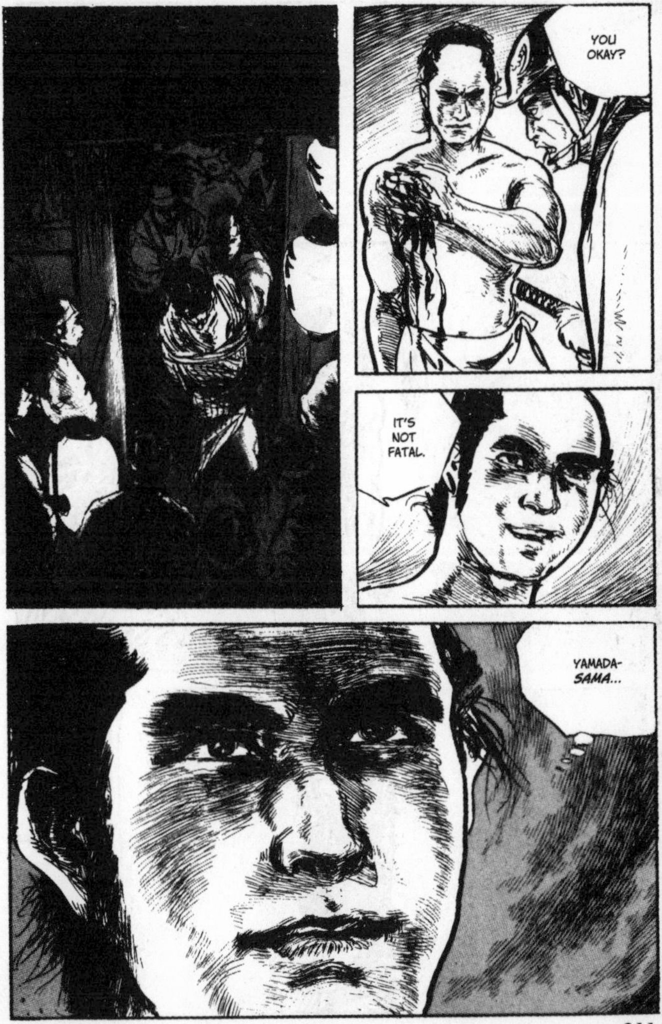
YOU OKAY?
IT'S NOT FATAL.
YAMADA-SAMA...

GLOSSARY

baku
Nothingness.

-bō
Affectionate suffix for boys' names.

bugei
Martial arts.

burei-uchi
Literally, "striking down the impolite." A samurai had the right to execute commoners for rudeness.

daimyō
Feudal lord.

dainagon
Chief councillor of state.

danna
Term of respect among commoners for a great man.

edo karō
Senior advisor in a *daimyō*'s edo residence.

gokenin
Lower grade retainer.

gyōkishin
Literally, "congealing energy heart."

han
A feudal domain.

hiyameshikui
Literally, "cold rice eater." Term of contempt for second sons who are not heirs.

hour of the horse
Between 11 A.M. and 1 P.M.

ihai
Buddhist mortuary tablet.

jizō
A bodhisattva comforting the common man. *Jizō* figures are guardian saints of travelers, children, women, and the weak and ailing.

jōmawari
Literally, "regular patrol(man)." A type of dōshin (constable).

kaginawa
Hook rope.

kan
A bundle of a thousand copper coins.

kasa
An umbrella.

kata-kesa
Buddhist robe worn on one shoulder (*kata*).

katana-ban
Guardian of a *katana* (sword).

kireaji
Literally "cutting taste." How well a blade cuts.

kobushin-gumi
Literally, "small builders group." Consisted of samurai without official appointments who still received a salary. They were in charge of obtaining laborers for official construction projects.

kodachi
Short sword.

koshi-ire
Literally, "palanquin entrance." The bride's entry into the groom's house.

kusari-jitte
A *jitte* (truncheon) with a retractable chain.

machi-bugyōsho
Office of the Edo city commissioner.

nanban
Westerners were known as "southern barbarians," after the first traders reaching Japan from the south.

nenban
Department of the city commissioner's office in charge of administration and finance.

o-jō-sama
Term of address for young ladies.

okakaeseki
Lowest rank of *gokenin* (lower grade retainer of the shōgun). Unlike other *gokenin* ranks, this rank is not hereditary.

okashiratsuki
Literally, "with tail and head." A whole fish.

o-koshimono-yaku
Overseer of swords.

o-memie
Daimyō with the right to meet the shōgun.

o-tameshiyaku
The swordmaster who performed *o-tameshi*, the testing of the shōgun's swords. The "o-" signifies respect for the shōgun.

rokumai
Rice given to samurai as a form of wages.

suemonogiri
Cutting through a stationary object.

Tanagobara
Sword tang shaped like a fish's belly. Characteristic of Muramasa swords.

tantō
A dagger.

Tokugawa Ieyasu
First of the Tokugawa shōguns.

tsuku
Rice.

wakizashi
Short sword.

yomi
The underworld.

yoriki
Police lieutenant.

KAZUO KOIKE

Though widely respected as a powerful writer of graphic fiction, Kazuo Koike has spent a lifetime reaching beyond the bounds of the comics medium. Aside from co-creating and writing such classic manga as *Lone Wolf and Cub* and *Crying Freeman*, Koike has hosted the popular *Shibi Golf Weekly* instructional television program; founded the *Albatross View* golf magazine; produced movies; written popular fiction, poetry, and screenplays; and mentored some of Japan's best manga talent.

Koike started the *Gekiga Sonjuku*, a college course aimed at helping talented writers and artists—such as *Ranma 1/2* creator Rumiko Takahashi—break into the comics field. His methods and teachings continue to influence new generations of manga creators, not to mention artists and writers around the world. Examples of Koike's influence range from the comics works of Frank Miller and Stan Sakai to the films of Quentin Tarantino.

The driving focus of Koike's narrative is character development, and his commitment to the character is clear: "Comics are carried by characters. If a character is well-created, the comic becomes a hit." Kazuo Koike's continued success in comics and literature has proven this philosophy true.

Kazuo Koike continues to work in the entertainment media to this very day, consistently diversifying his work and forging new paths across the rough roads of Edo-period history and the green swaths of today's golfing world.

GOSEKI KOJIMA

Goseki Kojima was born on November 3, 1928, the very same day as the godfather of Japanese comics, Osamu Tezuka. Art was a Kojima family tradition, his own father an amateur portrait artist and his great-great-grandfather a sculptor.

In 1950, Kojima moved to Tokyo, where the postwar devastation had given rise to special manga forms for audiences too poor to buy the new manga magazines just starting to reach the newsstands. Kojima created art for *kami-shibai*, or "paper-play" narrators, who would use manga story sheets to present narrated street plays, and later moved on to creating works for the *kashi-bon* market, bookstores that rented out books, magazines, and manga to mostly low-income readers.

In 1967, Kojima broke into the magazine market with his ninja adventure, *Dojinki*. As the manga magazine market grew and diversified, he turned out a steady stream of popular samurai manga series.

In 1970, in collaboration with Kazuo Koike, Kojima began the work that would seal his reputation, *Kozure Okami (Lone Wolf and Cub)*. Many additional series would follow, including this related series, *Samurai Executioner*.

In his final years, Kojima turned to creating original graphic novels based on the movies of his favorite director, the great Akira Kurosawa. Kojima passed away on January 5, 2000 at the age of 71.

LONE WOLF AND CUB
Kazuo Koike and
Goseki Kojima
*Collect the complete
28-volume series!*

LONE WOLF 2100
Mike Kennedy and
Francisco Ruiz Velasco
*The stylish, futuristic
re-imagining of the classic
Lone Wolf and Cub*

Available from your local comics shop or bookstore!

To find a comics shop in your area, call 1-888-266-4226 • For more information or to order direct:
•On the web: www.darkhorse.com •E-mail: mailorder@darkhorse.com
•Phone: 1-800-862-0052 or (503) 652-9701 Mon.-Sat. 9 A.M. to 5 P.M. Pacific Time
*Prices and availability subject to change without notice

*Dark Horse Comics: Mike Richardson publisher • Neil Hankerson executive vice president
Tom Weddle vice president of finance • Randy Stradley vice president of publishing • Chris Warner senior books editor
Anita Nelson vice president of sales & licensing & marketing • David Scroggy vice president of product development
Lia Ribacchi art director • Dale LaFountain vice president of information technology
Darlene Vogel director of purchasing • Ken Lizzi general counsel*